VOLUME II

The Way We Lived

Essays and Documents
in American Social History

Frederick M. Binder
City University of New York, College of Staten Island

David M. Reimers
New York University

D. C. HEATH AND COMPANY
Lexington, Massachusetts   Toronto

CREDITS

Cover painting: "Main Street, Gloucester, 1917" by John Sloan (New Britain Museum of American Art).

Chapter-opening photos: p. 5, Lightfoot Collection; p. 25, Nebraska State Historical Society; p. 44, The Library of Congress; p. 67, Culver Pictures, Inc.; p. 87, The Granger Collection; p. 103, Brown Brothers; p. 121, Brown Brothers; p. 137, The National Archives; p. 164, The Granger Collection; p. 181, The Wisconsin Center for Theatre Research; p. 203, The Library of Congress; p. 223, The Library of Congress; p. 238, The National Archives; p. 261, AP/Wide World Photos; p. 283, United Press International, Inc.; p. 304, Martin A. Levick/Black Star.

Published simultaneously in Canada.

Printed in the United States of America.

International Standard Book Number: 0-669-09031-X

Library of Congress Catalog Card Number: 87-81182

PREFACE

History courses have traditionally emphasized the momentous events of our past. Wars and laws, technological advances and economic crises, ideas and ideologies, and the roles of famous heroes and infamous villains have been central to these studies. Yet, what made events momentous is the impact they had on society at large, on people from all walks of life. The growing attention to social history is in part a recognition that knowledge of the experiences, values, and attitudes of these people is crucial to gaining an understanding of our past.

Thus America's history, as reflected in the everyday lives of its people, constitutes the focus of these volumes. In preparing a work of selected readings, we have had to make choices as to which episodes from our past to highlight. Each of those included, we believe, was significant in the shaping of our society. Each of the essays is followed by original documents that serve several purposes. They provide examples of the kinds of source materials used by social historians in their research; they help to illuminate and expand upon the subject dealt with in the essays; and they bring the reader into direct contact with the people of the past—people who helped shape, and people who were affected by, the "momentous events."

Our introduction to each essay and its accompanying documents is designed to set the historical scene and to call attention to particular points in the selections, raising questions for students to ponder as they read. A list of suggested readings has been included after each of the major divisions of the text. We trust that these volumes will prove to be what written history at its best can be—interesting and enlightening.

F. M. B.
D. M. R.

CONTENTS

PART II

Modern American Society, *1920–Present*
161

Contents

PART I

The Emergence of an Urban, Industrial Society

1865–1920

AFTER THE CIVIL WAR, AMERICANS TURNED THEIR ATTENTION to building a new social order for the defeated Confederacy. Former slaves hoped for a society in which they would be treated as equals and would enjoy the fruits of their labor. Following the stormy Reconstruction years, however, white Southern Democrats again took control of their state governments, imposing severe limitations on the rights of blacks. Later, around the turn of the century, Southern whites, with Northern compliance, relegated blacks to second-class citizenship, segregated them in public life, and removed them from political affairs. For most blacks the postwar labor system closely resembled the pre–Civil War one; by law, they were free, but their lives were not much improved over what they had been under slavery.

Elsewhere, westward expansion accelerated. The Indians of the Great Plains found their land coveted, just as the Cherokees and other eastern Indians had years before, and ultimately were no more successful in stopping the advance of white miners, cattlemen, and farmers. Even as the last of the Indian wars were coming to an end, Native Americans found themselves confined to reservations and subjected to pressures to reject their tribal culture and pattern their lives after those of white Americans.

In the nation's cities and towns, industrialization continued its rapid pace after 1865. The social and economic changes of this period were so substantial that by World War I a majority of Americans lived in urban areas, earning their living in factories and businesses. For those engaged in manual labor, working conditions were often extremely hazardous. A growing number of the new urban wage earners were women, but they were confined to certain "female" occupations, such as stenography, typing, teaching, retail selling, and nursing.

As in the years before the Civil War, people immigrated from Europe in search of new opportunities in the United States. Many immigrants continued to arrive from England, Ireland, and Germany, but after 1896 the majority of newcomers were from eastern and southern Europe. For the most part, they settled in the growing industrial cities of the Northeast and Middle West, but immigrants could be found in all regions of America, where they strove to adapt to new and sometimes strange and hostile environments.

Europeans were not the only people on the move in these years. Southern blacks, facing poverty and racial discrimination at home, began to emigrate north around 1880. When World War I curtailed European immigration and created a labor shortage in the nation's industries, the black move north dramatically increased. Although these migrants usually found a better life in their new settings, they nonetheless discovered that northern cities had their own forms of racial discrimination.

The readings that follow explore the major changes noted above. The essays and documents focus on the new Southern labor system, the settlement of the last frontier, the westward movement's impact upon Indian life and culture, the consequences of industrial growth for both men and women workers, and the migration of peoples from abroad and of blacks from the South to the North. The section concludes with a look at how America's participation in World War I affected the lives of its soldiers and civilians.

CHAPTER 1

Reconstruction and
Free Plantation Labor

The Civil War eliminated slavery but left undecided the question of what agrarian labor system would replace it in the devastated South. Peter Kolchin's essay "Free Plantation Labor" describes how Alabama freedmen (former slaves) and their erstwhile masters established relationships by which the productivity of the land could be maintained. As you read, consider the aspirations, fears, and misunderstandings that governed the behavior of blacks, Southern whites, and Southern-based representatives of the federal government working for the Freedmen's Bureau. Although salaried agricultural labor and tenant farming made an appearance on Alabama plantations, it was sharecropping that came to dominate agriculture in that state and much of the rest of the South. Sharecropping ultimately proved to be an unproductive system of land management, crushing black farmers and their families under a yoke of debt and poverty for generations to come. Yet, as Kolchin's essay

points out, both blacks and whites initially found the system attractive. Why was this so?

The first document is a letter from a freed slave to his former master. The letter speaks eloquently of the conditions and humiliations that he had endured in the past and also of the better life that he had built for himself. How would you describe the general tone of the letter?

Although even the most tenacious plantation owners recognized that slavery was finished and that a new system of labor was required, few white Southerners were ready to accept the freedmen as social and political equals. In 1865–66, Southern politicians established Black Codes to ensure the maintenance of white supremacy. The second document is the Black Code of St. Landry's Parish, Louisiana. To what extent does this document support the claim of some Northern Radical Republicans that the Black Codes amounted to nothing less than the continuation of slavery? Reading the code will help explain part of the motivation for the passage of the Reconstruction amendments and laws by the Republican-controlled federal government. It will also provide clues to the fate in store for Southern blacks after 1877, when the last federal troops were removed from the South and Reconstruction came to an end.

The third document consists of letters from two Northern schoolteachers, who were among the hundreds who went south after the war under the auspices of the Freedmen's Bureau and several private philanthropic agencies. What do these documents and the Kolchin essay indicate about the goals of the newly freed blacks? What actions did the freedmen take to achieve their objectives?

Beginning in the 1890s the freedmen lost the rights and opportunities they had won during the ten years following the Civil War, as Southern whites began systematically to disenfranchise blacks and to institutionalize segregationist and discriminatory practices. Whites prohibited blacks from voting, segregated them in public life, denied them justice in the courts, and placed their children in underfunded "colored schools." Though blacks never accepted these conditions as permanent, over half a century would pass before their march toward full equality resumed with the promise of significant success.

ESSAY

Free Plantation Labor

Peter Kolchin

I

Despite the migration of Negroes to Alabama's towns and cities, the most important question to blacks in 1865 concerned the role of the rural freedmen. The end of the Civil War found general confusion as to their status. "You have been told by the Yankees and others that you are free," one planter declared to his Negroes in April 1865. "This may be so! I do not doubt that you will be freed in a few years. But the terms and time of your ultimate freedom is not yet fully and definitely settled. Neither you nor I know what is to be the final result." Even if free, the Negroes' position in society remained to be determined. Presumably they would continue to till the land, for agriculture, especially cotton, was the mainstay of the state's economy and would continue as such for years. But it was not clear under what new system the land would be cultivated.

In the spring of 1865, before the arrival of Freedmen's Bureau officials, Union officers played the greatest role in establishing the new order. Throughout the state, they informed whites that the Negroes really were free and gathered blacks together to tell them of their new rights. "All persons formerly held as slaves will be treated in every respect as entitled to the rights of freedmen, and such as desire their services will be required to pay for them," announced Lieutenant Colonel C. T. Christensen in a typical statement from Mobile.

The army also served as the precursor of the Freedmen's Bureau in establishing the new agricultural labor system, according to which freedmen were to work under yearly contracts with their employers, supervised by federal officials. Varieties of this contract system had already been tested in certain Union-occupied portions of the South before the end of the war, and in April Thomas W. Conway, general superintendent of freedmen for the Department of the Gulf, arrived in Montgomery to inaugurate it in Alabama. But it was late summer before the Freedmen's Bureau was fully established throughout the state, and until then the task of supervising relations between planters and freedmen rested primarily with the army. Officers advised blacks to remain on their plantations "whenever the persons by whom they are employed recognize their rights and agree to compensate them for their services." Similar circulars,

SOURCE: Peter Kolchin, "Free Plantation Labor," in *First Freedom: The Responses of Alabama Blacks to Emancipation and Reconstruction* (Greenwood Press Inc., Westport, Conn.: 1972), 30–48. Copyright © 1972. Reprinted with permission of the author and publisher.

although not always so friendly in tone, were issued from other parts of the state. Brevet Major General R. S. Granger ordered that all contracts between freedmen and planters must be in writing. He added bluntly that "[t]hose found unemployed will be arrested and set to work." But officers were usually vague in recommending what the compensation of the freedmen, or their working relations with planters, should be. Conditions varied widely from one location to another during the first few months after the war as individual army officers, Freedmen's Bureau officials, and planters exercised their own discretion.

Observers generally noted a demoralization of labor during the spring and summer of 1865, which they frequently associated with the early migration of freedmen. Upon his arrival in Montgomery, Conway noted a "perfect reign of idleness on the part of the negroes." Other Bureau officials joined planters in declaring that blacks either would not work or would at best make feeble symbolic gestures toward work. Southern whites, and some Northern ones as well, complained that Negroes refused to work and were "impudent and defiant." In one piedmont county, the commander of the local militia warned that "[t]he negroes are becoming very impudent and unless something is done very soon I fear the consequences." White Alabamians frequently confused black "impudence" with outright revolt, but organized violence did occasionally occur.

Events on the Henry Watson plantation, a large estate in the blackbelt county of Greene, illustrate the behavior of freedmen during the first few months after the war. "About the first of June," wrote John Parrish to his brother-in-law Henry Watson, who was vacationing in Germany, "your negroes rebelled against the authority" of the overseer George Hagin. They refused to work and demanded his removal. As Parrish was ill at the time, he induced a friend of Watson's, J. A. Wemyss, to go to the plantation and attempt to put things in order. "He made a sort of compromise bargain with the negroes," Parrish reported, "agreeing that if they would remain he would give them part of the crop, they should be clothed and fed as usual, and that Mr. Hagan [*sic*] should have no authority over them. . . . All hands are having a good easy time, not doing half work." Six days later Parrish reported that "they have again rebelled." When Wemyss informed them firmly that they must submit to the overseer's authority, at first they "amiably consented," but soon they once again objected— "their complaints were universal, very ugly"—and seventeen of them left for nearby Uniontown, where a federal garrison was stationed. Meanwhile, a Freedmen's Bureau agent had arrived in Greensboro. Parrish brought him to the plantation, where he "modified the contract in the negroes['] fav[or] & made them sign it with their marks." The modified contract granted the laborers one-eighth of the crop.

When Watson finally returned from Germany to take charge of matters himself, he was totally disgusted with what he found. The Negroes "claim of their masters full and complete compliance on their part," he complained, "but forget that they agreed to do anything on theirs and are all idle, doing nothing, insisting that they shall be fed and are eating off their masters." Finding such a state of affairs more than he could tolerate, he decided to rent the plantation to overseer Hagin and "have nothing to do with the hiring of hands or the care of the plantation." Hagin, in turn, later broke up the plantation and sublet individual lots to Negro families.

II

Southern whites, long accustomed to thinking of their slaves as faithful and docile servants, were quick to blame outsiders for any trouble. As early as April 1862, a north Alabama planter had noted that the Union soldiers "to a great extent demoralized the negroes. . . . The negroes were delighted with them and since they left enough can be seen to convince one that the Federal army[,] the negroes and white Southern people cannot inhabit the same country." After the war, planters continued to complain about the harmful influence of the army. The presence of black troops was especially unpalatable to former slave owners. "[N]egroes will *not work* surrounded [by] black troops encouraging them to insubordination," complained one outraged resident of a blackbelt community.

Although Alabama whites were deeply humiliated by the presence of Yankees and black troops in their midst, there was little foundation to the complaints about outside agitation. Indeed, federal officials often cooperated directly with planters and local authorities in attempting to keep blacks in line. Army officers urged Negroes to stay on their plantations. Freedmen's Bureau agents frequently assisted in keeping order, too. "My predecessors here worked with a view to please the white citizens, at the expense of, and injustice to, the Freedmen," complained a shocked Bureau assistant superintendent shortly after his arrival in Tuskegee. "They have invariably given permission to inflict punishment for insolence or idleness, and have detailed soldiers to tie up and otherwise punish the laborers who have, in the opinion of the employers, been *refractory*." [Freedmen's Bureau] Commissioner [O. O.] Howard later explained that the Bureau "came to the assistance of the Planters" and succeeded in making the blacks "reliable laborers under the free system." He added that "[t]he good conduct of the millions of freedmen is due to a large extent to our officers of the Army and the Bureau."

A more substantial cause of the demoralization of labor was the mistrust existing between freedman and planter. Where this mistrust was minimal—that is, where planters and freedmen had relatively close ties and where planters readily acknowledged the changed condition of their relations—Negroes continued to work well. More often than not it was the small planter, who worked in the field beside his employees and knew them personally, who managed to remain on good terms with them. But few planters were willing to accept all the implications of the overthrow of slavery. "Thus far," pronounced the state's leading newspaper [*Daily Selma Times*] in October, "we are sorry to say that experience teaches that the negro in a free condition will not work on the old plantations." Another newspaper agreed that freedom had made the blacks "dissatisfied, listless, improvident, and unprofitable drones." Throughout the state, whites refused to believe that Negroes would work without the compulsion of slavery.

Some planters continued to hope that emancipation could either be rescinded or delayed, and "consequently told the negroes they were not free." Others recognized the de jure passing of slavery and concentrated on making the condition of the freedmen as near as possible to that of slaves. Upon his arrival in Montgomery, Conway noted that "the Planters appeared disinclined to offer employment, except with guarantees that would practically reduce the Freedmen again to a state of bondage."

Early contracts between planters and freedmen reflected the disbelief of whites in the possibility of free black labor and their desire to maintain slavery in fact, if not in name. Some planters reached "verbal agreements" with freedmen to continue as they had, without recompense. It was also relatively easy, before the Freedmen's Bureau was firmly established, for planters to lure former slaves into signing contracts that essentially perpetuated their condition. "Today I contracted with Jane and Dick to serve the remainder of the year, such being the federal law," Sarah Espy of the mountain county of Cherokee wrote in her diary in July. "I give them their victuals and clothing, the proceeds of their patches[,] and they are to proceed as heretofore." Similar contracts were made in other regions, and numerous Freedmen's Bureau officials reported upon arrival at their posts that Negroes were working without pay. The practice was summarized in a report to [Assistant Commissioner Wager] Swayne: "We find that the agreements they [the freedmen] have been working under (some of them since last April) are merely a paper drawn up by their late owners," wrote Captain J. W. Cogswell, "in which the negro promises to work for an indefinite time for nothing but his board and clothes, and the white man agrees to do nothing."

When some compensation was provided, as was the case more often than not, it almost always involved a share of the crop. There seems to have been little or no experimentation with wage labor during the first few months after the war. The initial reason for the immediate widespread adoption of sharecropping was simple: the defeated South did not have sufficient currency to pay laborers in cash. Cropping provided a convenient mode of paying freedmen without any money transactions.

Partly for the same reason and partly from tradition, most early contracts specified that food and medical care would be provided by the planter. In addition to being a continuation of the old plantation paternalism, this provision also conformed to the wishes of the Freedmen's Bureau. Shortly after his arrival in Montgomery, Swayne drew up a list of proposed labor regulations. One was that "[p]art of the compensation is required to be in food and medical attendance, lest the improvident leave their families to suffer or the weak are obliged to purchase at unjust rates what they must immediately have." The concern of the Freedmen's Bureau for the welfare of the freedmen, superimposed upon the legacy of slave paternalism and combined with the shortage of currency, insured that early contracts would give Negroes, in addition to their share of the crop, "quarters, fuel, necessary clothes, [and] medical attendance in case of sickness."

Although the size of the shares freedmen received in 1865 varied considerably, it was almost always very small. W. C. Penick agreed to pay his laborers one-quarter of the crop, but such liberality was rare during the summer of 1865. More typical was the contract between Henry Watson and his more than fifty adult blacks, which promised them one-eighth of the crop. In other cases shares varied from one-quarter to one-tenth of the crop.

In addition to appropriating the greater portion of the freedmen's labor, planters were concerned with maintaining control over their lives. "I look upon slavery as gone, gone, gone, beyond the possibility of help," lamented one planter. He added reassuringly, however, that "we have the power to pass stringent police laws to govern the negroes—This is a blessing—For they must be controlled in some way or white people cannot live amongst them." Such an outlook did not necessarily represent a conscious effort to thwart the meaning of freedom, for whites had been conditioned by years of slavery to look upon subservience as the only condition compatible with Negro, or any plantation, labor. Nevertheless, the effect was the same. Early contracts often included provisions regulating the behavior of laborers. A typical one provided that "all orders from the manager are to be promptly and implicitly obeyed under any and all circumstances" and added "[i]t is also agreed that none of the said negroes will under any circumstances leave the plantation without a written permission from the manager." If any of them quit work before the expiration of the contract, he was to forfeit all his wages. Some contracts gave planters authority to whip refractory Negroes.

It is only as a response to such attempts to perpetuate slave conditions that the seeming demoralization of black labor can be understood. Although whites pointed at idle or turbulent Negroes and repeated that they did not comprehend the meaning of freedom, the lack of comprehension was on the part of Alabama's whites. Blacks lost little time in demonstrating their grasp of the essentials of freedom and the tactical flexibility their new condition provided. Just as many felt compelled to leave their old plantations immediately after the war to prevent old relations from being perpetuated, so did they find it necessary to establish at the outset that they would not labor under conditions that made them free in name but slave in fact.

III

In December 1865 events reached something of a crisis as planters continued to strive for a return to the methods of prewar days and blacks continued to resist. Planter-laborer relationships were tense during the summer and fall, but with contracts entered into after the war due to expire on 31 December, the approach of the new year heralded an especially difficult time. Negroes now had the experience of over half a year as freedmen in dealing with planters. They also had the backing of the Freedmen's Bureau, which, if generally ambivalent about the precise position of the freedman in Southern society, refused to sanction his essential reenslavement. The culmination of the demoralization of labor and the mass migrations of 1865 was the refusal of many blacks to contract for the following year.

One reason Negroes were slow to contract was that many of them expected the plantations of their ex-masters to be divided among them at the start of the year. While this idea proved to be a total misconception, it was neither so ludicrous nor so far-fetched a notion as white Alabamians portrayed it. Southern whites themselves had contributed greatly to the expectation by warning during the war that defeat would result in the confiscation of their lands. Commissioner Howard had originally intended to turn over confiscated and abandoned lands to the freedmen, and it was only when President Johnson directly countermanded this policy in the autumn of 1865 that the Bureau reversed itself and began restoring the lands in its possession to the original owners. As the end of the year approached, Freedmen's Bureau officials carefully explained to Negroes that they were not to be given land and advised them to contract for moderate wages.

White Alabamians responded to the black desire for land by exaggerating the extent to which the freedmen expected confiscation, playing up every minor incident, and predicting ominously that New Year's would bring a black uprising. They complained of Negroes arming themselves, and in at least one area whites organized armed patrols to defend themselves against an imagined impending Negro insurrection. Other observers, however, denied any threat of an uprising, and according to [reformer] Carl Schurz rumors were "spread about impending negro insurrections evidently for no other purpose than to serve as a pretext for annoying police regulations concerning the colored people."

The refusal of the freedmen to contract in December in no way presaged a rebellion, but merely expressed their reluctance to repeat their unhappy experience of the past half-year. Without careful Freedmen's Bureau supervision, the contract system threatened to become little more than an opportunity for whites to take advantage of illiterate and ignorant blacks. As Swayne wrote, with what turned out to be something of an underestimation of the abilities of the newly freed slaves, "[c]ontracts imply bargaining and litigation, and at neither of these is the freedman a match for his Employer." For this reason, the assistant commissioner [Swayne] reported, planters "so vigorously demanded contracts there was danger they would not undertake to plant at all without them."

That the fears of insurrection consisted chiefly of groundless rumors became evident when New Year's day passed without the slightest hint of trouble. To the astonishment and relief of whites, freedmen rushed to contract during the first few days of 1866 and then settled down to work. "The praiseworthy conduct of the negroes has surprised many," declared the Selma *Morning Times* in an editorial that typified the general white response. The demoralizing effects of emancipation about which whites had complained so bitterly vanished in a matter of days. "One thing is obvious," recorded a surprised planter; "the negroes, who are hired are farming and working much better than any one predicted they would work." Other white Alabamians agreed. From Tuskegee, the local Freedmen's Bureau agent boasted that "the Freedmen have commenced work with such a zeal as to merit the praise and approbation of the Planters. Planters say to me [']my negroes have never done so well as they are doing now[']."

But if planters rejoiced that their laborers were hard at work, the freedmen had won a signal victory that was noticed by the more perceptive whites. "I think the negro hire was very high," complained future Democratic Governor George S. Houston; "[I] never had any idea of paying that much for negroes." He was right. Gone were the days when a typical contract gave the laborers one-eighth of the crop, or merely bed and board. By refusing to contract until the last moment, the freedmen had thrown their prospective employers into a panic and forced a significant alteration in the terms of the ultimate settlement. Although neither so well concerted nor organized, the process had essentially the same effect as a massive general strike.

Aside from the presence of the Freedmen's Bureau, which made blatant cheating by planters more difficult, the prevailing shortage of labor proved an inestimable boon to the freedmen. In 1866, as throughout most of the early postwar period, the pressure was on the planter to find laborers rather than on the Negro to find employment. Freedmen could feel relatively free in refusing to contract on what they regarded as unsatisfactory terms or in leaving employers with whom they were unhappy. Labor stealing, or enticing freedmen to change employers for higher wages, was a persistent complaint among planters. Occasionally, blacks were even able to strike for higher wages, as in the mountain county of Cherokee, "where they bound themselves together, under a penalty of fifty lashes, to be laid on

13

the naked back, not to contract to work for any white man during the present harvest, for less than two dollars per day."

As had been the case in 1865, the terms of working arrangements varied widely among plantations. Both the lower and upper limits of the pay scale, however, were substantially higher than they had been. Half, or perhaps slightly more than half, of the contracts provided for a division of the crop. In such cases, the laborer almost always received a larger share than he had in 1865. Although there are examples of freedmen receiving as little as one-sixth of the crop, the prevailing portion—when, as was usual in 1866, the laborer provided nothing but his own labor—was one-quarter. For the first time, many planters contracted to pay their employees money wages rather than a portion of the crop. A typical small planter recorded that he paid his eight field hands an average of ten dollars per month for men and fifty dollars a year for women, in addition to food. In other cases where Negroes worked for wages, the rate of compensation usually ranged from seven to fifteen dollars per month for men, and somewhat less for women.

IV

The economic disadvantage of sharecropping to the Negro became evident in 1866 as the bright prospects of winter and spring faded in the summer. By August the cotton crop, which once seemed so promising, had been reduced by unseasonal rains to half its usual size, and autumn saw the second straight crop failure. As the extent of the disaster became clear, whites across the state began to decide that free blacks were not working well after all. The *Clarke County Journal*, for example, noted that although freedmen had labored satisfactorily during the winter and spring, now they seemed stubborn and lazy. "What is the matter with the freedmen?" it queried.

The contract system provided innumerable opportunities for friction between planters and freedmen—especially sharecroppers—in time of crisis. True, there were occasional touching instances when planters looked after former slaves. One white wrote to Swayne that an ex-slave of his who had left him after the war "because he would not 'feel free' if he did not" was "about to be imposed upon by an unprincipled man, who is about to employ him for the next year for far less than he is worth. . . . Please write to me," begged the distressed planter in a letter asking the assistant commissioner for advice. "I am willing to put myself to some trouble to protect my former faithful slave." Most planters, however, were primarily interested in receiving the maximum possible labor from the freedmen at minimal cost, even if it involved cheating, violence, and brutality.

The most common complaint of the freedmen was that either after the main labor on the crop was done or when it came time to divide the crop, planters would drive them off the plantations, frequently charging them with some technical violation of contract. Unlike wage earners, who were relatively secure, sharecroppers could be discharged and deprived of any compensation whatsoever. Temporary laborers could then be hired either by the day or week to finish up any remaining work. From Greene County, in the blackbelt, a Freedmen's Bureau agent reported "I find many, many men who employed them [freedmen] are arresting them . . . in a large majority of cases without cause" and sending them to sit in jail until the crop was sold. Although in some instances Bureau officials, or even the courts, mediated between planters and freedmen and were able to secure for the latter some payment, many injustices went unnoticed or unredressed.

The cyclical pattern established in 1865–1866 was repeated with some variations the following year. In December 1866, blacks once again were reluctant to contract. Although many of them now had the additional experience of being cheated out of their share of the crop, the absence of any illusions over the possibility of land confiscation enabled most blacks and planters to come to agreements more quickly and with less bitter feeling on both sides than they had the previous year. By spring, whites were rejoicing over Alabama's good fortune and praising her Negroes for their hard work and reliability. "The freedmen, according to universal testimony, are working better than they did last year," reported the *Daily Selma Messenger* with satisfaction.

There was an almost universal return to sharecropping in 1867, although a very few planters and freedmen continued, despite the shortage of currency, to experiment with wages. Some Freedmen's Bureau officials, who felt that Negroes fared better economically on wages, and some white Alabamians, who supported the system under which blacks were most carefully supervised, continued to advocate wage labor. With very few exceptions, however, planters and freedmen ignored their pleas. Arrangements granting the laborers one-quarter of the crop were most widespread, although in a few instances freedmen contracted to provide their own food and receive half the crop.

Sharecropping triumphed because both planters and freedmen favored the system. To the average planter it continued to be a more feasible labor system than wages, if for no other reason than the shortage of currency. In addition, many whites felt that shares gave blacks an interest in the crop, thus providing them with an incentive to work. Most blacks apparently preferred cropping, despite the economic disadvantages, because it allowed them greater control of their own lives. Because of his interest in the crop, the sharecropper required less supervision. In contrast to the wage laborer, who was a hired hand clearly in a subordinate position to his employer, the cropper was the partner of the landowner in a joint business venture that provided the freedman with opportunities for greater individual discretion, dignity, and self-respect. For this reason, Negroes

15

considered the cropper a notch above the wage laborer in the social scale. "I am not working for wages," declared one freedman to his employer, as he explained why he had a right to leave the plantation at will to attend political meetings, "but am part owner of the crop and as I have all the rights that you or any other man has I shall not suffer them abridged."

V

As in 1866, the cotton crop of 1867 was a poor one. By fall, planters had once again begun to complain about the inefficiencies of freedmen as laborers. "The cause of the cotton crop being so inferior is the inefficiency of labor and the bad season [is] more on account of labor than anything else," lamented George Hagin, the ex-overseer who had rented Henry Watson's plantation. "There has been a few of the old negroes that lived on the place before that have worked very well but the younger ones are worth nothing." A correspondent of the Union Springs *Times* proclaimed free labor a failure.

Once again, planters drove freedmen from their homes without pay. "Negroes are now being dismissed from the plantations[,] there being nothing more for them to do," explained one blackbelt resident. He added calmly that "[t]hey will all be turned loose without homes[,] money or provisions[;] at least no meat." From the northwest corner of the state, 114 Negroes appealed for assistance to Major General John Pope, who in April had assumed command of the Third Military District, comprising Alabama, Georgia, and Florida. They explained that "unless some person in whom we can place the utmost confidence be appointed to superintend the settling up of our affairs, we do not feel that justice will be done us." In 1867, for the first time, many blacks were also fired for voting Republican or attending political meetings.

Occasionally, through unusual persistence or intelligence, blacks were able to enlist the aid of the Freedmen's Bureau and resist arbitrary discharge. Bernard Houston, a sharecropper on an Athens plantation, told his landlord, "I shall not suffer myself to be turned off[,] and under legal advice and the advice of assistant Commissioner of [the] Freedmans Bureau I shall stay there until the crop is matured[,] gathered and divided according to contract." The planter protested lamely that he objected to the Negro's being "disobedient" and denied that politics had anything to do with the situation, but a month later he complained to Swayne that the freedman was "yet on the place acting in utter and entire disobedience of orders & the necessary discipline of the plantation."

In numerous other cases, freedmen were less fortunate. Freedmen's Bureau agents tried to come to the assistance of persecuted blacks, but there were simply too few agents for the job. Furthermore, since the procedure for handling grievances was not clear, Bureau representatives were not sure how best to dispose of them. Some turned cases over to the civil courts. In general, however, this method proved unsatisfactory. "[B]esides the slow process of the Law, there stands in the way the difficulty of obtaining counsel," explained one Bureau agent. "The Freedmen as a general thing have no mean[s] to pay a fee: consequently they submit to the swindle simply because they cannot purchase justice." The sub-assistant commissioner at Huntsville sent discharged freedmen back to their plantations and told them to stay there. In other locations, officials tried to mediate between laborers and planters. "I notify the parties concerned to appear at this office together, and try either to effect an understanding, or a settlement," explained one Bureau official. He reported that he had "so far been fortunate, to prevent any injustice to be done." But for every such settlement, many other grievances undoubtedly went unheard.

The cumulative effects of three years of substandard crops became increasingly evident during the late autumn and early winter of 1867–1868, a period of considerable tension because of the meeting of the Radical Constitutional Convention in December and the election to ratify the new constitution in February. The problem was no longer that freedmen were reluctant to contract, but rather that planters were unwilling or unable to plant. Their universal reaction to poor crops and low profits was to plan to cut back on planting operations. Unemployment among Negroes threatened to reach serious proportions for the first time since the war. . . .

VI

Hidden behind the daily monotony of agricultural labor, significant changes occurred in the lives of black plantation workers during their first few years of freedom. These changes were evident both in their relations with their employers and in their relations with each other. All of them can, with little inaccuracy and only slight ambiguity, be called moves toward independence. These moves, as much class as racial in nature, represented not only the desire of blacks to be free of white control, but also of ex-slave plantation laborers to be free of planter control.

"Freedom has worked great changes in the negro, bringing out all his inherent savage qualities," proclaimed the Mobile *Daily Register* in 1869. Certainly a growing physical restlessness and self-consciousness among black plantation workers—reinforced by the political emancipation brought about under congressional Reconstruction—were very evident. They were no longer willing to be imposed upon by their former owners. From the end of the war laborers, such as those on the Henry Watson plantation, had revolted against working under their old overseers. But the increasing number of white complaints of Negro "impudence," "insolence," and "insubordination," and the increasing readiness of black laborers to resort to violence and organization when faced with an unpalatable situation, testified to their growing self-assertiveness and confidence. In December 1867, for example, planters in Russell County, who were forced to cut back on planting operations because of poor crops the previous year, complained that their laborers were "seizing and holding property upon some of the places. They are generally armed." A year later, a revolt in the same area had to be put down by military force.

This desire of agricultural laborers for independence, which led them to choose sharecropping over wages even though they usually fared better economically under a wage system, was one of the greatest causes of other changes in modes of life and labor on the plantation. Before the war, field hands on large plantations had usually lived in rows of cabins grouped together. They had worked together in a slave gang, under the authority of an overseer and perhaps a driver. Their lives had been, by and large, collective. After the war, black plantation laborers quickly indicated their preference for a more individual form of life. They objected to working under the control of an overseer. They also objected to the regimented nature of the work gang and the Negro quarters. These had been accepted "in the days of slavery, when laborers were driven by overseers by day, and penned like sheep at night, and not allowed to have any will of their own," reported one Freedmen's Bureau agent. "But now, being *free* to think and act for themselves, they feel their individual responsibility for their conduct, and the importance of maintaining a good character." He noted that fights frequently broke out among Negroes forced to live among others against their will.

Many planters found it necessary or useful to break up the former slave quarters and allow laborers to have individual huts, scattered across the plantations. The process was far from complete by the end of the 1860s, but the trend was unmistakable. As early as the spring of 1867, an article in the Montgomery *Daily Advertiser* described certain changes that had occurred in the appearance of one plantation community. "You do not see as large gangs together as of old times, but more frequently squads of five or ten in a place, working industriously without a driver," wrote the correspondent. "Several large land owners have broken up their old 'quarters' and have rebuilt the houses at selected points, scattered over the plantation. . . ."

Although most black sharecroppers continued to provide only their labor and receive food and clothing in addition to their usual quarter of the crop, the late 1860s saw the introduction of a new cropping arrangement that would, in a matter of years, be widely adopted. Early in 1868, a Freedmen's Bureau official noted that there "does not seem to be as much uniformity in the tenor of contracts as last year." He wrote that although "some give the freedmen one-fourth of the crop and provide rations as was customary last year . . . others give one third of [the] crop, and require the laborers to furnish their own rations; and some give one half, the laborers bearing an equal share of the expense." The result was to remove the cropper still further from the wage laborer, and accentuate his role as a partner of the planter in a joint business venture.

Such changes in working and living conditions were sometimes fostered by planters themselves. Some, like Henry Watson, found it impossible to adjust to a new situation in which they did not have total control over their labor force. Under such circumstances, it was tempting for them to adopt whatever system would permit the least contact between employer and laborer, even if it resulted in more of the very independence that so troubled them. A correspondent from the blackbelt county of Hale reported to the Mobile *Daily Register* in 1869 that "everything appears experimental. . . . Many planters have turned their stock, teams, and every facility for farming, over to the negroes, and only require an amount of toll for the care of their land, refusing to superintend, direct, or even, in some cases, to suggest as to their management."

By the late 1860s, then, old patterns of agricultural relationships had been irreparably shattered, and the outlines of new ones had emerged. The logical culmination of emancipation for the plantation workers—the acquisition of their own land—remained for most an illusory dream. But within the confines of the plantation system great changes had occurred in the lives of the black laborers. They themselves had helped bring about most of these changes by demonstrating that they were not willing to continue in a position of complete subservience to their former owners. As one white planter lamented succinctly of the freedmen, "[T]hey wish to be free from restraint." That wish was a potent one in the years immediately following the Civil War.

DOCUMENTS

A Letter
"To My Old Master . . . ," c. 1865

TO MY OLD MASTER, COLONEL P. H. ANDERSON,
BIG SPRING, TENNESSEE

Sir: I got your letter, and was glad to find that you had not forgotten Jourdon, and that you wanted me to come back and live with you again, promising to do better for me than anybody else can. I have often felt uneasy about you. I thought the Yankees would have hung you long before this, for harboring Rebs they found at your house. I suppose they never heard about your going to Colonel Martin's to kill the Union soldier that was left by his company in their stable. Although you shot at me twice before I left you, I did not want to hear of your being hurt, and am glad you are still living. It would do me good to go back to the dear old home

SOURCE: L. Maria Child, *The Freedmen's Book* (1865).

again, and see Miss Mary and Miss Martha and Allen, Esther, Green, and Lee. Give my love to them all, and tell them I hope we will meet in the better world, if not in this. I would have gone back to see you all when I was working in the Nashville Hospital, but one of the neighbors told me that Henry intended to shoot me if he ever got a chance.

I want to know particularly what the good chance is you propose to give me. I am doing tolerably well here. I get twenty-five dollars a month, with victuals and clothing; have a comfortable home for Mandy—the folks call her Mrs. Anderson—and the children—Milly, Jane, and Grundy—go to school and are learning well. The teacher says Grundy has a head for a preacher. They go to Sunday school, and Mandy and me attend church regularly. We are kindly treated. Sometimes we overhear others saying, "Them colored people were slaves" down in Tennessee. The children feel hurt when they hear such remarks; but I tell them it was no disgrace in Tennessee to belong to Colonel Anderson. Many darkeys would have been proud, as I used to be, to call you master. Now if you will write and say what wages you will give me, I will be better able to decide whether it would be to my advantage to move back again.

As to my freedom, which you say I can have, there is nothing to be gained on that score, as I got my free papers in 1864 from the Provost-Marshal-General of the Department of Nashville. Mandy says she would be afraid to go back without some proof that you were disposed to treat us justly and kindly; and we have concluded to test your sincerity by asking you to send us our wages for the time we served you. This will make us forget and forgive old scores, and rely on your justice and friendship in the future. I served you faithfully for thirty-two years, and Mandy twenty years. At twenty-five dollars a month for me, and two dollars a week for Mandy, our earnings would amount to eleven thousand six hundred and eighty dollars. Add to this the interest for the time our wages have been kept back, and deduct what you paid for our clothing, and three doctor's visits to me, and pulling a tooth for Mandy, and the balance will show what we are in justice entitled to. Please send the money by Adam's Express, in care of V. Winters, Esq., Dayton, Ohio. If you fail to pay us for faithful labors in the past, we can have little faith in your promises in the future. We trust the good Maker has opened your eyes to the wrongs which you and your fathers have done to me and my fathers, in making us toil for you for generations without recompense. Here I draw my wages every Saturday night; but in Tennessee there was never any pay-day for the Negroes any more than for the horses and cows. Surely there will be a day of reckoning for those who defraud the laborer of his hire.

In answering this letter, please state if there would be any safety for my Milly and Jane, who are now grown up, and both good-looking girls. You know how it was with poor Matilda and Catherine. I would rather stay here and starve—and die, if it come to that—than have my girls brought to shame by the violence and wickedness of their young masters. You will also please state if there has been any schools opened for the colored children in your neighborhood. The great desire of my life now is to give my children an education, and have them form virtuous habits.

Say howdy to George Carter, and thank him for taking the pistol from you when you were shooting at me.

FROM YOUR OLD SERVANT,
JOURDON ANDERSON

The Black Code of St. Landry's Parish, 1865

Whereas it was formerly made the duty of the police jury to make suitable regulations for the police of slaves within the limits of the parish; and whereas slaves have become emancipated by the action of the ruling powers; and whereas it is necessary for public order, as well as for the comfort and correct deportment of said freedmen, that suitable regulations should be established for their government in their changed condition, the following ordinances are adopted, with the approval of the United States military authorities commanding in said parish, viz:

SECTION 1.   *Be it ordained by the police jury of the parish of St. Landry,* That no negro shall be allowed to pass within the limits of said parish without a special permit in writing from his employer. Whoever shall violate this provision shall pay a fine of two dollars and fifty cents, or in default thereof shall be forced to work four days on the public road, or suffer corporeal punishment as provided hereinafter.

SECTION 2.   *Be it further ordained,* That every negro who shall be found absent from the residence of his employer after 10 o'clock at night, without a written permit from his employer, shall pay a fine of five dollars, or in default thereof, shall be compelled to work five days on the public road, or suffer corporeal punishment as hereinafter provided.

SECTION 3.   *Be it further ordained,* That no negro shall be permitted to rent or keep a house within said parish. Any negro violating this provision shall be immediately ejected and compelled to find an employer; and any person who shall rent, or give the use of any house to any negro, in violation of this section, shall pay a fine of five dollars for each offence.

SECTION 4.   *Be it further ordained,* That every negro is required to be in the regular service of some white person, or former owner, who shall be

SOURCE: U.S. Congress, *Senate Executive Document No. 2* (Washington, D.C., 1865), 93–94.

held responsible for the conduct of said negro. But said employer or former owner may permit said negro to hire his own time by special permission in writing, which permission shall not extend over seven days at any one time. Any negro violating the provisions of this section shall be fined five dollars for each offence, or in default of the payment thereof shall be forced to work five days on the public road, or suffer corporeal punishment as hereinafter provided.

SECTION 5.   *Be it further ordained,* That no public meetings or congregations of negroes shall be allowed within said parish after sunset; but such public meetings and congregations may be held between the hours of sunrise and sunset, by the special permission in writing of the captain of patrol, within whose beat such meetings shall take place. This prohibition, however, is not intended to prevent negroes from attending the usual church services, conducted by white ministers and priests. Every negro violating the provisions of this section shall pay a fine of five dollars, or in default thereof shall be compelled to work five days on the public road, or suffer corporeal punishment as hereinafter provided.

SECTION 6.   *Be it further ordained,* That no negro shall be permitted to preach, exhort, or otherwise declaim to congregations of colored people, without a special permission in writing from the president of the police jury. Any negro violating the provisions of this section shall pay a fine of ten dollars, or in default thereof shall be forced to work ten days on the public road, or suffer corporeal punishment as hereinafter provided.

SECTION 7.   *Be it further ordained,* That no negro who is not in the military service shall be allowed to carry fire-arms, or any kind of weapons, within the parish, without the special written permission of his employers, approved and indorsed by the nearest or most convenient chief of patrol. Any one violating the provisions of this section shall forfeit his weapons and pay a fine of five dollars, or in default of the payment of said fine, shall be forced to work five days on the public road, or suffer corporeal punishment as hereinafter provided.

SECTION 8.   *Be it further ordained,* That no negro shall sell, barter, or exchange any articles of merchandise or traffic within said parish without the special written permission of his employer, specifying the articles of sale, barter or traffic. Any one thus offending shall pay a fine of one dollar for each offence, and suffer the forfeiture of said articles, or in default of the payment of said fine shall work one day on the public road, or suffer corporeal punishment as hereinafter provided.

SECTION 9.   *Be it further ordained,* That any negro found drunk within the said parish shall pay a fine of five dollars, or in default thereof shall work five days on the public road, or suffer corporeal punishment as hereinafter provided.

SECTION 10.   *Be it further ordained,* That all the foregoing provisions shall apply to negroes of both sexes.

SECTION 11.   *Be it further ordained,* That it shall be the duty of every citizen to act as a police officer for the detection of offences and the apprehension of offenders, who shall be immediately handed over to the proper captain or chief of patrol.

SECTION 12.   *Be it further ordained,* That the aforesaid penalties shall be summarily enforced, and that it shall be the duty of the captains and chiefs of patrol to see that the aforesaid ordinances are promptly executed.

SECTION 13.   *Be it further ordained,* That all sums collected from the aforesaid fines shall be immediately handed over to the parish treasurer.

SECTION 14.   *Be it further ordained,* That the corporeal punishment provided for in the foregoing sections shall consist in confining the body of the offender within a barrel placed over his or her shoulders, in the manner practiced in the army, such confinement not to continue longer than twelve hours, and for such time within the aforesaid limit as shall be fixed by the captain or chief of patrol who inflicts the penalty.

SECTION 15.   *Be it further ordained,* That these ordinances shall not interfere with any municipal or military regulations inconsistent with them within the limits of said parish.

SECTION 16.   *Be it further ordained,* That these ordinances shall take effect five days after their publication in the *Opelousas Courier.*

Dedicated Teachers, Determined Students, 1869

RALEIGH, N.C., FEB. 22, 1869

It is surprising to me to see the amount of suffering which many of the people endure for the sake of sending their children to school. Men get very low wages here—from $2.50 to $8 per month usually, while a first rate hand may get $10, and a peck or two of meal per week for rations— and a great many men cannot get work at all. The women take in sewing and washing, go out by day to scour, etc. There is one woman who supports three children and keeps them at school; she says, "I don't care how hard I has to work, if I can only sen[d] Sallie and the boys to school looking respectable." Many of the girls have but one decent dress; it gets washed and ironed on Saturday, and then is worn until the next Saturday, provided they do not tear it or fall in the mud; when such an accident happens there is an absent mark on the register. . . . One may go into their cabins on

SOURCE: Edward L. Pierce, "The Freedmen at Port Royal," *Atlantic Monthly* 12 (September 1869): 306–7.

cold, windy days, and see daylight between every two boards, or feel the rain dropping through the roof; but a word of complaint is rarely heard.

They are anxious to have the children "get on" in their books, and do not seem to feel impatient if they lack comforts themselves. A pile of books is seen in almost every cabin, though there be no furniture except a poor bed, a table and two or three broken chairs.

MISS M. A. PARKER

CHARLOTTESVILLE, VA., OCT. 17, 1866

Mrs. Gibbins (a colored native teacher) is very much liked by the colored people here. Her nature is so noble, that she is not so liable to stimulate petty jealousy among her people as many might under similar circumstances. . . . I think she is doing well in her new sphere of duty, especially in the matter of government. She has a kind of magnetism about her which is a good qualification for a teacher. She is really a fine reader of easy readings, and I should choose her to prepare scholars for me in that line, from among nine-tenths of those engaged in this work, so far as I have known her. She intends to pursue her studies in the evening with my help.

ANNA GARDNER

CHAPTER 2

The Last Frontier

From eastern North Dakota, south to the Texas panhandle, and west to the Rocky Mountains lay the Great Plains, a region considered at one time so bleak and uninhabitable that travelers referred to it as the "Great American Desert." In time, however, it would prove to be a source of immense wealth in minerals, grains, and livestock. This last American frontier—the land of the miner, the farmer, and the cowboy—was by the late 1800s undergoing a transformation paralleling that in the urban-industrial East with its large cities and smoking factories.

American literature and folklore has immortalized those who tamed and settled the Great Plains—the miners and their wide-open boom towns; the sod-house farmers; and, above all, the cowboys. The cowboys spent long hours in the saddle, often in miserable weather, driving their cattle to market. All too often, little profit was made from the long and lonely livestock drives. In what ways does the life of the cowboy, as described in the Paul Horgan essay "The Last Frontiersman," contrast with popular depictions in western novels, in the movies, and on television?

The story of mining, like that of cattle raising and farming, was one of initial boom and prosperity for some, followed by bust for many. Like the other ventures, mining added to the nation's wealth—$1,242,872,032 in gold and $901,160,660 in silver were unearthed between 1860 and 1890—and at the same time enriched the nation's folklore. In 1862, before he took the pen name Mark Twain, Samuel Clemens worked as a reporter for the Virginia City (Nevada) Enterprise. *In the first document, taken from his book* Roughing It, *Clemens describes Virginia City, America's premier mining town and home of the world's greatest vein of silver, the Comstock Lode. What evidence does Clemens provide of a spirit of speculative business enterprise in this remote frontier mining town?*

The westward movement of farmers onto the Great Plains was steady once the prairie lands in the eastern portions of Minnesota, the Dakotas, Kansas, and Nebraska had been settled. The Homestead Act of 1862 made it possible to obtain 160 acres of land free simply by farming and living on the tract or "claim" for five years. In addition, the railroads owned enormous stretches of land along their rights of way, granted to them by the government; because they wanted to populate the region to develop customers for their services, they offered reasonable rates and credit terms to purchasers of land. The second document, from Harper's *Magazine, provides a traveler's view of wheat farming in the plains area of western Minnesota. Note the upbeat tone of the piece: the enthusiasm about transforming the "Great American Desert" and the determination to obtain land, even if it involved "dodging" the law.*

What the document does not *reveal is the expense of fortifying the semiarid land to produce crops. Required were steel plows to cut the tough sod, windmills to pump water from deep in the ground, and barbed wire to fence off land on the treeless plains. In order to obtain these and other new, American-built agricultural tools—threshers, harvesters, binders—the settlers had to borrow money. Loneliness, brutally harsh weather, insects, and even debt could be tolerated, given the certainty of a rich harvest. However, beginning in 1887, when a series of intensely dry summers devastated the region, hundreds of debt-ridden farmers abandoned their land, and many headed back east. The third document, an article by journalist William Allen White, describes such a scene. What can you conclude, from the documents reprinted here, about the impact of industrialization on agriculture and mining during the last half of the nineteenth century?*

ESSAY

The Last Frontiersman

Paul Horgan

The cowboy was the last of the clearly original types of Western American to draw his general tradition and character from the kind of land he worked in, and the kind of work he did. His forerunners were the trapper of the mountains and the trader of the plains. Of the three, he left the fullest legacy of romance and to see him as he first was, it would be necessary in a later century to clear a way back to him through a dense folk literature of the printed page, the moving picture film and the radio that in using all his symbols would almost never touch the reality that supported them.

His work was monotonous in hardship and loneliness, and occasionally it was shot through with excitement that rose from danger. The country where he worked was in its dimensions and character his enemy; and yet it was also in an intimate way almost a completion of his nature, that revelled in vast vacant privacies, and fixed its vision on the distance as though to avoid any social responsibility. He had for his most constant companion not a man or a woman, but an animal—his horse, on whom his work and his convenience and even at times his life depended. His duties took him endlessly riding over range country, where he sought for cattle to capture, calves or yearlings to brand, herds to drive to water, individual cows or bulls of a proper age or condition to cut out of a herd for segregation into another group. Such a group would then be driven to another location—a different pasture or a market.

In dealing with cows through the consent of his horse, the cow boy needed to know much of the nature of both animals. Through experience he learned to anticipate the behavior of cattle, and to judge the effect upon them of every stimulus. He saw that the laws that governed them were the laws of the crowd; and he developed extraordinary skill in handling great crowds of cattle at a time. His horse, broken to riding, and subject to his will, he had to know as an individual creature, and dominate relentlessly its nature by turns sensitive, stubborn and gentle. Living with these two animal natures, the cowboy seemed to acquire in his own certain of their traits, almost as though to be effective at living and working with them, he must open his own animal nature to theirs and through sympathy resemble them. If he could be as simple as a cow, he could also be as stubborn; as fearless as a wild mustang, and as suspicious of the unfamiliar;

SOURCE: Paul Horgan, *Great River: The Rio Grande in North American History*, vol. 2 (New York: Rinehart and Co., 1954), 873–86. Reprinted by permission of Farrax, Straus & Giroux, Inc.

as incurious as an individual bull, and as wild to run with a crowd when attracted. Even in his physical type, the cowboy might tend to resemble his animal companions—a certain flare of nostril and whiteness of eyelash could recall the thoughtless face of a calf; a leanness of leg and arm was a reminder of a horse's fine-boned supports and further suggested the physique best adapted to, and developed for, the horseman's job—the hard, sinewy body, light of weight but powerful, tall for high vision over the animal herd, long-legged for gripping the mount around its breathing barrel. His state of body and nerve had to be ready to fight, for his job sometimes included battle, when Indians or organized cattle and horse thieves came down upon his herd. Then like any soldier he had to shoot to kill, under the sanction of his duty. For his labors, he was paid in the 1870s from fifteen to twenty dollars a month in gold or silver. He saw himself at his task, and his self-image survived in his anonymous folk literature:

> All day long on the prairie I ride,
> Not even a dog to trot by my side:
> My fire I kindle with chips gathered round,
> My coffee I boil without being ground.

In any group of nineteenth century cowboys, more were bearded than clean-shaven. Their costumes were much alike, though with individual variations. But all their garments were "coarse and substantial, few in number and often of the gaudy pattern." The cowboy wore a wide-brimmed hat with its crown dented into a pyramid or flattened. If the brim in front was sometimes turned up off his face, it could be turned down to protect him from the pressing light of the sky under which he spent all day. Around his neck he wore a bandana of tough silk. It served many purposes. Tied over his face it filtered dust before his breath. It served to blindfold a calf or tie its legs. It was a towel, a napkin, a bandage, a handkerchief, or simply an ornament. His shirt was of stout cotton flannel, in a bright color or loud design of checks or stripes or plaids. Over it he sometimes wore a cloth or leather vest but rarely a jacket. His trousers were either of heavy denim, dyed dark blue, sewn with coarse yellow thread, and reinforced at points of great wear with copper rivets, or were of odd colors and materials, mostly dark, that could stand tough use. They fitted tightly. The trouser legs were stuffed into boots that reached almost to the knee. At work, the cowboy often wore leggings of thick cowhide. They were made after the pattern of Indian leggings—two long tubes, with wide flaps at each side cut into fringes or studded with silver disks, that reached from ankle to groin, and were tied to a belt as though to the string of a breechclout. Their purpose was to shield him against thorns in the brush he rode through, and the violent rub of haired animal hides, and the burn of rope when he pulled it against his leg as he turned his horse to control a lasso'd creature. On his boots he wore large spurs, of silver or iron. He wore gloves to work in, and around his tight hips he wore a cartridge belt from which depended his pistol—most often a Colt's single-action, .45-caliber revolver called the Peacemaker. He had no change of clothing. He went unwashed and unbathed unless he camped by a stream or a pond. "I wash," he said in his multiple anonymity,

> I wash in a pool and wipe on a sack;
> I carry my wardrobe all on my back. . . .

Like the object of his work and its chief instrument—the cow and the horse—his Texas saddle, in its essential form, came from Spain. Its high pommel and cantle, heavy stirrups and great weight suggested the squarish, chairlike saddle of the jousting knight, though its design was modified by Mexican saddlers until all contours were rounded and smoothed, and the pommel, of silver or other metal, was developed to serve as a cleat about which to secure the lariat whose other end was noosed about a captive cow or horse. When not in use the lariat was coiled and tied to the saddle. There was little other baggage on the saddle, except now and then a leather scabbard containing a short rifle. If two cowboys travelled together they carried their camp equipment and bedrolls on a pack animal. Otherwise, when a large group worked daily out of a central camp, their equipment was carried in the camp wagon to which they returned during the day for meals and at night for fire, food and companionship.

The wagon, pulled by four horses and driven by the camp cook, was a roving headquarters for the grazing party. Its form was invented by Charles Goodnight in the 1850s, who adapted an Army vehicle to the needs of the cow camp. Rolling in movement, it had a compact look, with its sheets over bows, that concealed the contents, which consisted of bedrolls for the workers and at its free end a high, square chest standing upright. Parked, free of its horses, and with its tongue propped level to serve as a rack for harness, and with its sheets extended and supported by poles to make a generous pavilion of shade to one side, the wagon seemed to expand into several times its own size. It was amazing how much it carried, and how much immediate ground its unpacked equipment could cover. The chest at the rear was faced with a wooden lid which when opened downward became a worktable supported by a central leg. Then were revealed in the chest many fitted drawers and hatches in which the cook kept every necessity for cooking and every oddment, including medicines. Behind it in the wagon bed, along with the bedrolls, he carried his heavy pots and skillets and tin dishes. Beneath the wagon frame hung buckets and to its sides were lashed water barrels.

The cooking fire, which at night served also to give its light to the camp gathering, was made a few feet from the wagon and its profuse scatter of equipment. There the cook prepared his meals, always the same. If brush or wood were scarce, he made his fire of dried animal droppings, . . . If he had no matches he could start his fire by pouring gunpowder into his pistol, wadding it loosely, and firing it with its muzzle close to a scrap of cloth or other dry kindling. He prepared a great pot of coffee boiled from whole beans. A cowboy drank a quart or more every day. Of such coffee it was said that "you would hesitate, if judging from appearance, whether to call it coffee or ink." It was drunk without cream or sugar. There was a kettle full of stew in which[,] using his pocketknife— his only table service—the cowboy probed for a lump of meat. With thick biscuit or cornbread he soaked up the gravy and like an Indian ate from his fingers. There were no green vegetables to be had. A pot of kidney beans finished the meal. The cowboys squatted near one another, or stood idling by the wagon, and ate in silence and with speed. A meal was not an occasion of social interest. It was an act of need, disposed of without grace or amenity. Inseparable from it were the taste and smell of dust and cow-hair and horse sweat and leather—sensory attributes of everything in the cowboy's working life.

> For want of an oven I cook bread in a pot,
> And sleep on the ground for want of a cot.

But before the bedrolls were opened up from their heavy canvas covers, and the work party went to sleep, there was a little while for talk and other diversion. Such a miniature society created its own theatre. There was always someone who would be moved to perform, while the rest gazed at the intimate, never-failing marvel of how one whom they knew—a man just like them—became before their very eyes somebody else. The campfire put rosy light over the near faces of the gathered men and their cluttered possessions, and threw their shadows like spokes out on the flat ground until the immense darkness absorbed all. At the very center of light a fellow rose. He had a joke to tell. He acted it out. It may have been well known to all, but they listened in fixity. It was likely to be an obscene jape. The cowboy, observed a cattleman of the 'seventies, "relishes . . . a corrupt tale, wherein abounds much vulgarity and animal propensity." His delight was a practical joke on one of his fellows. The joke was good if it made a fool of someone. It was better if it mocked the victim's personal peculiarity, and it was even better if it played upon "animal propensity"—for the sake of symbolic relief of the enforced continence under which the work party lived on the range.

There were other stories to hear—many dealt with experiences in the Civil War, to which the early cowboys were still close in time. There were wrestling and other trials of strength to perform. There were songs to sing, some of whose texts were lewd parodies of sentimental ballads. All knew the songs of the cattle trail, and could sing them together. If in one of his cubbyholes the cook carried a violin for its owner, there would be fiddle music of an astonishing legerity that yet managed to seem tuneless, while a cowboy danced a clog in firelighted dust, and the rest clapped hands. Often a mournful piety stirred in someone, and when he began to sing a hymn, others joined him, and like a sigh of innocence, their united voices rose over their lonely fire where they camped, a little knot of men with every potentiality, to one or another degree, for every human attribute. The bedrolls came out of the wagon and were spread. Nobody had a book to read, and in any case, the firelight was dying and would soon be down to coals.

> My ceiling's the sky, my floor is the grass,
> My music's the lowing of herds as they pass;
> My books are the brooks, my sermons the stones,
> My parson a wolf on his pulpit of bones. . . .

As his artless song implied, the cowboy belonged to the type of man who was not, actually, domesticated. He chose freedom in the wilds over responsibilities of hearth and home. He thought more about work than he did of a family. He made love on almost a seasonal schedule, as though in rut. He visited a prostitute, or took a sweetheart, only to leave her, with sighs about how he must go roaming, as though all would understand his natural state. He departed for work or went off to fight wherever he would find other men like himself. He preferred the society of men to that of women: for only with men could he live a daily life that was made up of danger, and hard exposure, and primitive manners. These did not seem like disadvantages to him, for he liked them for themselves, and, further, they brought into his life excitement, freedom and wilderness, all of which he sought.

If he saw himself as a simple creature, and if tradition so accepted him, both were wrong. His temperament and character were full of tempestuous contradictions and stresses. The life he chose resembled the Indian's more than any other, but it lacked the sustaining spiritual power of the Indian's nature-mythology, and so it could not really hold for him the unquestioned dignity of a system that tried to explain—in whatever error—the whole of human life. He was close to the frontiersman many of whose ways he repeated, but he was neither innovator, builder nor explorer. His love of hardness and primitive conditions could be turned either to serve his comrades in unbreakable loyalty, or to lead him, as it did in individual cases, to a career as gunman or cattle thief. His longing for love was so great that he felt an exaggerated chivalry for womankind, but in his worship he made women unreal; and yet through his song literature he lamented, ". . . between me and love lies a gulf very wide." He sanctioned his state by romanticizing it in ballad and story; but he refuted it symbolically by his periodic violent outbreaks of gunplay, drunkenness and venery. And with all his hardness, he gave in to a soft core of sentiment whose objects were the animals he worked with, and the comrades who worked with him.

"I and they were but creatures of circumstance," said a cowboy of his fellows in his domesticated old age, "the circumstances of an unfenced world." From their unfencedness came their main characteristics. Solitude was put upon them by their chosen environment, which thus modified their character. "Adhesiveness," in the jargon of the nineteenth-century parlor science, was a human trait. The nearest living being to whom the cowboy could turn with affection was his horse. It was his daylong companion and helper. It obeyed his orders and made him master of distance and took him in and out of danger. Responding to his signals, it seemed to him to possess more than animal intelligence. His horse, a masterpiece of anthropomorphism, joined him in a partnership, and was paid every honor due to such a position. "My horse," continued the retired cowboy, "my horse was something alive, something intelligent and friendly and true. He was sensitive, and for him I had a profound feeling. I sometimes think back on . . . remarkable horses I owned in much the same way that I think back on certain friends that have left me. . . . I went hungry sometimes, but if there was any possible way of getting food for my horse or if there was a place to stake him, even though I had to walk back a mile after putting him to graze"—and cowboys hated to walk—"I never let him go hungry. Many a time I have divided the water in a canteen with a horse." If it was expedient to take care of his horse in order to assure his own mobility and safety, and if it was ordinary human kindness to care for a dumb creature, there was yet more than such promptings in the cowboy's devotion to his mount, as many a song and story attested. The professional cowboy rarely had a cultivated mind; and in his incurious thought he was lowered and his horse was elevated until they drew together in common identity. It was a process typical of a juvenile stage of character, and it may have suggested why the cowboy and his legend should appeal forever after as a figure of play to little boys. In much the same sort of emotion the cowboy felt a mournful fondness for the animals he herded—the little "dogies" to whom he sang on the trail to keep them quiet, and to whom he attributed something of himself as they were objects of his vigilance and labor, day and night. In its innocence and pathos his system of projected sentimentality for his animals suggested that only by making of them more than they were could he have survived his lonely and arduous duty with them. One of his songs said of the cowboy that "his education is but to endure. . . ."

Another song celebrated the life of cowboys together in their wandering yet coherent community. "The boys were like brothers," they sang of themselves, "their friendship was great. . . ." Alike in their extreme individualism, their self-reliance, their choice of a life wild, free and rude, the companions of the cow camp gave to one another an extreme loyalty. It seemed like a tribute to the hard skills they had to master to do their jobs. A man who proved himself able at it deserved membership in a freemasonry unlike any other. Its physical tasks caused a high value to come upon the life of action, in which there was no place for the values of mind and spirit. These were relegated to the world of women; and in the towns and cities that later completed the settling of the last frontier West, for the better part of a century it would be the women's organizations that would try to rescue the fine arts, education, religion, and social amenity from being held as simply irrelevant to civilized life—an attitude even more withering to mankind's highest expressions than one of mere contempt. For its purpose in its time, the brotherhood of the cow camp was all that was needed to make an effective society. Diverse like all individuals, and sprung from various backgrounds and kinds of experience, the cowboys taken together seemed to merge into a type more readily than most workers in a common job. Their environment directly created the terms of their work, and their work in its uncomplicated terms created their attitudes and points of view. And if they were like one another in their principal traits, it was because so many of them chose their calling for the same general reason.

This—it was attested to again and again in the cowboy's anonymous ballad literature—this was flight from one kind of life to another. Many cowboys left home, "each," said a ballad,

> Each with a hidden secret well smothered in his breast,
> Which brought us out to Mexico, way out here in the West.

In this lay a suggestion of doom, a rude Byronism that was echoed in other songs by allusions to unhappiness, guilt, escape. Some were driven to the new society of the cow range by a faithless girl at home, or a dissolute life, or a criminal past; others by inability to become reconciled to their home societies following the Civil War, or by bitterness in family life, or even by a cruel stepmother. Romantic conventions of behavior in the nineteenth century could move the cowboy, who punished those who had betrayed him. "I'll go," he threatened,

> . . . to the Rio Grande,
> And get me a job with a cowboy band.

He did not mean a band of musicians, for not until the next century would the cowboy's public identity be chiefly that of an entertainer who in a commercial adaptation of the cowboy costume would spend more time with a microphone than with either horse or cow. No, with companions on the cattle range, the cowboy, deaf to dissuasion by loved ones who had proved faithless, promised to go

> . . . where the bullets fly,
> And follow the cow trail till I die.

Unable for whatever reason to accept the bindings of conventional society, within the one he sought and helped to make on the last frontier, he was capable of sure dependability in any cause for the common good of his comrades, whom he did not judge, even if sometimes a propensity to go wrong should overtake them in the very land where they had thought to escape their doom. Who knew when a man might encounter the moral frailty of one of his friends of the brushlands?

> As I walked out in the streets of Laredo,
> As I walked out in Laredo one day,
> I spied a dear cowboy wrapped up in white linen,
> Wrapped up in white linen as cold as the clay.

It was a dirge for a young man who in his dying words revealed a longing for a gentler land than the dusty empire of his work, and confessed his errors. "Oh," he said,

> Oh, beat the drum slowly and play the fife lowly.
> Play the dead march as you carry me along;
> Take me to the green valley, there lay the sod o'er me,
> For I'm a young cowboy and I know I've done wrong.

Unashamed of their grief that sprang from their close living, his bearers saw themselves in him, and if he had sinned, they could not condemn him.

> We beat the drum slowly and played the fife lowly,
> And bitterly wept as we bore him along;
> For we all loved our comrade, so brave, young and handsome,
> We all loved our comrade although he'd done wrong.

For here was a clan feeling, a solidarity, with a realistic view of character and its capacity for error. Idealizing one another in the all-male society of their work and play, the cowboys remained loyal above, or even because of, the weaknesses they shared and assuaged with violence. In conclusion, the dirge moved from the individual to the group.

> Then beat your drum lowly and play your fife slowly,
> Beat the Dead March as you carry me along;
> We all love our cowboys so young and so handsome,
> We all love our cowboys although they've done wrong.

In another valedictory the cowboy spirit, after reciting the perils of "some bad company" which could only lead to being "doomed for hell," ended in the presence of the hangman with an admonition to morality.

> It's now I'm on the scaffold,
> My moments are not long;
> You may forget the singer
> But don't forget the song.

In the cowboy's lonely character there were extremes of feeling and behavior. If in his work there seemed to be a discipline of dedicated steadfastness, a purity of vocation, then when he went to town, he threw himself into indulgence. Perhaps the town was a reminder of the coherent social life he had fled at home, and perhaps it was now a guilty joy to outrage it by his behavior. Certainly the town was the very opposite of the desolate open range from which even the cowboy needed periodic change.

His best chance for it came when men of the range party were told to drive a herd of cattle to the marketing and shipping towns. The main trails along which he drove went north from the Texan Rio Grande to Kansas, and another—the Goodnight-Loving Trail—led westward to New Mexico and California. It passed the Pecos River at Horsehead Crossing about a hundred miles above the Rio Grande, and presently divided into two forks. One pointed north to Colorado. The other crossed the Rio Grande at Las Cruces and followed the old road to San Diego.

The cattle made trails that showed many narrow grooves side by side— marks of the strict formation in which the animals in their thousands were driven for upwards of a thousand miles. A cowboy said that trail life was "wonderfully pleasant"—this in spite of continuing hazards. There still might be trouble with Indians. All the cattle were wild, and were easily stampeded by attacks, or by thunderstorms, or by hail. If the weather was wet, rivers rose, and to take thousands of cattle across swollen waters was at best a tedious job, and often a perilous one. Against the drovers on the move there pressed at one period a whole organized enterprise of thievery. Outlaws captured drovers, tortured them, sometimes killed them, and stole their herds. When one drover was captured, he tried to talk his way out of his trouble, but the bandits were immovable and a reporter of the incident said bitterly that "it was like preaching morality to an alligator."

But in swelling volume the animal trains passed through to their destinations, and the cowboys were happy on the trail. They played tricks on one another, and shot game on the prairies, and after supper sang, told stories, danced to a fiddle, lay back to look at the stars and speculate about them, and listened for the sounds of the herd settling down for the night. "I do not know anything more wholesome and satisfying," mused a cowboy long after his trail days, "than seeing cattle come in on their bed ground at night so full and contented that they grunt when they lie down."It was like a communion of creature comforts in which man and animal could meet. Three shifts of night guards were posted over the herds. A sleepy cowboy rubbed tobacco juice in his eyes to keep awake. Morning must come, and another day to be spent at the pace of cattle walking with odd delicacy in their narrow grooved trails, and after enough such days, the shipping town would take form like a few scattered gray boxes on the severe horizon, and the cowboy would feel his various hungers begin to stir.

It was in town that he got into most of his trouble. Every facility was there to help him do it. As a cattle shipper observed, in frontier towns "there are always to be found a number of bad characters, both male and female, of the very worst class in the universe, such as have fallen below the level of the lowest type of brute creation." These pandered to the cowboy's howling appetite for dissipation.

Sometimes he rode into town and without cleaning himself or changing his clothes but just as he had dismounted in hat, damp shirt, earth-caked trousers, and boots and spurs, he strode into a dance house, seized a "calico queen" or a "painted cat," as he called the dancing women, and with Indian yells and a wild eye went pounding about the dance floor under a grinding necessity to prove in public, most of all to himself, that he was at last having a good time. The music to which he danced was "wretched . . . ground out of dilapidated instruments, by beings fully as degraded as the most vile. Few more wild, reckless scenes of abandoned debauchery can be seen on the civilized earth," remarked the cattle shipper, "than a dance house in full blast in one of the many frontier towns. To say they dance wildly or in an abandoned manner is putting it mild. . . ."

And sometimes the cowboy, at large in town with his accumulated pay, went first to improve his looks. In a barbershop he had a bath, and then had his three to six months' growth of hair trimmed, and his full beard cut down, shaped and dyed black. In a clothing store he bought completely new clothes, from hat to boots, and then, strapping on his pistol, he was ready to impose himself like shock upon the town. Gambling rooms, saloons, a theatre, a row of prostitutes' quarters like cattle stalls, dance houses—from one to the next the cowboy could make his explosive way, to be catered to by "men who live a soulless, aimless life," and women who had "fallen low, alas! how low . . . miserable beings." Among the conventions of the cowboy's town manners was free use of his firearm, whether he might harm anyone or not. The pathos of folly long done and half forgotten would make his murderous antics seem unreal to later view. But they were real enough in the frontier towns of the 1870s. "It is idle," sighed the cattle shipper in that decade, "it is idle to deny the fact that the wild, reckless conduct of the cowboys while drunk . . . have brought the *personnel* of the Texan cattle trade into great disrepute, and filled many graves with victims, bad men and good men. . . . But by far the larger portion of those killed are of that class that can be spared without detriment to the good morals and respectability of humanity. . . ." And "after a few days of frolic and debauchery, the cowboy is ready, in company with his comrades, to start back to Texas, often not having one dollar left of his summer's wages." All he had was a memory that found its way into one of his songs, about "The way we drank and gambled and threw the girls around. . . ."

The cowboy triumphed at a lonely work in a beautiful and dangerous land. Those of his qualities that did the job were the good ones—courage, strength, devotion to duty. His worse traits, exercised for relief, were not judged in relation to his task. All aspects of his complex nature entered into his romance. He saw himself for his own achievement, and like the earliest individuals of the frontier, he consciously created his character and his tradition, and whether his emotion was honest or not, it was so energetic that by it he made his nation see him in his own terms. In him, the last American to live a life of wild freedom, his domesticated compatriots saw the end of their historical beginnings, and paid him nostalgic tribute in all their popular arts. Soon, like them, he would lose his nomadic, free and rough form of life before the westward sweep of machine technics by which Americans made their lives physically more easy—and socially less independent and self-reliant. In the very exercise of their genius for convenience in living, the Americans sacrificed to the social and commercial patterns of mass technics some part of the personal liberty in whose name the nation had been founded. The cowboy in his choice of solitude held on to his whole liberty as long as he could. But domestication of his West by machine technics began in the 1860s and, once started, went fast.

For in response to such technics, the cattle industry grew with suddenness, and then became stabilized. The first of these was the westward advance of the railroads with which the northbound cattle drives could make a junction. It was not easy to arrange for the earliest rail transport of western cattle. A young Illinois cattle shipper who was the first to establish a livestock market in Kansas was astonished to have his new idea rejected by two railroad presidents and the leading businessmen of several Kansas towns to whom he went in turn. Finally the Hannibal & St. Joe Railroad gave the young shipper a contract "at very satisfactory rates of freight from the Missouri River to Quincy, [Illinois] thence to Chicago." He selected Abilene, Kansas, as the site for his stockyards, and in 1867, the first cattle were driven there from Texas. During the next four years 1,460,000 head of cattle were brought to Abilene. Other trails and shipping centers were soon established, and it was estimated that during a period of twenty-eight years nearly ten million cattle worth almost a hundred million dollars were moved from the Texas ranges to market. In the process of developing so great a business, the whole practice of cattle raising became formalized through changes that sought greater efficiency.

One of these [innovations] used a technical machine product that soon conquered the open range where wild cattle once drifted according to weather. It was barbed wire, first used in 1875 to fence pastures in which with fewer and less skillful cowboys the herds could be restricted and more easily managed. When land was enclosed, ranch dwellings were needed. Permanent headquarters buildings followed. Cattle no longer were driven to rivers but found their water in earth tanks supplied by dug wells, with still another machine product to keep it flowing—the metal windmill. The main trunk lines of the railroads ran east to west across the continent; but soon feeder lines were built—sometimes following the flat terrain of the old trails—and machine transportation reached nearer and nearer to the great ranches of the border where the whole cattle industry had had its beginnings. The Missouri, Kansas and Texas Railroad was the great Texas cattle line. It tapped the Rio Grande brush country ranges. The Atchison, Topeka and Santa Fe main line crossed New Mexico and a branch line ran from Belen on the Rio Grande all the way down the valley to El Paso. The Texas and Pacific reached eastward from San Diego to El Paso in 1877, and bridges now came back to the Rio Grande to stay. The whole river empire was soon tied to the rest of the nation by rails. When packing houses were established at Kansas City, Fort Worth and other Southwestern cities, the final pattern of the organized beef cattle industry was realized. In it there was little room for the figure, the temperament, of the original cowboy, with his individual lordship over great unimpeded distances and his need of freedom as he defined it. His cow camp literature recorded yet another stage—the last—of his history. "The cowboy has left the country," he could sing, "and the campfire has gone out. . . ."

On barbed wire fences, like symbols of the new order of affairs over the controlled range lands, dead, skinned coyotes were impaled in a frieze—twenty or thirty of them at a time. They were stretched in midair with a lean, racing look of unearthly nimbleness, running nowhere; and their skulled teeth had the smile of their own ghosts, wits of the plains. In the dried varnish of their own amber serum they glistened under the sun. The day of unrestrained predators was over.

DOCUMENTS

Flush Times in Nevada,*
c. 1862

Six months after my entry into journalism that grand "flush times" of Silverland began, and they continued with unabated splendor for three years. All difficulty about filling up the "local department" ceased, and the only trouble now was how to make the lengthened columns hold the world of incidents and happening that came to our literary net every day. Virginia had grown to be the "livest" town, for its age and population, that America had ever produced. The sidewalks swarmed with people— to such an extent, indeed, that it was generally no easy matter to stem the human tide. The streets themselves were just as crowded with quartz-wagons, freight-teams, and other vehicles. The procession was endless. So great was the pack, that buggies frequently had to wait half an hour for an opportunity to cross the principal street. Joy sat on every countenance, and there was a glad, almost fierce, intensity in every eye, that told of the money-getting schemes that held sway in every heart. Money was as plenty as dust; every individual considered himself wealthy, and a melancholy countenance was nowhere to be seen. There were military companies, fire companies, brass bands, banks, hotels, theaters, "hurdy-gurdy houses,"** wide-open gambling-palaces, political pow-wows, civic processions, street-fights, murders, inquests, riots, a whiskeymill every fifteen steps, a Board of Aldermen, a Mayor, a City Surveyor, a City Engineer, a Chief of the Fire Department, with First, Second, and Third Assistants, a Chief of Police, City Marshal, and a large police force, two Boards of Mining Brokers, a dozen breweries, and a half dozen jails and station-houses in full operation, and some talk of building a church. The "flush times" were in magnificent flower! Large fireproof brick buildings were going up in the principal streets, and the wooden suburbs were spreading out in all directions. Town lots soared up to prices that were amazing.

The great "Comstock lode" stretched its opulent length straight through the town from north to south, and every mine on it was in diligent process of development. One of these mines alone employed six hundred and seventy-five men, and in the matter of elections the adage was, "as the 'Gould & Curry' [mine] goes, so goes the city." Laboring-men's wages were four and six dollars a day, and they worked in three "shifts" or gangs,

SOURCE: Samuel L. Clemens, *Roughing It* (New York: Harper and Brothers, 1890), II: 11–13, 16–19.

[*The term *flush times* refers to the silver and gold boom in Nevada in the 1860s.]
[**dance halls]

and the blasting and picking and shoveling went on without ceasing, night and day.

The "city" of Virginia roosted royally midway up the steep side of Mount Davidson, seven thousand two hundred feet above the level of the sea, and in the clear Nevada atmosphere was visible from a distance of fifty miles! It claimed a population of fifteen thousand to eighteen thousand, and all day long half of this little army swarmed the streets like bees and the other half swarmed the drifts and tunnels of the "Comstock," hundreds of feet down in the earth directly under those same streets. . . .

My salary was increased to forty dollars a week. But I seldom drew it. I had plenty of other resources, and what were two broad twenty-dollar gold pieces to a man who had his pockets full of such and a cumbersome abundance of bright half-dollars besides? (Paper money has never come into use on the Pacific coast.) Reporting was lucrative, and every man in the town was lavish with his money and his "feet."* The city and all the great mountainside were riddled with mining-shafts. There were more mines than miners. True, not ten of these mines were yielding rock worth hauling to a mill, but everybody said, "Wait till the shaft gets down where the ledge comes in solid, and then you will see!" So nobody was discouraged. These were nearly all "wildcat" mines, and wholly worthless, but nobody believed it then. The "Ophir," the "Gould & Curry," the "Mexican," and other great mines on the Comstock lode in Virginia and Gold Hill were turning out huge piles of rich rock every day, and every man believed that his little wildcat claim was as good as any on the "main lead" and would infallibly be worth a thousand dollars a foot when he "got down where it came in solid." Poor fellow! he was blessedly blind to the fact that he would never see that day. So the thousand wildcat shafts burrowed deeper and deeper into the earth day by day, and all men were beside themselves with hope and happiness. How they labored, prophesied, exulted! Surely nothing like it was ever seen before since the world began. Every one of these wildcat mines—not mines, but holes in the ground over imaginary mines—was incorporated and had handsome engraved "stock" and the stock was salable, too. It was bought and sold with a feverish avidity on the boards every day. You could go up on the mountainside, scratch around and find a ledge (there was no lack of them), put up a "notice" with a grandiloquent name on it, start a shaft, get your stock printed, and with nothing whatever to prove that your mine was worth a straw, you could put your stock on the market and sell out for hundreds and even thousands of dollars. To make money, and make it fast, was as easy as it was to eat your dinner. Every man owned "feet" in fifty different

[*shares of stock in wildcat mines, measured in feet]

wildcat mines and considered his fortune made. Think of a city with not one solitary poor man in it! One would suppose that when month after month went by and still not a wildcat mine (by wildcat I mean, in general terms, *any* claim not located on the mother vein, *i.e.,* the "Comstock") yielded a ton of rock worth crushing, the people would begin to wonder if they were not putting too much faith in their prospective riches; but there was not a thought of such a thing. They burrowed away, bought and sold, and were happy.

New claims were taken daily, and it was the friendly custom to run straight to the newspaper offices, give the reporter forty or fifty "feet" and get him to go and examine the mine and publish a notice of it. They did not care a fig what you said about the property so [long as] you said something. Consequently we generally said a word or two to the effect that the "indications" were good, or that the ledge was "six feet wide," or that the rock "resembled the Comstock" (and so it did—but as a general thing the resemblance was not startling enough to knock you down!). . .

There was *nothing* in the shape of a mining claim that was not salable. We received presents of "feet" every day. If we needed a hundred dollars or so, we sold some; if not we hoarded it away, satisfied that it would ultimately be worth a thousand dollars a foot. I had a trunk about half full of "stock." When a claim made a stir in the market and went up to a high figure, I searched through my pile to see if I had any of its stock—and generally found it.

Growing Wheat on the Great Plains, 1863

As one goes over the country in the fall of the year he sees vast tracts of "new breaking," where the virgin soil, black as ink, and rich almost to glutinousness, has been broken by the plow, and the soil turned bottom upward in long, dark bands or layers as far as the eye can reach. Here it is exposed for months to the wind and weather till it decomposes and becomes fit for agricultural purposes. Every year vast tracts of prairie are thus turned over, or "broken," and with the next the loam is leveled and the seed is cast in; and thus large additions are annually made to the aggregate amount of acres of wheat.

Take your stand on one of these "new breaking-pieces," and look perhaps in any direction, and you will find yourself enclosed by its dreary

SOURCE: "Among the Wheat-Fields of Minnesota," *Harper's New Monthly Magazine,* 212 (January 1863): 193–4.

strips of black loam; not a blade of grass nor a single leaf will appear. It is a picture of desolation and vacancy; nature and life are in their embryo; not a glimpse can be seen of their future creations. Nothing can exceed the contrast between this and what these same fields will present a year or two afterward, when they stand yellow with the harvest, an emblem of cheerfulness and prosperity.

Farms are generally 160 acres in extent—a "quarter section" being usually the quantity bought and worked. Under the Homestead Law lands are constantly taken up, the cost being a mere trifle for fees, etc. The settler is required to locate on it, put up a small house, do some fencing and "breaking," and pass a night on it at least once every six months.

Many amusing stories are told how persons of ingenious habits of mind and India-rubber consciences manage to conform to the letter, while they evade the more burdensome intents of the law. The merest apology for a house, and the least possible amount of residence and "improvements" are done. Still this dodging of the law works no serious violation of its contemplated objects. Lands are opened, destitute families are provided with a farm and means of attaining independence and prosperity, and the State is settled up. Sometimes a family is so constituted as to be able to take four quarters, or a full square mile of land. No single applicant can take out papers for more than one quarter section, and a man and his wife and young children are viewed as one party. But if he has a widowed mother and two unmarried sisters grown up living with him, each is regarded as a legal applicant; and they arrange it often thus: They select four quarter sections lying contiguous to each other, and put up a house right upon the centre where the four quarter sections touch, so that each quarter of the building stands on a different quarter section. Partitions divide the interior into rooms to correspond; and each party then fulfills his obligations to the law at one-fourth the expense he or she would otherwise incur. They are supposed to form four distinct families, dwelling apart, although practically they still form but one household as before.

These wild lands thus entered are worth about $5 per acre, and when "improved" rise to $15 or $25 according to circumstances. At the end of five years' residence Government gives a clean deed of the property. Many, however, having the means, prefer to buy the land outright at the start, paying the Government price, $1.25 per acre.

Wheat matures from about the beginning to the middle of August. The whole country then awakens from its long slothfulness. Business revives. Interest, energy, and happiness everywhere appear. No one who has never witnessed the dullness pervading all departments of business during the winter and spring can comprehend the great and sudden transformation which the incoming crop produces. Mechanics, tradesmen, wheat-buyers, railroads, steamboats—all seem to be indued with new life and vigor: . . .

Heading East
Out of Kansas, 1895

There came through Emporia yesterday two old-fashioned "mover wagons," headed east. The stock in the caravan would invoice four horses, very poor and very tired; one mule, more disheartened than the horses; and one sad-eyed dog, that had probably been compelled to rustle his own precarious living for many a long and weary day.

A few farm implements of the simpler sort were in the wagon, but nothing that had wheels was moving except the two wagons. All the rest of the impedimenta had been left upon the battlefield, and these poor stragglers, defeated but not conquered, were fleeing to another field, to try the fight again.

These movers were from western Kansas—from Gray County, a county which holds a charter from the state to officiate as the very worst, most desolate, God-forsaken, man-deserted spot on the sad old earth. They had come from that wilderness only after a ten years' hard, vicious fight, a fight which had left its scars on their faces, had beat their bodies, had taken the elasticity from their steps, and left them crippled to enter the battle anew.

For ten years they had been fighting the elements. They had seen it stop raining for months at a time. They had heard the fury of the winter wind as it came whining across the short burned grass, and their children huddling in the corner. They have strained their eyes watching through the long summer days for the rain that never came. They have seen that big cloud roll up from the southwest about one o'clock in the afternoon, hover over the land, and stumble away with a few thumps of thunder as the sun went down. They have tossed through hot nights wild with worry, and have arisen only to find their worst nightmares grazing in reality on the brown stubble in front of their sun-warped doors.

They had such high hopes when they went out there; they are so desolate now—no, not now, for now they are in the land of corn and honey. They have come out of the wilderness, back to the land of promise. They are now in God's own country down on the Neosho, with their wife's folks, and the taste of apple butter and good cornbread and fresh meat and pie—pie-plant [rhubarb] pie like mother used to make—gladdened their shrunken palates last night. And real cream, curdling on their coffee saucers last night for supper, was a sight so rich and strange that it lingered in their dreams, wherein they walked beside the still water, and lay down in green pastures.

SOURCE: From William Allen White, Emporia (Kansas) *Gazette*, June 15, 1895.

CHAPTER 3

Indian Schools: "Americanizing" the Native American

The white settlers' movement onto the Great Plains had devastating effects on the Native American tribes who had roamed the area for centuries. As on previous frontiers further east, the Indians resisted the encroachment with some initial success, their most notable victory being the defeat of General George Custer at the Little Bighorn River in 1876. However, the whites' superior manpower and technology, fueled by their desire to fulfill a "manifest destiny" to develop the entire continent, overcame the Native Americans, and in the end the whites removed them to reservations.

During the 1870s and 1880s, even while the last Indian wars were being waged, the federal government passed legislation and instituted policies designed to solve the "Indian problem" by "Americanizing" them—assimilating them into American society. The federal government encouraged them, sometimes forcefully, to exchange their lands, held by the tribe as a whole, for individual holdings on which they were expected to engage in farming. Equally important, the government sought to educate their children away from their traditional cultures and provide them with the skills, knowledge, and attitudes deemed necessary for the new way of life that the dominant white culture was dictating for them.

By 1881, the federal government was operating 106 Indian day and boarding schools to accomplish these objectives. Although most of the schools were on or adjacent to reservation land, white educators placed their greatest faith in nonreservation boarding schools far removed from parental and tribal influences. Robert A. Trennert's essay, "Educating Indian Girls at Nonreservation Boarding Schools, 1878–1920," provides a detailed view of this educational policy in action. What do you think the advocates of Indian education meant by "assimilation"? To what does the author attribute the failure of the government's Indian-school policies during this period?

The first document consists of excerpts from the "Rules for Indian Schools" set forth by the Bureau of Indian Affairs (1890). What attitudes toward their mission and toward Native American youth would likely be engendered in the minds of the teachers upon reading their instructions? In what ways does each of the rules cited contribute to the broad objectives of the government's Indian-education policies? What can you conclude about the immediate and long-term objectives of Indian education?

Although government land and educational policies were expressed in positive terms, they in fact reflected the prevailing belief that the Native American culture was inferior. At the turn of the century many social scientists had adapted Darwin's biological theories of evolution to an explanation of social development, drawing conclusions that are totally rejected by their counterparts of today. Specifically, they developed a theoretical hierarchy of superior and inferior races that placed northern Europeans at the top and Indians, blacks, and southern and eastern Europeans, among others, at the bottom. The second document, a 1905 report of the Board of Indian Commissioners, typifies the attitudes underlying governmental policies up until the 1930s. This report sheds light on the basis for Indian policy and reveals much of the rational for the immigration-restriction and racial-segregation laws of the era as well.

Many factors explain why, by the 1920s, Native Americans found themselves mired in poverty at the bottom of the economic ladder: the failure of the federal government's Indian-education policies, the poor land conditions under which they were expected to become independent farmers, and the racism and discrimination meted out by the dominant white culture. During the 1930s, however, conditions began to improve. The Indian Reorganization Act of 1934 called for the establishment of tribal governments and the election of tribal leaders, which exemplified a more enlightened view of Native American culture and reflected the New Deal government's concern for the poor and disadvantaged.

After World War II, Native Americans, like other minority groups, organized to proclaim their cultural identity and to demand full civil rights and economic *opportunity. The final document presents the findings and recommendations of the Minnesota Advisory Committee (1978), which investigated Indian education and employment in the Minneapolis–St. Paul area. What does it reveal about the recent status of Native American schooling and about attitudes toward Indians and their culture?*

E S S A Y

Educating Indian Girls at Nonreservation Boarding Schools, 1878–1920

Robert A. Trennert

During the latter part of the nineteenth century the Bureau of Indian Affairs made an intensive effort to assimilate the Indian into American society. One important aspect of the government's acculturation program was Indian education. By means of reservation day schools, reservation boarding schools, and off-reservation industrial schools, the federal government attempted to obliterate the cultural heritage of Indian youths and replace it with the values of Anglo-American society. One of the more notable aspects of this program was the removal of young Indian women from their tribal homes to government schools in an effort to transform them into a government version of the ideal American woman. This program of assimilationist education, despite some accomplishments, generally failed to attain its goals. This study is a review of the education of Indian women at the institutions that best typified the government program—the off-reservation industrial training schools. An understanding of this educational system provides some insight into the impact of the acculturation effort on the native population. Simultaneously, it illustrates some of the prevalent national images regarding both Indians and women.

The concept of educating native women first gained momentum among eighteenth-century New England missionaries who recommended that Indian girls might benefit from formal training in housekeeping. This idea matured to the point that, by the 1840s, the federal government had committed itself to educating Indian girls in the hope that women trained as good housewives would help their mates assimilate. A basic premise of this educational effort rested on the necessary elimination of Indian culture. Although recent scholarship has suggested that the division of labor

SOURCE: Robert A. Trennert, "Educating Indian Girls at Nonreservation Boarding Schools, 1878–1920," *Western Historical Quarterly,* 13 (July 1982): 169–90. Copyright by the Western History Association. Reprinted by permission.

between the sexes within Indian societies was rather equitable, mid-nineteenth-century Americans accepted a vision of Native American women as slaves toiling endlessly for their selfish, slovenly husbands and fathers in an atmosphere of immorality, degradation, and lust. Any cursory glance at contemporary literature provides striking evidence of this belief. Joel D. Steele, for example, in his 1876 history of the American nation described Indian society in the following terms: "The Indian was a barbarian. . . . Labor he considered degrading, and fit only for women. His squaw, therefore, built his wigwam, cut his wood, and carried his burdens when he journeyed. While he hunted or fished, she cleared the land . . . and dressed skins."

Government officials and humanitarian reformers shared Steele's opinion. Secretary of the Interior Carl Schurz, a noted reformer, stated in 1881 that "the Indian woman has so far been only a beast of burden. The girl, when arrived at maturity, was disposed of like an article of trade. The Indian wife was treated by her husband alternately with animal fondness, and with the cruel brutality of the slave driver." Neither Steele nor Schurz was unique in his day; both expressed the general opinion of American society. From this perspective, if women were to be incorporated into American society, their sexual role and social standing stood in need of change.

The movement to educate Indian girls reflected new trends in women's education. Radical changes in the economic and social life of late nineteenth-century America set up a movement away from the traditional academy education of young women. Economic opportunity created by the industrial revolution combined with the decline of the family as a significant economic unit produced a demand for vocational preparation for women. The new school discipline of "domestic science," a modern homemaking technique, developed as a means to bring stability and scientific management to the American family and provide skills to the increasing number of women entering the work force. In the years following the Civil War, increased emphasis was placed on domestic and vocational education as schools incorporated the new discipline into their curriculum. Similar emphasis appeared in government planning for the education of Indian women as a means of their forced acculturation. However, educators skirted the question of whether native women should be trained for industry or homemaking.

During the 1870s, with the tribes being confined to reservations, the government intensified its efforts to provide education for Indian youth of both sexes. The establishment of the industrial training schools at the end of the decade accelerated the commitment to educate Indian women. These schools got their start in 1878 when Captain Richard Henry Pratt, in charge of a group of Indian prisoners at Fort Marion, Florida, persuaded the government to educate eighteen of the younger male inmates at Hampton

Normal Institute, an all-black school in Virginia, run by General Samuel C. Armstrong. Within six months Pratt and Armstrong were pleased enough with the results of their experiment to request more students. Both men strongly believed that girls should be added to the program, and Armstrong even went so far as to stipulate that Hampton would take more Indian students only on condition that half be women. At first Indian Commissioner Ezra A. Hayt rejected the proposal, primarily because he questioned the morality of allowing Indian women to mix with black men, but Armstrong's argument that "without educated women there is no civilization" finally prevailed. Thus, when Pratt journeyed west in the fall of 1878 to recruit more students, he fully expected half to be women.

Pratt was permitted to enlist fifty Indian students on his trip up the Missouri River. Mrs. Pratt went along to aid with the enlistment of girls. Although they found very little problem in recruiting a group of boys, they had numerous difficulties locating girls. At Fort Berthold, for instance, the Indians objected to having their young women taken away from home. Pratt interpreted this objection in terms of his own ethnocentric beliefs, maintaining that Indian tribes made their "squaws" do all the work. "They are too valuable in the capacity of drudge during the years they should be at school to be spared to go," he reported. Ultimately it required the help of local missionaries to secure four female students. Even then there were unexpected problems. As Pratt noted, "One of the girls [age ten] was especially bright and there was a general desire to save her from the degradation of her Indian surroundings. The mother [age twenty-six] said that education and civilization would make her child look upon her as a savage, and that unless she could go with her child and learn too, the child could not come." Pratt included both mother and daughter. Not all the missionaries and government agents, however, shared Pratt's enthusiasm. At Cheyenne River and other agencies a number of officials echoed the sentiments of Commissioner Hayt regarding the morality of admitting girls to a black school, and they succeeded in blocking recruitment. As a result, only nine girls were sent to Hampton.

Although the educational experiences of the first Indian girls to attend Hampton have not been well documented, a few things are evident. The girls were kept under strict supervision and were separated from the boys except during times of classroom instruction. In addition, the girls were kept apart from black pupils. Most of the academic work was focused on learning the English language, and the girls also received instruction in household skills. The small number of girls, of course, made it difficult to implement a general educational plan. Moreover, considerable opposition remained to educating Indian women at Hampton. Many prominent reformers expected confrontations, or even worse, love affairs, between black and red. Others expressed concern that Indian students in an all-black setting would not receive sufficient incentive and demanded they have the benefit of direct contact with white citizens.

Captain Pratt himself wanted to separate the Indians and blacks, and despite the fact that no racial trouble surfaced at Hampton, he pressured the government to create a school solely for Indians. Indian contact with blacks did not fit in with his plans for native education, and he reminded Secretary Schurz that Indians could become useful citizens only "through living among our people." The government consented, and in the summer of 1879 Pratt was authorized to open a school at Carlisle Barracks, Pennsylvania, "provided both boys and girls are educated in said school." Thus, while Hampton continued to develop its own Indian program, it was soon accompanied by Carlisle and other all-Indian schools.

Under the guidance of General Armstrong at Hampton and Captain Pratt at Carlisle, a program for Indian women developed over a period of several years. Although these men differed on the question of racial mixing, they agreed on what Indian girls should be learning. By 1880, with fifty-seven Indian girls at Carlisle and about twenty at Hampton, the outlines of the program began to emerge. As rapidly as possible the girls were placed in a system that put maximum emphasis on domestic chores. Academic learning clearly played a subordinate role. The girls spent no more than half a day in the classroom and devoted the rest of their time to domestic work. At Carlisle the first arrivals were instructed in "the manufacture and mending of garments, the use of the sewing machine, laundry work, cooking, and the routine of household duties pertaining to their sex."

Discipline went hand in hand with work experience. Both Pratt and Armstrong possessed military backgrounds and insisted that girls be taught strict obedience. General Armstrong believed that obedience was completely foreign to the native mind and that discipline was a corollary to civilization. Girls, he thought, were more unmanageable than boys because of their "inherited spirit of independence." To instill the necessary discipline, the entire school routine was organized in martial fashion, and every facet of student life followed a strict timetable. Students who violated the rules were punished, sometimes by corporal means, but more commonly by ridicule. Although this discipline was perhaps no more severe than that in many non-Indian schools of the day, it contrasted dramatically with tribal educational patterns that often mixed learning with play. Thus, when Armstrong offered assurances that children accepted "the penalty gratefully as part of his [her] education in the good road," it might be viewed with a bit of skepticism.

Another integral part of the program centered on the idea of placing girls among white families to learn by association. The "outing" system, as it was soon called, began almost as quickly as the schools received

49

students. Through this system Pratt expected to take Indian girls directly from their traditional homes and in three years make them acceptable for placement in public schools and private homes. By 1881 both Carlisle and Hampton were placing girls in white homes, most of which were located in rural Pennsylvania or New England. Here the girls were expected to become independent, secure a working knowledge of the English language, and acquire useful domestic skills. Students were usually sent to a family on an individual basis, although in a few cases several young women were placed in the same home. Emily Bowen, an outing program sponsor in Woodstock, Connecticut, reveals something of white motives for participation in the service. Miss Bowen, a former teacher, heard of Pratt's school in 1880 and became convinced that God had called upon her to "lift up the lowly." Hesitating to endure the dangers of the frontier, she volunteered instead to take eight Indian girls into her home to "educate them to return and be a blessing to their people." Bowen proposed to teach the girls "practical things, such as housework, sewing, and all that is necessary to make home comfortable and pleasant." In this manner, she hoped, the girls under her charge would take the "true missionary spirit" with them on their return to their people.

Having set the women's education program in motion, Pratt and his colleagues took time to reflect on just what result they anticipated from the training. In his 1881 report to Commissioner Hiram Price, Pratt charted out his expectations. Essentially he viewed the education of native girls as a supportive factor in the more important work of training boys. To enter American society, the Indian male needed a mate who would encourage his success and prevent any backsliding. "Of what avail is it," Pratt asked, "that the man be hard-working and industrious, providing by his labor food and clothing for his household, if the wife, unskilled in cookery, unused to the needle, with no habits of order or neatness, makes what might be a cheerful, happy home only a wretched abode of filth and squalor?" Pratt charged Indian women with clinging to "heathen rites and superstitions" and passing them on to their children. They were, in effect, unfit as mothers and wives. Thus, a woman's education was supremely important, not so much for her own benefit as for that of her husband. Pratt did acknowledge that girls were required to learn more than boys. An Indian male needed only to learn a single trade; the woman, on the other hand, "must learn to sew and to cook, to wash and iron, she must learn lessons of neatness, order, and economy, for without a practical knowledge of all these she cannot make a home."

The size of the girls' program increased dramatically during the 1880s. The government was so taken with the apparent success of Carlisle and Hampton that it began to open similar schools in the West. As the industrial schools expanded, however, the women's program became institutionalized, causing a substantial deviation from the original concept. One reason for this change involved economic factors. The Indian schools, which for decades received $167 a year per student, suffered a chronic lack of funds; thus, to remain self-sufficient, they found themselves relying upon student labor whenever possible. Because they already believed in the educational value of manual labor, it was not a large step for school officials to begin relying upon student labor to keep the schools operating. By the mid-1880s, with hundreds of women attending the industrial schools, student labor had assumed a significant role in school operations. Thus, girls, originally expected to receive a useful education, found themselves becoming more important as an economic factor in the survival of the schools.

The girls' work program that developed at Hampton is typical of the increasing reliance on Indian labor. By 1883 the women's training section was divided into such departments as sewing, housekeeping, and laundry, each in the charge of a white matron or a black graduate. The forty-one girls assigned to the sewing department made the school's bedding, wardrobe, and curtains. At Winona Lodge, the dormitory for Indian girls that also supported the housework division, the matron described the work routine as follows: "All of the Indian girls, from eight to twenty-four years old, make their own clothes, wash and iron them, care for their rooms, and a great many of them take care of the teachers' rooms. Besides this they have extra work, such as sweeping, dusting, and scrubbing the corridors, stairs, hall, sewing-room, chapel, and cleaning other parts of the building." In addition, a large group of Indian girls worked in the school laundry doing the institution's wash.

Conditions were even more rigorous at western schools where a lack of labor put additional demands on female students. At Genoa, Nebraska, the superintendent reported that the few girls enrolled in that school were kept busy doing housework. With the exception of the laundry, which was detailed to the boys, girls were responsible for the sewing and repair of garments, including their own clothes, the small boys' wear, underwear for the large boys, and table linen. The kitchen, dining room, and dormitories were also maintained by women students. Similar circumstances prevailed at Albuquerque, where Superintendent P. F. Burke complained of having to use boys for domestic chores. He was much relieved when enough girls enrolled to allow "the making of the beds, sweeping, and cleaning both the boys' and girls' sleeping apartments." Because of inadequate facilities there were no girls enrolled when the Phoenix school opened in 1891; but as soon as a permanent building was constructed, Superintendent Wellington Rich requested twenty girls "to take the places now filled by boys in the several domestic departments of the school." Such uses of student labor were justified as a method of preparing girls for the duties of home life.

Some employees of the Indian Service recognized that assembly line chores alone were not guaranteed to accomplish the goals of the program.

Josephine Mayo, the girls' matron at Genoa, reported in 1886 that the work program was too "wholesale" to produce effective housewives. "Making a dozen beds and cleaning a dormitory does not teach them to make a room attractive and homelike," she remarked. Nor did cooking large quantities of a single item "supply a family with a pleasant and healthy variety of food, nicely cooked." The matron believed that Indian girls needed to be taught in circumstances similar to those they were expected to occupy. She therefore suggested that small cottages be utilized in which girls could be instructed in the care of younger students and perform all the duties of a housewife. Although Mayo expressed a perceptive concern for the inherent problems of the system, her remarks had little impact on federal school officials. In the meantime, schools were expected to run effectively, and women continued to perform much of the required labor.

Not all the girls' programs, of course, were as routine or chore oriented as the ones cited above. Several of the larger institutions made sincere efforts to train young Indian women as efficient householders. Girls were taught to care for children, to set tables, prepare meals, and make domestic repairs. After 1896 Haskell Institute in Kansas provided women with basic commercial skills in stenography, typing, and bookkeeping. Nursing, too, received attention at some schools. A number of teachers, though conventional in their views of Indian women's role, succeeded in relaxing the rigid school atmosphere. Teachers at Hampton, for instance, regularly invited small groups of girls to their rooms for informal discussions. Here girls, freed from the restraints of the classroom, could express their feelings and receive some personal encouragement. Many institutions permitted their girls to have a dress "with at least some imitation of prevailing style" and urged them to take pride in their appearance.

The industrial schools reached their peak between 1890 and 1910. During this period as many as twenty-five nonreservation schools were in operation. The number of Indian women enrolled may have reached three thousand per annum during this period and females composed between 40 and 50 percent of the student body of most schools. The large number of young women can be attributed to several factors: girls were easier to recruit, they presented fewer disciplinary problems and could be more readily placed in the "outing" system, and after 1892 they could be sent to school without parental consent.

Women's education also became more efficient and standardized during the 1890s. This was due in large part to the activities of Thomas J. Morgan, who served as Indian commissioner from 1889 to 1893. Morgan advocated the education of Indian women as an important part of the acculturation process, believing that properly run schools could remove girls from the "degradation" of camp life and place them on a level with "their more favored white sisters." The commissioner hoped to accomplish this feat by completely systematizing the government's educational program. "So far as possible," he urged, "there should be a uniform course of study, similar methods of instruction, the same textbooks, and a carefully organized and well understood system of industrial training." His suggestions received considerable support, and by 1890, when he issued his "Rules for Indian Schools," the standardization of the Indian schools had begun. Morgan, like Pratt before him, fully expected his concept of education to rapidly produce American citizens. The results were not what the commissioner expected. While standardization proved more efficient, it also exacerbated some of the problems of the women's educational program.

Under the direction of Morgan and his successors, the Indian schools of the era became monuments to regimentation from which there was no escape. This development is obvious in the increasing emphasis on military organization. By the mid-nineties most girls were fully incorporated into the soldierly routine. As one superintendent noted, all students were organized into companies on the first day of school. Like the boys, the girls wore uniforms and were led by student officers who followed army drill regulations. Every aspect of student life was regulated. Anna Moore, a Pima girl attending the Phoenix Indian School, remembered life in the girls' battalion as one of marching "to a military tune" and having to drill at five in the morning. Most school officials were united in their praise of military organization. Regimentation served to develop a work ethic; it broke the students' sense of "Indian time" and ordered their life. The merits of military organization, drill, and routine in connection with discipline were explained by one official who stated that "it teaches patriotism, obedience, courage, courtesy, promptness, and constancy."

Domestic science continued to dominate the women's program. Academic preparation for women never received much emphasis by industrial school administrators despite Morgan's promise that "literary" training would occupy half the students' time. . . . One reason for the lack of emphasis on academics was that by 1900 many school administrators had come to feel that Indians were incapable of learning more. One school superintendent did not consider his "literary" graduates capable of accomplishing much in white society, while another educator described the natives as a "child race."

The extent to which every feature of the girls' program was directed toward the making of proper middle-class housewives can be seen in the numerous directives handed down by the government. By the early twentieth century every detail of school life was regulated. In 1904 Superintendent of Indian Schools Estelle Reel issued a three-page circular on the proper method of making a bed. Much of this training bore little relationship to the reservation environment to which students would return. A few programs were entirely divorced from reality. The cooking course at Sherman Institute in California, for instance, taught girls to prepare formal meals including the serving of raw oysters, shrimp cocktails, and croquettes. In another instance, Hampton teachers devoted some of their energies to discussing attractive flower arrangements and the proper selection of decorative pictures.

Another popular program was the "industrial" cottage. These originated in 1883 at Hampton when the school enrolled several married Indian couples to serve as examples for the students. The couples were quartered in small frame houses while learning to maintain attractive and happy homes. Although the married students did not long remain at Hampton, school officials began to use the cottages as model homes where squads of Indian girls might practice living in white-style homes. By 1900 similar cottages were in use at western schools. The industrial cottage at Phoenix, for example, operated a "well-regulated household" run by nine girls under a matron's supervision. The "family" (with no males present) cleaned and decorated the cottage, did the regular routine of cooking, washing, and sewing, and tended to the poultry and livestock in an effort "to train them to the practical and social enjoyment of the higher life of a real home."

The outing system also continued to be an integral part of the girls' program. As time went on, however, and the system was adopted at western locations, the original purposes of the outings faded. Initially designed as a vehicle for acculturation, the program at many locations became a means of providing servants to white householders. At Phoenix, for example, female pupils formed a pool of cheap labor available to perform domestic services for local families. From the opening of the school in 1891, demands for student labor always exceeded the pool's capacity. One superintendent estimated that he could easily put two hundred girls to work. Moreover, not all employers were interested in the welfare of the student. As the Phoenix superintendent stated in 1894, "The hiring of Indian youth is not looked upon by the people of this valley from a philanthropic standpoint. It is simply a matter of business." In theory, school authorities could return pupils to school at any time it appeared they were not receiving educational benefits; but as one newspaper reported, "What a howl would go up from residents of this valley if the superintendent would exercise this authority."

Even social and religious activities served an educational purpose. When Mrs. Merial Dorchester, wife of the superintendent of Indian schools, made a tour of western school facilities in the early 1890s, she recommended that school girls organize chapters of the King's Daughters, a Christian service organization. Several institutions implemented the program. At these locations girls were organized by age into "circles" to spend spare time producing handcrafted goods for charity. School officials supported such activity because the necessity of raising their own funds to pay dues instilled in the girls a spirit of Christian industry. The manufacture of goods for charity also enhanced their sense of service to others. Said one school superintendent, the organization is "effective in furnishing a spur to individual effort and makes the school routine more bearable by breaking the monotony of it." Although maintaining a nonsectarian stance, the schools encouraged all types of religious activity as an effective method of teaching Christian values and removing the girls from the home influence.

An important factor in understanding the women's program at the industrial schools is the reaction of the girls themselves. This presents some problems, however, since most school girls left no record of their experiences. Moreover, many of the observations that have survived were published in closely controlled school magazines that omitted any unfavorable remarks. Only a few reliable reminiscences have been produced, and even these are not very informative. Despite such limitations, however, several points are evident. The reaction of Indian girls to their education varied greatly. Some came willingly and with the approval of their parents. Once enrolled in school, many of these individuals took a keen interest in their education, accepted discipline as good for them, and worked hard to learn the ways of white society. An undetermined number may have come to school to escape intolerable conditions at home. Some evidence suggests that schools offered safe havens from overbearing parents who threatened to harm their children. For other girls the decision to attend a nonreservation school was made at considerable emotional expense, requiring a break with conservative parents, relatives, and tribesmen. In a few cases young women even lost their opportunity to marry men of their own tribe as they became dedicated to an outside lifestyle.

Many girls disliked school and longed to return home. The reasons are not hard to find. The hard work, discipline, and punishment were often oppressive. One Hopi girl recalled having to get down on her knees each Saturday and scrub the floor of the huge dining hall. "A patch of floor was scrubbed, then rinsed and wiped, and another section was attacked. The work was slow and hard on the knees," she remembered. Pima schoolgirl [Anna] Moore experienced similar conditions working in the dining hall at Phoenix: "My little helpers and I hadn't even reached our teen-aged years yet, and this work seemed so hard! If we were not finished when the 8:00 a.m. whistle sounded, the dining room matron would go around strapping us while we were still on our hands and knees. . . . We just dreaded the sore bottoms." In a number of instances, teachers and matrons added to the trauma by their dictatorial and unsympathetic attitudes. A few girls ran away from school. Those who were caught received humiliating punishment. Runaway girls might be put to work in the school yard cutting grass with scissors or doing some other meaningless drudgery. In a few cases recalcitrant young ladies had their hair cut off. Such experiences left many girls bitter and anxious to return to the old way of life.

The experiences of Indian girls when they returned home after years of schooling illustrate some of the problems in evaluating the success of the government program. For many years school officials reported great success for returned students. Accounts in articles and official documents maintained that numbers of girls had returned home, married, and established good homes. The Indian Bureau itself made occasional surveys purporting to show that returned students were doing well, keeping neat homes, and speaking English. These accounts contained a certain amount of truth. Some graduates adapted their education to the reservation environment and succeeded quite well. Many of these success stories were well publicized. There is considerable evidence to suggest, however, that the reports were overly optimistic and that most returning girls encountered problems.

A disturbingly large number of girls returned to traditional life upon returning home. The reasons are rather obvious. As early as 1882, the principal of Hampton's Indian Division reported that "there is absolutely no position of dignity to which an Indian girl after three years' training can look forward to with any reasonable confidence." Although conditions improved somewhat as time went on, work opportunities remained minimal. Girls were usually trained in only one specialty. As the superintendent of the Albuquerque school reported, girls usually returned home with no relevant skills. Some spent their entire school stay working in a laundry or sewing room, and though they became expert in one field, they had nothing to help them on the reservation. As the Meriam report* later noted, some Indian girls spent so much time in school laundries that the institutions were in violation of state child labor laws. In another instance, one teacher noted how girls were taught to cook on gas ranges, while back on the reservation they had only campfires.

Moreover, the girls' educational achievements were not always appreciated at home. Elizabeth White tells the story of returning to her Hopi home an accomplished cook only to find that her family shunned the cakes and pies she made in place of traditional food, called her "as foolish as a white woman," and treated her as an outcast. As she later lamented, her school-taught domestic skills were inappropriate for the Hopis. Girls who refused to wear traditional dress at home were treated in like manner. Under these circumstances, many chose to cast off their learning, to marry, and return to traditional living. Those young women who dedicated themselves to living in the white man's style often found that reservations were intolerable, and unable to live in the manner to which they had become accustomed, they preferred to return to the cities. Once there the former students tended to become maids, although an undetermined number ended up as prostitutes and dance hall girls.

[*a 1928 report of an intense study of the conditions of American Indians and the operations of the Bureau of Indian Affairs, conducted by the Institute for Government Research under the auspices of the Department of the Interior]

Employment opportunities for educated Indian women also pointed up some of the difficulties with the industrial schools. In fairness, it must be admitted that trained women probably had more opportunities than their male counterparts. Most of those who chose to work could do so; however, all positions were at the most menial level. If a girl elected to live within the white community, her employment choices were severely limited. About the only job available was that of domestic service, a carry-over from the outing system. In this regard, the Indian schools did operate as employment agencies, finding jobs for their former students with local families. Despite the fact that some Indian women may have later come to feel that their work, despite its demeaning nature, provided some benefits for use in later life, many of their jobs proved unbearably hard. After being verbally abused, one former student wrote that "I never had any Lady say things like that to me." Another reported on her job, "I had been working so hard ever since I came here cleaning house and lots of ironing. I just got through ironing now I'm very tired my feet get so tired standing all morning." Unfortunately, few respectable jobs beyond domestic labor were available. Occasionally girls were trained as nurses or secretaries only to discover that they could find no work in Anglo society.

The largest employer of Indian girls proved to be the Indian Bureau. Many former students were able to secure positions at Indian agencies and schools; in fact, had it not been for the employment of former students by the paternalistic Indian service, few would have found any use for their training. The nature of the government positions available to Indian girls is revealing. Almost all jobs were menial in nature; only a few Indian girls were able to become teachers, and none worked as administrators. They were, rather, hired as laundresses, cooks, seamstresses, nurses' helpers, and assistant matrons. Often these employees received little more than room, board, and government rations, and even those who managed to be hired as teachers and nurses received less pay than their white counterparts. . . . Indian girls could find work, but only in the artificial environment of Indian agencies and schools located at remote western points and protected by a paternalistic government. Here they continued to perform tasks of domestic nature without promise of advancement. Nor were they assimilated into the dominant society as had been the original intent of their education.

School administrators were reluctant to admit the failings of the system. As early as the 1880s some criticism began to surface, but for the most part it was lost in the enthusiasm for training in a nonreservation environment. After 1900, however, critics became more vocal and persistent, arguing that the Indian community did not approve of this type of education, that most students gained little, and that employment opportunities were limited at best. More important, this type of education contributed little to the acculturation effort. As one opponent wrote, "To educate the Indian out of his [or her] home surroundings is to fill him with false ideas and to endow him with habits which are destructive to his peace of mind and usefulness to his community when the educational work is completed." Commissioner Leupp (1905–1909) was even more vocal. He generally accepted the increasingly prevalent theory that Indians were childlike in nature and incapable of assimilating into white society on an equal basis. Leupp suggested that the system failed to produce self-reliant Indians and, instead of giving Indian children a useful education, protected them in an artificial environment. Other school officials echoed the same sentiments. In this particular respect it was suggested that boarding school students were provided with all the comforts of civilization at no cost and thus failed to develop the proper attitude toward work. Upon returning to the reservations, therefore, they did not exert themselves and lapsed into traditionalism.

Despite increasing criticism, the women's educational program at the nonreservation schools operated without much change until after 1920. Girls were still taught skills of doubtful value, were hired out as maids through the outing system, did most of the domestic labor at the schools, and returned to the reservation either to assume traditional life or accept some menial government job. By the late twenties, however, the movement to reform Indian education began to have some impact. Relying upon such studies as the 1928 Meriam Report, reformers began to demand a complete change in the Indian educational system. Among their suggestions were that industrial boarding schools be phased out and the emphasis on work training be reduced. Critics like [former Commissioner of Indian Affairs] John Collier argued that the policy of removing girls from their homes to educate them for a life among whites had failed. Instead, girls were discouraged from returning to the reservation and had received little to prepare them for a home life. Collier's arguments eventually won out, especially after he became Indian commissioner in 1933. Thus ended this particular attempt to convert Native American women into middle-class American housewives. . . .

DOCUMENTS

Rules for Indian Schools, 1890

General Rules

39. The Sabbath must be properly observed. There shall be a Sabbath school or some other suitable service every Sunday, which pupils shall be required to attend. The superintendent may require employés to attend and participate in all the above exercises; but any employé declining as a matter of conscience shall be excused from attending and participating in any or all religious exercises. . . .

41. All instruction must be in the English language. Pupils must be compelled to converse with each other in English, and should be properly rebuked or punished for persistent violation of this rule. Every effort should be made to encourage them to abandon their tribal language. To facilitate this work it is essential that all school employés be able to speak English fluently, and that they speak English exclusively to the pupils, and also to each other in the presence of pupils.

42. Instruction in music must be given at all schools. Singing should be a part of the exercises of each school session, and wherever practicable instruction in instrumental music should be given.

43. Except in cases of emergency, pupils shall not be removed from school either by their parents or others, nor shall they be transferred from a Government to a private school without special authority from the Indian Office.

44. The school buildings should be furnished throughout with plain, inexpensive, but substantial furniture. Dormitories or lavatories should be so supplied with necessary toilet articles, such as soap, towels, mirrors, combs, hair, shoe, nail, and tooth brushes, and wisp brooms, as to enable the pupils to form exact habits of personal neatness.

45. Good and healthful provisions must be supplied in abundance; and they must well cooked and properly placed on the table. A regular bill of fare for each day of the week should be prepared and followed. Meals must be served regularly and neatly. Pains should be taken not only to have the food healthful and the table attractive, but to have the bill of fare varied.The school farm and dairy should furnish an ample supply of vegetables, fruits, milk, butter, cottage cheese, curds, eggs, and poultry. Coffee and tea should be furnished sparingly; milk is preferable to either, and children can be taught to use it. Pupils must be required to attend meals promptly after proper attention to toilet, and at least one employé must be in the dining room during each meal to supervise the table manners of

SOURCE: U.S. Bureau of Indian Affairs, "Rules for Indian Schools," *Annual Report of the Commissioner of Indian Affairs, 1890* (Washington, D.C., 1890), cxlvi, cl–clii.

the pupils and to see that all leave the table at the same time and in good order. . . .

47. So far as practicable, a uniform style of clothing for the school should be adopted. Two plain, substantial suits, with extra pair of trousers for each boy, and three neat, well-made dresses for each girl, if kept mended, ought to suffice for week-day wear for one year. For Sunday wear each pupil should be furnished a better suit. The pupils should also be supplied with underwear adapted to the climate, with night clothes, and with handkerchiefs, and, if the climate requires it, with overcoats and cloaks and with overshoes.

48. The buildings, outhouses, fences, and walks should at all times be kept in thorough repair. Where practicable, the grounds should be ornamented with trees, grass, and flowers.

49. There should be a flag staff at every school, and the American flag should be hoisted, in suitable weather, in the morning and lowered at sunset daily.

50. Special hours should be allotted for recreation. Provision should be made for outdoor sports, and the pupils should be encouraged in daily healthful exercise under the eye of a school employé; simple games should also be devised for indoor amusement. They should be taught the sports and games enjoyed by white youth, such as baseball, hopscotch, croquet, marbles, bean bags, dominoes, checkers, logomachy, and other word and letter games, and the use of dissected maps, etc. The girls should be instructed in simple fancy work, knitting, netting, crocheting, different kinds of embroidery, etc.

51. Separate play grounds, as well as sitting rooms, must be assigned the boys and the girls. In play and in work, as far as possible, and in all places except the school room and at meals, they must be kept entirely apart. It should be so arranged, however, that at stated times, under suitable supervision, they may enjoy each other's society; and such occasions should be used to teach them to show each other due respect and consideration, to behave without restraint, but without familiarity, and to acquire habits of politeness, refinement, and self-possession. . . .

53. Corporal punishment must be resorted to only in cases of grave violations of rules, and in no instances shall any person inflict it except under the direction of the superintendent, to whom all serious questions of discipline must be referred.* Employés may correct pupils for slight misdemeanors only.

---

*In some of the more advanced schools it will be practicable and advisable to have material offenses arbitrated by a school court composed of the advanced students, with school employés added to such court in very aggravated cases. After due investigation, the amount of guilt should be determined and the quantity of punishment fixed by the court, but the approval of the superintendent shall be necessary before the punishment is inflicted, and the superintendent may modify or remit but may not increase the sentence.

54. Any pupil twelve years of age or over, guilty of persistently using profane or obscene language; of lewd conduct; stubborn insubordination; lying; fighting; wanton destruction of property; theft; or similar misbehavior, may be punished by the superintendent either by inflicting corporal punishment or imprisonment in the guardhouse; but in no case shall any unusual or cruel or degrading punishment be permitted. . . .

Industrial Work

56. A regular and efficient system of industrial training must be a part of the work of each school. At least half of the time of each boy and girl should be devoted thereto—the work to be of such character that they may be able to apply the knowledge and experience gained, in the locality where they may be expected to reside after leaving school. In pushing forward the school-room training of these boys and girls, teachers, and especially superintendents, must not lose sight of the great necessity for fitting their charges for the every-day life of their after years.

57. A farm and garden, if practicable an orchard also, must be connected with each school, and especial attention must be given to instruction in farming, gardening, dairying, and fruit growing.

58. Every school should have horses, cattle, swine, and poultry, and when practicable, sheep and bees, which the pupils should be taught to care for properly. The boys should look after the stock and milk the cows, and the girls should see to the poultry and the milk.

59. The farm, garden, stock, dairy, kitchen, and shops should be so managed as to make the school as nearly self-sustaining as practicable, not only because Government resources should be as wisely and carefully utilized as private resources would be, but also because thrift and economy are among the most valuable lessons which can be taught Indians. Waste in any department must not be tolerated.

60. The blacksmith, wheelwright, carpenter, shoemaker, and harness maker trades, being of the most general application, should be taught to a few pupils at every school. Where such mechanics are not provided for[,] the school pupils should, so far as practicable, receive instruction from the agency mechanics.

61. The girls must be systematically trained in every branch of housekeeping and in dairy work; be taught to cut, make, and mend garments for both men and women; and also be taught to nurse and care for the sick. They must be regularly detailed to assist the cook in preparing the food and the laundress in washing and ironing.

62. Special effort must be made to instruct Indian youth in the use and care of tools and implements. They must learn to keep them in order, protect them properly, and use them carefully.

A Government Official Describes Indian Race and Culture, 1905

We believe that the strength of our American life is due in no small part to the fact that various and different race elements have entered into the making of the American the citizen of the United States in the twentieth century. No one racial stock is exclusively in control in our land. The typical modern American is a fine "composite," with race elements drawn from many sources. We do not believe that the Government of the United States in dealing with its Indian wards would act righteously or wisely if it were to attempt to crush out from those who are of Indian descent all the racial traits which differentiate the North American Indian from the other race stocks of the world. Certain conceptions of physical courage, a certain heroic stoicism in enduring physical pain, an inherited tendency to respect one's self, even if that tendency shows itself at times in unwarrantable conceit, are race traits which have value, if the people who have them become civilized and subject themselves to the laws of social morality and to the obligation of industrial efficiency, which are essential if any race stock or any group of families is to hold its own in the modern civilized world.

But the facts seem to us to be that good results are to be hoped for not by keeping the North American Indians peculiar in dress or in customs. We think that the wisest friends of the Indian recognize with great delight and value highly the art impulse in certain Indian tribes, which has shown itself in Indian music, in Indian art forms—such as the birchbark canoe, in Indian basketry, and more rarely in Indian pottery. But we firmly believe that the way to preserve the best of what is distinctively characteristic in the North American Indians is to civilize and educate them, that they may be fit for the life of the twentieth century under our American system of self-government. Because we value the elements for good which may come into our American life through the stock of North American Indians, we wish to see children of Indian descent educated in the industrial and practical arts and trained to habits of personal cleanliness, social purity, and industrious family life. We do not believe that it is right to keep the Indians out of civilization in order that certain picturesque aspects of savagery and barbarism may continue to be within reach of the traveler and the curious, or even of the scientific observer. In the objectionable "Indian dances" which are breaking out afresh at many points we see not a desirable maintenance of racial traits, but a distinct reversion toward barbarism and superstition. We believe that while the effort should never be made to "make

SOURCE: U.S. Department of Interior, "Board of Indian Commissioner's Reports," in *Annual Reports* (June 30, 1905), H. Doc. 20: 59th Cong., 1st sess., 17–18.

a white man out of an Indian," in the sense of seeking to do violence to respect to parents or a proper or intelligent regard for what is fine in the traits and the history of one's ancestors, it is still most desirable that all the Indians on our territory should come as speedily as possible to the white man's habits of home-making, industry, cleanliness, social purity, and family integrity.

Precisely as all intelligent American patriots have seen danger to our national life in the attempt, wherever it has been made, to perpetuate in the United States large groups of foreign-born immigrants who try to keep their children from learning English and seek to perpetuate upon our territory (at the cost of true Americanism for their children) what was characteristic in the life of their own people on other continents and in past generations, precisely as in such cases we feel that the hope of our American system lies in the public schools and such educational institutions as shall maintain standards of public living that inevitably bring the children of foreign-born immigrants into the great body of English-speaking, home-loving, industrious, and pure-minded Americans—precisely so does it seem to us that all the efforts of the Government, and far more of distinctive missionary effort on the part of the Christian people of this country than has ever yet been used with this end in view, should be steadily employed in the effort to make out of the Indian children of this country intelligent, English-speaking, industrious, law-abiding Americans. We believe that the breaking up of tribal funds as rapidly as practicable will help toward this end. Even if many of the Indians do for a time misuse money while they are learning how to use it properly, even if some of them squander it utterly, we believe that there is hope for the Indians in the future only as by education, faith in work, and obedience to Christian principles of morality and clean living, their children shall come to have the social standards and the social habits of our better American life throughout the land.

Our task is to hasten the slow work of race evolution. Inevitably, but often grimly and harshly by the outworking of natural forces, the national life of the stronger and more highly civilized race stock dominates in time the life of the less civilized, when races like the Anglo-Saxon and the Indian are brought into close contact. In our work for the Indians we want to discern clearly those influences and habits of life which are of the greatest advantage in leading races upward into Christian civilization; and these influences and habits we wish to make as strongly influential as possible, and as speedily as possible influential upon the life of all these American tribes. It is not unreasonable to hope that through governmental agencies and through the altruistic missionary spirit of one of the foremost Christian races and governments of the world much can be done to hasten that process of civilization which natural law, left to itself, works out too slowly and at too great a loss to the less-favored race. We want to make the conditions for our less-favored brethren of the red race so favorable that the social forces which have developed themselves slowly and at great expense of time and life in our American race and our American system of government shall be made to help in the uplifting of the Indians and to shorten that interval of time which of necessity must elapse between savagery and Christian civilization.

A Recent View of Native Americans, 1978

Findings—Education

The Minnesota Advisory Committee to the U.S. Commission on Civil Rights finds that:

1. Virtually no progress has been made to reduce the Indian dropout rate since the Minnesota Advisory Committee first examined this issue in 1974. The dropout rate of Indian students continues to be significantly higher than for students of other races. While Indians constituted 5.3 percent of total enrollments in 1976, they accounted for almost 10 percent of all dropouts in the Minneapolis public schools.

2. According to certain indicators of educational participation, Indians receive a better education when they attend schools with a concentration of Indian students than when they are a small minority within the school. Indians attending schools with a concentration of Indian students have a lower dropout rate and are less likely to be assigned to special education classes than Indian students in general within the Minneapolis public schools.

3. While public school officials are generally supportive of alternative Indian schools, some believe that encouraging such schools within the public school system would constitute a violation of State and Federal civil rights laws.

4. Alternative Indian education programs operated or assisted by public school districts do not violate Federal civil rights laws, provided such programs are open to students of all racial and ethnic backgrounds and are not restricted to Indian students. This conclusion is supported by the attorney for the Midwestern Regional Office of the U.S. Commission on Civil Rights and also by a former Acting Director of HEW's [Department of Health, Education, and Welfare] Office for Civil Rights.

SOURCE: Minnesota Advisory Committee to the U.S. Commission on Civil Rights, *Bridging the Gap: A Reassessment*, January 1978, 22–23.

5. Little progress has been made towards incorporating Indian studies into the curriculum in most public schools.

6. Both public and private Indian alternative schools lack adequate data to assess their educational programs.

  a. All schools lack follow-up information on students who have graduated, which is necessary to evaluate the marketability of the schools' diplomas and how that marketability varies by sex and ethnic group.
  b. All private Indian alternative schools and some public schools lack data on graduation and dropout rates.

Recommendations—Education

1. The Minnesota Advisory Committee recommends to the Minneapolis and St. Paul public school systems that they establish alternative Indian education programs at both the elementary and secondary levels.

  a. Indian educators should be centrally involved in developing the program, Indian administrators should have key administrative positions, and Indian teachers should be well represented on the faculty.
  b. Such programs should be open to students of all racial and ethnic backgrounds in order to be in full compliance with Federal civil rights requirements.
  c. Officials must ensure that the alternative Indian education programs do not become a first step towards more exclusionary and discriminatory practices, whereby minorities and women become restricted to racially or sexually identifiable educational programs. The establishment of alternative Indian education programs must in no way hinder the effectiveness of Federal and State civil rights efforts to guarantee equal educational opportunity for all individuals. . . .

3. The Minnesota Advisory Committee recommends to the State board of education that it establish a policy whereby all students in Minnesota schools will be able to take Indian studies as part of their course of study.

  a. The State board of education should instruct local school districts that this is the policy and should provide all possible assistance to ensure that it is carried out.
  b. Indian studies should be included in the regular curriculum. They should not be treated simply as extracurricular activities available to students before or after normal school hours.

4. The Minnesota Advisory Committee recommends to the Minneapolis and St. Paul public schools and to the private Indian alternative schools

that they do a more complete assessment of their educational programs by:

a. Developing procedures for more accurately measuring the dropout rate of Indian students;

b. Conducting follow-up studies that would enable them to determine the activities (e.g., college, work, military service) of former students, at least for the first year upon leaving school;

c. Maintaining records of the number and percentage of its students who graduate, drop out, or transfer to another school, by race and sex; and

d. Conducting any other research deemed appropriate to obtain an objective assessment of their educational programs.

CHAPTER 4

Woman's Sphere: Woman's Work

During the final decades of the nineteenth century, America's urban growth and expanding industrial economy led to the creation of innumerable jobs in the private and public sectors. For many white men with ambition, intelligence, and education, the choice of careers was broad and the chance of success promising. For immigrants, for blacks, for poor youth off the farm, and for women, however, opportunities expanded in a much more limited way. The barriers of ethnicity, race, sex, and inadequate schooling were formidable.

Margery W. Davies's essay "Office Work After the Civil War" recounts the feminization of clerical work during these decades. She illustrates the relationship between the increasing numbers of women in the office workforce and significant developments in American society: the rise of urban industrialism, the decline of the family farm, the impact of technology on the home and workplace, and the "drastic changes in the scale and shape of business enterprise." At the same time, she illuminates how, despite expanding employment opportunities, the popular perception of a separate woman's sphere continued to restrict women to particular occupations. What does Davies identify as the most significant factors in trans-

forming clerical work from a male-dominated to a female-dominated occupation? What made this kind of work attractive to women?

The popular belief in a grouping of occupations considered to be "women's work" required some justification for admitting them to certain jobs. Teaching, as Davies notes, preceded office work as the first "literacy-required" occupation deemed suitable to women's nature. In the first document, from Horace Mann's report as Secretary of the Board of Education in Massachusetts in 1844, the famous crusader for public education applauds the entry of women as teachers in the primary grades, a position for which he believed they were particularly fit. Note his references to woman's special qualities with which "the Author of nature preadapted her." The persuasiveness of Mann's argument is reflected in the fact that by the Civil War, the schoolmistress had almost completely replaced the schoolmaster in the nation's public elementary schools. Of course, differences in salaries might also have been a factor: in 1861, the average salary for male teachers in rural districts was $6.30 per week; for women, it was $4.05. In urban districts, it was $18.00 for men and $6.91 for women.

Women attempting to enter more prestigious, traditionally male occupations often experienced considerable resistance and displayed no small amount of courage by their perseverance. The second document is a 1916 newspaper account of the recollections of Dr. Anna Manning Comfort, who graduated in the first class of the New York Medical College and Hospital for Women in 1865. How was the perception of a separate place for women within the medical profession modified between 1865 and 1916?

Although popular beliefs about women's natural capacities supported their entry into teaching, clerical jobs, nursing, factory work, librarianship, social work, and even medicine, they were also used to exclude women from positions of leadership in those fields, deny them the right to vote, and bar their entry into other professions. In 1872, the United States Supreme Court upheld a decision of the Illinois courts denying Myra Bradwell a license to practice law on the grounds of her sex. The third document presents Supreme Court Justice Bradley's majority opinion in support of the Court's decision. Notice that his argument rested heavily upon traditional perceptions of woman's nature.

The Court's decision in Bradwell v. Illinois was a setback for women's rights. Yet, there were victories as well. That same year (1872), the Illinois legislature removed all restrictions to women's entry into the professions. Similar actions were taken in other states. In 1869, Arabella Mansfield of Iowa had become the first woman licensed to practice law. By 1891, there were two hundred licensed women lawyers in the nation; of course, the figure represented less than 1 percent of all the nation's attorneys. The struggle has continued well into our own century. How would you describe popular beliefs today concerning separate spheres for men and women in the home, in politics, and the world of work?

ESSAY

Office Work After the Civil War

Margery W. Davies

The last third of the nineteenth century witnessed drastic changes in the scale and shape of business enterprise. The small and highly competitive firms that had dominated production in the antebellum United States gave way to giant corporations integrated vertically and horizontally in the merger movement that swept through industry during the 1890s. In the steel, oil, tobacco, food, and meat-packing sectors, to name just a few, such corporations enjoyed virtual monopolies.

As is now well known, profound changes in production techniques accompanied the rise of the trusts. But innovation was not restricted to the shop floor. It also reached upwards into the office, for the increase in the volume of business, coupled with the development of regional, national, and international markets, led to a proliferation of correspondence and inspired the need for more accurate record keeping. As the amount and geographic range of a firm's activities grew, it became more difficult for that firm to conduct the bulk of its transactions in person. While face-to-face business contacts by no means disappeared, a businessman might choose to pay a bill, order merchandise, or confirm an appointment in writing rather than in person, particularly when the transaction took place between cities. Even after the invention of the telephone, many businesses preferred to keep a written record of transactions rather than having to rely on memory.

As a firm's operations expanded and became more complex, accurate records of its transactions became more important. A small entrepreneurial butcher did not need very complex records. He might keep a list of which customers owed him money and how much, and of how many pounds of beef and how many pounds of pork he could expect each week from various meat-slaughterers, but he would not need much more. A large meat-packing firm, however, required more complex records: how many head of cattle were fattening in pens in Omaha or Kansas City, and how many were being driven across the plains from points farther west; how much the workers in the slaughterhouses were being paid; how many refrigerated cars were on their way to the eastern cities, and how many on their way back. These records had to be accurate and up-to-date, for the managers needed detailed information at their fingertips in order to make plans for the future. Furthermore, . . . firms required elaborate records to guard

SOURCE: Margery W. Davies, *Women's Place Is at the Typewriter: Office Work and Office Workers, 1870–1930.* Copyright © 1982 by Temple University. Reprinted by permission of Temple University Press.

against fraud both by their own employees and by the companies with which they did business.

Among the outstanding features of the reorganization of the office was the division of businesses into departments. This became necessary as firms grew so large and complex that it was no longer possible for one capitalist, or even a small group, to make all the decisions. The ultimate control of a firm's capital and direction still rested with the owner or owners, but the more mundane operations were decentralized into various functionally defined departments. The Pennsylvania Railroad management, for example, one of the first to introduce this method of organization, instituted separate offices for accounting and for the supervision of roadbeds and moving stock. It also worked out a more elaborate structure of relations between the major departments and their ancillary units.

These organizational innovations were accompanied by the subdivision of clerical labor. Before the Civil War there had been four basic clerical jobs in the office: copyist, bookkeeper, messenger or office boy, and clerk. This relatively simple range of occupations was expanded and elaborated following the war, with the division of labor most pronounced in the largest offices. File clerks, shipping clerks, billing clerks and other "semiskilled" workers began to appear. The exact pattern that the division of labor followed in a particular office depended, of course, on the nature of the business at hand. An insurance company might have many billing or file clerks, but no shipping clerks whatsoever; a mail-order house would use an army of shipping and file clerks, but no billing clerks since orders were paid in advance.

Not surprisingly, the most popular change resulted from the introduction of the typewriter. Once it was adopted, stenographers and typists quite rapidly replaced copyists. A stenographer's job consisted of taking dictation, usually from a firm's manager or owner, although occasionally also from a higher-level clerical worker, and then transcribing the notes into a letter, report, or whatever. For a while, it was considered rude or disrespectful for a firm to type its correspondence, and some dictation was at first transcribed in a fine longhand. Before long, however, typewriting became the accepted mode of business correspondence, and handwritten letters yielded to typewritten ones. The stenographer was in effect a direct replacement for a copyist, since in general stenography encompassed transcription as well as dictation. The integration of these tasks came about not only because many different systems of shorthand were in use, but also because stenographers tended to add individual quirks or shortcuts to the system being used. Hence the stenographer might be the only one who could read his or her notes. At first glance it would seem that the shift from copyist to stenographer involved no further division of labor. But the fact that typists were being hired as well as stenographers suggests even greater specialization. Take the example of a manufacturer with outstanding debts from thirty customers. He might decide to send each of them a dunning letter couched in the strongest language instead of an invoice with "Third and Final Notice" stamped on it in red ink. He might dictate this letter to a stenographer, who would transcribe it in longhand and pass it on, along with the names and addresses of the overdue debtors, to two or three typists, who would produce as many copies of the letter as necessary. The result was that what had once been done by one kind of clerk, a copyist, was now done by two, a stenographer and a typist. In this example, the typists execute the bulk of the task at hand, and the manufacturer congratulates himself on the efficiency of his system and on the money saved by using a stenographer only where necessary and by using typists whenever possible.

This increasing division of labor constituted a basic change in the organization of office work. In antebellum offices clerical workers were responsible for a wide range of tasks and in some cases their work bore the aspects of a craft. But the division and redivision of clerical tasks meant that an individual clerical worker performed only a small number of tasks in a larger range of operations. This reorganization of work was uneven. It first appeared immediately before the Civil War (the Erie Railroad) and was clearly taking hold by the 1870s. Thus the post–Civil War expansion and consolidation of capitalism drastically rearranged the office by partitioning firms into departments and dividing up clerical work into specialized tasks. Another factor which did much to alter the appearance of clerical work, and which had some influence on the changing nature of that work, was technological innovation, with the typewriter being far and away the most important of the new office machines. . . .

One of the ways women entered clerical work was by mastering the typewriter and then finding a job as a typist. When Mark Twain bought his first typewriter in early 1875, the salesman had a "type girl" on hand to demonstrate the machine to prospective customers. And in late 1875 this ad for the Remington typewriter appeared in the *Nation*:

CHRISTMAS PRESENT
for a boy or girl

And the benevolent can, by the gift of a "Type-Writer" to a poor, deserving young woman, put her at once in the way of earning a good living as a copyist or corresponding clerk.

No invention has opened for women so broad and easy an avenue to profitable and suitable employment as the "Type-Writer," and it merits the careful consideration of all thoughtful and charitable persons interested in the subject of work for woman.

Mere girls are now earning from $10 to $20 per week with the "Type-Writer," and we can at once secure good situations for one hundred expert writers on it in court-rooms in this city.

The public is cordially invited to call and inspect the working of the machine, and obtain all information at our showrooms.

But in 1875 and for a few years thereafter, the typewriter was still thought of as a frill by most businessmen. It was not until the 1880s that typewriters were manufactured and sold in large numbers.

In the 1880s, also, the employment of women in offices began to climb sharply. . . . This coincidence has led some analysts to conclude that the invention of the typewriter was basically responsible for the employment of women in offices in the United States. For example, a pamphlet put out by the Women's Bureau of the United States Department of Labor asserts that "not only . . . has the typewriter revolutionized modern business methods but it has *created* an occupation calling for more women than have been employed as a result of any other invention." Bruce Bliven, the author of a history of the typewriter, recounts the story of how the New York YWCA started training young women typists in 1881. Far from succumbing to mental and physical breakdowns under the strain of their new occupation, as some observers had warned, these women quickly found jobs. The YWCA was soon deluged with many more requests for typists than it could fill. Bliven concludes that "the revolution came rather quietly, on high-buttoned shoes, accompanied not by gunfire or bombs bursting in air, but by a considerable amount of rather obnoxious snickering."

Just as it would be a mistake to say that the typewriter was responsible for the growth of offices after the Civil War, so would it be erroneous to credit it with the employment of women in those offices. . . . [F]emale employment was increasing rapidly throughout the clerical occupations, and not just among stenographers and typists.

Although the typewriter was not responsible for the employment of women as clerical workers, its existence probably facilitated or eased the entrance of women into offices. It was such a new machine that it had not been "sex-typed" as masculine. Thus women who worked as typists did not face the argument that a typewriter was a machine fit only for men. In fact, it was not too long afterwards that women were claimed to be more manually dexterous and tolerant of routine than men and therefore more suited, by virtue of their very natures, to operate typewriters.

Changes in the structure of capitalism in the United States brought women into offices. The expansion and consolidation of capitalist firms after the Civil War caused a rapid increase in the amount of correspondence and record keeping required by those firms. This in turn resulted in the growth of offices and an immediate increase in the need for clerical workers. That, in short, explains the demand. Where was the supply to come from?

The basic skill required of clerical workers was literacy. The supply therefore had to come from those segments of the population that had some education, and at this time[,] women, as well as men, had advanced schooling. In fact, . . . the number of women high school graduates exceeded that of men during the last decades of the nineteenth century.

And women's labor was cheaper than men's. Patriarchal social relations devalued the labor of women compared to that of men from similar backgrounds. The reasons for this are legion. First of all, there was the widespread belief that women were simply, and by the very nature of things, inferior to men. In addition, women were often thought to be working for "pin money" with which to make frivolous purchases. Since they were not thought to be supporting themselves or their families, there was nothing the matter with paying them low wages. Then there was the argument that women were not serious members of the labor force: they would be returning to an exclusively domestic life either as soon as they married or, at the very latest, as soon as they bore children. Such transient workers did not deserve the higher wage with which an employer might try to attract and keep a more steadfast male worker. Finally, women's depressed wages did drive them back into the home, where they again became available to fill a subordinate position within the domestic division of labor. Whether or not this worked to the ultimate benefit of men, it certainly provided them with short-term benefits.

On the face of it, the cheapness of labor ought to explain why employers preferred women over men. But women's labor in the United States has always come cheaper than men's, so that it is not immediately obvious why employers did not always show preference for females. There must be a further reason why employers started to favor women for certain clerical positions.

The supply of literate male labor was simply not large enough to fill the great demand for office workers. The expansion of capitalist firms created not only a much larger need for clerical workers, but also an increased demand for managerial personnel. As is clear from the discussion of the proliferation of hierarchical structures within late nineteenth-century firms, the managerial corps necessitated by this new system of finely delegated authority expanded mightily. An educated man, faced with the choice among positions within the office hierarchy, was unlikely to choose to be a typist instead of a manager, who was higher-paid and invested with a fair degree of authority and power. The expansion of capitalist firms, coupled with the growth of cities at the end of the nineteenth century, also led to a rise in the number of jobs ancillary to business operations. Lawyers are an excellent example: in 1870 there were 40,736 lawyers in the United States, all but five of whom were men. By 1900 there were almost three times as many lawyers, 114,640, over 99 percent of whom were men. There had been one lawyer for every 307 people employed in all occupations in the United States in 1870; by 1900 there was one lawyer for every 254 such persons. Thus a man who had enough education and literacy skills (the ability to spell reasonably well, to write [in] a legible hand, to do basic arithmetic accurately) to obtain a job as a clerical worker was also probably educated enough to at least aspire to, and in many cases to attain, a managerial or professional position. As a consequence, the supply of men available for clerical work was considerably diminished.

Furthermore, fewer boys than girls were graduating from high school in the United States. . . . If high school and college graduations are considered together, more men than women were receiving secondary school diplomas or better during the years 1870 and 1880. But in 1890 and 1900, the number of women receiving high school diplomas or better had outstripped the number of men. Despite the fact that consistently far more men than women graduated from college, the number of women finishing high school grew to so outweigh the number of men that the surplus of male over female college graduates was cancelled out. In addition, the men who were reaching those high educational levels were likely to be supplying the demand for managers and professionals. Thus the demand for managers and professionals and the fact that more women than men were reaching relatively high levels of formal education combine to explain why it was that the ever-increasing demand for clerical workers was met by women.

Other factors, though secondary, also influenced feminization. First of all, the employment of women as clerks in the United States Treasury Department during the Civil War established a precedent that may have eased the entrance of women into offices ten and fifteen years later. The employment of female clerks in the Treasury Department showed that it was possible for women to work in offices. Women had gotten a toe in the office door. As a result, when structural changes in capitalism produced a dramatic rise in the demand for clerical workers, it was slightly easier for women to push the door wide open.

A second factor that facilitated—as opposed to caused—the employment of women was the invention and production of the typewriter. Women were employed in increasing numbers throughout the entire gamut of clerical occupations, and not just as typists. The process that underlay the employment of women in offices was similar to that which underlay the successful manufacture of a typewriter in the first place—the expansion and consolidation of capitalist firms. But the fact that the typewriter was sex-neutral, without historical ties to workers of either sex, meant that female typists did not have to meet the argument that they were operating a man's machine.

Finally, the reorganization of the division of labor within the office may have abetted its feminization. It is possible that if offices had simply expanded without being reorganized, women would have had a more difficult time entering clerical work. The reorganization of many offices often resulted in a redivision of clerical labor and in the creation of new jobs, from stenographers and typists to file clerks, billing clerks, and the like. Since many of these jobs, or at least their labels, had not existed before the growth of the office, they were not defined as men's jobs. Women who took such positions did not face the argument that they were taking over men's work.

Nonetheless, the roots of the feminization of clerical work lay in political-economic conditions that were independent of the job itself. Changes in the structure of capitalism caused a rapid increase in the demand for clerical workers, a demand that was met in part by an available supply of literate women. Furthermore, it seems that many employers were only too glad to employ female labor in place of more costly male labor. The feminization of clerical work was not intrinsic to the job itself, despite ideological justifications that arose after the fact. By its very nature, clerical work was neither men's work nor women's work.

Clerical jobs were available to women, but, for feminization to occur, women had to be available to take the jobs. A variety of factors produced a supply of women to fill the demand. The economic decline of small, family-owned farms and businesses frequently forced daughters into the labor force. Clerical work was generally seen as more desirable than industrial work, and this spurred women of working-class origins to seek clerical jobs. Productive work in the home was on the decline, making the labor of both working-class and non-working-class women available for jobs outside the domestic sphere. And clerical work was one of the few options for literate women seeking jobs that required literate workers. . . .

Although the decline of the small, independent farmer as a class had hardly begun in earnest, by the end of the nineteenth century the large cities of the East were already beginning to feel the effects. The new homesteads of the West absorbed only some of the eastern farmers forced off their land. Others who found they could no longer make ends meet were already moving into the cities in the waning years of the nineteenth century, although it was not until the twentieth that displaced small farmers really began to swell the urban labor force. The ranks of clerical workers included people of small-farm origins from the outset.

The situation of small-business proprietors differed significantly from that of farmers. From 1870 to 1930 they not only held their own numerically and as a proportion of the labor force but, in fact, grew. Although the class as a whole maintained itself through the years, . . . individual members of the classic petite bourgeoisie did not always manage to make ends meet, much less prosper. Thousands of fledgling businesses were started by hopeful entrepreneurs; almost as many failed.

These small entrepreneurs lived in constant dread of failure and imposed long hours on themselves and their families in order to fend off financial disaster. "But the average life of these old middle-class, especially urban, units in the twentieth century is short; the coincidence of family unit and work-situation among the old middle class is a pre-industrial fact. So even as the centralization of property contracts their 'independence,' it liberates the children of the old middle class's smaller entrepreneurs."

Some of those children were "liberated" to become clerical workers. The endemic financial insecurity of many small businessmen often meant not only that their children were reluctant to follow them in an unstable occupation, but also, in many cases, that the children were forced to support themselves. Thus the classic petite bourgeoisie contributed to the pool of people available for work in offices. . . .

For many daughters of working-class families, however, membership in the labor force was nothing new. The vast majority of working-class families were unable to afford the luxury of keeping out of the labor force an unmarried daughter whose labor was not essential to the maintenance of the home. Single working-class women were expected to enter the labor force as a matter of course. In fact, a writer in 1929 considered it a sign of the improved condition of the working class that its children were staying in school longer and longer, rather than entering the labor force out of economic necessity:

> The rising standard of living of manual workers has made it possible for more of them to provide their children with the high school education necessary to clerical positions, and the popular belief in education as the open sesame to opportunity has been an incentive to increased high school attendance. This increase in the high school population—the rate of which, within the last thirty years, has been about twenty times the rate of the increase in the population—has thrown upon the vocational market thousands of girls with a high school education, a large proportion of whom aspire to clerical positions.

The main reason working-class girls "aspired" to clerical work was that it paid better than most jobs open to women. In 1883, at the very beginning of the influx of large numbers of women into clerical work, female office workers in Boston were relatively well off compared to women in other working-class occupations. Copyists in personal service earned an average weekly wage of $6.78, bookkeepers earned $6.55, cashiers earned $7.43, and clerks (it is not clear from the available information whether "clerks" refers to clerks in offices or stores, or both) earned $5.28. Although a highly skilled craft-worker in manufacturing, such as a button-hole-maker for men's shirts, could earn as much as $10.00, most women working in manufacturing did not make over $5.00, and some made considerably less. These wages do not take into account the shorter hours women in offices enjoyed, a factor that would make their average hourly wage even better when compared to that of other working-class women. In 1910 a study of the incomes and expenditures of 450 Boston working women found that clerical work was second only to professional occupations in annual net income.

In addition to better wages, clerical work brought higher status than many other "female" occupations, such as factory work, domestic service, and clerking in stores. The argument has been made that this higher status was a result of a cleaner work environment, shorter hours, such benefits as vacation and sick leave, and the notion that clerical work could lead to promotions of some importance in the business world. Whether or not such analyses are correct, the fact that clerical work enjoyed higher status does not seem to be in question. . . . [A]t least some working-class women saw clerical work not only as more prestigious, but even as a means of rising out of the working class itself. . . .

In *The Long Day: The Story of a New York Working Girl*, Dorothy Richardson also saw clerical work as a means of escaping the drudgery of working-class jobs. Her heroine started out in jobs that were typical of most turn-of-the-century working women: making artificial flowers or paper boxes and working first as a sales clerk and then as a demonstrator of a new brand of tea or coffee in a department store. Determined to better her position, she took a night-school course in stenography and studied English grammar and composition on her own. After having attained a typing speed of one hundred words a minute, she sought her first clerical job. It "paid me only six dollars a week, but it was an excellent training-school, and in it I learned self confidence, perfect accuracy, and rapidity. Although this position paid me two dollars less than what I had been earning brewing tea and coffee and handing it over the counter, and notwithstanding the fact that I knew of places where I could go and earn ten dollars a week, I chose to remain where I was." Armed with clerical experience, she then moved on to a fifteen-dollar-a-week stenographic position at a publishing house. It was at this point in her life that Richardson's heroine started writing and selling articles. Richardson's account shows not only that she considered clerical work to be a cut above other kinds of working-class jobs, but also that she believed that one could use office work as a means of moving from a purely working-class job to a higher position with some autonomy.

The number of women available to work in offices was also augmented by the decline of productive work in the home. For farm families, there was ample work both in the field and in the home to keep the various family members busy. In addition to all of the chores that accompanied farming itself, there was a lot of work that served to keep the family self-sufficient and relatively independent of the market. Even after rural Americans no longer performed such tasks as weaving cloth or making candles, which had been part of the normal household's work in the seventeenth and eighteenth centuries, much still remained. Vegetables and fruits were preserved, butter and cheese were made, some furniture was constructed from scratch, and almost everyone's clothes were handmade. In addition, the absence of running water, central heating, and electricity meant that water had to be carried from a well or pump, wood chopped to supply cooking and heating needs, and kerosene lamps filled and kept in good running order. There was plenty of work to keep parents and children occupied most of the time.

But with the move from country to city that was well under way by the end of the nineteenth century, productive work done in the home began to decrease. The same growth of industrialism that drew a labor force to the cities resulted in the mass production of consumer goods. Items that had been produced in the home were now available in stores. Canned goods, bakery bread, and readymade clothing gained gradual acceptance in more and more urban homes, despite the fact that a kitchen garden plot was a common feature of many urban dwellings into the twentieth century. Even more important changes, perhaps, were running water and indoor plumbing, central heating, and electrical wiring, all of which became standard features of more and more urban homes, beginning with those of the well-to-do.

The decrease of productive work in the home had its most dramatic effect on women. "Woman's place is in the home" made economic sense when there was plenty of work to be done. But as domestic work diminished, women who remained there began to lose their productive function in society. In fact, as [historian] Gerda Lerner has pointed out, one of the long-term developments of the nineteenth century was the elevation of this non-productive function of women to a symbol of high status and wealth. The "lady" was living testament to her husband's or father's ability to earn money and to a relatively high place in the class structure.

A woman's ability to enjoy nonproductive leisure was determined, of course, by her family's economic position. Booth Tarkington's Alice Adams and her parents were anxious that she should enjoy just as much leisure and luxury as the town's bourgeois daughters.* A good example of the way Alice liked to spend her time is this account of her activities on the morning of a high-class dance given by one of the girls in town.

> "Where are you going?" [asked her mother].
> "Oh, I've got lots to do. I thought I'd run out to Mildred's to see what she's going to wear tonight, and then I want to go down and buy a yard of chiffon and some narrow ribbon to make new bows for my slippers—you'll have to give me some money."

Alice would have preferred to spend her time on such frivolous errands, but her family's financial straits sent her into the labor market, her hopes of rising into the bourgeoisie dashed. The relatively small amount of productive work done in the Adams home permitted the grown daughter to

[*Booth Tarkington's novel *Alice Adams* was published in 1921.]

spend most of her time in leisure activities, at least for a while. And when Alice entered the labor force, she was able to do so because her labor was not needed in the home.

During the period from 1870 to 1930, the number of occupations open to women was relatively limited. In general, women found employment in factory work of various kinds, in the smaller manufacturing concerns that employed sweated labor, behind the counter in retail stores, in domestic service, in nursing, in clerical work, in teaching, and to a very small degree in some of the higher-level professions. Manufacturing and other factory work, as well as domestic service, did not require literacy. And in positions where neither bills nor orders were written out, neither did retail selling. A literate woman who used her education in her work was restricted to a narrow range of occupational choices. Among these options, the better-paid were clerical work, teaching, and the various professions.

The teaching and professional positions that were open to women absorbed a small proportion of the female labor force. . . . In fact, teaching was the only occupation requiring literacy that in any way rivaled clerical work as an employer of women after the Civil War. . . . [T]eaching employed more women than did the clerical occupations until 1900, after which the number of female clerical workers rose so dramatically that teaching fell far behind. [Scholar] Elizabeth Baker argues that women may have preferred clerical work to teaching because of the severe restrictions placed on the personal and social life of teachers. Women teachers were not allowed to smoke, to drink, or, in some instances, to "keep company" with men. Those who married were often asked to leave their jobs. And sometimes "the new view of science and religion which they were bringing to the classroom from their college and university experience was opposed. Conditions such as these prompted many young girls to take up stenography instead of teaching when they graduated from high school; and it is not surprising that more than 100,000—a sixth of the teachers—were reported to have left the profession every year."

There is also some evidence that teachers were paid less than clerical workers. In 1912 the superintendent of schools in Council Bluffs, Iowa, argued that the student who completed the high school's business course was in a better economic position than the one who chose the classical course: "If a graduate of the classical course in the . . . high school had decided to teach in the public schools of the same city, under the most favorable circumstances possible[,] she could not have commenced teaching until one year after graduation. Her salary for the third year after graduation could not have been more than fifty dollars per month for nine months, or $450 per year. The average pupil (female) who graduated from the business department of the high school would have received for the same year an annual salary of slightly over $660. A male graduate of the same year would have received an annual salary of slightly over $840. You may judge for yourself of the economic efficiency from the standpoint of salary."

That women's low level of employment in the professions was due in part to outright discrimination is made clear by a study of women in government service published in 1920. It indicates that the federal government primarily hired women as clerical workers and goes on to demonstrate that the civil service examinations themselves (a prerequisite to government employment) discriminated against women and shunted them into clerical positions. . . .

Some of the very institutions where literacy skills were taught and polished led directly to clerical work. Both private commercial schools and the commercial track of public high schools trained girls and young women for clerical work. Commercial schools, where skills such as arithmetic, penmanship, and bookkeeping were taught, had been established in the United States by the 1840s and 1850s. Their doors were open to both men and women. Men were urged to obtain an education that would give them a solid start in their climb to success in the business world. Women were encouraged to apply their brains to pursuits other than gracing the domestic circle, or, in the case of working-class women, to aspire to jobs that would liberate them from the drudgery of the factory or sweatshop. In the latter half of the nineteenth century, such institutions were very successful. By 1890 there were over 80,000 students enrolled in commercial schools (by comparison enrollment in grades nine to twelve of public and private high schools totaled 298,000). Women made up only 4 percent of the 6,460 students enrolled in commercial schools in 1871, but they accounted for 32 percent of the 96,135 enrolled in 1894–95.

By the twentieth century, private business schools were being supplanted by other institutions. University business schools were offering training to aspiring capitalists and managers, while public high schools were initiating commercial education departments to teach clerical skills. By 1915 enrollment in the commercial courses of public high schools outstripped that in private commercial schools. In these high school courses girls predominated. In 1902–3 they already made up 54 percent of the total; in 1930 this had increased to 67 percent. It has been argued that public commercial education furthered the feminization of clerical work. Not only did the commercial courses provide clerical training for girls, but school guidance materials often funneled girls into commercial courses and advised them to plan for clerical jobs. . . .

For some women, participation in the labor force afforded psychological benefits such as increased independence and self-reliance. This, however, should not distract attention from the central fact of working-class life: most women worked because they had to.

DOCUMENTS

"Is Not Woman Destined to Conduct the Rising Generation?" 1844

One of the most extraordinary changes which have taken place in our schools, during the last seven years, consists in the great proportionate increase in the number of female teachers employed.

In 1837, the number of male teachers in all our public schools, including
summer and winter terms, was, ...2370
Of females. 3591
In the school year 1843–4, it was,—males, ...2529
Females. 4581
Increase in the number of male teachers 159
Increase in the number of female teachers 990
During the same time, the number of schools, in the State, has
increased only. 418

This change in public sentiment, in regard to the employment of female teachers, I believe to be in accordance with the dictates of the soundest philosophy. Is not woman destined to conduct the rising generation, of both sexes, at least through all the primary stages of education? Has not the Author of nature preadapted her, by constitution, and faculty, and temperament, for this noble work? What station of beneficent labor can she aspire to, more honorable, or more congenial to every pure and generous impulse? In the great system of society, what other part can she act, so intimately connected with the refinement and purification of the race? How otherwise can she so well vindicate her right to an exalted station in the scale of being; and cause that shameful sentence of degradation by which she has so long been dishonored, to be repealed? Four-fifths of all the women who have ever lived, have been the slaves of man—the menials in his household, the drudges in his field, the instruments of his pleasure, or, at best, the gilded toys of his leisure days in court or palace. She has been outlawed from honorable service, and almost incapacitated, by her servile condition, for the highest aspirations after usefulness and renown. But a noble revenge awaits her. By a manifestation of the superiority of moral power, she can triumph over that physical power which has hitherto subjected her to bondage. She can bless those by whom she has been

SOURCE: Horace Mann, *"Eighth Annual Report of the Secretary of the Board of Education (1844),"* in *Life and Words of Horace Mann*, vol. 3, ed. Mary Mann (Boston, 1891), 426–29.

wronged. By refining the tastes and sentiments of man, she can change the objects of his ambition; and, with changed objects of ambition, the fields of honorable exertion can be divided between the sexes. By inspiring nobler desires for nobler objects, she can break down the ascendency of those selfish motives that have sought their gratification in her submission and inferiority. All this she can do, more rapidly, and more effectually than it can ever be done in any other way, unless through miracles, by training the young to juster notions of honor and duty, and to a higher appreciation of the true dignity and destiny of the race.

The more extensive employment of females for educating the young, will be the addition of a new and mighty power to the forces of civilization. It is a power, also, which, heretofore, to a very great extent, has been unappropriated; which has been allowed, in the administration of the affairs of men, to run to waste. Hence it will be an addition to one of the grandest spheres of human usefulness, without any subtraction from other departments—a gain without a loss. For all females—the great majority—who are destined, in the course of Providence, to sustain maternal relations, no occupation or apprenticeship can be so serviceable; but, in this connection, it is not unworthy of notice, that, according to the census of Massachusetts, there are almost eight thousand more females than males belonging to the State.

But if a female is to assume the performance of a teacher's duties, she must be endowed with high qualifications. If devoid of mental superiority, then she inevitably falls back into that barbarian relation, where physical strength measures itself against physical strength. In that contest, she can never hope to succeed; or, if she succeeds, it will be only as an Amazon, and not as a personification of moral power. Opportunities, therefore, should be everywhere opened for the fit qualification of female teachers; and all females possessing in an eminent degree, the appropriate natural endowments, should be encouraged to qualify themselves for this sacred work. Those who have worthily improved such opportunities, should be rewarded with social distinction and generous emoluments. Society cannot do less than this, on its own account, for those who are improving its condition; though for the actors themselves, in this beneficent work, the highest rewards must forever remain where God and nature have irrevocably placed them—in the consciousness of well-doing.

Could public opinion, on this one subject, be rectified, and brought into harmony with the great law of Christian duty and love, there are thousands of females amongst us, who now spend lives of frivolity, of unbroken wearisomeness and worthlessness, who would rejoice to exchange their days of painful idleness for such ennobling occupations; and who, in addition to the immediate rewards of well-doing, would see, in the distant prospect, the consolations of a life well spent, instead of the pangs of remorse for a frivolous and wasted existence.

Only Heroic Women Were
Doctors Then (1865), 1916

Changes in the position of women in the world in the last fifty years were emphasized by Dr. Anna Manning Comfort, graduate of the New York Medical College and Hospital for Women in its first class in 1865, at a luncheon in her honor, given by the Faculty and Trustees of the college at Delmonico's yesterday. Dr. Comfort was graduated at the age of 20, and she is only in the early seventies, alert and well preserved, though she has had a vigorous career, has been married, and is the mother of three children.

"Students of today have no idea of conditions as they were when I studied medicine," said Dr. Comfort. "It is difficult to realize the changes that have taken place. I attended the first meeting when this institution was proposed, and was graduated from the first class. We had to go to Bellevue Hospital for our practical work, and the indignities we were made to suffer are beyond belief. There were 500 young men students taking post-graduate courses, and we were jeered at and catcalled, and the 'old war horses,' the doctors, joined the younger men.

"We were considered aggressive. They said women did not have the same brains as men and were not trustworthy. All the work at the hospital was made as repulsively unpleasant for us as possible. There were originally six in the class, but all but two were unable to put up with the treatment to which we were subjected and dropped out. I trembled whenever I went to the hospital and I said once that I could not bear it. Finally the women went to the authorities, who said that if we were not respectfully treated they would take the charter from the hospital!

"As a physician there was nothing that I could do that satisfied people. If I wore square-toed shoes and swung my arms they said I was mannish, and if I carried a parasol and wore a ribbon in my hair they said I was too feminine. If I smiled they said I had too much levity, and if I sighed they said I had no sand.

"They tore down my sign when I began to practice, the drug stores did not like to fill my prescriptions, and the older doctors would not consult with me. But that little band of women made it possible for the other women who have come later into the field to do their work. When my first patients came and saw me they said I was too young, and they asked in horrified tones if I had studied dissecting just like the men. They were shocked at that, but they were more shocked when my bills were sent in to find that I charged as much as a man.

SOURCE: "Only Heroic Women Were Doctors Then," *The New York Times*, 9 April 1916.

"I believe in women entering professions," said Dr. Comfort, "but I also believe in motherhood. For the normal woman it is no more of a tax to have a profession as well as family life than it is for a man to carry on the multitudinous duties he has outside the family. I had three sons of my own and two adopted ones, and I am as proud of my motherhood as of my medical career. I gave as much of my personality to my children in an hour as some mothers do in ten. My children honored me and have been worth while in the world."

There were many expressions of esteem for Dr. Comfort and she was overcome when it was announced that money had been raised for an Anna Manning Comfort scholarship in the hospital.

Letters of regret were read from John Burroughs and Colonel Theodore Roosevelt among others.

"I believe in women in the medical profession, and in politics, and in all worthy pursuits," said John Burroughs.

"I am amazed to learn that this is the only institution in this State, and one of two in the United States, exclusively for the woman medical student," said Colonel Roosevelt. "There should be others and women of refinement would be drawn into the profession who will not study medicine in a co-educational college, and more women doctors are needed."

Dr. Walter G. Crump, who spoke of the need for medical colleges exclusively for women, said:

"We learn from the [1910] Flexner report that there is an overproduction of doctors, but nine out of ten of the women doctors practice. There are demands continually for women physicians which cannot be filled. They are needed in many places where women and girls are to be under a physician's care."

Dr. Mary A. Brinkman, who was one of the early graduates of the college, spoke. She said she could corroborate many of the things told by Dr. Comfort. . . .

Women's Separate Sphere, 1872

The claim of the plaintiff, who is a married woman, to be admitted to practice as an attorney and counsellor-at-law, is based upon the supposed right of every person, man or woman, to engage in any lawful employment for a livelihood. The Supreme Court of Illinois denied the application on the ground that, by the common law, which is the basis of the laws of Illinois, only men were admitted to the bar, and the legislature had not made any change in this respect, but had simply provided that no person

SOURCE: Justice Bradley's majority opionion in *Bradwell* v. *Illinois* (December 1872).

should be admitted to practice as attorney or counsellor without having previously obtained a license for that purpose from two justices of the Supreme Court, and that no person should receive a license without first obtaining a certificate from the court of some county of his good moral character. In other respects it was left to the discretion of the court to establish the rules by which admission to the profession should be determined. The court, however, regarded itself as bound by at least two limitations. One was that it should establish such terms of admission as would promote the proper administration of justice, and the other that it should not admit any persons, or class of persons, not intended by the legislature to be admitted, even though not expressly excluded by statute. In view of this latter limitation the court felt compelled to deny the application of females to be admitted as members of the bar. Being contrary to the rules of the common law and the usages of Westminster Hall* from time immemorial, it could not be supposed that the legislature had intended to adopt any different rule.

The claim that, under the fourteenth amendment of the Constitution, which declares that no State shall make or enforce any law which shall abridge the privileges and immunities of citizens of the United States, the statute law of Illinois, or the common law prevailing in that State, can no longer be set up as a barrier against the right of females to pursue any lawful employment for a livelihood (the practice of law included), assumes that it is one of the privileges and immunities of women as citizens to engage in any and every profession, occupation, or employment in civil life.

It certainly cannot be affirmed, as an historical fact, that this has ever been established as one of the fundamental privileges and immunities of the sex. On the contrary, the civil law, as well as nature herself, has always recognized a wide difference in the respective spheres and destinies of man and woman. Man is, or should be, woman's protector and defender. The natural and proper timidity and delicacy which belongs to the female sex evidently unfits it for many of the occupations of civil life. The constitution of the family organization, which is founded in the divine ordinance, as well as in the nature of things, indicates the domestic sphere as that which properly belongs to the domain and functions of womanhood. The harmony, not to say identity, of interests and views which belong, or should belong, to the family institution is repugnant to the idea of a woman adopting a distinct and independent career from that of her husband. So firmly fixed was this sentiment in the founders of the common law that it became a maxim of that system of jurisprudence that a woman had no legal existence separate from her husband, who was regarded as her head and representative in the social state; and, notwithstanding some recent

[*the ancient seat of English law, established in the twelfth century] modifications of this civil status, many of the special rules of law flowing from and dependent upon this cardinal principle still exist in full force in most States. One of these is, that a married woman is incapable, without her husband's consent, of making contracts which shall be binding on her or him. This very incapacity was one circumstance which the Supreme Court of Illinois deemed important in rendering a married woman incompetent fully to perform the duties and trusts that belong to the office of an attorney and counsellor.

It is true that many women are unmarried and not affected by any of the duties, complications, and incapacities arising out of the married state, but these are exceptions to the general rule. The paramount destiny and mission of woman are to fulfil the noble and benign offices of wife and mother. This is the law of the Creator. And the rules of civil society must be adapted to the general constitution of things, and cannot be based upon exceptional cases.

The humane movements of modern society, which have for their object the multiplication of avenues for woman's advancement, and of occupations adapted to her condition and sex, have my heartiest concurrence. But I am not prepared to say that it is one of her fundamental rights and privileges to be admitted into every office and position, including those which require highly special qualifications and demanding special responsibilities. In the nature of things it is not every citizen of every age, sex, and condition that is qualified for every calling and position. It is the prerogative of the legislator to prescribe regulations founded on nature, reason, and experience for the due admission of qualified persons to professions and callings demanding special skill and confidence. This fairly belongs to the police power of the State; and, in my opinion, in view of the peculiar characteristics, destiny, and mission of woman, it is within the province of the legislature to ordain what offices, positions, and callings shall be filled and discharged by men, and shall receive the benefit of those energies and responsibilities, and that decision and firmness which are presumed to predominate in the sterner sex.

For these reasons I think that the laws of Illinois now complained of are not obnoxious to the charge of abridging any of the privileges and immunities of citizens of the United States.

CHAPTER 5

Immigrant Life and Labor

New factories and growing cities drew millions to America in search of opportunities. The half-century from 1880 to 1930 was the period of greatest immigration to the United States. During that time, over 25 million newcomers arrived in America. Before the mid-1890s, Germans, Irish, and other northern and western Europeans dominated the immigration statistics. After 1896, the majority of immigrants hailed from southern and eastern Europe, with Jews, Italians, Poles, and Slavs accounting for the largest numbers.

Most of these people left Europe to escape the wretched economic conditions in their native lands. Farm workers with no land of their own and city workers earning meager wages and crowded into slums heard of better conditions across the ocean. Jews also escaped from vicious anti-Semitism, including laws that limited their civil rights, restricted their employment and educational opportunities, and banned them from living in designated areas. As harsh as these restrictions were, worse things awaited Jews who lived in Russia. After 1880, anti-Semitic violence, in the form *of pogroms, erupted periodically. During these outbursts, Jews were murdered and their possessions were destroyed or confiscated. It is not surprising that they eagerly sought a new life in another country.*

Although the millions leaving Europe did not all settle in the United States (many went to Canada or South America), it was the country favored by the majority of emigrants, most of whom passed by the Statue of Liberty and through Ellis Island. However, not all of the newcomers intended to stay in America. Many young males migrated in search of work, with the hope of saving funds to return home and buy land. In the end, however, millions decided to make their new homes in the United States because they found that conditions were better, if not for themselves, then at least for their children.

The essay by Gary R. Mormino and George E. Pozzetta, "Immigrant Women in Tampa: The Italian Experience, 1890–1930," explores the experiences of one group of newcomers. What motivated them to immigrate to the United States and how did they adjust to life in America? For most groups, there were a number of reasons for leaving their native lands, but often a single overriding cause ultimately led to the decision to emigrate. In what ways was this true of the Sicilian immigrants in Tampa? How did the work routines of Tampa's cigar factories preserve Italian social and cultural patterns? What are the most significant examples of the blending of traditional ways and new practices?

Although elderly Italian women in Tampa today may "yearn nostalgically for the halcyon days of yesteryear," the first document, from journalist Jacob Riis's How the Other Half Lives, *reveals that the experiences of immigrant cigar makers in New York were not the kind likely to produce fond memories. What were the key differences in living and working conditions in immigrant communities between Tampa and New York during this era?*

In the second document, a Chinese immigrant writes of his experiences at the turn of the century. As with the Italians in Tampa, his transition to living in America combined elements of both cultural continuity and adaptation to new ways of life. What are your reactions to the author's explanations of why the Chinese faced such severe prejudice in the United States?

ESSAY

Immigrant Women in Tampa:
The Italian Experience, 1890–1930

Gary R. Mormino and George E. Pozzetta

The historical study of women, particularly immigrant women, has advanced dramatically over the past decade. Recent scholarship has rescued from neglect a great deal of historical material and has placed in clearer perspective the important roles played by women in American society. Ultimately, women's history will be fully integrated into the pageantry of the American experience. Sufficient specialized studies to accomplish this goal, however, do not yet exist. More regional and local investigations detailing the histories of women in many different locations, time periods, and life situations are required.

During the period 1890–1930 the state of Florida possessed no more cosmopolitan mix of population and culture than that which existed in Tampa. Residing there, and working primarily in Tampa's cigar industry, were thousands of immigrant Spanish, Cuban, and Italian men and women. The necessities of coming to a new land, coping with a strange culture, and adapting to new demands resulted in the creation of a unique ethnic community called Ybor City. Immigrant women added their own distinctive contributions to the quality of life existing in this enclave. During the tumultuous [cigar makers'] strike of 1910, one reporter took note of "bevies of gayly dressed Spanish, Cuban, and Italian women," waving their red bandanas as striking cigar makers marched to the *Internationale*. In 1931, the year of Tampa's last great cigar strike, a German visitor marveled at the city's "Spanish India [Ybor City]. . . . What a colorful, screaming, shrill and turbulent world! Spanish and Cuban women and cats—both equally beautiful, equally exotic . . . a veritable narrow ghetto, rich with life's smells." The hints of romance and radicalism that such images put forth belie the more fundamental roles played by women.

The Italian women who came to Florida traced their roots back to a cluster of small villages in the western part of Sicily; it was here that the outlooks and values of the immigrants took shape. These remote, hill-top settlements had a history that was tinctured with fatalism and gloom. For them, the unification of Italy in 1870 had only changed rulers not masters; power emanated from wealthy landowners who controlled the area's wheat, olives, vines, and sheep. From these urban-villages numbering

SOURCE: Gary R. Mormino and George E. Pozzetta, "Immigrant Women in Tampa: The Italian Experience, 1890–1930," *Florida Historical Quarterly*, Vol. LXI (January 1983): 196–312. Reprinted courtesy of the *Florida Historical Quarterly*.

6,000 or more inhabitants, peasants walked several miles each day to tend their plots of earth. . . . because of this rural-urban mixture, a crude middle class of artisans and shopkeepers had evolved.

"If you want a large family," a Sicilian proverb instructed, "begin with a girl, but she may not live beyond the first year." The bittersweet message this folk wisdom imparted is evocative of the vital role played by women in the Sicilian agri-urban system. Peasant women derived their esteem from their domestic prowess and economic contributions. In general, Sicilian men preferred that women not work outside the home, since the women's status as a wage earner jeopardized family honor and male prestige. In 1907 only fifteen per cent of all Sicilian women labored outside the home in non-agrarian occupations. A 1909 government survey conducted in Tampa found similar patterns in force: 10.5 per cent of the city's Italian women had worked outside the home for wages before coming to America, and another 18.4 per cent had toiled as farm laborers. The work experience for these women, therefore, resided principally in the context of the family.

The key point basic to understanding the Sicilian family is its function as a collective producer, a common pool of familial resources. The family was the Sicilians' state. The Church had joined forces with the *galantuomini* (upper classes), the government had betrayed the people, justice was corrupt, only the family could be trusted. Sicilians denigrated and denied individualism for the greater family good. Parents regarded their children as economic assets whose incomes helped stave off disaster and added to the family fortunes.

An overabundance of children, however, exacerbated the island's many problems. In 1800, Sicily's population stood at 1,000,000; by 1900 the island groaned to support 3,500,000 inhabitants. Emigration functioned as an endemic rather than epidemic phenomenon, decimating some villages while leaving others untouched by its pressures. One of Tampa's points of origin, the village of Santo Stefano Quisquina, provides a textbook case of the dynamics of demography. Local birth and census records, preserved in the parish church and town hall, reveal the classic pattern: in 1861 Santo Stefano listed 5,464 citizens, the number climbing to 6,315 in 1881, but falling to 6,087 in 1901, and 5,897 in 1931. The decline after 1881 points to heavy rates of emigration beginning in that decade. Birth records reinforce this picture. In 1867, 232 births were recorded at the parish church, La Madre della Chiesa. In 1887 a near record 292 babies were born; but in 1907—at the very climax of Italian emigration—only 160 children were registered, the fewest births in three generations. Santo Stefano confirmed historian Frank Thistlethwaite's thesis that "there is a direct correlation between the rates of emigration and the natural increase twenty years previously."

Emigration severely dislocated the rhythms of village life in the old country. In the process women accepted new challenges and assumed new responsibilities. This was particularly true in light of the heavy male predominance in the early phases of the immigration experience. The masculine imbalance wrought by migration altered sexual roles in the villages. When the men left, women often became managers for the estates, handling business needs and working in the fields. Oftentimes with husbands away in Tampa, women held together the unbroken international circle, underscoring the peasant proverb, "If the father should die, the family would suffer; if the mother should die, the family ceases to exist." Other women chose to chart entirely new directions for themselves.

The case of Salvatore and Agatina Cannella illustrates the immigrant experience and its effects upon the participants. Salvatore Cannella operated a dry goods store in Santo Stefano, a business which he resumed in New Orleans after emigration. Like many of the early immigrants, the Cannellas returned to Sicily after earning several thousand dollars. Unfortunately, Salvatore died shortly after repatriating. Agatina Cannella, shrouded in black, contemplated a life of mourning as custom dictated, but she opted to break away from convention. Rosalia Cannella Ferlita, her daughter, explained her mother's decision, an alternative inconceivable to an earlier generation: "My mother was used to the business. . . . Well in Italy she had to stay in the house. There was nothing to do. . . . There was no communication. Sit and sit. Finally she decided to come back to America. But she didn't want to go back to New Orleans—too many memories—so she came to Tampa."

In Tampa, Sicilians joined Spaniards and Cubans to develop Ybor City. The creation of Vicente Martinez Ybor, this enclave was carved out of palmetto scrubland in 1886 to become the capital of hand-rolled cigarmaking in the United States. Incorporated into Tampa in 1887, this ethnic settlement by 1905 was composed of about 6,000 foreign-born "Latins." In order of numerical importance, they included Cubans, Italians, and Spaniards. Ybor City evolved into a unique experiment: a company town financed by foreign capital; an industrial community amidst a rural South; and a Latin workforce in a state dominated by WASPs. Such was the environment which greeted the Sicilian immigrants who arrived between the late 1880s and the 1920s.

Evidently, and the records are sparse, the period of predominantly male settlement was short-lived. Several early records document the female presence in Tampa. In May 1892, the Italian consul of New Orleans reported nearly 300 Sicilians in Tampa, approximately one-third of whom were women. The 1900 manuscript census provides a more in-depth portrait of an emerging Italian community. The fraction of females in 1900 remained at one-third, but the overall colony numbers had increased to over 1,300. The typical Sicilian female was sixteen, reflecting the youthful character of the colony. A scant two per cent of the Italian women were listed age fifty and older. Most Italians, men and women, were illiterate. Husbands on the average were five years older than wives. The 1905 Florida State Census listed 2,574 Italians in Tampa—1,370 males and 1,204 females. By 1909, one report indicated that ninety-nine per cent of the Italian husbands in its survey had been reunited with their wives.

Curiously missing from the 1900 census, as it related to Italians, were two standard immigrant institutions, the boarding house and the extended family living under one roof. Several explanations may clarify this absence. The year 1900 may have been too early to capture the extended family, since the Italian community was in the process of establishing itself. The census did reveal a pattern of boarding on the part of Italian men, but not in homes managed by Italian women. This again is undoubtedly a function of the early stage of family immigration then in place for Italians. Provision must be made also for the presence of boarding houses that went unrecorded because of bureaucratic omission or group commission. Census takers have always had difficulty in recording the newest immigrants. Given the abominable spelling of Italian names by census takers, there would be difficulty in obtaining completely reliable information from the mobile residents of a boarding house, particularly if a group felt a sense of alienation.

Nearly sixteen per cent of Tampa's Italian households maintained boarders in 1909, as documented by a United States Senate Immigration Commission survey. In these arrangements, women played a central role. The owner's wife, oftentimes with the support of female children, tended to the boarders' many needs, including washing, cooking, mending, and various other household tasks. These jobs were added, of course, to the duties required in caring for the woman's own family. Among Italian households supporting boarders in the survey year, an average of seven boarders were found per residence. While at home, Italian women somehow found time to continue the handicraft arts of sewing, crocheting, and embroidering.

· Italians were counted most heavily where their presence was courted— at the city's burgeoning workplace. Ybor City boasted in the early twentieth century nearly 200 cigar factories which, by 1911, were producing in excess of 1,000,000 hand-rolled cigars daily. Each week the more than 10,000 workers earned $250,000 dollars in wages. Women played a significant role in making Tampa synonymous with quality cigars, a function that went beyond just posing for the comely cigar labels that advertised Tampa Girl and Farnesia [cigars] to the world.

Latin *patrones* [employers] such as V. Martinez Ybor and Ignacio Haya welcomed women on a number of levels. Their presence stabilized what once appeared as a wild, male frontier community; more importantly, women demonstrated their expertise in the cigar factories. Unlike the Spanish and Cubans, Italians brought with them no previous experience in the tobacco industry save a sheer doggedness to work hard and long. Their tenacious commitment to work, combined with values such as frugality, dependability, and abstention from hard liquor, made Italians ideal workers. Women shared this acceptance of the work ethic. "Work hard, work always, and you will never know hunger," a proverb promised. As early as June 1900, nearly seventy per cent of all gainfully employed Italians in Ybor City were engaged in the cigar industry. By 1909 Italians accounted for almost twenty per cent of the total cigar workforce. If one added the numbers involved in *chinchales* (storefront workshops), the figures would be even greater.

The 1900 census revealed patterns characteristic of Italian immigrants. Italians, whether in New York, San Francisco, or Tampa, almost always started at the bottom of the occupational ladder and faced a long upward climb. In 1900 most female Italian cigar workers labored as unskilled tobacco strippers, widely regarded as the least desirable position in the industry. Tobacco stripping involved removal of the hard stems from the tobacco leaves, a job that many observers felt was particularly suited to the nimble fingers of women. Because of poor pay, unhealthy working conditions, and lowly status, the positions of stripper often fell to those women who could find no other employment. One Tampa labor newspaper observed in 1917 that stripping attracted "[o]rphan girls, maids who have no male helper, widows with young children, the victims of divorce, the daughters of large families, the victims of vicious men or of sick and disabled men." Italian women, however, used the stripping tables in the early years . . . to launch themselves upward into the ranks of cigarmakers. So successful were they that by the second decade of the new century they posed a serious threat to displace male cigarmakers.

To become a skilled cigar worker, many Italians underwent a long apprenticeship lasting at a minimum eight months but sometimes extending to well over a year. An Italian consul once suggested that this requirement reduced the number of prospective Italian cigarmakers because, while apprenticed, candidates received no [financial] assistance. Having endured the training period, however, Italians could expect handsome wages. "Italian women have become very adept at this craft," noted the same consul in 1909, with some earning $25.00 a week. "On average, the workers average sixteen to eighteen dollars a week." Those cigarworkers who received pay on a piecework basis earned substantial wages compared to other skilled workers during this period. The curious fact that apparently Tampa's Italian women earned more than men (certainly a rarity in industrial history) was buttressed by a 1913 report in *Bolletino dell'Emigrazione* indicating that Italian men averaged $15.00 to $18.00 a week while women earned $15.00 to $20.00 a week, but some "even to twenty-three dollars a week." Children earned between $6.00 and $12.00 a week.

If women were limited in their work roles—no woman was ever elected to the prestigious post of *lector* (reader)* and few have been discovered in the leadership of the local labor movement—a remarkable number of Italian women did work. In 1909, sixteen per cent of the foreign-born women in America were employed for wages; in Tampa, just under one quarter of the Italian-born women were so occupied. The latter figure was almost certainly undercounted. The 1900 census, for instance, revealed many examples of Italian girls, aged ten to sixteen, whose occupation (one could generally expect "at school") was left blank. One surmises that these girls worked but, because of minimum age work laws, the figure went unreported. Government reports further substantiated the Italian proclivity for work. In 1900 substantially more Ybor City Italian women were employed in cigar factories than their male counterparts. Fully sixty per cent of the foreign-born women employed in the cigar industry were Italian. . . .

The cigar industry offered a congenial atmosphere punctuated by frequent doses of *cafe con leche* [coffee with milk], dramatic readings from popular *novelle* [novels], the companionship of *paesani* [countrymen], and the heady solidarity of strong unions. Furthermore, there existed in Tampa no established native or immigrant class, such as the Irish or Germans, to supervise or intimidate Latin women—at least in Ybor City. Thus, in this setting traditional Italian values could survive, albeit in somewhat altered form, and rapid economic development could occur within the context of social conservatism.

Even the city's turbulent, fractious labor history failed to dislodge Italian women from the cigar factories. Strikes became benchmarks of time in Ybor City. A series of violent and protracted strikes led by fiercely militant unions enveloped Ybor City between 1899 and 1931. Conflicts generally revolved around challenges to pre-industrial fringe benefits and sovereignty of the workplace. The workers' embrace of popular leftist causes, such as socialism and anarchism, intensified the struggle.

Italian men and women clearly supported the cause. During the general strike occurring in 1900, the *Tampa Tribune* observed the following scene: "The hall was literally packed with women who work daily in the branch of the cigarmaking industry. There were Americans, Cubans, Spaniards and Italians in the mass of feminine toilers . . . 1248 women members. . . . It was the largest body of women ever assembled in Tampa. It was a sight worth seeing."

In 1910 the *Tribune* described as "ludicrous," nine Italian women who picketed the factory of Arguelles, Lopez and Brothers. "The misguided ones, armed with clubs," an observer wrote, "paraded the streets about the factory. Their weapons they brandished and their tongues they did

[*Cigar makers commonly elected one of their number to read from books and journals while work progressed.]

wag, giving vent to threats that they would beat all to death who would work." Tampa-born author Jose Yglesias, in his reminiscences with Studs Terkel, confirmed the pattern: "People date their lives from various strikes in Tampa. When they refer to a scab, they say, 'It's no surprise he's going to break the strike since his mother did it in 1921.' In my hometown strikes were passionate affairs. . . . Women beat up women scabs."

Italian women earned their place in the rank and file [of labor]. And yet in historical perspective, their essential group experience embodied a conservative lifestyle. How does one explain the relationship of labor radicalism and domestic conservatism? The work choices made by Italian women[,] which took them out of homes, gave them higher wages than their menfolk, and placed them in militant unions[,] must be understood in the context of their family obligations. The individual's identity assumed importance only as it contributed to the group well being. Sicilian women—and girls—worked not to enhance their self-identification, nor to achieve a share of American independence, but to maintain and sustain the family unit. The general pattern was to utilize cigar factory jobs as a means to an end rather than as permanent employment selections. While women labored for wages in the factories, often for extended periods of time, men began to move in different directions. Typically men labored for a few years to build a small amount of investment capital, usually put toward some form of property. "The Italian cigar makers are not content until they own their own homes," wrote an official in 1909. Soon men began to purchase dairies, truck farms, and cattle herds on the fringes of Ybor City. Others invested in the first small beginnings of a trade or business—a fruit stand, fish store, grocery, confectionary, bakery, or import house. Women and children often provided steady wages until these ventures matured. The elderly and very young also contributed. Old women cared for children during the work day, and youngsters of six, seven, or eight years acquired rudimentary cigarmaking skills at home. The strategy reaped dividends.

Italians achieved extraordinary progress in the street trades compared to their Latin [Hispanic] counterparts in Ybor City. In 1909 Italians boasted forty-seven fruit and vegetable vendors, seven fish markets, and fourteen ice and ice cream dealers as compared to a total of only three such Cuban and Spanish enterprises. Many of these business ventures were launched on precisely the basis described above. The case of Alex and Josephine Scaglione typified this paradigm. The couple met while rolling cigars in Ybor City. Soon Alex left the factories and opened a grocery store. Josephine continued to roll cigars until the business stabilized. Their son became a high school principal and college president, characteristic of the generation after 1930, once Italians had struggled to carve themselves a niche in the bourgeois world.

Family obligations extended to the unit's more junior members as well. "A family's wealth," an Old World proverb reminded immigrants, "depended upon the number of hands it has," and Italians were not reluctant to enlist all available support. Parents directed the vocations of their children and during the period 1890–1930, work began early. Few Italian children in Tampa—as elsewhere—entered high school before the Depression. "The education of children is almost altogether neglected," complained one official. Reflecting Old World priorities, girls fared much worse than their brothers in educational opportunity and achievement. "Education was out of the question for a single girl," explained Mary Italiano. "I went to school as far as the fourth or fifth grade." The necessity of going to work, either at a factory work bench or in the home, came soon to the lives of most Italian women.

Tampa's Italians exercised patience and persistence in their efforts to achieve success. When strikes depressed the local economy, Italians proved particularly adept at probing the urban and rural economies, finding work mining phosphate, picking oranges, gardening, or peddling. Tina Provenzano remembered fleeing her cigar factory in Tampa during the 1920 strike and living with her father, who then was working for a Clearwater farmer. A taste of tenant farming did not cheapen the family dignity. "Italians were more interested in building something for ourselves," explained Nick Nuccio, one of Tampa's most successful Latin politicians: "The Spanish and Cuban people . . . they come here to make a little money and go back to Spain and Cuba. The Italian people knew they were going to live [here] for the rest of their lives, raise a family. I lived in the same house for thirty-eight years."

Just as Italians adjusted to the new demands of the workplace, so too did the patterns of Italian domestic life reflect the impact of a new environment. Old World fathers soon discovered their daughters saw little romance or utility in Sicilian-style marriages. While mothers rarely handpicked their daughter's future mate, neither did they play an inactive role. The chaperone entered the scene. Courtship followed a strict code of ethics. Friday and Saturday evenings climaxed around Ybor City's main thoroughfare, Seventh Avenue. Throngs of Latins converged during the evening hours for shopping, indulging in guava tarts with coffee, and dancing at one of the four mutual aid societies: L'Unione Italiana, Centro Asturiano, Centro Español, and Círculo Cubano. Young couples were allowed to flirt and dance, but always under the watchful eye of mother or an older sister. In Ybor City there were no privileged sanctuaries. "Mother would take us walking up and down Seventh Avenue," smiled Angelina Spoto Comescone, "and all the boys would be standing on the curb and the mothers would be like little hens watching her chicks. So that nobody would look at us or touch us. . . . The boys would go wild trying to get a word with us. . . . It was beautiful. It was entertainment. It was beautiful."

Helen Martinez Spoto concurred: "We had to have a chaperone, always. . . . It was nicer then. We were more together . . . the family together." Rosemary Scaglione Crapraro offered her insights into the institution: "Marriage was the only way, the only way to get . . . out from under the skirts of the mother. . . . We thought that by getting married young—you see we couldn't see a fella, couldn't sit on the porch with the light on at night—so the first [male] to come along and smile at us, we would marry him. *And* there was not divorce."

More structured recreation took place within the mutual aid society, but women typically operated at the fringes of this institution. Organized in 1894, L'Unione Italiana ministered to the social and economic needs of Italian immigrants. It dispensed cradle-to-grave benefits, from unemployment compensation to burial expenses. In 1914, a magnificent clubhouse was erected [and] replaced a few years later, after a fire, by an even more resplendent four-story structure. The club served, however, as the principal domain of men. Club rules allowed women to join in the 1920s and participate in medical benefits, but their role was explicitly defined by their committee names: the Women's Auxiliary Committee and Women's Recreational Committee. Yet, even before formal entry, women participated fully in the numerous Sunday picnics and outings sponsored by the club. They also labored diligently in the many fund-raising drives for various civic and national causes highlighting the club's existence.

If Italian women seldom frequented the *cantina* [barroom] of the social club, they were invisible at the ballot box. No woman possessed the vote until 1920, of course, but even as late as 1930 Tampa's Latins—men and women—wielded little leverage in the city's ward system. For good reasons, Italians declined the franchise. In the old country, the peasantry was virtually disfranchised until 1892, and a universal male franchise was not won until 1912. Moreover, most of Tampa's Sicilians never learned to read or write English, a requirement for registering to vote in Florida. For example, in 1909, only six per cent of Tampa's foreign-born Italian women who were employed could speak English, as opposed to twenty per cent of their Cuban counterparts. Ironically, this figure belies the very rapid linguistic adaptation achieved by Italian women in adjusting to the dominant language of Ybor City. In this ethnic enclave, the *lingua franca* was Spanish, not English, and because of their heavy representation in the cigar factories, Italian women may well have acquired facility in Spanish more quickly than men. Fluency in Spanish, however, did not translate into a high rate of voting or naturalization. Indeed, by 1930, only twenty-four per cent of Tampa's foreign born population was naturalized, easily the lowest percentage of any large city in the United States.

In general, women accommodated to the social dictates of this period. The Italian family was father-dominated but mother-centered, a delicate balance of wills. Few women challenged this arrangement. Today elderly Italian women yearn nostalgically for the halcyon days of yesteryear. "Ybor City was one big family," sobbed Angelina Comescone. "In the evenings our parents would take us walking. . . . Ybor City was all one big family. We all loved one another. It was beautiful. We could go walking, singing all the way, Italian, Spanish, and American songs. Nobody walks anymore. It was beautiful then. Nobody sings anymore. . . . Today, you don't hear anybody sing anymore."

When asked to summarize the role of women in Ybor City, seventy-year-old Nelson Palermo pondered, and then said, "Cigarmaking, kitchen, raising children. And respect." In the broadest terms, his characterization speaks accurately. And yet, Italian women in Ybor City played a myriad of roles, many of them undefined and unrecorded. One is reminded of an observation in Ann Cornelisen's classic work on Italian life, *Women in the Shadows*. "As for the women," the speaker explained, "put any label you want on it. It amounts to the same thing. . . . Men work and talk about politics. We do the rest. . . . We decide, but we don't have to talk about it in the Piazza."

Italian women were thus significant forces in determining the nature of immigrant adjustments to life in Tampa. Their tenacious efforts helped to preserve a culture, with its emphasis on hard work, frugality, and strong family bonds. Yet, at the same time, they often played a leading role in flexibly adapting Old World ways to cope with the new conditions encountered in Florida. In the end, both the immigrant group itself and the urban environment in which it existed were reshaped as a result of this delicate balance between the old and new. . . .

DOCUMENTS

Tenement Cigar Makers, c. 1890

Take a row of houses in East Tenth Street. . . . They contained thirty-five families of cigarmakers, with probably not half a dozen persons in the whole lot of them, outside of the children, who could speak a word of English, though many had been in the country half a lifetime. This room with two windows giving on the street, and a rear attachment without windows, called a bedroom by courtesy, is rented at $12.25 a month. In the front room[,] man and wife work at the bench from six in the morning till nine at night. They make a team, stripping the tobacco leaves together; then he makes the filler, and she rolls the wrapper on and finishes the cigar. For a thousand they receive $3.75, and can turn out together three thousand cigars a week. The point has been reached where the rebellion comes in, and the workers in these tenements are just now on a strike,

SOURCE: Jacob Riis, *How the Other Half Lives* (New York: Scribner's, 1903), 103–8.

demanding $5.00 and $5.50 for their work. The manufacturer having refused, they are expecting hourly to be served with notice to quit their homes, and the going of a stranger among them excites their resentment, until his errand is explained. While we are in the house, the ultimatum of the "boss" is received. He will give $3.75 a thousand, not another cent. Our host is a man of seeming intelligence, yet he has been nine years in New York and knows neither English nor German. Three bright little children play about the floor.

His neighbor on the same floor has been here fifteen years, but shakes his head when asked if he can speak English. He answers in a few broken syllables when addressed in German. With $11.75 rent to pay for like accommodation, he has the advantage of his oldest boy's work besides his wife's at the bench. Three properly make a team, and these three can turn out four thousand cigars a week, at $3.75. This Bohemian has a large family; there are four children, too small to work, to be cared for. . . . [T]his Bohemian's butcher's bill for the week, with meat at twelve cents a pound . . . is from two dollars and a half to three dollars. . . . Here is a suite of three rooms, two dark, three flights up. The ceiling is partly down in one of the rooms. "It is three months since we asked the landlord to fix it," says the oldest son, a very intelligent lad who has learned English in the evening school. His father has not had that advantage, and has sat at his bench, deaf and dumb to the world about him except his own, for six years. He has improved his time and become an expert at his trade. Father, mother, and son together, a full team, make from fifteen to sixteen dollars a week. . . .

Probably more than half of all the Bohemians in this city are cigar-makers, and it is the herding of these in great numbers in the so-called tenement factories, where the cheapest grade of work is done at the lowest wages, that constitutes at once their greatest hardship and the chief grudge of other workmen against them. . . .

Men, women and children work together seven days in the week in these cheerless tenements to make a living for the family, from the break of day till far into the night. Often the wife is the original cigarmaker from the old home, the husband having adopted her trade here as a matter of necessity, because, knowing no word of English, he could get no other work. As they state the cause of the bitter hostility of the trades unions, she was the primary bone of contention in the day of the early Bohemian immigration. The unions refused to admit the women, and, as the support of the family depended upon her to a large extent, such terms as were offered had to be accepted. The manufacturer has ever since industriously fanned the antagonism between the unions and his hands, for his own advantage. The victory rests with him, since the Court of Appeals decided that the law, passed a few years ago, to prohibit cigarmaking in tenements was unconstitutional, and thus put an end to the struggle. While it lasted, all sorts of frightful stories were told of the shocking conditions under which people lived and worked in these tenements, from a sanitary point of view especially, and a general impression survives to this day that they are particularly desperate. The Board of Health, after a careful canvass, did not find them so then. I am satisfied from personal inspection, at a much later day, guided in a number of instances by the union cigarmakers themselves to the tenements which they considered the worst, that the accounts were greatly exaggerated. Doubtless the people are poor, in many cases very poor; but they are not uncleanly, rather the reverse; they live much better than the clothing-makers in the Tenth Ward, . . .

The Experiences of a Chinese Immigrant, 1880–1903

My father gave me $100, and I went to Hong Kong with five other boys from our place and we got steerage passage on a steamer, paying $50 each. Everything was new to me. All my life I had been used to sleeping on a board bed with a wooden pillow, and I found the steamer's bunk very uncomfortable, because it was so soft. The food was different from that which I had been used to, and I did not like it at all. I was afraid of the stews, for the thought of what they might be made of by the wicked wizards of the ship made me ill. Of the great power of these people I saw many signs. The engines that moved the ship were wonderful monsters, strong enough to lift mountains. When I got to San Francisco, which was before the passage of the Exclusion act [1882], I was half starved, because I was afraid to eat the provisions of the barbarians, but a few days' living in the Chinese quarter made me happy again. A man got me work as a house servant in an American family, and my start was the same as that of almost all the Chinese in this country.

The Chinese laundryman does not learn his trade in China; there are no laundries in China. The women there do the washing in tubs and have no washboards or flat irons. All the Chinese laundrymen here were taught in the first place by American women just as I was taught.

When I went to work for that American family I could not speak a word of English, and I did not know anything about housework. The family consisted of husband, wife and two children. They were very good to me and paid me $3.50 a week, of which I could save $3.

I did not know how to do anything, and I did not understand what the lady said to me, but she showed me how to cook, wash, iron, sweep,

SOURCE: *Independent* 60 (19 February 1903): 417–23.

dust, make beds, wash dishes, clean windows, paint and [polish] brass, polish the knives and forks, etc., by doing the things herself and then overseeing my efforts to imitate her. She would take my hands and show them how to do things. She and her husband and children laughed at me a great deal, but it was all good natured. . . .

In six months I had learned how to do the work of our house quite well, and I was getting $5 a week and board, and putting away about $4.25 a week. I had also learned some English, and by going to a Sunday school I learned more English and something about Jesus, who was a great Sage, and whose precepts are like those of Kong-foo-tsze.

It was twenty years ago when I came to this country, and I worked for two years as a servant, getting at the last $35 a month. I sent money home to comfort my parents, but tho I dressed well and lived well and had pleasure, going quite often to the Chinese theater and to dinner parties in Chinatown, I saved $50 in the first six months, $90 in the second, $120 in the third and $150 in the fourth. So I had $410 at the end of two years, and I was now ready to start in business.

When I first opened a laundry it was in company with a partner, who had been in the business for some years. We went to a town about 500 miles inland, where a railroad was building. We got a board shanty and worked for the men employed by the railroads. Our rent cost us $10 a month and food nearly $5 a week each, for all food was dear and we wanted the best of everything—we lived principally on rice, chickens, ducks and pork, and did our own cooking. The Chinese take naturally to cooking. It cost us about $50 for our furniture and apparatus, and we made close upon $60 a week, which we divided between us. We had to put up with many insults and some frauds, as men would come in and claim parcels that did not belong to them, saying they had lost their tickets, and would fight if they did not get what they asked for. Sometimes we were taken before Magistrates and fined for losing shirts that we had never seen. On the other hand, we were making money, and even after sending home $3 a week I was able to save about $15. When the railroad construction gang moved on we went with them. The men were rough and prejudiced against us, but not more so than in the big Eastern cities. It is only lately in New York that the Chinese have been able to discontinue putting wire screens in front of their windows, and at the present time the street boys are still breaking the windows of Chinese laundries all over the city, while the police seem to think it a joke.

We were three years with the railroad, and then went to the mines, where we made plenty of money in gold dust, but had a hard time, for many of the miners were wild men who carried revolvers and after drinking would come into our place to shoot and steal shirts, for which we had to pay. One of these men hit his head hard against a flat iron and all the miners came and broke up our laundry, chasing us out of town. They were going to hang us. We lost all our property and $365 in money, which members of the mob must have found. . . .

I have found out, during my residence in this country, that much of the Chinese prejudice against Americans is unfounded, and I no longer put faith in the wild tales that were told about them in our village, tho some of the Chinese, who have been here twenty years and who are learned men, still believe that there is no marriage in this country, that the land in infested with demons and that all the people are given over to general wickedness.

I know better. Americans are not all bad, nor are they wicked wizards. Still, they have their faults, and their treatment of us is outrageous.

The reason why so many Chinese go into the laundry business in this country is because it requires little capital and is one of the few opportunities that are open. Men of other nationalities who are jealous of the Chinese, because he is a more faithful worker than one of their people, have raised such a great outcry about Chinese cheap labor that they have shut him out of working on farms or in factories or building railroads or making streets or digging sewers. He cannot practice any trade, and his opportunities to do business are limited to his own countrymen. So he opens a laundry when he quits domestic service.

The treatment of the Chinese in this country is all wrong and mean. It is persisted in merely because China is not a fighting nation. The Americans would not dare to treat Germans, English, Italians or even Japanese as they treat the Chinese, because if they did there would be a war.

There is no reason for the prejudice against the Chinese. The cheap labor cry was always a falsehood. Their labor was never cheap, and is not cheap now. It has always commanded the highest market price. But the trouble is that the Chinese are such excellent and faithful workers that bosses will have no others when they can get them. If you look at men working on the street you will find an overseer for every four or five of them. That watching is not necessary for Chinese. They work as well when left to themselves as they do when some one is looking at them.

CHAPTER 6

The High Cost of Earning
a Living

By the close of the nineteenth century, the benefits of industrialization to the United States were apparent. It had become a wealthy and powerful nation, a leader among the countries of the world. But there was a price for this growth in terms of human suffering, and it was only beginning to be realized. Working conditions were often abysmal; immigrant families engaged in cigar manufacturing, for example, lived and worked in overcrowded, foul-smelling tenements. Factories and mines were designed with minimal concern for worker health and safety. Workers toiled hours at bare-subsistence wages, and they lacked virtually any compensation benefits or legal safeguards to protect their well-being.

Bonnie Mitelman's article "Rose Schneiderman and the Triangle Fire" describes one of the most horrible examples of the consequences of such conditions. Although it focuses primarily on the tragedy of an industrial fire, the article also offers insights into working conditions in the garment industry, the attitudes of management toward their employees and workers toward their unions, and the circumstances that finally gained public support and government action for workplace reform.

The first document, an excerpt from "Memoirs of a Sweatshop Girl," relates the story of a young woman, seventeen-year-old Sadie Frome, who labored in the garment industry of New York City. Her memoir reveals details about her life as a laborer and the hopes she had for the future. Sadie had arrived with her mother from Poland four years earlier. In the intervening time, her mother had died of tuberculosis and Sadie had moved from the Lower East Side of Manhattan to the Brownsville section of Brooklyn, where she obtained a room and a job in a garment factory.

The other two documents illustrate the hazards of the workplace, by no means restricted to the garment industry of New York City. In the second document, a coal miner describes the economic hardships and health hazards suffered by those who labored below the earth's surface. How do you explain the attitude of the miner expressed in the statement "We are American citizens and we don't go to hospitals and poorhouses"?

With funding from the Russell Sage Foundation, a group of scholars and social workers early in the twentieth century carried out an extensive investigation of social and economic conditions in Allegheny County, Pennsylvania, an area populated by many Polish and Slavic workers employed in the region's steel mills. The final document is from the **Pittsburgh Survey**, which was published in 1910 as the final report of the investigation. What does it reveal about the risks of working in the steel industry at that time?

In response to conditions such as those described in the essay and documents, state and federal governments have progressively moved against industrial hazards. However, do you know of any recent incidents indicating that worker safety is still an unresolved issue today in some industries?

ESSAY

Rose Schneiderman and the Triangle Fire

Bonnie Mitelman

On Saturday afternoon, March 25, 1911, in New York City's Greenwich Village, a small fire broke out in the Triangle Waist Company, just as the 500 shirtwaist employees were quitting for the day. People rushed about, trying to get out, but they found exits blocked and windows to the fire escape rusted shut. They panicked.

As the fire spread and more and more were trapped, some began to jump, their hair and clothing afire, from the eighth and ninth floor windows. Nets that firemen held for them tore apart at the impact of the falling bodies. By the time it was over, 146 workers had died, most of them young Jewish women.

A United Press reporter, William Shepherd, witnessed the tragedy and reported, "I looked upon the heap of dead bodies and I remembered these girls were the shirtwaist makers. I remembered their great strike of last year in which these same girls had demanded more sanitary conditions and more safety precautions in the shops. These dead bodies were the answer."

The horror of that fire touched the entire Lower East Side ghetto community, and there was a profuse outpouring of sympathy. But it was Rose Schneiderman, an immigrant worker with a spirit of social justice and a powerful way with words, who is largely credited with translating the ghetto's emotional reaction into meaningful, widespread action. Six weeks following the tragedy, and after years of solid groundwork, with one brilliant, well-timed speech, she was able to inspire the support of wealthy uptown New Yorkers and to swing public opinion to the side of the labor movement, enabling concerned civic, religious, and labor leaders to mobilize their efforts for desperately needed safety and industrial reforms.

The Triangle fire, and the deaths of so many helpless workers, seemed to trigger in Rose Schneiderman an intense realization that there was absolutely nothing or no one to help working women except a strong union movement. With fierce determination, and the dedication, influence, and funding of many other people as well, she battled to regulate hours, wages, and safety standards and to abolish the sweatshop system. In so doing, she brought dignity and human rights to all workers.

SOURCE: Bonnie Mitelman, "Rose Schneiderman and the Triangle Fire," *American History Illustrated* 16 (July 1981): 38–47. Reprinted through the courtesy of Historical Times, Inc., publishers of *American History Illustrated*.

The dramatic "uprising of the 20,000" of 1909–10, in which thousands of immigrant girls and women in the shirtwaist industry had endured three long winter months of a general strike to protest deplorable working conditions, had produced some immediate gains for working women. There had been agreements for shorter working hours, increased wages, and even safety reforms, but there had not been formal recognition of their union. At Triangle, for example, the girls had gained a 52 hour week, a 12–15 percent wage increase, and promises to end the grueling subcontracting system. But they had not gained the only instrument on which they could depend for lasting change: a viable trade union. This was to have disastrous results, for in spite of the few gains that they seemed to have made, the workers won no rights or bargaining power at all. In fact, "The company dealt only with its contractors. It felt no responsibility for the girls."

There were groups as well as individuals who realized the workers' impotence, but their attempts to change the situation accomplished little despite long years of hard work. The Women's Trade Union League [WTUL] and the International Ladies' Garment Workers' Union, through the efforts of Mary Dreier, Helen Marot, Leonora O'Reilly, Pauline Newman, and Rose Schneiderman, had struggled unsuccessfully for improved conditions: the futility that the union organizers were feeling in late 1910 is reflected in the WTUL minutes of December 5 of that year.

A scant eight months after their historic waistmakers' strike, and three months before the deadly Triangle fire, a Mrs. Malkiel (no doubt Theresa Serber Malkiel, who wrote the legendary account of the strike, *The Diary of a Shirtwaist Striker: A Story of the Shirtwaist Makers' Strike in New York*) is reported to have come before the League to urge action after a devastating fire in Newark, New Jersey, killed twenty-five working women. Mrs. Malkiel attributed their loss to the greed and negligence of the owners and the proper authorities. The WTUL subsequently demanded an investigation of all factory buildings and it elected an investigation committee from the League to cooperate with similar committees from other organizations.

The files of the WTUL contain complaint after complaint about unsafe factory conditions; many were filled out by workers afraid to sign their names for fear of being fired had their employers seen the forms. They describe factories with locked doors, no fire escapes, and barred windows. The New York *Times* carried an article which reported that fourteen factories were found to have no fire escapes, twenty-three that had locked doors, and seventy-eight that had obstructed fire escapes. In all, according to the article, 99 percent of the factories investigated in New York were found to have serious fire hazards.

Yet no action was taken.

It was the Triangle fire that emphasized, spectacularly and tragically, the deplorable safety and sanitary conditions of the garment workers. The tragedy focused attention upon the ghastly factories in which most immigrants worked; there was no longer any question about what the strikers had meant when they talked about safety and sanitary reform, and about social and economic justice.

The grief and frustration of the shirtwaist strikers were expressed by one of them, Rose Safran, after the fire: "If the union had won we would have been safe. Two of our demands were for adequate fire escapes and for open doors from the factories to the street. But the bosses defeated us and we didn't get the open doors or the better fire escapes. So our friends are dead."

The families of the fire victims were heartbroken and hysterical, the ghetto's *Jewish Daily Forward* was understandably melodramatic, and the immigrant community was completely enraged. Their Jewish heritage had taught them an emphasis on individual human life and worth; their shared background in the *shtetl* [Jewish village in eastern Europe] and common experiences in the ghetto had given them a sense of fellowship. They were, in a sense, a family—and some of the most helpless among them had died needlessly.

The senseless deaths of so many young Jewish women sparked within these Eastern Europeans a new determination and dedication. The fire had made reform absolutely essential. Workers' rights were no longer just socialist jargon: They were a matter of life and death.

The Triangle Waist Company was located on the three floors of the Asch Building, a 10-story, 135-foot-high structure at the corner of Greene Street and Washington Place in Greenwich Village. One of the largest shirtwaist manufacturers, Triangle employed up to 900 people at times, but on the day of the fire, only about 500 were working.

Leon Stein's brilliant and fascinating account of the fire, entitled simply *The Triangle Fire*, develops and documents the way in which the physical facilities, company procedures, and human behavior interacted to cause this great tragedy. Much of what occurred was ironic, some was cruel, some stupid, some pathetic. It is a dramatic portrayal of the eternal confrontation of the "haves" and the "have-nots," told in large part by those who survived.

Fire broke out at the Triangle Company at approximately 4:45 P.M. (because time clocks were reportedly set back to stretch the day, and because other records give differing times of the first fire alarm, it is uncertain exactly what time the fire started), just after pay envelopes had been distributed and employees were leaving their work posts. It was a small fire at first, and there was a calm, controlled effort to extinguish it. But the fire began to spread, jumping from one pile of debris to another, engulfing the combustible shirtwaist fabric. It became obvious that the fire could not be snuffed out, and workers tried to reach the elevators or stairway. Those who reached the one open stairway raced down eight flights of stairs to safety; those who managed to climb onto the available passenger elevators also got out. But not everyone could reach the available exits. Some tried to open the door to a stairway and found it locked. Others were trapped between long working tables or behind the hordes of people trying to get into the elevators or out through the one open door.

Under the work tables, rags were burning; the wooden floors, trim, and window frames were also afire. Frantically, workers fought their way to the elevators, to the fire escape, and to the windows—to any place that might lead to safety.

Fire whistles and bells sounded as the fire department raced to the building. But equipment proved inadequate, as the fire ladders reached only to the seventh floor. And by the time the firemen connected their hoses to douse the flames, the crowded eighth floor was completely ablaze.

For those who reached the windows, there seemed to be a chance for safety. The New York *World* describes people balancing on window sills, nine stories up, with flames scorching them from behind, until firemen arrived: "The nets were spread below with all promptness. Citizens were commandeered into service, as the firemen necessarily gave their attention to the one engine and hose of the force that first arrived. The catapult force that the bodies gathered in the long plunges made the nets utterly without avail. Screaming girls and men, as they fell, tore the nets from the grasp of the holders, and the bodies struck the sidewalks and lay just as they fell. Some of the bodies ripped big holes through the life nets."

One reporter who witnessed the fire remembered how,

A young man helped a girl to the window sill on the ninth floor. Then he held her out deliberately, away from the building, and let her drop. He held out a second girl the same way and let her drop. He held out a third girl who did not resist. They were all as unresisting as if he were helping them into a street car instead of into eternity. He saw that a terrible death awaited them in the flames and his was only a terrible chivalry. He brought around another girl to the window. I saw her put her arms around him and kiss him. Then he held her into space—and dropped her. Quick as a flash, he was on the window sill himself. His coat fluttered upwards—the air filled his trouser legs as he came down. I could see he wore tan shoes.

Those who had rushed to the fire escape found the window openings rusted shut. Several precious minutes were lost in releasing them. The fire escape itself ended at the second floor, in an airshaft between the Asch Building and the building next door. But too frantic to notice where it ended, workers climbed onto the fire escape, one after another until, in one terrifying moment, it collapsed from the weight, pitching the workers to their death.

Those who had made their way to the elevators found crowds pushing to get into the cars. When it became obvious that the elevators could no longer run, workers jumped down the elevator shaft, landing on the top of the cars, or grabbing for cables to ease their descent. Several died, but incredibly, some did manage to save themselves in this way. One man was found, hours after the fire, beneath an elevator car in the basement of the building, nearly drowned by the rapidly rising water from the firemen's hoses.

Several people, among them Triangle's two owners, raced to the roof, and from there were led to safety. Others never had that chance. "When Fire Chief Croker could make his way into the [top] three floors," states one account of the fire, "he found sights that utterly staggered him . . . he saw as the smoke drifted away bodies burned to bare bones. There were skeletons bending over sewing machines."

The day after the fire, the New York *Times* announced that "the building was fireproof. It shows hardly any signs of the disaster that overtook it. The walls are as good as ever, as are the floors: nothing is worse for the fire except the furniture and 141 [*sic*] of the 600 men and girls that were employed in its upper three stories."

The building *was* fireproof. But there had never been a fire drill in the factory, even though the management had been warned about the possible hazard of fire on the top three floors. Owners Max Blanck and Isaac Harris had chosen to ignore these warnings in spite of the fact that many of their employees were immigrants who could barely speak English, which would surely mean panic in the event of a crisis.

The New York *Times* also noted that Leonora O'Reilly of the League had reported Max Blanck's visit to the WTUL during the shirtwaist strike, and his plea that the girls return to work. He claimed a business reputation to maintain and told the Union leaders he would make the necessary improvements right away. Because he was the largest manufacturer in the business, the League reported, they trusted him and let the girls return.

But the improvements were never made. And there was nothing that anybody could or would do about it. Factory doors continued to open in instead of out, in violation of fire regulations. The doors remained bolted during working hours, apparently to prevent workers from getting past the inspectors with stolen merchandise. Triangle had only two staircases where there should have been three, and those two were very narrow. Despite the fact that the building was deemed fireproof, it had wooden window frames, floors, and trim. There was no sprinkler system. It was not legally required.

These were the same kinds of conditions which existed in factories throughout the garment industry; they had been cited repeatedly in the complaints filed with the WTUL. They were not unusual nor restricted to Triangle; in fact, Triangle was not as bad as many other factories.

But it was at Triangle that the fire took place.

The *Jewish Daily Forward* mourned the dead with sorrowful stories, and its headlines talked of "funerals instead of weddings" for the dead young girls. The entire Jewish immigrant community was affected, for it seemed there was scarcely a person who was not in some way touched by the fire. Nearly everyone had either been employed at Triangle themselves, or had a friend or relative who had worked there at some time or another. Most worked in factories with similar conditions, and so everyone identified with the victims and their families.

Many of the dead, burned beyond recognition, remained unidentified for days, as searching family members returned again and again to wait in long lines to look for their loved ones. Many survivors were unable to identify their mothers, sisters, or wives; the confusion of handling so many victims and so many survivors who did not understand what was happening to them and to their dead led to even more anguish for the community. Some of the victims were identified by the names on the pay envelopes handed to them at quitting time and stuffed deeply into pockets or stockings just before the fire. But many bodies remained unclaimed for days, with bewildered and bereaved survivors wandering among them, trying to find some identifying mark.

Charges of first- and second-degree manslaughter were brought against the two men who owned Triangle, and Leon Stein's book artfully depicts the subtle psychological and sociological implications of the powerful against the oppressed, and of the Westernized, German-Jewish immigrants against those still living their old-world, Eastern European heritage. Ultimately, Triangle owners Blanck and Harris were acquitted of the charges against them, and in due time they collected their rather sizable insurance.

The shirtwaist, popularized by Gibson girls, had come to represent the new-found freedom of females in America. After the fire, it symbolized death. The reaction of the grief-stricken Lower East Side was articulated by socialist lawyer Morris Hillquit:

> The girls who went on strike last year were trying to readjust the conditions under which they were obliged to work. I wonder if there is not some connection between the fire and that strike. I wonder if the magistrates who sent to jail the girls who did picket duty in front of the Triangle shop realized last Sunday that some of the responsibility may be theirs. Had the strike been successful, these girls might have been alive today and the citizenry of New York would have less of a burden upon its conscience.

For the first time in the history of New York's garment industry there were indications that the public was beginning to accept responsibility for the exploitation of the immigrants. For the first time, the establishment seemed to understand that these were human beings asking for their rights, not merely troublemaking anarchists.

The day after the Triangle fire a protest meeting was held at the Women's Trade Union League, with representatives from twenty leading labor and civic organizations. They formed "a relief committee to cooperate with the Red Cross in its work among the families of the victims, and another committee . . . to broaden the investigation and research on fire hazards in New York factories which was already being carried on by the League."

The minutes of the League recount the deep indignation that members felt at the indifference of a public which had ignored their pleas for safety after the Newark fire. In an attempt to translate their anger into constructive action, the League drew up a list of forceful resolutions that included a plan to gather delegates from all of the city's unions to make a concerted effort to force safety changes in factories. In addition, the League called upon all workers to inspect factories and then report any violations to the proper city authorities and to the WTUL. They called upon the city to immediately appoint organized workers as unofficial inspectors. They resolved to submit the following fire regulations suggestions: compulsory fire drills, fireproof exits, unlocked doors, fire alarms, automatic sprinklers, and regular inspections. The League called upon the legislature to create the Bureau of Fire Protection and finally, the League underscored the absolute need for all workers to organize themselves at once into trade unions so that they would never again be powerless.

The League also voted to participate in the funeral procession for the unidentified dead of the Triangle fire.

The city held a funeral for the dead who were unclaimed. "More than 120,000 of us were in the funeral procession that miserable rainy April day," remembered Rose Schneiderman. "From ten in the morning until four in the afternoon we of the Women's Trade Union League marched in the procession with other trade-union men and women, all of us filled with anguish and regret that we had never been able to organize the Triangle workers."

Schneiderman, along with many others, was absolutely determined that this kind of tragedy would never happen again. With single-minded dedication, they devoted themselves to unionizing the workers. The searing example of the Triangle fire provided them with the impetus they needed to gain public support for their efforts.

They dramatized and emphasized and capitalized on the scandalous working conditions of the immigrants. From all segments of the community came cries for labor reform. Stephen S. Wise, the prestigious reform rabbi, called for the formation of a citizens' committee. Jacob H. Schiff, Bishop David H. Greer, Governor John A. Dix, Anne Morgan (of *the* Morgans) and other leading civic and religious leaders collaborated in a mass meeting at the Metropolitan Opera House on May 2 to protest factory conditions and to show support for the workers.

Several people spoke at that meeting on May 2, and many in the audience began to grow restless and antagonistic. Finally, 29-year-old Rose Schneiderman stepped up to the podium.

In a whisper barely audible, she began to address the crowd.

I would be a traitor to these poor burned bodies, if I came here to talk good fellowship. We have tried you good people of the public and we have found you wanting. The old Inquisition had its rack and its thumbscrews and its instruments of torture with iron teeth. We know what these things are today: the iron teeth are our necessities, the thumbscrews the high-powered and swift machinery close to which we must work, and the rack is here in the fire-proof structures that will destroy us the minute they catch on fire.

This is not the first time girls have burned alive in the city. Every week I must learn of the untimely death of one of my sister workers. Every year thousands of us are maimed. The life of men and women is so cheap and property is so sacred. There are so many of us for one job it matters little if 140-odd are burned to death.

We have tried you, citizens; we are trying you now, and you have a couple of dollars for the sorrowing mothers and daughters and sisters by way of a charity gift. But every time the workers come out in the only way they know to protest against conditions which are unbearable, the strong hand of the law is allowed to press down heavily upon us.

Public officials have only words of warning to us—warning that we must be intensely orderly and must be intensely peaceable, and they have the workhouse just back of all their warnings. The strong hand of the law beats us back when we rise into the conditions that make life bearable.

I can't talk fellowship to you who are gathered here. Too much blood has been spilled. I know from my experience it is up to the working people to save themselves. The only way they can save themselves is by a strong working-class movement.

Her speech has become a classic. It is more than just an emotional picture of persecution; it reflects the pervasive sadness and profound understanding that comes from knowing, finally, the cruel realities of life, the perspective of history, and the nature of human beings.

The devastation of that fire and the futility of the seemingly successful strike that had preceded it seemed to impart an undeniable truth to Rose Schneiderman: They could not fail again. The events of 1911 seemed to have made her, and many others, more keenly aware than they had ever been that the workers' fight for reform was absolutely essential. If they did not do it, it would not be done.

In a sense, the fire touched off in Schneiderman an awareness of her own responsibility in the battle for industrial reform. This fiery socialist worker had been transformed into a highly effective labor leader.

The influential speech she gave did help swing public opinion to the side of the trade unions, and the fire itself had made the workers more aware of the crucial need to unionize. Widespread support for labor reform and unionization emerged. Pressure from individuals, such as Rose Schneiderman, as well as from groups like the Women's Trade Union League and the International Ladies' Garment Workers' Union, helped form the New York State Factory Investigating Commission, the New York Citizens' Committee on Safety, and other regulatory and investigatory bodies. The League and Local 25 (the Shirtwaist Makers' Union of the ILGWU) were especially instrumental in attaining a new Industrial Code for New York State, which became "the most outstanding instrument for safeguarding the lives, health, and welfare of the millions of wage earners in New York State and . . . in the nation at large."

It took years for these changes to occur, and labor reform did not rise majestically, Phoenix-like, from the ashes of the Triangle fire. But that fire, and Rose Schneiderman's whispered plea for a strong working-class movement, had indeed become the loud clear call for action.

DOCUMENTS

Memoirs of a Sweatshop Girl, 1902

Two years ago I came to this place, Brownsville, [a section in Brooklyn, New York], where so many of my people are, and where I have friends. I got work in a factory making underskirts—all sorts of cheap underskirts, like cotton and calico for the summer and woolen for the winter, but never the silk, satin or velvet underskirts. I earned $4.50 a week and lived on $2 a week, the same as before.

I got a room in the house of some friends who lived near the factory. I pay $1 a week for the room and am allowed to do light housekeeping—

SOURCE: *Independent* 54 (September 25, 1902): 2279–82.

that is, cook my meals in it. I get my own breakfast in the morning, just a cup of coffee and a roll, and at noon time I come home to dinner and take a plate of soup and a slice of bread with the lady of the house. My food for a week costs a dollar, just as it did in Allen street, and I have the rest of my money to do as I like with. I am earning $5.50 a week now, and will probably get another increase soon.

It isn't piecework in our factory, but one is paid by the amount of work done just the same. So it is like piecework. All the hands get different amounts, some as low as $3.50 and some of the men as high as $16 a week. The factory is in the third story of a brick building. It is in a room twenty feet long and fourteen broad. There are fourteen machines in it. I and the daughter of the people with whom I live work two of these machines. The other operators are all men, some young and some old.

At first a few of the young men were rude. When they passed me they would touch my hair and talk about my eyes and my red cheeks, and make jokes. I cried and said that if they did not stop I would leave the place. The boss said that that should not be, that no one must annoy me. Some of the other men stood up for me, too, especially Henry, who said two or three times that he wanted to fight. Now the men all treat me very nicely. It was just that some of them did not know better, not being educated.

Henry is tall and dark, and he has a small mustache. His eyes are brown and large. He is pale and much educated, having been to school. He knows a great many things and has some money saved. I think nearly $400. He is not going to be in a sweatshop all the time, but will soon be in the real estate business, for a lawyer that knows him well has promised to open an office and pay him to manage it.

Henry has seen me home every night for a long time and makes love to me. He wants me to marry him, but I am not seventeen yet, and I think that is too young. He is only nineteen, so we can wait.

I have been to the fortune teller's three or four times, and she always tells me that tho I have had such a lot of trouble I am to be very rich and happy. I believe her because she has told so many things that have come true. So I will keep on working in the factory for a time. Of course it is hard, but I would have to work hard even if I was married.

I get up at half-past five o'clock every morning and make myself a cup of coffee on the oil stove. I eat a bit of bread and perhaps some fruit and then go to work. Often I get there soon after six o'clock so as to be in good time, tho the factory does not open till seven. I have heard that there is a sort of clock that calls you at the very time you want to get up, but I can't believe that because I don't see how the clock would know.

At seven o'clock we all sit down to our machines and the boss brings to each one the pile of work that he or she is to finish during the day, what they call in English their "stint." This pile is put down beside the machine and as soon as a skirt is done it is laid on the other side of the machine. Sometimes the work is not all finished by six o'clock and then the one who is behind must work overtime. Sometimes one is finished ahead of time and gets away at four or five o'clock, but generally we are not done till six o'clock.

The machines go like mad all day, because the faster you work the more money you get. Sometimes in my haste I get my finger caught and the needle goes right through it. It goes so quick tho, that it does not hurt much. I bind the finger up with a piece of cotton and go on working. We all have accidents like that. Where the needle goes through the nail it makes a sore finger, or where it splinters a bone it does much harm. Sometimes a finger has to come off. Generally, tho, one can be cured by a salve.

All the time we are working the boss walks about examining the finished garments and making us do them over again if they are not just right. So we have to be careful as well as swift. But I am getting so good at the work that within a year I will be making $7 a week, and then I can save at least $3.50 a week. I have over $200 saved now.

The machines are all run by foot power, and at the end of the day one feels so weak that there is a great temptation to lie right down and sleep. But you must go out and get air, and have some pleasure. So instead of lying down I go out, generally with Henry. Sometimes we go to Coney Island, where there are good dancing places, and sometimes we go to Ulmer Park to picnics. I am very fond of dancing, and, in fact, all sorts of pleasure. I go to the theater quite often, and like those plays that make you cry a great deal. "The Two Orphans" is good. Last time I saw it I cried all night because of the hard times that the children had in the play. I am going to see it again when it comes here.

For the last two winters I have been going to night school at Public School 84 on Glenmore avenue. I have learned reading, writing and arithmetic. I can read quite well in English now and I look at the newspapers every day. I read English books, too, sometimes. The last one that I read was "A Mad Marriage," by Charlotte Braeme. She's a grand writer and makes things just like real to you. You feel as if you were the poor girl yourself going to get married to a rich duke.

I am going back to night school again this winter. Plenty of my friends go there. Some of the women in my class are more than forty years of age. Like me, they did not have a chance to learn anything in the old country. It is good to have an education; it makes you feel higher. Ignorant people are all low. People say now that I am clever and fine in conversation.

We have just finished a strike in our business. It spread all over and the United Brotherhood of Garment Workers was in it. That takes in the cloakmakers, coatmakers, and all the others. We struck for shorter hours, and after being out four weeks won the fight. We only have to work nine and a half hours a day and we get the same pay as before. So the union does good after all in spite of what some people say against it—that it just takes our money and does nothing.

I pay 25 cents a month to the union, but I do not begrudge that because it is for our benefit. The next strike is going to be for a raise of wages, which we all ought to have. But tho I belong to the union I am not a Socialist or an Anarchist. I don't know exactly what those things mean. There is a little expense for charity, too. If any worker is injured or sick we all give money to help.

Some of the women blame me very much because I spend so much money on clothes. They say that instead of a dollar a week I ought not to spend more than twenty-five cents a week on clothes, and that I should save the rest. But a girl must have clothes if she is to go into high society at Ulmer Park or Coney Island or the theatre. Those who blame me are the old country people who have old-fashioned notions, but the people who have been here a long time know better. A girl who does not dress well is stuck in a corner, even if she is pretty, and Aunt Fanny says that I do just right to put on plenty of style.

I have many friends and we often have jolly parties. Many of the young men like to talk to me, but I don't go out with any except Henry.

Lately he has been urging me more and more to get married—but I think I'll wait.

"Our Daily Life Is Not a Pleasant One," 1902

I am thirty-five years old, married, the father of four children, and have lived in the coal region all my life. Twenty-three of these years have been spent working in and around the mines. My father was a miner. He died ten years ago from "miners' asthma [black lung disease]."

Three of my brothers are miners; none of us had any opportunities to acquire an education. We were sent to school (such a school as there was in those days) until we were about twelve years of age, and then we were put into the screen room of a breaker to pick slate. From there we went inside the mines as driver boys. As we grew stronger we were taken on as laborers, where we served until able to call ourselves miners. We were given work in the breasts and gangways. There were five of us boys. One lies in the cemetery—fifty tons of top rock dropped on him. He was killed three weeks after he got his job as a miner—a month before he was to be married.

SOURCE: *Independent* 54 (June 12, 1902): 1407–10.

In the fifteen years I have worked as a miner I have earned the average rate of wages any of us coal heavers get. To-day I am little better off than when I started to do for myself. I have $100 on hand; I am not in debt; I hope to be able to weather the strike without going hungry.

I am only one of the hundreds you see on the street every day. The muscles on my arms are no harder, the callous on my palms no deeper than my neighbors' whose entire life has been spent in the coal region. By years I am only thirty-five. But look at the marks on my body; look at the lines of worriment on my forehead; see the gray hairs on my head and in my mustache; take my general appearance, and you'll think I'm ten years older.

You need not wonder why. Day in and day out, from Monday morning to Saturday evening, between the rising and the setting of the sun, I am in the underground workings of the coal mines. From the seams water trickles into the ditches along the gangways; if not water, it is the gas which hurls us to eternity and the props and timbers to a chaos.

Our daily life is not a pleasant one. When we put on our oil soaked suit in the morning we can't guess all the dangers which threaten our lives. We walk sometimes miles to the place—to the man way or traveling way, or to the mouth of the shaft on top of the slope. And then we enter the darkened chambers of the mines. On our right and on our left we see the logs that keep up the top and support the sides which may crush us into shapeless masses, as they have done to many of our comrades.

We get old quickly. Powder, smoke, after-damp, bad air—all combine to bring furrows to our faces and asthma to our lungs.

I did not strike because I wanted to; I struck because I had to. A miner—the same as any other workman—must earn fair living wages, or he can't live. And it is not how much you get that counts. It is how much what you get will buy. I have gone through it all, and I think my case is a good sample.

I was married in 1890, when I was 23 years old—quite a bit above the age when we miner boys get into double harness [married]. The woman I married is like myself. She was born beneath the shadow of a dirt bank; her chances for school weren't any better than mine; but she did have to learn how to keep house on a certain amount of money. After we paid the preacher for tying the knot we had just $185 in cash, good health and the good wishes of many friends to start us off.

Our cash was exhausted in buying furniture for housekeeping. In 1890 work was not so plentiful, and by the time our first baby came there was room for much doubt as to how we would pull out. Low wages, and not much over half time in those years, made us hustle. In 1890–91, from June to May, I earned $368.72. That represented eleven months' work, or an average of $33.52 per month. Our rent was $10 per month; store not less than $20. And then I had my oil suits and gum boots to pay for. The result was that after the first year and a half of our married life we were in debt. Not much, of course, and not as much as many of my neighbors, men of larger families, and some who made less money, or in whose case there had been sickness or accident or death. These are all things which a miner must provide for.

I have had fairly good work since I was married. I made the average of what we contract miners are paid; but, as I said before, I am not much better off than when I started.

In 1896 my wife was sick eleven weeks. The doctor came to my house almost every day. He charged me $20 for his services. There was medicine to buy. I paid the drug store $18 in that time. Her mother nursed her, and we kept a girl in the kitchen at $1.50 a week, which cost me $15 for ten weeks, besides the additional living expenses.

In 1897, just a year afterward, I had a severer trial. And mind, in those years, we were only working about half time. But in the fall of that year one of my brothers struck a gas feeder. There was a terrible explosion. He was hurled downward in the breast and covered with the rush of coal and rock. I was working only three breasts away from him and for a moment was unable to realize what had occurred. Myself and a hundred others were soon at work, however, and in a short while we found him, horribly burned over his whole body, his laborer dead alongside of him.

He was my brother. He was single and had been boarding. He had no home of his own. I didn't want him taken to the hospital, so I directed the driver of the ambulance to take him to my house. Besides being burned, his right arm and left leg were broken, and he was hurt internally. The doctors—there were two at the house when we got there—said he would die. But he didn't. He is living and a miner today. But he lay in bed just fourteen weeks, and was unable to work for seven weeks after he got out of bed. He had no money when he was hurt except the amount represented by his pay. All of the expenses for doctors, medicine, extra help and his living were borne by me, except $25, which another brother gave me. The last one had none to give. Poor work, low wages and a sickly woman for a wife had kept him scratching for his own family.

It is nonsense to say I was not compelled to keep him, that I could have sent him to a hospital or the almshouse. We are American citizens and we don't go to hospitals and poorhouses. . . .

Risking Life and Limb in Pittsburgh's Steel Mills, 1910

In a year when industrial activity was at its height—that is, from July 1, 1906, to June 30, 1907—526 men were killed by work-accidents in Allegheny County, Pennsylvania. During three months, April, May and June, of the same year, the hospitals of the county received over 509 men injured in such accidents. It is impossible to state the total number of injuries during that quarter, because there is no available record except of cases received at the hospitals. But even were an accurate estimate of the number of injuries in a year possible, it would be of little value. A scratched finger and a lost leg can not be added together if you look for a useful truth in the sum. It is better, therefore, not to try to estimate the total number of injuries in a year, but to concentrate our attention on the permanent loss of health and power involved in the injuries we are sure of. In 294 of the 509 non-fatal accident cases of which we have record (those received at the hospitals during the three selected months), it was possible to learn the nature and extent of the injury. One hundred and twenty-seven of the men escaped without permanent injury. Ninety-one sustained what is here called a slight permanent injury; for instance, a lame leg, arm, foot, hand, or back, not serious enough to disable a man, the loss of a finger, slight impairment of sight or hearing, and the like. Seventy-six men (25.5 per cent) suffered a serious permanent injury. Lest there should be doubt as to what is meant here by "serious," it will be better to state exactly what these injuries were. Seven men lost a leg, sixteen men were hopelessly crippled in one or both legs, one lost a foot, two lost half a foot, five lost an arm, three lost a hand, ten lost two or more fingers, two were left with crippled left arms, three with crippled right arms, and two with two useless arms. Eleven lost an eye, and three others had the sight of both eyes damaged. Two men have crippled backs, two received internal injuries, one is partially paralyzed, one feebleminded, and two are stricken with the weakness of old age while still in their prime. Finally three men suffer from a combination of permanent injuries. One of these has a rupture and a crippled foot; another a crippled left leg, and the right foot gone; the third has lost an arm and leg. These 76 are the wrecks of 294 hospital cases. . . .

Estimating the hospital cases for a year on the same basis we have the Pittsburgh District annually sending out from its mills, railroad yards, factories, and mines, 45 one-legged men; 100 hopeless cripples walking with crutch or cane for the rest of their lives; 45 men with a twisted, useless

SOURCE: Crystal Eastman, *The Pittsburgh Survey: Work-Accidents and the Law* (New York: Charities Publication Committee, 1910), 11–14.

119

arm; 30 men with an empty sleeve; 20 men with but one hand; 60 with half a hand gone; 70 one-eyed men—500 such wrecks in all. Such is the trail of lasting miseries work-accidents leave behind.

Five hundred and twenty-six men dead does not necessarily mean 526 human tragedies. We all know men who would give more happiness by dying than they gave by living. But 500 men mutilated—here there can be no doubt. And time goes on. There has been no respite. Each year has turned them out as surely as the mills ran full and the railroads prospered—as surely as times were "good." In five years there would be 2,500. Ten years would make 5,000, enough to people a little city of cripples, a number noticeable even among Greater Pittsburgh's 600,000. It is no wonder that to a stranger Pittsburgh's streets are sad.

This steady march of injury and death means suffering, grief, bitterness, thwarted hopes incalculable. These things cannot be reckoned, they must be felt. But the loss of youth and strength and wealth-producing power in those 500 yearly deaths, can be set forth to some extent in figures.

From the point of view of social welfare, the gravest feature of the situation is that the men killed in industry are young men. Eighty-four per cent of the men in the year's list of deaths were not over forty; 58 per cent were not over thirty. . . .

It is a mistake, also, to suppose that it is the cheap, unskilled labor which suffers most from industrial accidents. In the Pittsburgh District, generally speaking, $1.65 a day, or $9.90 a week is "good pay" for common labor. Only 16 per cent of the men killed during the year (whose earnings were ascertainable) were in this class of labor. And even including as unskilled those men in the steel mills who work seven days a week for $1.65 a day, making a weekly wage of $11.55, we have but 32 per cent unskilled. . . .

There is no bright side to this situation. By industrial accidents, Allegheny County loses more than 500 workmen every year, of whom nearly half are American born, 70 per cent are workmen of skill and training, and 60 per cent have not yet reached the prime of their working life. Youth, skill, strength—in a word, human power—is what we are losing.

Is this loss a waste? This is a question which Pittsburgh and every industrial district must answer. If it is merely an inevitable loss in the course of industry, then it is something to grieve over and forget. If it is largely, or half, or partly unnecessary—a waste of youth and skill and strength—then it is something to fight about and not forget. . . .

CHAPTER 7

Bound for the Promised Land: The Black Migration North

America's rapid industrialization in the late nineteenth century and first decade of the twentieth occurred primarily in the urban North and thus provided few opportunities for black Americans, most of whom lived and worked in the rural South. There the Jim Crow system—racial discrimination inflicted through both legal and informal means—kept Southern blacks powerless and poor. As the essay "Going into Canaan" by William Tuttle discusses, many of these people began to believe around the turn of the century that jobs, and therefore a better life, awaited them in the North. As Tuttle notes, there were jobs; World War I created an industrial labor shortage because many young men were in the military, and at the same time the conflict severely curtailed immigration from Europe. Thus, although blacks had been moving to the North since about 1880, migration to Northern urban centers

substantially increased after war broke out in Europe. To what factors does Tuttle attribute Chicago's popularity among northbound black migrants?

The first document is a letter from a black Mississippi mechanic to the Chicago Defender, *an influential black newspaper. The letter reflects the determination of blacks to find a better life in the North, the reluctance of Southern whites to let them leave, and the key role the* Defender *played in encouraging northward migration.*

Although the black migrants did find jobs in the North, their hopes for economic, political, and social equality were shattered by deep-seated racism, manifested in attempts to confine them to the worst housing and poorest-paying jobs. The second document, from the Chicago Property Owners' Journal, *a magazine devoted to maintaining all-white neighborhoods, reveals how some whites felt about the influx of blacks; this racism sometimes resulted in ugly confrontations.*

The third document shows how a conflict on Chicago beaches in the summer of 1919 led to a race riot that left 23 blacks and 15 whites dead and 537 people injured. Race riots were not limited to Chicago. East St. Louis had experienced a bloody riot in 1917, and another occurred in the nation's capital in 1919. If Southern blacks thought that moving north would lead to equality, their experiences quickly taught them otherwise. Yet they continued to come. What, then, were the gains to be made by migrating?

ESSAY

Going Into Canaan

William M. Tuttle

"What the past year has held for us we know," editorialized Chicago's militant black newspaper, the *Defender*, on New Year's Day. But "what the year of 1916 will bring no man knows. . . ." A black man in the South, receiving a copy of this *Defender* in the mail from a friend, would find little hint of the mass migration which would begin that year.

The news in Chicago on New Year's Day was not of the future but of the immediate holiday season. It told of lodge parties, family reunions, and church socials, and despite the frigid and gusty weather, there was much to celebrate. The Pullman car conductors and porters, for example, boasted of the ten per cent wage increases which the company had just announced. Local personages from the black community were in the news.

SOURCE: Excerpted from William M. Tuttle, Jr., *Race Riot: Chicago in the Red Summer of 1919*. Copyright © 1970 William M. Tuttle, Jr. Reprinted with permission of Atheneum Publishers, a division of Macmillan, Inc.

There was a photograph in the *Defender* of Binga Dismond, track star at the University of Chicago, who was studying for admission to medical school; and reporters noted from Boston that the fiery Ida B. Wells-Barnett had been elected to the executive committee of the National Equal Rights League at its annual convention. Yet there was sufficient discouraging news to offset the good. Jack Johnson, the "Greatest Boxer of Them All," according to the local press, had suffered an unexpected defeat at the hands of the "Great White Hope," Jess Willard, the previous spring, and blacks that winter were increasingly suspicious that federal agents had arranged the outcome; Mound Bayou, an all-black town in Mississippi, was in financial collapse because of crop failures; and racial violence had erupted in Muskogee, Oklahoma. The determined black men in that unhappy Oklahoma community, however, claimed that they had "got their spirit from the *Defender*," and that they had decided to die if necessary to rid their neighborhood of the "filth" of prostitution and the white men it attracted.

This news of the outside world, coming to a man born and raised on a piece of land he had never left, might have been an opening shaft of light to one in darkness as to the realities of the larger world. The *Defender* in those days, however, was not encouraging men to move to Chicago, as it was later to do; in fact, on New Year's Day 1916 it even questioned the wisdom of a black's trying to live in that city, where "conditions make it practically impossible . . . to secure a flat or a house in a desirable neighborhood at anything like a moderate rental, if, in fact, they can be had at all."

But 1916 was the year that heralded the advent of a migration of hundreds of thousands of blacks to the urban industrial North. Chicago's black population practically doubled in the next four years. The school census of May 1914 counted 54,557 black people, and some blacks estimated that at least that many more arrived between 1916 and 1918. Perhaps this latter estimate is inflated, and certainly it does not accord with the federal census; but it is also apparent that a sizable portion of the black minority has, even in recent and more sophisticated censuses, proved itself to be invisible to the enumerators. At any rate, by 1920, according to the federal census, the number of blacks in Chicago had soared to 110,000, and the vast preponderance of this increase was made up of migrants who had been Southern and to a large extent rural up to World War I.

Other Northern urban industrial complexes were almost as magnetic in their appeal as Chicago; altogether over 450,000 blacks flocked to the North between 1916 and 1918. But it was Chicago more than any other northern city that represented "the top of the world" and "freedom" to Southern blacks. It was Chicago, renowned for its World's Columbian Exposition of 1893 and famous for its mail order houses, mass-production industries, and vast railroad network, that was "a synonym for the

'North.' " To Southern blacks, Chicago was not only a city; it was a state of mind.

One 1916 migrant to Chicago was Shot Pinckney. A sharecropper, Pinckney farmed with his own family and 300 others on a 2,000-acre Mississippi plantation. "We were never paid money," he later recalled, "only credit at the Commissary." Naturally he had thought about leaving the plantation and Mississippi, but because of the size of his family (a wife and six children) and because of the surveillance of the overseers and guards (". . . they wouldn't let us go anywhere except to work. . . ."), he had become resigned to living out the rest of his years there. But in the autumn of 1916 "a new comer" working in one of the cotton gins approached him and asked: "How would you like to leave this plantation and go up north and make some money?" Fearful that they might be overheard, Pinckney quickly replied: "You are either drunk or just a plain, simple, damn fool." That evening, however, the stranger visited his shack, and Pinckney and his wife agreed to leave for the North if the stranger could suggest a way to escape. But, Pinckney asked, "How are we to get by the guard at the 'Big Gate'?" The next morning Pinckney followed the stranger's instructions and asked the overseer for permission for his family to leave the plantation "so we could see a circus which we heard would be in town" on Saturday. The overseer looked at Pinckney with "a squinting, suspicious expression in his eyes," but he finally consented. The stranger had persuaded other families to request permission, and they, too, were issued passes to show the guards at the "Big Gate." "We all left walking Friday night about midnight," each family having with it only a meager amount of personal belongings "lest we arouse suspicion and jeopardize our chances of escape." Waiting a mile away at "the little station on the branch track" was something that Pinckney and his family had never seen before—a train. They boarded it, and at about 5:30 felt it lurch and then creep forward, "as if to make less noise as possible; gradually picking up more and more speed after it had reached the main line." Occasionally the train would jerk to a stop, but Pinckney and his family did "not know what station it was, as we were not allowed to look outside the train, or even raise the window-blinds until the train had crossed the Mason and Dixon line." But even before it had left Mississippi, each car in the train was "packed to every available foot of . . . space," and thus jammed together the migrants traveled to Chicago. Employment was awaiting Pinckney at the stockyards. The stranger probably profited as well as the workers, for he was doubtless a labor agent for Northern industries.

Pinckney's departure from the South was rather unique, but historically there was nothing unusual about the interstate migration of Southern blacks. A series of migrations had followed the withdrawal of federal troops from the South after Reconstruction. In 1879, . . . thousands migrated to Kansas, idealized as the home of John Brown and free-soil victories. Blacks in 1889 moved from southern Alabama to Arkansas and Texas; and during the 1890's they flowed into the mineral regions around Birmingham, Alabama. The spread of the boll weevil produced a migration from Southern cotton fields to the canebrakes of Louisiana, and when sugar planters reduced their acreage in 1914 because of the prospect of free sugar, another movement commenced.

In a sense, the World War I migration was merely an acceleration of this longstanding process. Between 1916 and 1918, however, not only did far more blacks migrate than ever before, but the direction of the migration shifted as well. The decennial movement of black people from 1880 to 1910 had been 20.5 miles southwest, 9.5 miles southwest, and 5.8 miles southwest; but, in 1920, the movement was 21.5 miles northeast. It was the forces that reversed the direction of the migration which, above all, distinguished the "Great Northern Drive" from the earlier migrations.

Of these forces, one set compelled countless blacks to flee the South, while the other lured them to the North. "I am in the darkness of the south," lamented a dweller of Alabama in pleading for a train ticket to Chicago, ". . . o please help me to get out of this low down country [where] i am counted no more thin a dog." Disfranchisement, segregated facilities, inequality before the courts, mistreatment by police, lynchings and other kinds of physical violence, abuse and verbal insults to women, and governmental neglect of sanitation, lighting, and streets—these were among the social and political forces driving blacks out of the South. "Anywhere north will do us," wrote a Louisianian who epitomized the zeal to escape the caste system of the South; and, he added, "I suppose the worst place there is better than the best place here." A Texas black voiced a similar sentiment when he indicated that although he preferred to migrate to Chicago, he primarily wanted "to leave the South and go and [any] Place where a man will be any thing Except a Ker. . . ."

Education, or rather the inaccessibility of it, was a potent driving force. Black parents longed to provide better opportunities for their children, and basic to this desire was schooling. "I want a good paying job," wrote a Mississippian, "that I may be able to educate my children." In Southern districts, however, and especially in areas with high percentages of cotton tenancy, the school terms for blacks were as much as two months shorter than those for whites. It was not sufficient simply to pay taxes, for as one Louisianian complained: "Our poll tax paid, state and parish taxes yet . . . we cannot get schools." Investment in public school property and equipment in the South was five to ten times more per white child than per black child, and the disparity between salaries for teachers of whites and teachers of blacks was equally great. An extreme example of this was a portion of Louisiana in which the annual salaries averaged $28.89 per white pupil and $.87 per black pupil. It was thus effective advertising for Chicago when the *Defender* displayed in its pages two photographs, one of a frame, single-room "Jim Crow School" in Abbeville, Louisiana, the other of an expansive, stone-columned building housing Chicago's Robert Lindblom High School, "where no color line is drawn" and "one of the many reasons why members of the Race are leaving the south."

The incomes of most Southern blacks, especially agricultural wage hands, sharecroppers, and tenant farmers, had never been more than paltry. Immediately before America's entry into World War I, natural disasters exacerbated this economic driving force, and hunger, malnutrition, and pellagra burgeoned as indices of these misfortunes. The boll weevil in 1915 and 1916 ravaged the cotton crops of Louisiana, Mississippi, Alabama, Georgia, and Florida; and of these five states all but Louisiana also experienced disastrous rains and floods. The resultant destitution prompted blacks to moan: "De white man he got ha'f de crap [crop]. Boll-weevill took de res'. Ain't got no home. Ain't got no home." In southwestern Perry County, Alabama, for example, cotton was the sole crop. "We see starvation ahead of us," wrote a black Alabamian, and at least 6,000 of the 24,000 blacks laboring in the immediate region left after the destructive arrival of the boll weevil. The infestation also visited southwestern Georgia, inflicting immense damage to crops in 1916. This along with flooding rains convinced planters that they must turn to such food products as peanuts, corn, velvet beans, oats, sorghum, and sweet potatoes—all crops that required substantially less labor than cotton; the excess in the labor supply was then either turned out penniless or left without any provision being made for its subsistence. Other planters, moreover, would not and sometimes could not advance funds to sharecroppers and tenants with which to plant the next year's crops. "Heavy rains and Boll weavel," a black farmer from southwestern Georgia observed sadly, had caused the loss of thousands of bales of cotton, and now the local planter was "going to see that his personal losses are minimized as far as possible and this has left the average farm laborer with nothing to start out with to make a crop for next year. . . ." And since "nobody wants to carry him till next fall . . . he wants to migrate to where he can see a chance to get work."

Despite the labor depression in the South in 1915 and 1916, there was a contemporaneous increase in the cost of living. "Everything is gone up but the poor colerd peple wages," concluded a black in New Orleans, and it was clear that, whether afflicted by no wages or low wages, the blacks' standard of living was wretched. "Wages is so low and grocery is so high," complained a Mississippian, "untill all I can do is to live." Similar reports from all over the South flowed into the offices of the *Defender*, the Chicago Urban League, and employment offices.

Obviously, these driving forces were not unique to the World War I years. Inequality in its multitudinous forms had been the perennial scourge of Southern blacks, and debt peonage, dispossession, and the increasing unproductivity of the land through natural disaster, poor cultivation, and the planting of a single crop were virtually as old as the cotton culture itself. During the war, however, the abundance of Northern jobs provided escape. As A. L. Jackson, executive secretary of Chicago's all-black Wabash Avenue YMCA, explained to members of the City Club of Chicago: "The negro had wanted to come north all the time and he came when at last he had a chance to earn a living." Jobs were abundant in Chicago, for at the very time that its industries cried out for workers to satisfy the insatiable demands for war products, two factors depleted the labor force. On the one hand, the war caused immigration to the United States to dwindle from 1,218,480 in fiscal year 1914 to 366,748 in 1916, and to 110,618 in 1918. To restrict further the availability of immigrant labor, foreign belligerents conscripted their eligible nationals residing in the United States. In 1918 the net immigration had ebbed to only 6,023. The result in Chicago was a decline in the foreign-born percentage of the population from 33.5 per cent in 1910 to 28.4 per cent in 1920. On the other hand, 4,791,172 Americans served in the armed forces during World War I, creating additional voids in the labor force. The sources from which industries obtained replacements for immigrants and servicemen were women, machines, Southern whites, and, above all, blacks.

Chicago was the logical destination of many of the migrants. Jobs were plentiful there and wages were high, especially in industries like slaughtering and meat packing, iron and steel forging, electrical machinery, and machine-shop products. Moreover, Chicago's employment opportunities, particularly in the stockyards, were well publicized in the South. A frequent rumor was that the stockyards needed 50,000 men and women immediately, and that the packers would provide temporary quarters. "The packing houses in Chicago for a while seemed to be everything," a black in Hattiesburg, Mississippi, recalled; ". . . you could not rest in your bed at night for Chicago." Throughout the war Southern blacks discussed the migration, and more often than not the discussions centered on Chicago. A common evening pastime in Hattiesburg was sauntering to the depot to ask the Chicago porters on the Gulf and Ship Island Railroad numberless questions about the city. Hastily formed conclaves then spread news about such topics as Chicago's climate, the public schools, voting, and jobs throughout the black community. Out of these discussions, representatives were often appointed whose function it was to notify Chicago industries, newspapers, and placement agencies that a certain number of black people were available for employment and to request train tickets. These groups ranged in size from two or three families to more than 1,000 persons.

The massive railroad network emanating from Chicago made it the most accessible destination for numerous blacks, especially those from Mississippi, Arkansas, Alabama, Louisiana, and Texas. Although the majority of the migrants paid their own fares, others traveled to the city on train passes, and club rates often eased the financial burden of the trip for still others. Regardless of the travel arrangements, the incontrovertible fact was that thousands of black migrants had boarded trains for Chicago. ". . . I have seen it on Saturdays and Sundays when there wasn't standing room in the negro car," wrote a white railroad man from Hattiesburg in the spring of 1917, "and some days we would pull a special car for them." Every weekend for the past six months, he noted, "There would be a bunch collect here, sometimes as many as 150 at a time, and leave in parties. Most have gone to Chicago. . . ."

In addition, Chicago's railroad lines connected it with practically every Southern town where lynchings occurred; and there was, as T. Arnold Hill of the Chicago Urban League observed, a correlation between Southern mob violence and the influx of migrants to Chicago. "Every time a lynching takes place in a community down south," he told a reporter, "you can depend on it that colored people will arrive in Chicago within two weeks. We have seen it happen so often that whenever we read newspaper dispatches of a public hanging or burning . . . we get ready to extend greetings to the people from the immediate vicinity of the lynchings."

Letters from migrants to relatives and friends generated "the moving fever," especially when they contained money, which was concrete proof of prosperity and could easily be converted into a train ticket. A carpenter supplied glowing reports about Chicago to his brother in Hattiesburg, telling him that he had just been promoted and received a raise. "I should have been here 20 years ago. I just begun to feel like a man." His children were enrolled in "the same school with the whites and I don't have to umble to no one." Moreover, he had registered to vote, and he proudly announced that "there isnt any 'yes sir' and 'no sir'—its all yes and no and Sam and Bill." Similarly, a laborer from Chicago's Calumet region informed a friend in Alabama that the city fulfilled all the hopes with which he had undertaken his migration. The people were patriotic, the schools integrated, and he wondered sometimes how the industries could afford to be so generous with salaries "the way they work labors, they do not hurry or drive you." Work was plentiful, and money was abundant "and it is not hard to get." Mrs. Rosena Shephard heard her neighbor boasting about her daughter who had gone to Chicago. Six weeks had gone by with no news at all; then came word that she was earning $2.00 a day as a sausage-packer. "If that lazy, good-for-nothing gal kin make $2 a day," Mrs. Shephard exclaimed when she heard this news, "I kin make four," and she left for Chicago. Dr. Alexander H. Booth watched his patients set out from his Southern community, and he wondered whether he would ever be paid the fees that the departing migrants had long owed him. To his surprise, the payments started to arrive in letters from the North which told him that "home ain't nothing like this." The doctor packed his bags to join them. Because of letters, visits home by migrants, and rumors, the South was, as a Floridian remarked, "ringing with news from Chicago," news that could transform indecision into an affirmation to try it for oneself.

In addition to spontaneous responses to the driving forces and to the lure of Chicago, the process of migration was also stimulated by a government agency, private labor agents, certain industries, and the press. Until Southern planters protested, for example, the United States Employment Service sought to fill the requisitions of Northern employers with Southern blacks. Independent labor agents also scoured the South, inducing blacks to pull up stakes. To stem this flow, Southern states, counties, and city councils began to exact prohibitive license fees to discourage the recruiters. Birmingham required a $2,500 tax of labor agents, as did the State of Alabama, thus making it a $5,000 proposition before an agent could begin recruiting in that city; and when Alabama's courts of county commissioners or county boards of revenues began to exact their fees, the cost would spiral still higher. Other areas were equally apprehensive, but, as practically every strange face in Southern towns was identified as a labor agent, much of this legislation was directed at phantoms. Other recruiters were actually bunco artists who would vanish after collecting $2.00 per head in exchange for promises of train tickets and jobs in Chicago.

Labor agents affiliated with certain Northern industries, however, did pose a real threat to the maintenance of the Southern labor force. Between July 1916 and January 1917, for example, the Pennsylvania Railroad imported 12,000 blacks to do unskilled labor; but it ceased to do this when it became a much less expensive operation simply to hire blacks after they had arrived on their own tickets. The Illinois Central Railroad also issued passes on which hundreds of blacks traveled to Chicago, and steel mills and tanneries in the Chicago area did likewise. But passes and prepaid tickets were essential only during the initial stage of the migration, for after that it became a self-generating movement.

It is possible that the largest employers of black labor in Chicago, the meat packers, also enticed numerous blacks away from the South. This, at any rate, was the contention of many observers familiar with the Chicago labor market. The packers vehemently denied the charge of importation, asserting that, aside from bringing North from Southern branches a few blacks for "specific temporary work," they had "not found importation necessary. . . ."

Perhaps the most effective institution in stimulating the migration was the *Defender*, which prompted thousands to venture North. It was the *Defender's* emphatic denunciation of the Southern treatment of blacks and its emphasis on pride in the race that increased its circulation tenfold between 1916 and 1918. "Turn a deaf ear to everybody," a typical editorial advised in 1916. "You see they are not lifting their laws to help you. Are they? Have they stopped their Jim Crow cars? Can you buy a Pullman sleeper where you wish? Will they give you a square deal in court yet?" Blacks were slaves in the South, and they have remained slaves, so to the South "we have said, as the song goes, 'I hear you calling me,' and have boarded the train singing, 'Good-bye, Dixie Land.' "

"MILLIONS TO LEAVE SOUTH," was the *Defender*'s banner headline on January 6, 1917. "Northern Invasion Will Start in Spring—Bound for the Promised Land." That coming May 15 was to be the date of "The Great Northern Drive," and its announcement precipitated a massive outpouring of letters to the *Defender*, the Urban League, and various churches requesting and indeed pleading for jobs, information, transportation, and housing. And when the *Defender* declared later that there were no special trains designated to leave Southern stations on May 15, and that this date had been set simply because it was "a good time to leave for the north, so as to become acclimated," it was already too late. The exodus, the hegira, "The Flight Out of Egypt," the "Black Diaspora," had begun.

Reinforcing the desire to migrate were the success stories, the photographs of Chicago's public facilities to which all had equal access, and the advertisements of job openings and of rooms to rent and houses to buy which the *Defender* prominently displayed in its pages. As a rebuttal to "southern propagandists who . . . painted harrowing pictures of dire conditions suffered here," the *Defender* told its readers of Robert A. Wilson, formerly of Atlanta, who arrived in Chicago with a nickel and a penny. He spent the nickel for streetcar fare to the *Defender*'s offices and the penny for a bag of peanuts "to satisfy that pang of hunger." The newspaper directed him to the Urban League, which found him work at a foundry. Since that happy day, the *Defender* added, Wilson had acquired an automobile, house, and bank account, and had brought his family from the South; and "thus ends the romance of the lone nickel, the Lincoln penny, and the man who made opportunity a realization." That blacks could and did make good in Chicago was a constant theme of the *Defender*; it was the South, not the North, that was unfit for human habitation.

To blacks the *Defender* symbolized the freedom attainable in the North; its exhortations to depart "the land of suffering" impelled countless people to peddle household goods and personal belongings accumulated over a lifetime in order to purchase tickets for the North. Its validity rested with the knowledge that it was not controlled by the white community as was much of the local black press, and with the violent reactions it provoked among white Southerners. To the persistent rumor that blacks would freeze to death in the North, the *Defender* countered that this was "all 'bosh.' IF YOU CAN FREEZE TO DEATH in the north and be free, why FREEZE to death in the south and be a slave, where your mother, sister and daughter are raped. . . . where your father, brother and son are . . . hung to a pole, [and] riddled with bullets. . . ." For whites and blacks who praised the South or held the North in contempt, the *Defender* had nothing but disdain. It used to be preachers, the *Defender* asserted, but now there was a teacher, in Tallulah, Louisiana, who was "licking the white man's hand," and getting "his name in the white papers as 'good nigger'" for "asking that our people remain here and be treated like dogs. . . ."

Such utterances, of course, outraged whites. Letters arrived at the *Defender*'s offices threatening to kill "some of your good Bur heads" unless the newspaper started advising blacks "to be real niggers instead of fools," and Southern towns outlawed its circulation. The whites of Madison County, Mississippi, adopted a resolution claiming that the *Defender* was German propaganda designed to "revive sectional issues and create race antagonism," and thus "condemned its circulation in this county." Other whites confiscated issues of it, and at least one rural community permitted no correspondence between its black residents and the newspaper. All of this served to elevate the *Defender*'s value and to heighten its persuasiveness. A black leader in Louisiana confided to an official of the Labor Department that each issue of the *Defender* was so eagerly awaited that "my people grab it like a mule grabs a mouthful of fine fodder." And failure to receive a copy could cause real anguish. "I feel so sad in hart," a girl in Macon, Georgia, disconsolately wrote a friend in Chicago, "my definder diden come yesterday."

Blacks who heeded the *Defender* brought with them to Chicago a vision of opportunity, of "a better chance," and of "feeling like a man." Yet for many, perhaps most, the *Defender* had held out false promises. Their aspirations for economic, political, and social rebirth were soon shattered by their reception in the city.

The World War I migration of blacks was, according to a black minister in Atlanta, "the most unique movement in history." For "the colored race, known as the race which is led, has broken away from its leaders." Other observers agreed that a striking characteristic of the migration was its individualism. It was "a leaderless mass-movement," wrote black sociologist Charles S. Johnson, and it burst forth "only after a long period of gestation." Aggravated by decades of debasing social and political inequality and economic deprivation, the migrants of 1916 to 1919 were, Johnson added, "ready for the spark of suggestion which touched them off and sped them blindly northward." They were so ready, in fact, that they deserted their established leaders.

Numerous black business and professional men, who had derived social status and relative prosperity from Southern segregation, had remained silent in the past and had not remonstrated against the inhumane treatment and subsistence wages which the race had had to endure. Other blacks forfeited their credibility and positions of influence by heaping inflated and transparent praise upon the South as "our home" and upon the Southern white man as "our friend," and by damning the North as a place where blacks could do little but freeze or starve to death. But younger blacks were restless and dissatisfied, and would not accept the plantation and caste system under which their parents had suffered. Blacks naturally felt that they were powerless to object to mistreatment by whites. "We dare not resent . . . or show even the slightest disapproval," lamented a minister in rural Alabama. Being powerless, however, did not mean that blacks had to continue to endure indignity; and whether black leaders could have protested against the system or not, the migrants disregarded their advice when opportunity beckoned from the North.

The migrants, [journalist] Ray Stannard Baker noted, were "acting for themselves, self consciously. . . ." And in doing so they had to combat much more than resistance from members of their own race; they had to overcome the efforts of whites to check the migration. Blacks "are being snatched off the trains . . . and a rested [*sic*]," a Mississippian reported to the Chicago *Defender*, "but in spite of all this, they are leaving every day and every night. . . ." Despite threats even of death, the flow of migrants continued undeterred.

The migration was a positive movement in other ways. Although jobs and better wages were usually the initial stimulant, the migrants were searching for a share in the freedom that had been denied them for so long. Many blacks viewed the migration as a divinely inspired deliverance from the land of suffering. During the era of the Civil War, the Biblical story of the exodus of the Israelites from Egypt had fueled the hopes of the slaves for freedom, and plantation songs abounded with predictions of a new Moses to free them from their oppressors. But there was no exodus to the Promised Land after the war. There was emancipation, but for millions of blacks this was a cruel hoax which turned out to be but another form of bondage. Then came World War I and the migration to "Beulah Land"; countless blacks again saw God's hand at work pointing the way to freedom. A group of 147 blacks from Hattiesburg, for example, knelt down, kissed the ground, and held a prayer service after "Crossing over Jordan," the Ohio River. The men stopped their watches, the women sobbed, and then all sang the songs of deliverance, beginning with, "I done come out o' de land of Egypt; ain't that good news."

DOCUMENTS

"I Want to Come North," 1917

GRANVILLE, MISSISSIPPI, MAY 16, 1917

Dear Sir: This letter is a letter of information of which you will find stamp envelop for reply. I want to come north some time soon but I do not want to leve here looking for a job where I would be in dorse all winter. Now the work I am doing here is running a guage edger in a saw mill. I know

SOURCE: Emmett J. Scott, "Letters of Negro Migrants of 1916–1918," *Journal of Negro History*, 4 (July 1919): 435.

all about the grading of lumber. I have been working in lumber about 25 or 27 years. My wedges here is $3.00 a day 11 hours a day. I want to come North where I can educate my 3 little children also my wife. Now if you cannot fit me up at what I am doing down here I can learn anything any one els can. also there is a great deal of good women cooks here would leave any time all they want is to know where to go and some way to go. please write me at once just how I can get my people where they can get something for their work. There are women here cookeing for $1.50 and $2.00 a week. I would like to live in Chicago or Ohio or Philadelphia. Tell Mr. Abbott [owner of the *Defender*] that our pepel are tole that they can not get anything to do up there and they are being snatched off the trains here in Greenville and a rested but in spite of all this, they are leaving every day and every night 100 or more is expecting to leave this week. Let me here from you at once.

"Protect Your Property!" (1919), 1920

To damage a man's property and destroy its value is to rob him. The person who commits that act is a robber. Every owner has the right to defend his property to the utmost of his ability with every means at his disposal.

Any property owner who sells property anywhere in our district to undesirables is an enemy to the white owner and should be discovered and punished.

Protect your property!

Property conservatively valued at $50,000,000 owned by some 10,000 individuals is menaced by a possible Negro invasion of Hyde Park. The thing is simply impossible and must not occur. . . .

As stated before, every colored man who moves into Hyde Park knows that he is damaging his white neighbors' property. Therefore, he is making war on the white man. Consequently, he is not entitled to any consideration and forfeits his right to be employed by the white man. If employers should adopt a rule of refusing to employ Negroes who persist in residing in Hyde Park to the damage of the white man's property, it would soon show good results.

The Negro is using the Constitution and its legal rights to abuse the moral rights of the white. . . .

There is nothing in the make-up of a Negro, physically or mentally, which should induce anyone to welcome him as a neighbor. The best of them are insanitary, insurance companies class them as poor risks, ruin

SOURCE: *Property Owner's Journal*, cited in Chicago Commission on Race Relations, *The Negro in Chicago* (Chicago: University of Chicago Press, 1927), 121.

alone follows in their path. They are as proud as peacocks, but have nothing of the peacock's beauty. Certain classes of the Negores, such as the Pullman porters, political heelers and hairdressers are clamoring for equality. They are not content with remaining with the creditable members of their race, they seem to want to mingle with the whites. Their inordinate vanity, their desire to shine as social lights caused them to stray out of their paths and lose themselves. We who would direct them back where they belong, towards their people, are censured and called "unjust." Far more unjust are their actions to the members of their race who have no desire to interfere with the homes of the white citizens of this district. The great majority of the Negroes are not stirred by any false ambition that results only in discord. Wherever friction arises between the races, the suffering is usually endured by the innocent. If these misleaders are sincere in their protestations of injustice, if they are not hypocritical in their pretence of solving the race question, let them move.

Race Riot in Chicago, 1919

Sunday afternoon, July 27, 1919, hundreds of white and Negro bathers crowded the lake-front beaches at Twenty-sixth and Twenty-ninth streets. This is the eastern boundary of the thickest Negro residence area. At Twenty-sixth Street Negroes were in great majority; at Twenty-ninth Street there were more whites. An imaginary line in the water separating the two beaches had been generally observed by the two races. Under the prevailing relations, aided by wild rumors and reports, this line served virtually as a challenge to either side to cross it. Four Negroes who attempted to enter the water from the "white" side were driven away by the whites. They returned with more Negroes, and there followed a series of attacks with stones, first one side gaining the advantage, then the other.

Eugene Williams, a Negro boy of seventeen, entered the water from the side used by Negroes and drifted across the line supported by a railroad tie. He was observed by the crowd on the beach and promptly became a target for stones. He suddenly released the tie, went down and was drowned. Guilt was immediately placed on Stauber, a young white man, by Negro witnesses who declared that he threw the fatal stone.*

White and Negro men dived for the boy without result. Negroes demanded that the policeman present arrest Stauber. He refused; and at this crucial moment arrested a Negro on a white man's complaint. Negroes

SOURCE: Chicago Commission on Race Relations, *The Negro in Chicago* (Chicago: University of Chicago Press, 1927), 596–98.

[*The coroner's jury found that Williams had drowned from fear of stone-throwing which kept him from the shore.]

then attacked the officer. These two facts, the drowning and the refusal of the policeman to arrest Stauber, together marked the beginning of the riot.

Two hours after the drowning, a Negro, James Crawford, fired into a group of officers summoned by the policeman at the beach and was killed by a Negro policeman. Reports and rumors circulated rapidly, and new crowds began to gather. Five white men were injured in clashes near the beach. As darkness came Negroes in white districts to the west suffered severely. Between 9:00 P.M. and 3:00 A.M. twenty-seven Negroes were beaten, seven stabbed, and four shot. Monday morning was quiet, and Negroes went to work as usual.

Returning from work in the afternoon many Negroes were attacked by white ruffians. Street-car routes, especially at transfer points, were the centers of lawlessness. Trolleys were pulled from the wires, and Negro passengers were dragged into the street, beaten, stabbed, and shot. The police were powerless to cope with these numerous assaults. During Monday, four Negro men and one white assailant were killed, and thirty Negroes were severely beaten in street-car clashes. Four white men were killed, six stabbed, five shot, and nine severely beaten. It was rumored that the white occupants of the Angelus Building at Thirty-fifth Street and Wabash Avenue had shot a Negro. Negroes gathered about the building. The white tenants sought police protection, and one hundred policemen, mounted and on foot, responded. In a clash with the mob the police killed four Negroes and injured many.

Raids into the Negro residence area then began. Automobiles sped through the streets, the occupants shooting at random. Negroes retaliated by "sniping" from ambush. At midnight surface and elevated car service was discontinued because of a strike for wage increases, and thousands of employees were cut off from work.

On Tuesday, July 29, Negro men en route on foot to their jobs through hostile territory were killed. White soldiers and sailors in uniform, aided by civilians, raided the "Loop" business section, killing two Negroes and beating and robbing several others. Negroes living among white neighbors in Englewood, far to the south, were driven from their homes, their household goods were stolen, and their houses were burned or wrecked. On the West Side an Italian mob, excited by a false rumor that an Italian girl had been shot by a Negro, killed Joseph Lovings, a Negro.

Wednesday night at 10:30 Mayor Thompson yielded to pressure and asked the help of the three regiments of militia which had been stationed in nearby armories during the most severe rioting, awaiting the call. They immediately took up positions throughout the South Side. A rainfall Wednesday night and Thursday kept many people in their homes, and by Friday the rioting had abated. On Saturday incendiary fires burned forty-nine houses in the immigrant neighborhood west of the Stock Yards. Nine

135

hundred and forty-eight people, mostly Lithuanians, were made homeless, and the property loss was about $250,000. Responsibility for the fires was never fixed.

The total casualties of this reign of terror were thirty-eight deaths—fifteen white, twenty-three Negro—and 537 people injured. Forty-one per cent of the reported clashes occurred in the white neighborhood near the Stock Yards between the south branch of the Chicago River and Fifty-fifth Street, Wentworth Avenue and the city limits, and 34 per cent in the "Black Belt" between Twenty-second and Thirty-ninth streets, Wentworth Avenue and Lake Michigan. Others were scattered.

Responsibility for many attacks was definitely placed by many witnesses upon the [white] "athletic clubs," including "Ragen's Colts," the "Hamburgers," "Aylwards," "Our Flag," the "Standard," the "Sparklers," and several others. The mobs were made up for the most part of boys between fifteen and twenty-two. Older persons participated, but the youth of the rioters was conspicuous in every clash. Little children witnessed the brutalities and frequently pointed out the injured when the police arrived.

CHAPTER 8

War and Society, 1917–18

In April 1917, after months of debate and disagreement on whether to become involved in the war in Europe, the United States declared war on Germany. Unlike the major European powers embroiled in the conflict since 1914, America's participation in the war was brief—only about a year and a half. Nevertheless, the war had a tremendous impact on Americans, soldiers and civilians alike. For the first time, Americans were fighting on European soil, and they were certain their participation would be crucial in defeating the Germans and their allies.

The essay, drawn from David M. Kennedy's book Over Here: The First World War and American Society, *describes the experiences and impressions of the American soldiers of World War I, the "doughboys." By and large, according to Kennedy, these soldiers held a highly romantic view of the war, thinking of it in terms of heroism and adventure. In contrast were the depictions of battle by Europeans during and after the conflict: tales of destruction of towns and cities, the slaughter of hundreds of thousands of soldiers and civilians, and the misery of trench warfare. How do you account for the differences between the American soldiers' descriptions of the war and those of their European allies?*

The Kennedy essay points out that actual combat could have a sobering effect upon the doughboy, a conclusion supported by the first document—an excerpt from the diary of an unknown American flier, who was later shot down and killed over Germany.

During the war, the federal government, through propaganda, strove to convince the public that this was a noble cause, a clash between the forces of good and evil. Victory required the absolute loyalty and support of all citizens; questionable patriotism prompted great concern. For German-Americans particularly, the patriotic near-hysteria of these times proved to be a terrible burden. In restaurants sauerkraut was renamed "liberty cabbage," and hamburger emerged as "liberty steak." Cincinnati's German Street was renamed English Street, and Pittsburgh banned the playing of Ludwig von Beethoven's music. German-Americans were harassed and threatened with physical harm if they failed to demonstrate their commitment to the American war effort. The pressure on German-Americans to declare their loyalty is vividly reflected in the second document, a statement distributed by the Committee on Public Information, an agency created by the federal government to generate public support for the war. How did the author's assessment of blame for the war enable him to demonstrate his enthusiasm for the American cause without cutting his emotional ties to his native land?

Although a large segment of the population opposed entry into the war right up until 1917, support for the war effort was overwhelming once the United States joined the conflict. Nevertheless, not all Americans supported the war; those who did not and refused to serve in the armed forces on the grounds of religion or conscience suffered a good deal of intolerance. The final document reveals the experiences and convictions of Mennonites, who, despite their profound religious objections to the war, were drafted into the army. What relationship, if any, can you discern between the patriotic fervor of wartime society and increased intolerance?

ESSAY

The Doughboys' War: "An Extraordinary Interlude"

David M. Kennedy

It is easy to forget how vivid the Civil War seemed to Americans in the World War I era. Many men yet living had fought under Grant or Lee. More men still, especially those of an age to occupy influential positions in American life—including Theodore Roosevelt and Woodrow Wilson— had been impressionable boys when [General] Beauregard's batteries fired on Sumter. They were raised by hearthsides where fathers and uncles passed on the lore of Bull Run and Vicksburg, Chickamauga and the Wilderness, Cold Harbor and the Sunken Road, Antietam and the Bloody Angle. On registration day, June 5, 1917, Wilson addressed a convention of Confederate veterans, and spoke evocatively of "the old spirit of chivalric gallantry." That rhetoric and the attitude toward war it bespoke were comfortably familiar to two generations of Americans; but even while Wilson talked, both the language and the sentiment were as near to death as the graying men he faced.

Many of those aging veterans, and even more of their Union counterparts, remained powerful arbiters of popular values. Among the images they urged the young to regard reverently was that of war as an adventurous and romantic undertaking, a liberating release from the stultifying conventions of civilized society. No one had more eloquently articulated that sentiment than Oliver Wendell Holmes, Jr., a young Civil War officer in the 20th Massachusetts, veteran of Fredericksburg and Antietam, and for thirty years after 1902 a magisterial figure on the United States Supreme Court. Only in war, he told Harvard's graduating class in 1895, could men pursue "the divine folly of honor." From war "the ideals of the past for men have been drawn. . . . I doubt if we are ready to give up our inheritance." War might be terrible when you were in it, he said, but with time "you see that its message was divine." In the generation succeeding Holmes's, the charismatic Theodore Roosevelt whole-heartedly embraced those precepts and preached them to his countrymen with unflagging gusto. What American had not heard the account of the old Rough Rider waving his hat and charging up San Juan Hill, gleefully projecting an image of battle as a kind of pleasingly dangerous gentlemen's sport?

This irrepressibly positive and romantic view of war belonged particularly to an older elite, people like Holmes and Roosevelt: old-stock, Northeastern, often Anglophilic or Francophilic. In his study of prewar American culture, [historian] Henry May has called them "the beleaguered defenders of nineteenth-century tradition . . . the professional custodians of culture." From this quarter came some of the strongest pressure both for a permanent system of military training and for American intervention in the war. Almost unanimously, says May, "the leading men of letters, the college presidents, the old-line publishers, the editors of standard magazines, and their friends knew where they stood from the start" in 1914. "Instead of seeing the war as the doom of their culture, they believed it would bring about its revival: the war was a severe but necessary lesson in moral idealism." Thus did Princeton [University] President John Grier Hibben speak of the chastening and purifying effect of armed conflict. Thus did novelist Robert Herrick write of war's "resurrection of nobility. . . ." Everywhere, the venerable custodians of traditional culture spoke as if with a single voice: war was glorious, adventurous; it was manhood's destiny, a strenuous and virile antidote to the effete routine of modern life. And, as May has noted, it was the "young acquaintances of these elder idealists who were early in the field. The older colleges and the more exclusive prep schools contributed far more than their share to the volunteer units." Young men from the most prominent families and the most prestigious universities fought with the French or the English, joined the Lafayette Escadrille air unit, or the Norton-Harjes Ambulance Service.* It was, in short, the nation's most carefully cultivated youths, the privileged recipients of the finest education, steeped in the values of the genteel tradition, who most believed the archaic doctrines about war's noble and heroic possibilities.

Of all the young men who so believed, none did more passionately than Alan Seeger. A 1910 Harvard graduate given to writing florid and portentous verses, Seeger had gone to Paris in 1912, "in the spirit," says a sympathetic biographer, "of a romanticist of the eighteen-forties." Swelling with Byronic yearning for glory ("it is for glory alone that I am engaged," he wrote) and for a poetic death at an early age, in 1914 he joined the French Foreign Legion. For the next two years, huddled in billets in Champagne, he wrote of the war, in verse, in his diary, in letters to his

*Organized in March 1915 and privately financed by Americans, the Lafayette Escadrille was officered by French commanders and integrated into the French military service. The Escadrille was made up mostly of well-to-do young Americans. One famous "alumnus" was James R. Doolittle, who in 1942 led the first American airstrike of World War II against Tokyo. . . . Of the several volunteer ambulance units, the most publicized was founded in 1914 by Richard Norton, son of Harvard professor Charles Eliot Norton. Another unit, the American Ambulance Field Service, also attracted many volunteers. Among the later celebrated persons who served in one or another of the units were Ernest Hemingway, John Dos Passos, E. E. Cummings, and Malcolm Cowley. Most volunteers were college graduates. . . .

family, and in articles sent to the New York *Sun* and the *New Republic*. He was, he said candidly, "of a sentimental and romantic nature." His writing alternated between lyrical tributes to the charms of the French countryside and awe-filled descriptions of the grandeur of war. "Will never forget the beauty of this winter landscape," he noted in his diary, "the delicate skies, the little villages under their smoking roofs. Am feeling perfectly happy and contented." He was no less happy to hear "the magnificent orchestra of war" in an artillery cannonade, and he wrote his mother: "You have no idea how beautiful it is to see the troops undulating along the road in front of one in *colonnes par quatre* as far as the eye can see with the captains and lieutenants on horseback at the head of their companies. . . ."

When Seeger was killed in 1916, the custodians of culture instantly transformed him into America's first genuine war hero. His uplifting descriptions of war, cast in the literary conventions of the medieval romance, admirably fitted their own views. Indeed, so admirably did Seeger suit the tastes of the traditional keepers of culture that in 1915 they were already calling him America's Rupert Brooke (the English poet killed in combat). They hastened to complete the comparison by prematurely announcing Seeger's heroic demise in October 1915. When he died in fact on July 23, 1916, some were so eager to invest his memory with all the symbolic freight it would bear that he was often erroneously said to have met his fate—that would have been the phrase—on the Fourth of July.

Seeger's poems were published soon after his death, to extravagant praise from established critics, and his *Letters and Diary* was released to the public the following summer. Theodore Roosevelt, the hero of "A Message to America" ("I would go through fire and shot and shell . . . if ROOSEVELT led"), eulogized him in appropriately archaic accents as "gallant, gifted young Seeger." A Wellesley [College] student surpassed even the medieval metaphors of the dead poet himself: "Had he lived in centuries past," she wrote, "he would have lived a knight, true to his 'idols—Love and Arms and Song.' In the twentieth century he still lived as true as was possible to those idols. So he will live in our hearts—Alan Seeger, Knight."

Seeger's was the authentic voice of late nineteenth-century American high culture, and it spoke powerfully of war's ennobling glory. Other writers couched a similar message in a more popular idiom. Robert W. Service, for example, in *Rhymes of a Red Cross Man*, sang of the

> . . . dream that War will never be ended;
> That men will perish like men, and valour be splendid;
>
> ·
>
> That though my eye may be dim and my beard be hoary,
> I'll die as a soldier dies on the Field of Glory.

When [Senator] Hiram Johnson read Service's poems to his family in the evenings, "all of us at times have been rather choked up." When he read them to his fellow Senators, he said, "you could have heard a pin drop."

Seeger's *Poems* and Service's *Rhymes* were both best sellers in 1917, as was Arthur Guy Empey's *"Over the Top,"* a runaway success that sold 350,000 copies in its first year of release and was later made into a movie. Empey became a featured speaker at countless Liberty bond rallies. Those developments no doubt pleased his publisher, George Haven Putnam of G. P. Putnam's Sons, a founder of the pro-preparedness National Security League. *"Over the Top"* was a go-get-'em confection in the Richard Harding Davis vein, a snappy autobiographical account of the New Jersey boy's adventures with the British Army in France. Disappointed that his own country had been "too proud to fight" after the sinking of the *Lusitania*, Empey went to England to become a "Tommy." Though his account of his exploits among the English was replete with condescending national comparisons—British trains had "matchbox" cars; Americans had "energy and push," the English mere "tenacity"—Empey clearly intended to convey affection for the British soldier and sympathy for the Allied cause. "Tommy Atkins," he said, "has proved himself to be the best of mates, a pal, . . . a man with a just cause who is willing to sacrifice everything but honor in the advancement of the same. It is my fondest hope," he added, "that Uncle Sam and John Bull, arms locked, as mates, good and true . . . will wend their way through the years to come, happy and contented in each other's company."

Empey provided the American public with a kind of primer on life at the front. In a bright, wisecracking style, liberally sprinkled with colorful British Army slang, Empey recounted his initiation into British Army ways, his arrival at the front, his first encounters with "Fritz" (the Germans), his wounding in a trench raid, and his trip back to "blighty" (home). The narrative was not without its accounts of horrors and of gut-grinding fears. In a grudging and stiffly jocular way, Empey even admitted to tears at the death of a mate: "I, like a great big boob, cried like a baby. I was losing my first friend of the trenches." But the tone of *"Over the Top"* was overwhelmingly positive. Even the scenes of terror and fright could not really terrify or frighten, so briskly were they related, and so swiftly did they sink beneath the glinting surface of Empey's quick-paced story. With unrelenting good humor, Empey portrayed the war as a kind of thrillful sporting adventure, where all the players, on his side at least, were good fellows who knew how to "die game." In the climactic battle scene, Empey was wounded, but his outfit "took the trench and the wood beyond, all right." The story faithfully followed the formula of the popular adventure tale: men expired with athletic grace, the hero proved his manhood by receiving a wound in virtual hand-to-hand combat, as convention required, and in the end his fellows triumphantly seized their objective. . . .

From accounts like these, many departing doughboys formed expectations of what awaited them in France. An affirmative and inspiring attitude toward war, preached by guardians of tradition like Holmes and

Roosevelt, nurtured by popular writers like Seeger and Empey, filled men's imaginations in 1917. That attitude was sufficiently strong to counter three years of news and propaganda about the atrocities of modern warfare; it was strong enough, even, to temper men's natural fear of death. Historian William L. Langer, for example, went to war as a young man in 1917, and later recalled with wonder "the eagerness of the men to get to France and above all to reach the front." . . .[Writer] John Dos Passos recollected similar sentiments from 1917: "We had spent our boyhood in the afterglow of the peaceful nineteenth century. . . . What was war like? We wanted to see with our own eyes. We flocked into the volunteer services. I respected the conscientious objectors, and occasionally felt I should take that course myself, but hell, I wanted to see the show."

Brimming with eagerness and enthusiasm, hundreds of thousands of young men embarked in 1917 and 1918 upon what Theodore Roosevelt alluringly called the "Great Adventure." Secretary [of War] Newton D. Baker consciously strove to model the stateside training camps on "the analogy of the American college," and countless contemporary observers noted the keen sense of schoolboyish anticipation and excitement that infected the fresh recruits. "As in similar encampments," said one trainee, "Fort Sheridan was alive with enthusiastic recruits, with an atmosphere somewhat like that of a college campus on the eve of a big game."

Even more than college boys, the young men in the Army were to be protected from wickedness and vice. Temperance crusaders, long devoted to changing the nation's drinking habits, were at war's outbreak riding a wave of recent successes. By 1917 nineteen states had adopted prohibition, and the increasingly powerful Anti-Saloon League was pressing for a prohibition amendment to the federal Constitution. Passionate "drys" shuddered at the opportunities for debauchery that army life might put in the path of the nation's manhood. Their political muscle helped convince the War Department to ban the sale of liquor in the vicinity of the training camps, and to forbid (on paper at least) any man in uniform from buying a drink. These measures imparted further momentum to the temperance cause, and contributed to the ratification of the Eighteenth Amendment in 1919.

The Army also undertook a campaign against sexual vice that had substantial influence on postwar life. The American Social Hygiene Association had urged as early as 1914 that the public be educated about venereal disease, though the Association cautioned that the effort should go forward "conservatively and gradually . . . without impairing modesty and becoming reticence in either young or old." Despite widespread concern about the debilitating effects of the "social disease," little had happened by 1917 to advance the Association's cause. Then the Army, determined to get the maximum number of "effectives" from the mass of inductees, and not troubled by questions of modesty, launched a great anti-VD campaign. It assigned the task to the Commission on Training Camp Activities (CTCA), a consortium of civilian service organizations, like the YMCA, Knights of Columbus, and Jewish Welfare Board, that worked under official Army auspices. Wanting results, the Army and the Commission cared little for reticence, and they minced no words about sexual matters. Speaking frankly of "balls" and "whores," one CTCA pamphlet carefully explained that wet dreams were normal and that masturbation, common folk wisdom notwithstanding, would not lead to insanity. The clear implication was that natural emission, or even masturbation, was greatly preferable to potentially infectious liaisons. In the same vein, the Commission placarded the camps with posters proclaiming: "A German Bullet is Cleaner than a Whore." Pamphlets urged sexual purity in the name of patriotism: "How could you look the flag in the face," asked one, "if you were dirty with gonorrhea?" "A Soldier who gets a dose," warned a poster, "is a Traitor!"

The campaign continued with the doughboys in France. The Commander in Chief gave special attention to the venereal report every morning, and venereal infection was made a matter for discipline. "Keeping our men clean," said [General John] Pershing, was a matter of the highest importance, "not only from the standpoint of effectives, but from that of morals." But, as elsewhere, Pershing's efforts in the battle for sexual purity were hampered by what the general daintily termed "the difference between the French attitude and our own." In February 1918, [French] Premier [Georges] Clemenceau magnanimously offered to help establish licensed houses of prostitution, customary in the French army, for what he obviously regarded as the long-suffering American troops. Pershing passed the letter containing the offer to Raymond Fosdick, head of the CTCA. Fosdick, in turn, showed Clemenceau's letter to Secretary Baker, who reportedly exclaimed: "For God's sake, Raymond, don't show this to the President or he'll stop the war." The Americans declined this bit of gracious Gallic generosity, and continued to mete out stern punishment to soldiers suffering from VD. The Army congratulated itself that the campaign drastically lowered the venereal infection rate among the doughboys. The educational drive had further import as well. For many young men, the Commission's pamphlets, films, and lectures no doubt constituted the first thorough sex education they had received. Surely very few had ever been exposed to such frank and open scientific discussion of matters about which the society had been notoriously mute. In its own blunt way, the Army contributed to the demythologizing of erotic life by bringing sexual matters into the arena of public discourse, which was to become a characteristic feature of twentieth-century American culture.

The Army cooperated less eagerly with another social experiment in 1917–18: intelligence testing and classification by mental ability of men who passed through the training camps. Testing people's intelligence was a novel procedure in the prewar era. First developed by French psychologist Alfred Binet in the early years of the century, the method was adopted and improved by Stanford University's Lewis Terman in 1916, and became known in the United States as the Stanford-Binet test. When America entered the war, the American Psychological Association pressured the War Department to use the tests to screen mental incompetents from the Army and to classify all inductees on the basis of their intelligence. Not incidentally, this plan would provide the professional psychologists with data-sets of previously undreamed-of size, the raw material for countless further studies.

The Army at first responded tepidly to these "mental meddlers," as one general called them. But by early 1918 trained psychological examiners were posted to all the camps. There they administered thousands of "alpha" tests to the literate inductees, and "beta" tests to the illiterate. The results were used to designate the recruits "superior," "average," or "inferior," so that personnel officers might then select potential officer trainees and distribute the remainder of the men proportionately, with reference to their tested intelligence, throughout the various units.

The testers were struck by the extent of illiteracy their examinations revealed—as many as 25 percent of the draftees could be so classified. Examiners were also unsettled by the meager educational backgrounds of the recruits. Most enlisted men had left school between the fifth and seventh grades. The median number of years of education ranged from 6.9 for native whites and 4.7 for immigrants to 2.6 for Southern blacks. In one large sample of native white draftees, fewer than 18 percent had attended high school, and most of those men had not graduated. The typical enlisted soldier, concludes one student, was "an ill-educated unsophisticated young man . . . the opposite of the Harvard boys who volunteered for ambulance duty before America entered the war."

The psychologists were less surprised by their correlation of test performances with racial and national backgrounds. Invariably, men from "native" or "old" immigrant stock scored heavily in the "superior" range, while draftees from "new" immigrant backgrounds fell disproportionately into the "inferior" category. More than half the Russian, Italian, and Polish draftees, for example, showed up as "inferior." Nearly 80 percent of the blacks who took the alpha test were labeled "inferior," and their illiteracy rates were significantly higher than those for whites.

The psychologists, striving for scientific objectivity, denied that their examinations were biased toward certain educational or cultural backgrounds, or toward a particular kind of scholastic skill. Yet it may be doubted whether the native intelligence of recent immigrants or poor rural blacks was fairly tested by questions about the authorship of "The Raven," the talents of the painter Rosa Bonheur, or the city in which the Overland car was manufactured—all standard queries on the alpha test. These examinations were the crudest devices of an infant psychological "science" that even in its maturity has not escaped criticism on grounds of cultural bias. The Army, to its credit, never lost its suspicion of the psychologists, and ended the testing program at the first opportunity, January 1919. But what the Army rejected, the nation's educational system eagerly adopted in the postwar era, as intelligence testing became a familiar procedure in the schools. And to many old-stock, white Americans, the widely publicized results of the wartime tests conveniently reinforced their already disparaging appraisal of the new immigrant groups and blacks.

Forewarned about disease, tested and labeled, introduced to the manual of arms, trained to drill, drill, drill, fitted out with a new-fangled safety razor (the war would change the shaving techniques of a generation), and saddled with packs, the doughboys marched out of the camps and up the ramps of the ships of the "Atlantic Ferry." Most left from Hoboken, [New Jersey], and nearly half sailed in British vessels. A lucky few cruised in some style on the *Leviathan*, the former Hamburg-American luxury liner *Vaterland*, impounded in New York harbor since 1914, and in 1917 seized and made to carry troops to battle against the men who built her. Others traveled on various Cunard [British] ships and American ocean liners, but a great many were shipped in converted freighters, hastily refitted, stark, and dirty. "Assigned quarters on lower deck," said a private put on board the British ship *Kashmir*; "the blackest, foulest, most congested hole that I ever set foot into." On arrival in France, the men were shoehorned into the notorious "40-and-8's"—diminutive French railway freightcars supposedly able to carry 40 men or 8 horses—and rumbled slowly away from the ports along the choked rail system to their forward training areas in the interior of France. Once off the train, the men began to walk, and for many it must have seemed that they walked forever. *Stars and Stripes* [the soldiers' newspaper in France] found no more fertile subjects for humor than the length of hikes and the weight of packs. Billetted in widely scattered areas that required lengthy walks to training facilities, and prodded by officers under orders not to let the troops become restless while Pershing's idle army grew to sufficient size, the men moved constantly—often, it seemed, just to be moving. As the diary of one reads:

> Sat. June 22, 1918: Left Colembert in A.M. and hiked with full packs about 7 kilos to Bellebrune.
> Wed. June 26, 1918: Hiked with full packs back to Colembert.
> Thur. June 27, 1918: Hiked back to Bellebrune.
> Sat. June 29, 1918: Hiked with light packs about 14 kilos to gas school.
> Wed. July 3: Hiked about 20 kilos to Bouinngues.

Thur. July 4: Hiked 10 kilos to rifle range.
Fri. July 5: Hiked 18 kilos to Buysschure.
Sat. July 6: Hiked 15 kilos to Oudezeele.

Two million men served in the AEF [American Expeditionary Force]. The experience struck nearly all of them as an extraordinary moment in their lives—while they passed through it, and when they later remembered it. That they considered it an extraordinary interlude at the time is evidenced by the diaries and journals and strikingly "literary" letters so many of them wrote during their period of service. Americans in 1917, especially those of the age and class who qualified for the AEF, were not the diary-keeping people they had once been. Yet thousands of men who had never before recorded in writing their daily doings, and never would again, faithfully kept journals while they were in the Army. Most of these records began with induction and ended with discharge, neatly delineating the time spent in uniform as a peculiar interval, a moment stolen from ordinary life and forever after sealed off in the memory as a bundle of images that sharply contrasted with "normal" experience. The reactions to France and to war were, of course, as varied as the men who recorded them. But even a modest sampling of the personal documents left behind—a few of them published, many deposited in libraries, more still passed down reverently as family heirlooms to later generations—reveals common responses to the shared enterprise, and common conventions of perception and language to which these men resorted in the effort to comprehend their experience and relate it to others.

They were, first of all, as much tourists as soldiers. Later reflections, governed by the masculine need to emphasize prowess at martial exploits, would tend to blot that fact from the record. But the average doughboy spent more peacetime than wartime in France. And, though as many as 1.3 million Americans came under enemy fire, few saw sustained or repeated battle. Virtually none was subjected to the horror and tedium of trench warfare for years on end, the typical lot of the European soldier. The Americans fought no major defensive battles. Their two chief engagements were relatively brief, mobile attacks in the closing weeks of the conflict.*

Hence, to a remarkable extent—remarkable at least when compared with the war writings of European combatants—the doughboys' accounts deal with topics other than war. It was AEF policy to rotate leave zones "in order to give all an equal chance to see as much of France as possible." Most coveted of all were the pink tickets that permitted a trip to Paris.

[*In September 1918, the Americans at Saint Mihiel and Meuse-Argonne joined in the last great Allied offensive.]

Stars and Stripes felt obliged to caution arriving troops against the "oo-la-la" idea of France as a great tourist playground. Too many men, said the journal, came over "expecting to find a sort of international Coney Island, a universal pleasure resort." "We have been all over France and seen and learn [sic] a lot," said one awe-struck New Yorker. After the Armistice [1918], the Army organized sporting events and provided educational opportunities for the idle troops. It also endlessly compelled them to solve "problems"—sham attacks against an imaginary enemy. Many men fought more of these mock battles than real ones. One long-suffering soldier reported in April 1919 that "every hill in this vicinity has been captured or lost at least ten times." But the same enlisted man spoke the sentiments of many when, describing his post-Armistice leave to Nice and Monte Carlo, he called it "the most important event in my life over here (from a social standpoint)."

Like previous generations of their traveling countrymen, the doughboys were impressed with the *age* of the Old World. "Its old cathedrals, chateaux and ancient towns have been quite wonderful to my eyes so accustomed to the look of the New World," said one. In countless diaries and letters the soldiers dwelt on the quaint antiquity of this town, or that church or chateau, their imaginations especially fired by the evocation of names from the history books. "The church here," wrote another doughboy, "is very, very old, probably built sometime in the 12th or 13th century. Saint Louis the Crusader, King of France, attended service there on three occasions and Jeanne d'Arc was there several times." "The architecture for the most part seems to represent a period several hundred years past," wrote another. "We are living, for the present, in barracks built about the time of Louis XIV, though no one here knows anything about them prior to Napoleon."

The France they described was rich with history, an old country inhabited by old people. No observation of French life was more common than remarking the elderly women in black who seemed to be the only residents of the ruined towns behind the front. A tired people in a blighted land, the French pursued antiquated ways. "My but the people are old fashioned," observed one enlisted man. "They still harvest with cradles and sickles. Once in a while you see a binder or mower. I've never saw [sic] a real wagon, they use carts." All signs, in short, confirmed the American myth of the Old World as an exhausted place, peopled by effete and even effeminate races. All this, of course, served as a useful foil for the image of American energy and "pep." "What an impression our boys are making on the French," enthused Raymond Fosdick, head of the Commission on Training Camp Activities. "They are the greatest lot of sheer boys you ever saw. . . . The French, who love to sit and meditate, are constantly gasping at the exuberance and tirelessness of our fellows." "Never was there such a spectacle in all history," exclaimed a *New York Times* correspondent, "as that of the fresh millions of free Americans flocking to the rescue of be-leaguered and exhausted Europe."

But if Europe was exhausted, it was still splendid to behold. Numerous accounts expressed rapt wonder at the sheer physical beauty of France. "Picturesque" was perhaps the most commonly used word in these de-scriptions. One is struck too by the frequency of panoramic portraits of nature, of efforts to translate a long sweep of the eye into a string of words. If sunrise and sunset were the characteristic themes in the writings of trench-bound British troops in Flanders, as Paul Fussell has observed in his study *The Great War and Modern Memory*, it was the panoramic landscape that most attracted the eye of Americans. . . .

Common to many Americans' perceptions of France was a sense of ceremony, which often had religious overtones. *Stars and Stripes* declared that France was "holy ground," and that more than once in history the French "at Chalons, at Tours, at the Marne—'saved the soul of the world.' " To many of the doughboys, the great war in which they were now engaged amounted to a ritual reenactment of those historic dramas. To the largely Protestant Americans, the exotic rites of French Catholicism fittingly ex-emplified the ceremonial attitude they deemed appropriate to the occasion. Alan Seeger had noted that "the Catholic religion with its idealization of the spirit of sacrifice makes an almost universal appeal in these times," and many members of the AEF agreed with him. The "Marseillaise" [French national anthem], too, had the power to "set you quivering." When French religion and patriotic music were combined, the effect was deeply moving. One American soldier attended high mass on Bastille Day, 1918, and a band at the flag-draped church played the "Marseillaise": "Rene, talk about throwing up your hat and shouting 'To Hell with the Kaiser.' The scene and music impressed me so much that I could hardly get my breath. I cannot describe how grand the whole thing was."

Time and again in the personal narratives of these touring provincials one suddenly hears a different voice. The rough and often wise-cracking American idiom abruptly gives way to a grandiloquent tone that speaks, for example, of the "red-tiled roofs resplendent in the sunlight, resembling huge cameos set conspicuously on the vine covered slopes." This strange diction was the language of the tourist brochures, or of the ubiquitous YMCA guides who shepherded the gawking troops about the various sights. It was not a natural voice. Those wondrous foreign scenes often exceeded the native American capacity for authentic speech, and the con-frontation with the unfamiliar was thus almost automatically rendered in clichés and highly stylized prose. To a significant degree, the same was true of descriptions of the war itself.

Reverence toward France and the "cause" was not carried over to the Army. Fellowship of arms gave certain consolation, but the physical con-ditions of life and the restrictions of the military regime were constant causes of complaint. Most pestiferous were the lice—"cooties"—that occasioned frequent trips to the delousing stations, and almost daily "shirt readings," or close inspections of clothing for nits. Equally wearing on men's bodies and spirits was army food—or lack of it. In vivid contrast with the wooden descriptions of tourist sights are the lively and lavish descriptions of those rare meals eaten somewhere—anywhere—other than the military mess. The careful recording of menus, indeed, took up a great deal of space in many soldiers' diaries and letters. Men frequently noted losses of more than ten percent of their body weight in the weeks after arrival in France. These accounts confirmed [British] Field Marshal [Douglas] Haig's observation that the Americans "hardly knew how to feed their troops." They also suggest that undernourishment may have dulled the fighting effectiveness of the AEF.

But the worst feature of military life was the discipline. Military hierarchy and subordination chafed against ingrained American values of equality and individualism. Anti-German propaganda harped on the supposedly slavish subservience of the "Hun" in order to enhance an image of the German soldier as an eminently bayonetable alien. The American resentment of martial authority could be found in all ranks, and sometimes manifested itself in striking ways. Even a pillar of traditional authority such as once and future Secretary of War Henry L. Stimson complained to his diary, while a staff officer in France, that "I am getting a little tired of kowtowing to regulars just because they are regulars." On the returning troop carriers in 1919, the doughboys enacted a ritual "funeral of Sam Browne." To the throaty cheers of the enlisted men, the officers solemnly marched to the ship's rail and threw their leather girth-and-shoulder "Sam Browne" belts, hated symbols of military caste, into the sea. Even the hierarchy of different services prompted resentment, as infantry officers often took potshots at airborne American pilots, the elite and haughty "Knights of the Air." "It is just a gesture of irritation at the air service," opined the commander of an observation balloon squadron, "something like boys throwing a rock at a limousine which is dashing by when they are having to work."

Long idle behind the lines, and then only briefly exposed to battle, the great mass of the American soldiers in France were spectators in the theater of war. They had come to see the "Big Show," and were not disappointed. Nothing in that show was more exciting than the aerial battles. Men approaching the front strained their eyes and ears for signs of aircraft, more out of curiosity than fear. Always they referred to aerial "duels," or "wonderful air battles," or "thrilling air fights." One balloonist described seeing "Richthofen's *circus*." The famed "Red Baron's" formation approached, "some of the planes with red bodies, and they fly along with some planes climbing and some dropping and give the effect of being on the rim of a giant wheel which is rolling thru the sky."

Artillery fire, too, provided visual spectacle on a colossal scale. In the rear training area, reported one young officer, "the most fun is going out to the artillery range." There, secure in a bomb-proof observation shelter near the target, "you can see the shot appear as a little black speck and follow it down to the earth when it bursts.". . .

But the big guns also brought death. Worse, they brought it without warning, from an unseen distance. In descriptions of shelling, one occasionally finds the faintly dawning realization that modern military combat was something quite different from what the eager troops had been led to expect. And its worst feature was its impersonality. Many men wrote of their sense of outraged helplessness while being shelled. Indeed, "shell shock" may have had as much to do with this feeling of impotence as it did with the physical effects of concussion. Even the irrepressible Alan Seeger found bombardment "distressing," because he was "being harried like this by an invisible enemy and standing up against all the dangers of battle without any of its exhilaration or enthusiasm." William Langer wrote that shellfire "has always seemed a bit unfair to me. Somehow it makes one feel so helpless, there is no chance of reprisal for the individual man. The advantage is all with the shell, and you have no comeback." Enduring shellfire often prompted fantasies of bloody personal reprisal. As one draftee wrote: "we cannot fight artillery. Jerry is a rotten sport. . . . Poor Frank Carr, he was hit with a shell and broken all up. I'll remember that and when it comes my time to run a bayonet into one of the skunks I'll look to heaven and cry out to Frank to watch me do the job up."

But negative notes in the contemporary reactions to the war were relatively rare. What most strikes the reader of these personal war records is their unflaggingly positive, even enthusiastic, tone. Seeger's sanguine reflection that war was affording him "the supreme experience" was reiterated countless times by those who followed him to France. . . .

These expressions of exhilaration, wonder, and glory are notable not only for what they say but also for the way in which they say it. The sights of France elicited mostly tourist-brochure boilerplate from the doughboy writers. Similarly, the war itself seemed to overwhelm the power of the imagination to grasp directly, and of language to describe authentically. It is not especially surprising to find *Stars and Stripes* assuring a soldier-reader that he was the "spiritual successor" to "the Knights of King Arthur's Round Table." But it is to be remarked when countless common soldiers wrote privately of themselves in the same vein. American war narratives, with unembarrassed boldness, speak frequently of "feats of valor," of "the cause" and the "crusade." The memoirs and missives penned in France are shot through with images of knight-errantry and of grails thrillingly pursued. A truck driver in the aviation section of the AEF exclaimed that "war's great caldron of heroism, praise, glory, poetry, music, brains, energy, flashes and grows, rustles and roars, fills the heavens with its mighty being. . . .Oh! War as nothing else brings you back to the adventurous times of old." One of Lillian Wald's "boys" from the Henry Street Settlement proudly announced his enlistment in the "battle to throw down the shackles of Honensollern [sic] and Junkerism."

The ghost of Alan Seeger, and of the nineteenth-century literary conventions he exemplified, haunted these and innumerable similar passages. Faced with the unfamiliar reality of modern war, many young American soldiers tried to comprehend it in the comfortably familiar verbal formulae of their childhood storybooks. In the homeliest lines scribbled by the humblest privates, the war was frequently couched in language that appears to have been lifted verbatim from the pages of G. A. Henty or, more often, those of Sir Walter Scott. That language echoed, however pathetically, the epic posturings of George Creel* and the elaborately formal phrasing of [President] Woodrow Wilson. Those accents may ring strangely in the modern ear, but they flowed easily from the tongues and pens of the doughboys in 1918. The ubiquity of that idiom, from the White House to the trenches, suggested a widely made equation between the official and the personal definitions of the war's significance. If the war was to redeem Europe from barbarism, it would equally redeem individual soldiers from boredom; if the fighting in France was the "Great Adventure," the doughboys were the great adventurers; if Creel and Wilson could speak of the "Crusade," then it followed that American troops were crusaders. Not only did many doughboys accept without reflection the official definition of the war's meaning, but, perhaps more important, they translated that meaning into their understanding of their personal experiences, and described those experiences in language transported directly from the pious and inflated pronouncements of the spokesmen for traditional culture. That language pervaded all the vast "literature" produced during the war by members of the AEF. . . .

DOCUMENTS

Diary of an Unknown Aviator, 1918

We've lost a lot of good men. It's only a question of time until we all get it. I'm all shot to pieces. I only hope I can stick it. I don't want to quit. My nerves are all gone and I can't stop. I've lived beyond my time already.

It's not the fear of death that's done it. I'm still not afraid to die. It's this eternal flinching from it that's doing it and has made a coward out of

[*Chairman of the U.S. Committee on Public Information]
SOURCE: *War Birds: Diary of an Unknown Aviator* (New York: George H. Doran Co., 1926), 267–71.

me. Few men live to know what real fear is. It's something that grows on you, day by day, that eats into your constitution and undermines your sanity. I have never been serious about anything in my life and now I know that I'll never be otherwise again. But my seriousness will be a burlesque for no one will recognize it. Here I am, twenty-four years old, I look forty and I feel ninety. I've lost all interest in life beyond the next patrol. No one Hun will ever get me and I'll never fall into a trap, but sooner or later I'll be forced to fight against odds that are too long or perhaps a stray shot from the ground will be lucky and I will have gone in vain. Or my motor will cut out when we are trench straffing or a wing will pull off in a dive. Oh, for a parachute! The Huns are using them now. I haven't a chance, I know, and it's this eternal waiting around that's killing me. I've even lost my taste for licker. It doesn't seem to do me any good now. I guess I'm stale. Last week I actually got frightened in the air and lost my head. Then I found ten Huns and took them all on and I got one of them down out of control. I got my nerve back by that time and came back home and slept like a baby for the first time in two months. What a blessing sleep is! I know now why men go out and take such long chances and pull off such wild stunts. No discipline in the world could make them do what they do of their own accord. I know now what a brave man is. I know now how men laugh at death and welcome it. I know now why Ball went over and sat above a Hun airdrome and dared them to come up and fight with him. It takes a brave man to even experience real fear. A coward couldn't last long enough at the job to get to that stage. What price salvation now?

War is a horrible thing, a grotesque comedy. And it is so useless. This war won't prove anything. All we'll do when we win is to substitute one sort of Dictator for another. In the meantime we have destroyed our best resources. Human life, the most precious thing in the world, has become the cheapest. After we've won this war by drowning the Hun in our own blood, in five years' time the sentimental fools at home will be taking up a collection for these same Huns that are killing us now and our fool politicians will be cooking up another good war. Why shouldn't they? They have to keep the public stirred up to keep their jobs and they don't have to fight and they can get soft berths for their sons and their friends' sons. To me the most contemptible cur in the world is the man who lets political influence be used to keep him away from the front. For he lets another man die in his place.

The worst thing about this war is that it takes the best. If it lasts long enough the world will be populated by cowards and weaklings and their children. And the whole thing is so useless, so unnecessary, so terrible! . . .

The devastation of the country is too horrible to describe. It looks from the air as if the gods had made a gigantic steam roller, forty miles wide and run it from the coast to Switzerland, leaving its spike holes behind as it went. . . .

I've lost over a hundred friends, so they tell me—I've seen only seven or eight killed—but to me they aren't dead yet. They are just around the corner, I think, and I'm still expecting to run into them any time. I dream about them at night when I do sleep a little and sometimes I dream that some one is killed who really isn't. Then I don't know who is and who isn't. I saw a man in Boulogne the other day that I had dreamed I saw killed and I thought I was seeing a ghost. I can't realize that any of them are gone. Surely human life is not a candle to be snuffed out. . . .

German-American Loyalty, 1917

My emotions tell me one thing at this awful time, but my reason tells me another. As a German by birth it is a horrible calamity that I may have to fight Germans. That is natural, is it not? But as an American by preference, I can see no other course open. . . .

For 25 years Germany has shown dislike for the United States—the Samoan affair, the Hongkong contretemps, the Manila Bay incident, the unguarded words of the Kaiser himself, and, lastly, the Haitian controversy in 1914. . . . And it has not been from mere commercial or diplomatic friction. It is because their ideals of government are absolutely opposite. One or the other must go down. It is for us to say now which it shall be.

Because of my birth and feelings beyond my control I have no particular love for the French and less for the British. But by a strange irony of fate I see those nations giving their blood for principles which I hold dear, against the wrong principles of people I individually love. It is a very unhappy paradox, but one I can not escape. I do not want to see the allies triumph over the land of my birth. But I very much want to see the triumph of the ideas they fight for.

It sickens my soul to think of this Nation going forth to help destroy people many of whom are bound to me by ties of blood and friendship. But it must be so. It is like a dreadful surgical operation. The militaristic, undemocratic demon which rules Germany must be cast out. It is for us to do it—now. I have tried to tell myself that it is not our affair, that we should have contented ourselves with measures of defense and armed neutrality. But I know that is not so. The mailed fist has been shaken under our nose before. If Prussianism triumphs in this war the fist will continue

SOURCE: C. Kotzenabe, "German-American Loyalty," in Committee on Public Information, War Information Series, *American Loyalty* (Washington, D.C.: Government Printing Office, 1917), 5–6.

to shake. We shall be in real peril, and those ideas for which so much of the world's best blood has been spilled through the centuries will be in danger of extinction. It seems to me common sense that we begin our defense by immediate attack when the demon is occupied and when we can command assistance.

There is much talk of what people like me will do, and fear of the hyphen. No such thing exists. The German-American is as staunch as the American of adoption of any other land and perhaps more so. Let us make war upon Germany, not from revenge, not to uphold hairsplitting quibbles of international law, but let us make war with our whole heart and with all our strength, because Germany worships one god and we another and because the lion and the lamb can not lie down together. One or the other must perish.

Let us make war upon the Germany of the Junkerthum,* the Germany of frightfulness, the Germany of arrogance and selfishness, and let us swear not to make peace until the Imperial German Government is the sovereign German people.

Letters from Mennonite Draftees, 1918

DEAR BROTHER ———:

I went to Camp Cody, N. Mex., June 25, 1918. At first I drilled without a rifle, but later was asked to take one, explaining that the President's orders concerning the C. O.'s [conscientious objectors] required it, and I would get into non-combatant service in due time. I accepted it, and in two weeks was transferred to the infantry where, of course, I was asked again to take the rifle, and I saw that I had been deceived. I refused and explained why. Several nights after this, while I was in bed, some privates threw water into my bed, put a rope around my neck and jerked me out on the floor.

The next day two sergeants came to my tent and took me out, tied a gun on my shoulder and marched me down the street, one on each side of me, kicking me all the way. I was asked again whether I would take the rifle and drill. I refused and was taken to the bath-house, put under the shower bath where they turned on the water, alternating hot and cold, until I was so numb that I could scarcely rise. Just then one of the higher

[*the Prussian military aristocracy]
SOURCE: J. S. Hartzler, *Mennonites in the World War or Nonresistance Under Test* (Scottdale, Pa.: Mennonite Publishing House, 1922), 124–27.

officers came in and asked what they were about. They explained that they were giving me a bath. The officer told me to dress and go to my tent, that he wanted to interview me himself. He asked if I would take a rifle and drill. I told him that I could not. He ordered my sergeant to put me on company street work until they got my transfer, and in three weeks I was given non-combatant service.

VERY TRULY YOURS,——

DEAR BROTHER:

I came home Wednesday evening, Feb. 5. To get home, receive a hearty welcome and many expressions of joy for the effort made to maintain the faith, was alone worth the hardships which we endured.

I had been gone a few days more than ten months, of which I spent twenty-four days in our company, ten days in detention camp, seventy-eight days in the guard-house, one night in the Kansas City Police "lock-up," one hundred ninety-seven days in the disciplinary barracks (Fort Leavenworth, Kans.) and two days on the way home. . . .

I do not approve of such practices as the world was engaged in, and will give them neither moral nor material support though it may mean imprisonment or even death for not doing so. If the army would never kill a man, I can not see how a person could become a part of it, giving moral and material support to its maintenance and still retain a Christian character. The standards it upholds and the injustices it practices are unbelievable to a man who never saw them. . . . The only part that I can have in the army is suffering its punishments. Its purposes and those of Christianity are as different as night and day. The aims of the army are coercion, terrorism, carnal force; the ideals of Christianity are love, meekness, gentleness, obedience to the will of God, etc. When these ideals are maintained to the best of our ability, by God's grace He will provide care and protection in ways not imagined by man.

As to noncombatant service: all branches of service have one purpose; viz., to make the whole system a stronger organization of terrorism, destruction, and death. While I would not have been directly killing any one, I would have been doing a man's part in helping another do the act, and lending encouragement to the same. To support a thing and refuse to do the thing supported is either ignorance or cowardice. To refuse to go to the trenches and still give individual assistance to another doing so, is either an improper knowledge of the issues at stake or downright fear to face the bullets. I have a greater conscientious objection against noncombatant than against combatant service. I feel that the principle is the same, and that both are equally wrong. I would feel guilty toward the other man to accept service where the danger was not so great. . . .

To an observer it may have seemed ridiculous to refuse to even plant flowers at the base hospital. In the first place, that was the duty of the working gang under the quartermaster's department. Technically I would not have been doing military duty for I had not "signed up;" virtually I would have been rendering service because I was at work. . . . The farther one went with the military officers the farther they demanded him to go. I felt that the farther I went the less reason I could give for stopping, so I concluded that the best place to stop was in the beginning. It was on the charge of refusing to plant flowers that I received my court-martial sentence of ten years of hard labor in the disciplinary barracks at Fort Leavenworth, Kans.

FRATERNALLY YOURS,——

PART I

Suggestions for Further Reading

On southern black Americans after the Civil War, consult Eric Foner, *Nothing But Freedom: Emancipation and Its Legacy* (1983); John Hope Franklin, *Reconstruction After the Civil War* (1961); Leon Litwack, *Been in the Storm So Long: The Aftermath of Slavery* (1979); and Howard Rabinowitz, *Race Relations in the Urban South, 1865–1890* (1980). On black poverty, see Jay R. Mandle, *The Roots of Black Poverty* (1978). C. Vann Woodward, *The Strange Career of Jim Crow* (1966) remains an important work.

For the migration of blacks to the north, Forette Henri, *Black Migration: Movement North, 1900–1920* (1976) provides a general overview. For particular cities, see Gilbert Osofsky, *Harlem: The Making of a Ghetto, 1890–1930* (1968); David Katzman, *Before the Ghetto: Black Detroit in the Nineteenth Century* (1973); Allan Spear, *Black Chicago: The Making of a Ghetto, 1890–1920* (1967); Thomas Lee Philpott, *The Slum and the Ghetto: Neighborhood Deterioration and Middle Class Reform, Chicago, 1880–1930* (1978); and Kenneth Kusmer, *A Ghetto Takes Shape: Black Cleveland, 1870–1930* (1976). Two excellent studies of white racism are George Frederickson, *The Black Image in the White Mind: The Debate on Afro-American Character and Destiny, 1817–1914* (1971) and Joel Williamson, *The Crucible of Race* (1984). An outstanding study of black culture is Lawrence Levine, *Black Culture and Black Consciousness: Afro-American Folk Thought from Slavery to Freedom* (1977).

For industrialization and American workers, see Herbert Gutman, *Work, Culture and Society in Industrializing America* (1976); Stephan Thernstrom, *The Other Bostonians* (1973); and Melvyn Dubofsky, *Industrialism and the American Worker, 1865–1920* (1975). David Brody, *Steelworkers in America: The Non-Union Era* (1976) is an excellent book.

For the frontier, a general work is Richard Bartell, *The New Country: A Social History of the American Frontier, 1776–1890* (1974). An older book of value is Everett Dick, *Sod House Frontier: 1854–1890* (1937). See also W. Eugene Hollon, *The Great American Desert* (1966) and Joe B. Frantz and Julian E. Choate, Jr., *The American Cowboy: The Myth and the Reality* (1955).

For women after the Civil War, there are a number of useful works. General books are Peter Filene, *Him/Her Self: Sex Roles in Modern America* (1975) and Sheila M. Rothman, *Woman's Proper Place: A History of Changing Ideals and Practices, 1870 to the Present* (1978). On women and education, see Barbara Solomon, *In the Company of Educated Women* (1985). On women and work, see David Katzman, *Seven Days a Week: Women and Domestic Service in Industrializing America* (1978); Leslie Tentler, *Wage-Earning Women: Industrial Work and Family in the United States, 1900–1930* (1979); Dee Garison, *Apostles of Culture: The Public Libraries and American Society, 1876–1920* (1979); Barbara Harris, *Beyond Her Sphere: Women and the Professions in American History* (1978); and Nancy Dye, *As Equals and Sisters: The Labor Movement and the Women's Trade Union League of New York* (1980). On changing attitudes and practices about birth control, see Linda Gordon, *Woman's Body, Woman's Right: A Social History of Birth Control in America* (1979) and James Reed, *From Private Vice to Public Virtue: The Birth Control Movement and American Society Since 1830* (1977). On feminism, the standard work is Eleanor Flexner, *Century of Struggle: The Women's Rights Movement in the United States* (1959). Also helpful are William O'Neill, *Everyone Was Brave: A History of Feminism in America* (1971) and William Leach, *True Love and Perfect Union: The Feminist Reform of Sex and Society* (1980).

On immigration, Stephan Thernstrom (ed.), *The Harvard Encyclopedia of American Ethnic Groups* (1980) is outstanding. Two general works are Leonard Dinnerstein and David Reimers, *Ethnic Americans: A History of Immigration and Assimilation* (1987) and John Bodnar, *The Transplanted: A History of Immigrants in Urban America* (1985). John Higham, *Strangers in the Land: Patterns of Nativism, 1860–1925* (1955) is an especially good study of nativism. On the Italians, see Virginia Yans-McLaughlin, *Family and Community: Italian Immigrants in Buffalo, 1880–1930* (1977) and Humbert Nelli, *Italians in Chicago, 1880–1930: A Study in Ethnic Mobility* (1970). On Jews, see Moses Rischin, *The Promised City: New York's Jews, 1870–1914* (1962) and Irving Howe, *World of Our Fathers: The Journey of the East European Jews to America and the Life They Found and Made* (1976). For the Chinese, see Jack Chen, *The Chinese of America* (1981). Useful comparative studies are Thomas Kessner, *The Golden Door: Italian and Jewish Mobility in New York City, 1880–1915* (1977) and John Bodnar et al., *Lives of Their Own: Blacks, Italians and Poles in Pittsburgh, 1900–1960* (1982). On New York City, consult Nathan Glazer and Daniel Patrick Moynihan, *Beyond the Melting Pot: The Negroes, Puerto Ricans, Jews, Italians and Irish of New York City* (1963).

On American Indians, consult Francis Paul Prucha, *The Great White Father: The United States Government and the American Indians* (1984); Angie Debo, *A History of the Indians of the United States* (1970); and Vine Deloria, Jr., *Custer Died for Your Sins: An Indian Manifesto* (1969). On reform and assimilation, see Robert W. Mardock, *Reformers and the American Indians* (1971) and Frederick E. Hoxie, *A Final Promise: The Campaign to Assimilate the Indians, 1880–1920* (1984). On the New Deal and the Indians, see Philip Kenneth, *John Collier's Crusade for Indian Reform, 1920–1954* (1977). On education, see Margaret Szasz, *Education and the American Indian: The Road to Self-Determination, 1928–1973* (1974).

On World War I, Frederick Luebke, *Bonds of Loyalty: German Americans and World War I* (1974) is informative. For the home front, see David Kennedy, *Over Here: The First World War and American Society* (1980). On women during the war, see Maurine W. Greenwald, *Women, War and Work: The Impact of World War I on Women Workers in the United States* (1980). For military aspects of the war, the standard treatment is Edward Coffman, *The War to End All Wars: The American Military Experience in World War I* (1968).

PART II

Modern American Society

1920–Present

WITH THE END OF WORLD WAR I, AMERICANS TURNED THEIR attention to affairs at home. The nation experienced a rising standard of living as the changes that marked post–Civil War America—urbanization, industrialization, immigration, the movement of women into the paid workforce and the rapid development of the West—continued unabated. Yet, many were repelled by changes in American society wrought by these developments and looked back with nostalgia to the mid-nineteenth century. Some adopted ugly forms of protest and joined organizations such as the revived Ku Klux Klan to fight unwanted changes, while others attempted to outlaw behavior that they viewed as undesirable—for example, the consumption of alcoholic beverages. Although the Klan saw some of its goals (such as the restriction of immigration) achieved, it was clear that a new social morality was emerging.

The collapse of the stock market in 1929 and the onslaught of the Great Depression of the 1930s forced Americans to deal with unemployment, bankruptcies, farm foreclosures and a host of other economic problems. The New Deal tried many innovative methods of stimulating the ailing economy, but not until World War II did unemployment recede and a long period of economic growth, characterized by high consumption, begin. Not everyone fared equally at home during the war; Japanese Americans on the West Coast were interned in dreary and isolated camps.

As the nation prospered in the years following World War II, many people sought a better life by buying homes in the mushrooming suburbs and by becoming members of the consumer society. Yet postwar prosperity did not end social and economic injustice; during this period, blacks turned to protest to achieve their rights, as did American women, beginning in the late 1960s. Although neither blacks nor women had achieved economic status equal to that of white males as the 1980s drew to a close, they nonetheless had expanded their range of opportunities and roles in American society.

The essays and documents in the chapters that follow illuminate the major developments in American life since the end of World War I. They focus on the intolerance and the manners and morals of the 1920s, the impact of the Depression and World War II on American society, the internment of Japanese-Americans during the war, the suburbanization of America during the 1950s and 1960s, and the struggles of blacks and women for equality up to the present day.

CHAPTER 9

Intolerance: A Bitter Legacy of Social Change

At the turn of the century, few other issues caused so much debate and concern as the large-scale immigration to the United States from Southern and Eastern Europe. To many native-born Americans, whose roots lay in Northern and Western Europe, these millions of newcomers came to symbolize the disappearance of an older, simpler American society. Native-born Americans feared that the new immigrants would not adapt to established ways and values; in addition, they feared that the newcomers would lower the standard of living by taking jobs from American citizens or by working for low wages. During World War I, several prominent leaders also expressed apprehension about the potential for divided loyalties on the part of immigrants. Leaders such as Theodore Roosevelt believed that immigrants, especially German Americans, might have loyalties to Germany, the nation's wartime enemy. Roosevelt wanted absolute patriotism—what he called "100 percent Americanism."

Fear and dread of foreigners increased in the postwar years, with Eastern European Jews and Roman Catholics being blamed for many of the nation's social problems. One result of this mood was the revival of the Ku Klux Klan, a post–Civil War vigilante group that had first directed its hatred toward blacks, and later also toward immigrants it feared and despised. Within a few years of its revival after the war, the Klan was spreading its message of bigotry not only in the South, where it originated, but throughout the rest of the country, as well. The Klan's growth and influence was imposing but brief. David Chalmers's essay "The Hooded Knights Revive Rule by Terror in the 'Twenties" examines the revival and eventual decline of the Klan during that decade. According to the essay, what attractions did the Klan hold for the thousands who joined it?

The first document is from a 1926 article, "The Klan's Fight for Americanism," by Klan leader Hiram Evans. Notice how Evans's message combines bigotry and a supposed adherence to traditional American values. How does the document help to explain the Klan's appeal in sections of the country as different from each other in racial and ethnic makeup as Oregon, Georgia, and Massachusetts?

Although Evans's rantings seem outrageous to modern sensibilities, many people during this period, even in the highest levels of government, echoed the Klan philosophy. Evidence of this is found in the second document, an excerpt from Congressional testimony in 1921 concerning U.S. immigration policy. Although those testifying do not refer to any specific countries of origin in their condemnation of immigrants, federal legislation passed in 1924 (the National Origins Act) makes it clear that legislators believed immigrants from some countries to be less desirable than those from others. The new approach, generally referred to as the "national-origins system," gave preference to immigrants from Northern and Western Europe; it severely limited immigration from the rest of the Continent, and virtually barred Asians.

In 1952 Congress passed the McCarran-Walter Act, which was also based on the national-origins system. The final document reveals how the Senate subcommittee introducing the bill continued to defend this system; both the Senate and the House demonstrated their concurrence through passage of the Act. Finally, in 1965, Congress replaced this law with a nondiscriminatory one.

ESSAY
_____

The Hooded Knights Revive Rule by Terror in the 'Twenties

David Chalmers

D. W. Griffith's 1915 melodrama, *The Birth of a Nation*, was a blockbuster of a motion picture, and it helped revive the Ku Klux Klan. The Kentucky-born Griffith created his pioneering film from a novel written by a North Carolinian named Thomas Dixon. Dixon's life was built on eloquence and passion. A fellow-student and friend of Woodrow Wilson at Johns Hopkins graduate school, Dixon had been a legislator, Baptist preacher, lecturer, novelist, playwright, and actor, always reaching out to a larger audience. Griffith gave him his biggest one.

Dixon's 1905 book, *The Clansman: An Historical Romance of the Ku Klux Klan*, was one of three that he wrote on the Invisible Empire which his uncle had helped lead in the Carolina piedmont. The story evolved around two star-crossed families, the Camerons and the Stonemans, one from the South and the other from the North. Their sons and daughters fell in love, but the War Between the States separated them and Reconstruction brought them disaster. Congressman Stoneman, copied from life after Radical Republican leader Thaddeus Stephens, was presented as a crippled, hate-filled villain, urged on by his mulatto mistress to degrade the captured South. With the murder of "The Great Soul," Abraham Lincoln, there was nothing to stop him. Black tyranny ruled the South, black corruption stained its legislative halls, and brutish black lust stalked its womanhood. However, at this darkest moment, the hooded knights of the Ku Klux Klan, led by young Ben Cameron, Civil War hero and beloved of Stoneman's daughter, rode forth to save the South and its downtrodden people.

D. W. Griffith took Dixon's story and made it into the movies' first colossal spectacular. In place of the usual fifteen-minute flicker, Griffith created a three-hour epic, dramatically restaging the war's battles, Sherman's March to the Sea, and Lincoln's assassination at Ford's Theater. Congressman Stoneman comes to the Southern town of Piedmont to oversee his schemes for melding the races. Cameron's "Little Sister," as he called her, and her mother, Mrs. Lenoir, leap from a cliff to their deaths after ravishment by a black renegade soldier. Cameron is arrested and sentenced to death for murder; Stoneman's son, in love with Cameron's sister, takes his place. Just in time, the Klan arrives to save the living, avenge the fallen, and reunite the lovers.

SOURCE: David Chalmers, "The Hooded Knights Revive Rule by Terror in the 'Twenties," *American History Illustrated* 14 (February, 1980): 28–37. Reprinted through the courtesy of Historical Times, Inc., publishers of *American History Illustrated*.

Breaking the former static role of the camera, using angles, movement, and changing focus, expanding irises, reaching in and out of close-ups, juxtaposing, and paralleling, Griffith created his masterpiece. As the bugle call rang out and the Klan rode to the rescue, theater orchestras pounded out themes from Wagner and "The Hall of the Mountain King." Audiences rose cheering in the South, and crowds demonstrated in protest in the North. The picture was seen by President Woodrow Wilson, members of Congress and the Supreme Court, and millions of spectators at $2 apiece, while William J. Simmons, a fraternal organizer, colonel in the Woodmen of the World, and failed Methodist minister, dreamed of a revival of the Klan itself.

"Colonel" Simmons' plan for the Klan was revealed in the words of the advertisement which he inserted in the December 7, 1915, Atlanta *Journal*. The "Knights of the Ku Klux Klan" was "A High Class Order for Men of Intelligence and Character." It was to be "The World's Greatest *Secret*, Social, Patriotic, Fraternal, Beneficiary Order." In other words, it was to be a lodge, a fraternity. The fact that it was to exclude all who were not white, native-born, or Protestant did not make it substantially different from other such organizations and most college fraternities. It was the chance factor of its Southern origin that provided the dynamic element— the name and legend of the Ku Klux Klan. In *The Birth of a Nation,* whose Atlanta advertisement shared the page with Simmons' hand-drawn announcement of the Klan, Thomas Dixon and D. W. Griffith had engraved an image of flowing robes and mystic, masked, night-riding, patriotic violence on the national imagination. While most fraternities guarded their lodge hall secrets against outsiders and aliens, the vigilante heritage of the Klan took it out into the cow-pastures and city streets to protect its version of American values.

Simmons' initial plans had been less extravagant. His specialty was lodge ritual. He had hoped for a mildly successful organization in the Southeast to which he could sell memberships, regalia, and insurance. World War I enabled the Klan to do a little public marching and patriotic snooping. After the war the Klan, with a small membership in Georgia and Alabama, emerged into a time of opportunity. The heightened emotions and restlessness that were not immediately stilled by an end to the fighting, the manly camaraderie of the war and the habit of violence, people going home and not going home, black men who had served in the Army or who had left the farms for the cities and Northern factories— all were unsettling elements.

There were race riots in Chicago, Omaha, and Knoxville, in Duluth, Springfield, and Tulsa, in Texas, Arkansas, Kansas, and Florida. Large numbers of immigrants were arriving from the Southern and Eastern European dwelling places of the Roman Catholic, Jew, Slav, and Bolshevik.

Life in the cities was confusing; the war to end war had turned sour, and the attempt to make society better by prohibition was either being flouted or downright corrupted. As with the original Ku Klux Klan, the unsettled times and the mysterious name (now potent with the legacy of its vigilante role during Reconstruction) undoubtedly shaped the direction the Klan would take for years to come.

Simmons engaged a pair of fund raisers, Edward Young Clarke and Mrs. Elizabeth Tyler, who were the Southern Publicity Association, to handle recruitment. Simmons was to receive $2 of the $10 initiation fee paid by each new member. The rest was to go to Clarke, Tyler, and their salesmen. The results were phenomenal. The Klan made good copy and the press rushed to spread reports of its doings. Within a year membership was nationwide and soared to almost 100,000.

The basic Southern emphasis on patriotism and white supremacy was expanded into the protection of basic morality and 100 percent American-ism. The American way of life and moral values were to be guarded not only against the Negroes, but from Roman Catholics, Jews, and Orientals, from aliens and immigrants, from bootleggers and road houses, from crime and corrupt politicians, from marital infidelity and sexual immorality, and from scoffers and unbelievers. Salesman, or "kleagles," were selected from the Masonic and other lodges, touring lecturers from the evangelical min-istry, and the country was divided and subdivided into sales districts. Local groups brought the Klan into town to combat bootlegging or corrupt city government, and Atlanta's usual advice to new chapters was to "clean up the town." Crosses burned on nearby hillsides, sheeted horsemen paraded down Main Street on Saturday night and the next morning marched down church aisles to make donations while choirs sang "The Old Rugged Cross" or "Onward Christian Soldiers."

Georgia . . . was the cradle for the reborn Klan. Colonel Simmons' blazing cross on Stone Mountain had been its first annunciation and Peach-tree Street in Atlanta brought the robed faithful to its Imperial Palace. For fifty years Georgians would march in its parades and elect its candidates, as well as fight against its violence and intolerance. Nathan Bedford Forrest Klan No. 1 was the Imperial Empire's mother lodge, and in 1920 when Simmons triumphantly attended the annual reunion of the United Con-federate Veterans in Houston, its Exalted Cyclops Nathan Bedford Forrest III rode beside him.

The Klan spread through the cities and small towns of Georgia. The mighty Robert E. Lee No. 1 of Birmingham was the heart of its strength in Alabama and Sam Houston No. 1 led the way in Texas, although prob-ably outstripped in size and violence by Dallas' No. 66 and Beaumont's No. 7. Klan organizers did well in northern Louisiana and throughout Arkansas, but the Imperial Empire's earliest bastion of terror was in Texas and Oklahoma. Klan salesmen jumped across the continent to California, selling patriotism, fraternity, and moral enforcement. They spread out from Los Angeles, and moved northward across the border to power in Oregon, offering anti-Catholicism to the descendants of the New England and Mid-western Puritans. Its legions grew in Missouri and Kansas, and its salesmen worked their way up the Mississippi Valley, across the Great Plains, and into the mountain states. In 1924 Colorado became even a greater success story than Oregon, as the Klan helped elect the mayor of Denver, the governor, and both senators.

But in no realm did Klan political power become greater than in Indiana. Its ambitious Grand Dragon D. C. Stephenson, built his organization on a bloc by bloc basis throughout the state, carrying in tow the governor and both senators, negotiating for the purchase of Valparaiso University, and working his own way toward the White House. The Klan's fraternal appeal to what its Ohio Grand Dragon described as "the submerged majority of Protestants" swelled the tide of its membership in Cincinnati, Columbus, Toledo, Akron, and the steel centers of the Mahoning Valley. The Klan did well in the small towns and industrial cities of central Michigan and among the anti-Catholic socialists of Wisconsin. It signed up its thousands in Chicago and the suburbs, battling against an anti-Klan city administra-tion. In "Bloody Herrin" County down in fundamentalist southern Illinois, where the mountain people from Kentucky and Tennessee shared their country uneasily with French and Italian immigrant coal miners, labor conflict turned into a murderous Klan and anti-Klan war that brought in the National Guard some eight times in four years.

Nor was the East immune from the recruitments of the Invisible Em-pire. Torn from its past as an instrument by which the post–Civil War Reconstruction was undone, the Klan, which was mainly Democratic in the South, was Republican in the North. In both sections it represented the old moral values against the newcomers and social change. There was the same concern about foreigners, the Roman Catholic "threat" to the public schools, and the enforcement of prohibition. Klan marchers brought in by chartered trains "to give the micks something to think about" were attacked by mobs in the western Pennsylvania mill towns of Carnegie, Lilly, and Scottdale, but in the Philadelphia suburbs and down in Lancaster County, once the Klan got organized, it stayed organized.

While New York City was generally enemy territory, Klan weddings, christenings, church visits, volunteer fire departments, parades, rallies, county fair days, and local political victories marked the Klan as a leading organization in Long Island's Suffolk and Nassau counties. Upstate, Klan domain stretched from its Binghamton headquarters to Buffalo. It entered New Jersey from New York and Pennsylvania and despite denunciation at church conferences, it found a home among Methodist prohibitionists and along the seacoast from Atlantic City to Cape May. Portions of the Klan-infiltrated National Guard were disarmed in Rhode Island. Boston's Mayor Michael Curley cracked down on Klan meetings with the same sternness he had shown to the birth control crusader Margaret Sanger (despite American Civil Liberties Union protest in both cases), and Klansmen and Irishmen fought on summer nights in central Massachusetts. On the other side of the ethnic line, the prominent Boston blue-blood author Lothrop Stoddard found no conflict between his Americanism and that of the Klan, which also helped elect *Mayflower* descendant William Owen Brewster governor of Maine.

Simmons' talents lay in the area of lodge ritual and florid oratory, and many of his rising territorial leaders felt that he was not fully capitalizing on the Klan's potential. Led by the Dallas dentist Hiram Wesley Evans, whom Simmons had brought to Atlanta to help run things at the Imperial Palace, they staged a coup on the eve of the first national Klonvokation in 1922. When Simmons realized that he had been pushed upstairs out of control of the Klan, he was furious. Evans only laughed and replied, "Let's get the money, colonel."

There has never been a reliable tally of the number who belonged to the Klan. Between its veil of secrecy and its public boastings, the estimates run from two to four million members. During its peak years in the early 'twenties, members were streaming in and out in such numbers that the Klan itself probably never knew its own size. The consensus of historians is that Indiana took the lead with perhaps several hundred thousand Klansmen, Klanswomen, Tri-K's, and Junior Klansmen, with Texas, Oklahoma, Illinois, Ohio, and Pennsylvania probably close to 100,000 each. At one time or another in the 1920's, perhaps at least one out of every ten white, native-born, Protestant adult males belonged to the Invisible Empire. While sheer size did not necessarily mean political domination or long life for a Klan realm, in communities all across the country its strength gave a sense of power and immunity from the law. The mayor of Enid, Oklahoma, explained to the American Civil Liberties Union that since the Klan had 1,500 members and he had ten policemen, there was no point in investigating a reported Klan flogging.

A part of the fraternal excitement of the Klan was violence, a heritage from its Reconstruction days and not out of keeping with the Klan's vigilante role as a fighter against crime and immorality. The Klan was secret, masked, decentralized, and righteous, often operating with community approval and police participation. Although some Northern realms such as Ohio and Pennsylvania had their "Night Riders" and "Triple S" ("Super-Secret-Society") squads, the Southwest particularly liked "a little rough stuff." In the early 'twenties there were regular whippings and tar-and-feather parties in the meadows along Dallas' Trinity River bottoms. The

Mer Rouge murders* brought a portion of Louisiana close to civil war, and Governor Jack Walton got himself impeached when he called out the National Guard and imposed martial law on much of Klan-ridden Oklahoma. Texas and Oklahoma led the way, but Klan floggers were also active in Georgia, Alabama, Florida, North Carolina, and Kern County, California, with scattered incidents elsewhere. In those areas where the Klan dominated, however, it was the fellow white, native-born, Anglo-Saxon, Protestant rather than the Negro, Roman Catholic, Jew, or alien who was on the receiving end—which may be a commentary on the extent of the alien danger against which the Klan warned.

What drew its scores of thousands to the Klan? Later generations have looked upon the hooded knights as sour, defensive, bigoted, and something of a joke. To their contemporaries, they were serious business. Famed juvenile court judge, Ben Lindsey, who fought the Klan in Denver, commented, "They paid ten dollars to hate somebody and they were determined to get their money's worth." Julian Harris, son of the creator of the Uncle Remus tales, won a Pulitzer Prize for the anti-Klan campaign of his Columbus, Georgia, *Enquirer-Sun*. Taking the popular booster slogan "It's Great To Be a Georgian," he asked, "Is it great to be a citizen of a state whose governor is a member of and subservient to that vicious masked gang?" New Jersey Methodist Bishop E. H. Hughes found it necessary to remind his fellow ministers that "It is not Anglo-Saxon blood but the blood of Jesus Christ that has made us what we are."

However, to the Klansmen, their purpose was a positive expression of good fellowship and what America was all about. The Klan was a reform movement, even as prohibition was. It was a means to protect society, to keep things good "the way they had been," to get rid of criminals and corrupt politicians, dangerous radicals and those who scoffed at or violated church and home, bought illegal alcohol, or threatened racial purity and the Anglo-Saxon heritage of America.

People prefer simple explanations and scapegoats. Presidents Warren Harding and Calvin Coolidge, the Congress, and the Supreme Court hardly seemed dangerous forces for change. The Klansman found a symbol that he enjoyed blaming: the outsider-alien, personified in the Roman Catholic Church and personalized in the Roman Pope. Ex-priests and "escaped" nuns were popular on the Klan lecture circuit where stories of papal intrigue, convent sin, guns hidden in church basements, and the menace of the Knights of Columbus were staples. From Maine to California, the Klan girded its emotional loins against the Roman menace. While no Episcopal,

---

*On August 24, 1922, in Mer Rouge, Louisiana, two white critics of the Ku Klux Klan were brutally tortured and then hanged by Klan members.

Methodist, or Baptist convention approved of the Klan and many church leaders denounced it, the Klan appeared to be taking a noisy leadership in protecting community morality. In short, it was doing what the churches talked about: the Klan spoke their language, made donations, and filled their benches. So it was very difficult for many ministers and parishioners to turn it down.

In addition to fraternalism, nativism, and the protection of basic moral Americanism, the Invisible Empire offered fellowship, excitement, and a sense of power—and advantage. The ritual and life of the Klan were those of the lodge, and the Ku Klux Klan was the fastest growing fraternity of the 1920's, far outdistancing the newly formed American Legion. Through the early years, Klansmen gathered at monster initiations, cross burnings and rallies, at Klan Day at the state fair in Dallas or the inauguration of Grand Dragon D. C. Stephenson at Kokomo. From the lodge halls of Birmingham's Robert E. Lee No. 1 to Phoenix's Kamelback Klan No. 6, from Shreveport and Grand Island, Portland, New Haven, Beaumont, Bangor, Billings, Binghamton, and Bakersfield, Klansmen felt that they were part of a full-throated, rising, powerful force in the nation.

Of course there was always the possibility of more than the psychological advantage of being in on it. Merchants put "TWK" (Trade With a Klansman) and "SYMWA" (Spend Your Money With Americans) stickers in their shop windows. Rising young politicians such as lawyer Hugo Black in Alabama, joined, and county judge hopeful Harry Truman of Independence, Missouri, went through the first steps before he withdrew. With its soaring membership, the Klan seemed to have the votes.

Earle Mayfield in Texas was its first genuine U.S. Senator, and in Arkansas the Klan had its own primary first to decide which brother to support in the regular Democratic party one. Success whetted the appetites of the imperial potentates in Atlanta, and other eager hopefuls, from Maine to California. Altogether, the Klan substantially helped elect both senators from Colorado, Indiana, Oklahoma, and Alabama, and one each from Iowa, Oregon, Texas, Georgia, Tennessee, and Kentucky, as well as governors in Maine, Kansas, California, Wisconsin, Colorado, Indiana, Ohio, Tennessee, Alabama, Georgia, and Oregon. While some only accepted Klan support, at least five of the senators and four of the governors were Klan members.

In 1924, the Klan played a major role in presidential politics. The two candidates battling it out at the Democratic Convention in Madison Square Garden were the "wet," Catholic, New York Governor, Al Smith, and the Georgia-born Senator from California, William Gibbs McAdoo. McAdoo was not a bigot, but he had important support from Klan regions. The Platform Committee presented a plank opposing racial or religious discrimination, but the Smith supporters, and others, wanted the Klan denounced by name. As the Convention fought over the three crucial syllables, the supporters in the galleries chanted "Ku, Ku, McAdoo!" and "Booze! Booze! Booze!" at each other. The party's elder statesman and three times nominee, William Jennings Bryan, was hissed and booed when he asked for party unity and compassion, not condemnation, for those who belonged to the Klan. By an embittered 542 3/20 to 541 3/20 vote, the angry, shouting delegates failed to name the Klan. It was the climax of the Convention. Afterward it took nine days and 103 ballots to eventually send out John W. Davis as the compromise candidate to lose the election to Calvin Coolidge, who kept silent about it all.

In many communities, as the mayor of Enid, Oklahoma, had told the American Civil Liberties Union, the Klan held unchallenged power. That power, however, was unimaginative and soon squandered. The Klan was conservative, not revolutionary, and had little program other than to enjoy the spoils of office. Its members were a mixed bag of town and city blue- and white-collar workers, shopkeepers, and professional men. Although a potent force in politics, the Klan probably knew as little about economics as Warren G. Harding. Where it became involved, the Klan was pro-business and manipulated. Its leaders were friends to the electrical utilities in Oregon, and to the oil companies in Texas. In Kansas its top attorney also represented the anti-labor Associated Industries, and the Klan opposed street car regulation in Denver, public power ownership in Minneapolis, and the United Mine Workers in Kentucky. In the zones of emergence of the Northern cities, instead of organizing exclusionist neighborhood improvement associations, Klansmen spent their time at parades, church socials, fried chicken dinners, and lectures by Klan clergymen from Atlanta. The Klan's prime concern was fellowship and morality, not economics and urban dynamics.

On the national scene, the Klan supported immigration restriction, Federal aid to public education (as a counter to parochial schools), and non-participation in such "foreign" organizations as the League of Nations and the World Court. In state legislatures, Klansmen concentrated on protecting the flag, the Bible, racial purity, and the little red schoolhouse. This meant patriotic observances and readings from the King James Bible in the schools, and the exclusion of Roman Catholic teachers, or at least their wearing of religious garb. In Oregon the Klan combined with other fraternal lodges to pass a compulsory public school law, which the U.S. Supreme Court soon overruled.

But politics helped to undo the Klan's imperium. Leadership from Atlanta and in the state realms was remarkably inept. Conflict over which Klan candidate was going to be endorsed in Texas, Arkansas, and Oregon left bitter feelings. A jump to the Republican party did help produce a Klan senator from Oklahoma and a shift the other way elected a Democratic governor in Oregon, but the internal costs were high. State realms did not like being dictated to from Atlanta, and local Klansmen were no happier with the divisive, manipulative politics and authoritarian candidate-picking of their own Grand Dragons, who, in turn, had been imposed on the membership. Generally, the Klan was not successful in replacing other political associations and loyalties, and the men Klansmen elected, as well as those who told the Klansmen whom to elect, turned out to be of equally poor quality.

Although the Klan numbers and power often grew impressively, there was almost always someone to fight it, an editor such as Julian Harris or the Emporia, Kansas *Gazette's* William Allen White to expose it, or a district attorney such as future Texas Governor Dan Moody, Denver's Philip Van Cise, or Alabama Attorney General Charles McCall to investigate and indict it. The New York *World*, Memphis *Commercial Appeal*, Columbus, Georgia *Enquirer-Sun*, Montgomery, Alabama *Advertiser*, and Indianapolis *Times* received Pulitzer Prizes for their anti-Klan campaigns.

Initially, all press coverage helped spread the Klan, and violence gave the Klan a "hell-of-a-fellow" sense of power. By the mid-1920's, almost everything the Klan did or that was reported about it revealed its ineptitude, immorality, corruption, and community destructiveness. When Indiana Grand Dragon D. C. Stephenson, the most powerful leader of the Northern Klan, went to prison for a sex murder, the Klan's reputation was further badly damaged. The more the Klan's linen was hung out in public, the dirtier it appeared for all to see, and the Invisible Empire was almost continually in court to settle internal disputes. Colonel Simmons and "Doc" Evans fought over who would be Imperial Wizard; Grand Dragons struggled against Imperial headquarters, and local klaverns against their state realms. The leadership on most levels ruled dictatorially and was out for the money. This struggle for the spoils and the exploitation of the membership wrecked the Klan in practically every state where it existed. By the latter half of the 1920's, membership was melting away. In 1926, when the Klan staged its second national parade down Pennsylvania Avenue in Washington, D.C., only half as many Klansmen and women came, and they marched in columns of four instead of sixteen and twenty abreast as they had done the year before.

During its years of glory, the Klan produced no statesmanlike leaders or social programs, but rather violence, local turmoil, and scandal. By the latter 1920's the country had settled down—even if the Klan had not—to enjoy Republican prosperity. The dangers of Rome or Russia seemed more distant and less real. The Klan's role in the American fraternal world had been irreparably damaged by its mismanagement and extremism. The self-confidence of the great early days had become a sour defensiveness laboring under a damaged reputation, which contrasted badly with a more dominant American optimism.

Even in 1928 when the Democrats picked the Irish Catholic Al Smith as [their] presidential candidate, Klan leaders could not produce a revival. With the crash and Great Depression of the 1930's, the Klan ranks thinned to even fewer thousands. Shrunken to the Southeastern United States, the Klan sometimes had friends in power and engaged in occasional night riding and anti-union violence. It denounced the New Deal as communistic, but offered no alternatives.

At the end of the 1930's, Imperial Wizard Hiram Evans sold the Klan's Peachtree Street Palace to the Roman Catholic Church and the Klan itself to a veterinarian, Jimmy Colescott, from Terre Haute in the once potent realm of Indiana. A joint meeting with the German-American bund, in New Jersey, drew bad publicity. World War II, gas rationing, and a lien from the Internal Revenue Service for back taxes temporarily put the Imperial Empire out of business.

It was brought back to life after the end of the greater war in Europe, and maintains a fragmented existence mainly in the Southeast today, unmasked by state and local laws and watched by the F.B.I. It failed as a resistance movement during the civil rights days of the 1950's and 1960's in the South. Despite the annual compulsion of the press, wire services, and television to rediscover the Klan and announce its "revival," the Klan endures but has not regained any of the unity, numbers, or influence it once had in the 1920's. It was still capable of violence, but at the end of the 1970's, the most serious Klan watcher, the Anti-Defamation League, computed the strength of the various contending Klans at no more than 10,000.

DOCUMENTS

The Klan's Fight for "Americanism," 1926

The real indictment against the Roman Church is that it is, fundamentally and irredeemably, in its leadership, in politics, in thought, and largely in membership, actually and actively alien, un-American and usually anti-American. The old stock Americans, with the exception of the few such of Catholic faith—who are in a class by themselves, standing tragically torn between their faith and their racial and national patriotism—see in the Roman Church today the chief leader of alienism, and the most dangerous alien power with a foothold inside our boundaries. It is this and nothing

SOURCE: Reprinted from Hiram Evans, "Klan's Fight for Americanism," *North American Review* 123 (March–May 1926): 33–63, by permission of the University of Northern Iowa.

else that has revived hostility to Catholicism. By no stretch of the imagination can it fairly be called religious prejudice, though, now that the hostility has become active, it does derive some strength from the religious schism.

We Americans see many evidences of Catholic alienism. We believe that its official position and its dogma, its theocratic autocracy and its claim to full authority in temporal as well as spiritual matters, all make it impossible for it as a church, or for its members if they obey it, to coöperate in a free democracy in which Church and State have been separated. It is true that in this country the Roman Church speaks very softly on these points, so that many Catholics do not know them. It is also true that the Roman priests preach Americanism, subject to their own conception of Americanism, of course. But the Roman Church itself makes a point of the divine and unalterable character of its dogma, it has never seen fit to abandon officially any of these un-American attitudes, and it still teaches them in other countries. Until it does renounce them, we cannot believe anything except that they all remain in force, ready to be called into action whenever feasible, and temporarily hushed up only for expediency.

The hierarchical government of the Roman Church is equally at odds with Americanism. The Pope and the whole hierarchy have been for centuries almost wholly Italian. It is nonsense to suppose that a man, by entering a church, loses his race or national loyalties. The Roman Church today, therefore, is just what its name says—Roman; and it is impossible for its hierarchy or the policies they dictate to be in real sympathy with Americanism. Worse, the Italians have proven to be one of the least assimilable of people. The autocratic nature of the Catholic Church organization, and its suppression of free conscience or free decision, need not be discussed; they are unquestioned. Thus it is fundamental to the Roman Church to demand a supreme loyalty, overshadowing national or race loyalty, to a power that is inevitably alien, and which at the best must inevitably inculcate ideals un-American if not actively anti-American. . . .

The facts are that almost everywhere, and especially in the great industrial centers where the Catholics are strongest, they vote almost as a unit, under control of leaders of their own faith, always in support of the interests of the Catholic Church and of Catholic candidates without regard to other interests, and always also in support of alienism whenever there is an issue raised. They vote, in short, not as American citizens, but as aliens and Catholics! They form the biggest, strongest, most cohesive of all the alien *blocs*. On many occasions they form alliances with other alien *blocs* against American interests, as with the Jews in New York today, and with others in the case of the recent opposition to immigrant restriction. . . .

There are three of these great racial instincts, vital elements in both the historic and the present attempts to build an America which shall fulfill the aspirations and justify the heroism of the men who made the nation.

These are the instincts of loyalty to the white race, to the traditions of America, and to the spirit of Protestantism, which has been an essential part of Americanism ever since the days of Roanoke and Plymouth Rock. They are condensed into the Klan slogan: "Native, white, Protestant supremacy."

First in the Klansman's mind is patriotism—America for Americans. He believes religiously that a betrayal of Americanism or the American race is treason to the most sacred of trusts, a trust from his fathers and a trust from God. He believes, too, that Americanism can only be achieved if the pioneer stock is kept pure. . . .

Americanism, to the Klansman, is a thing of the spirit, a purpose and a point of view, that can only come through instinctive racial understanding. It has, to be sure, certain defined principles, but he does not believe that many aliens understand those principles, even when they use our words in talking about them. Democracy is one, fairdealing, impartial justice, equal opportunity, religious liberty, independence, self-reliance, courage, endurance, acceptance of individual responsibility as well as individual rewards for effort, willingness to sacrifice for the good of his family, his nation and his race before anything else but God, dependence on enlightened conscience for guidance, the right to unhampered development—these are fundamental. But within the bounds they fix there must be the utmost freedom, tolerance, liberalism. In short, the Klansman believes in the greatest possible diversity and individualism within the limits of the American spirit. But he believes also that few aliens can understand that spirit, that fewer try to, and that there must be resistance, intolerance even, toward anything that threatens it, or the fundamental national unity based upon it.

The second word in the Klansman's trilogy is "white." The white race must be supreme, not only in America but in the world. This is equally undebatable, except on the ground that the races might live together, each with full regard for the rights and interests of others, and that those rights and interests would never conflict. Such an idea, of course, is absurd; the colored races today, such as Japan, are clamoring not for equality but for their supremacy. The whole history of the world, on its broader lines, has been one of race conflicts, wars, subjugation or extinction. This is not pretty, and certainly disagrees with the maudlin theories of cosmopolitanism, but it is truth. The world has been so made that each race must fight for its life, must conquer, accept slavery or die. The Klansman believes that the whites will not become slaves, and he does not intend to die before his time.

Moreover, the future of progress and civilization depends on the continued supremacy of the white race. The forward movement of the world for centuries has come entirely from it. Other races each had its chance and either failed or stuck fast, while white civilization shows no sign of having reached its limit. Until the whites falter, or some colored civilization has a miracle of awakening, there is not a single colored stock that can claim even equality with the white; much less supremacy.

The third of the Klan principles is that Protestantism must be supreme; that Rome shall not rule America. The Klansman believes this is not merely because he is a Protestant, nor even because the Colonies that are now our nation were settled for the purpose of wresting America from the control of Rome and establishing a land of free conscience. He believes it also because Protestantism is an essential part of Americanism; without it America could never have been created and without it she cannot go forward. Roman rule would kill it.

Congress Debates Immigration Restriction, 1921

HOUSE OF REPRESENTATIVES

Mr. [Lucian Walton] PARISH [D.-Tex.]. We should stop immigration entirely until such a time as we can amend our immigration laws and so write them that hereafter no one shall be admitted except he be in full sympathy with our Constitution and laws, willing to declare himself obedient to our flag, and willing to release himself from any obligations he may owe to the flag of the country from which he came.

It is time that we act now, because within a few short years the damage will have been done. The endless tide of immigration will have filled our country with a foreign and unsympathetic element. Those who are out of sympathy with our Constitution and the spirit of our Government will be here in large numbers, and the true spirit of Americanism left us by our fathers will gradually become poisoned by this uncertain element.

The time once was when we welcomed to our shores the oppressed and downtrodden people from all the world, but they came to us because of oppression at home and with the sincere purpose of making true and loyal American citizens, and in truth and in fact they did adapt themselves to our ways of thinking and contributed in a substantial sense to the progress and development that our civilization has made. But that time has passed now; new and strange conditions have arisen in the countries over there; new and strange doctrines are being taught. The Governments of the Orient are being overturned and destroyed, and anarchy and bolshevism are threatening the very foundation of many of them, and no one

SOURCE: *Congressional Record*, April 20, 1921, 450, December 10, 1921, 177.

can foretell what the future will bring to many of those countries of the Old World now struggling with these problems.

Our country is a self-sustaining country. It has taught the principles of real democracy to all the nations of the earth; its flag has been the synonym of progress, prosperity, and the preservation of the rights of the individual, and there can be nothing so dangerous as for us to allow the undesirable foreign element to poison our civilization and thereby threaten the safety of the institutions that our forefathers have established for us.

Now is the time to throw about this country the most stringent immigration laws and keep from our shores forever those who are not in sympathy with the American ideas. It is the time now for us to act and act quickly, because every month's delay increases the difficulty in which we find ourselves and renders the problems of government more difficult of solution. We must protect ourselves from the poisonous influences that are threatening the very foundation of the Governments of Europe; we must see to it that those who come here are loyal and true to our Nation and impress upon them that it means something to have the privileges of American citizenship. We must hold this country true to the American thought and the American ideals. . . .

Mr. [James V.] McCLINTIC [D.-Okla.]. Some time ago it was my privilege to visit Ellis Island, not as a member of the committee but as a private citizen interested in obtaining information relative to the situation which exists at that place. I stood at the end of a hall with three physicians, and I saw them examine each immigrant as they came down the line, rolling back the upper eyelid in order to gain some information as to the individual's physical condition. I saw them place the chalk marks on their clothing which indicated that they were in a diseased condition, so that they could be separated when they reached the place where they were to undergo certain examinations. Afterwards I went to a large assembly hall where immigrants came before the examiners to take the literacy test, and the one fact that impressed me more than anything else was that practically every single immigrant examined that day had less than $50 to his credit. . . .

Practically all of them were weak, small of stature, poorly clad, emaciated, and in a condition which showed that the environment surrounding them in their European homes were indeed very bad.

It is for this reason that I say the class of immigrants coming to the shores of the United States at this time are not the kind of people we want as citizens in this country. It is a well-known fact that the majority of immigrants coming to this country at the present time are going into the large industrial centers instead of the agricultural centers of the United States, and when it is taken into consideration that the large centers are already crowded to the extent that there is hardly sufficient living quarters to take care of the people it can be readily seen that this class of people, instead of becoming of service to the communities where they go, they will become charges to be taken care of by charitable institutions. The week I visited Ellis Island I was told that 25,000 immigrants had been unloaded at that port. From their personal appearance they seemed to be the offcasts of the countries from which they came. . . .

National-Origins Formula Reaffirmed, 1951

The subcommittee [on immigration and naturalization] is cognizant of the facts existing at the time of the adoption of the national origins formula and the bitter charges of discrimination hurled at the incorporation of the principle in our immigration laws. The formula is still subjected to such charges but they seem to have lost some of their force over the intervening period of years. Experience has demonstrated that the national origins formula has been more of a numerically restrictive measure than a means of automatically selecting immigrants from the various nationalities in desired proportions.

Without giving credence to any theory of Nordic superiority, the subcommittee believes that the adoption of the national origins formula was a rational and logical method of numerically restricting immigration in such a manner as to best preserve the sociological and cultural balance in the population of the United States. There is no doubt that it favored the peoples of the countries of northern and western Europe over those of southern and eastern Europe, but the subcommittee holds that the peoples who had made the greatest contribution to the development of this country were fully justified in determining that the country was no longer a field for further colonization, and henceforth, further immigration would not only be restricted but directed to admit immigrants considered to be more readily assimilable because of the similarity of their cultural background to those of the principal components of our population. . . .

SOURCE: U.S. Congress, Senate Committee on the Judiciary, *U.S. Immigration and Naturalization*, S. Rept. 1515, 82d Cong., 1st sess., 1951, 455.

CHAPTER 10

Morals and Manners in the 1920s

Following World War I, many Americans eagerly embraced what President Warren G. Harding called "a return to normalcy." The term conveyed a nostalgic vision of an America of small towns and farms, with men and women pursuing traditional roles, largely unconcerned about events in other parts of the world. But the clock could not be turned back. Indeed, this image of the "good old days" was not an accurate view of the nation even prior to the war. The sweeping urban-industrial revolution of post–Civil War America had profoundly altered the social fabric, and would continue to do so.

The 1920 census provided dramatic evidence of the changes, revealing that for the first time a majority of Americans lived in urban areas. More Americans than ever before, including many women, now worked in factories and offices, and found their style of living affected by the automobile, the movies, a vast array of new consumer goods, and better housing. *For many of the younger generations, the good days were not in some distant past; they were now.*

In the essay from his book Only Yesterday, *Frederick Lewis Allen discusses the "revolution" in manners and morals during the 1920s. Although more recent historians have shown us that some of these changes were in evidence before 1920, there is no doubt that Allen distilled the essence of a new society. What does he identify as the major shifts in attitudes, lifestyles, and behavior during this period, and to what does he attribute them?*

The first document, from a 1925 magazine article, provides a contemporary view of one aspect of the "revolution" in morals. Do these practices seem innocent by today's standards?

Americans in the 1920s were well aware of the societal changes, and many who were alarmed by them offered solutions. The second document, a speech by Senator Henry Myers of Montana, singles out for criticism the movies (and the messages they conveyed), to which millions—especially the young—flocked weekly. Could the movies have been as influential as the senator claimed? What would his proposal of censorship have accomplished?

Criticism of the social climate in the United States did not originate in the 1920s; neither did attempts at reform. Nonetheless, in 1920 reformers had great hopes for a new age about to dawn. In that year the century-old battle against the consumption of alcoholic beverages appeared to have been won with the passage of the Eighteenth (Prohibition) Amendment. However, the third document—an excerpt from a statement issued in 1931 by a government commission established to investigate the effectiveness of the amendment and its accompanying legislation— provides findings to the contrary. What forms of behavior, though illegal, are nonetheless widely practiced today? What are the difficulties involved in outlawing forms of behavior deemed acceptable by a large segment of the public?

ESSAY

The Revolution in Manners and Morals
Frederick Lewis Allen

A first-class revolt against the accepted American order was certainly taking place during those early years of the Post-war [World War I] Decade, but it was one with which Nikolai Lenin had nothing whatever to do. The

SOURCE: Abridgement of pp. 78–108 from *Only Yesterday*, by Frederick Lewis Allen. Copyright © 1931 by Frederick Lewis Allen, renewed 1959 by Agnes Rogers Allen. Reprinted by permission of Harper & Row, Publishers, Inc.

shock troops of the rebellion were not alien agitators, but the sons and daughters of well-to-do American families, who knew little about Bolshevism and cared distinctly less, and their defiance was expressed not in obscure radical publications or in soap-box speeches, but right across the family breakfast table into the horrified ears of conservative fathers and mothers. Men and women were still shivering at the Red Menace when they awoke to the no less alarming Problem of the Younger Generation, and realized that if the Constitution were not in danger, the moral code of the country certainly was.

This code, as it currently concerned young people, might have been roughly summarized as follows: Women were the guardians of morality; they were made of finer stuff than men and were expected to act accordingly. Young girls must look forward in innocence (tempered perhaps with a modicum of physiological instruction) to a romantic love match which would lead them to the altar and to living-happily-ever-after; and until the "right man" came along they must allow no male to kiss them. It was expected that some men would succumb to the temptations of sex, but only with a special class of outlawed women; girls of respectable families were supposed to have no such temptations. Boys and girls were permitted large freedom to work and play together, with decreasing and well-nigh nominal chaperonage, but only because the code worked so well on the whole that a sort of honor system was supplanting supervision by their elders; it was taken for granted that if they had been well brought up they would never take advantage of this freedom. And although the attitude toward smoking and drinking by girls differed widely in different strata of society and different parts of the country, majority opinion held that it was morally wrong for them to smoke and could hardly imagine them showing the effects of alcohol.

The war had not long been over when cries of alarm from parents, teachers, and moral preceptors began to rend the air. For the boys and girls just growing out of adolescence were making mincemeat of this code.

The dresses that the girls—and for that matter most of the older women—were wearing seemed alarming enough. In July, 1920, a fashion-writer reported in the *New York Times* that "the American woman . . . has lifted her skirts far beyond any modest limitation," which was another way of saying that the hem was now all of nine inches above the ground. It was freely predicted that skirts would come down again in the winter of 1920–21, but instead they climbed a few scandalous inches farther. The flappers wore thin dresses, short-sleeved and occasionally (in the evening) sleeveless; some of the wilder young things rolled their stocking below their knees, revealing to the shocked eyes of virtue a fleeting glance of shin-bones and knee-cap; and many of them were visibly using cosmetics. "The intoxication of rouge," earnestly explained Dorothy Speare in *Dancers in the Dark*, "is an insidious vintage known to more girls than mere man can ever believe." Useless for frantic parents to insist that no lady did such things; the answer was that the daughters of ladies were doing it, and even retouching their masterpieces in public. Some of them, furthermore, were abandoning their corsets. "The men won't dance with you if you wear a corset," they were quoted as saying.

The current mode in dancing created still more consternation. Not the romantic violin but the barbaric saxophone now dominated the orchestra, and to its passionate crooning and wailing the fox-trotters moved in what the editor of the Hobart College *Herald* disgustedly called a "syncopated embrace." No longer did even an inch of space separate them; they danced as if glued together, body to body, cheek to cheek. Cried the *Catholic Telegraph* of Cincinnati in righteous indignation, "The music is sensuous, the embracing of partners—the female only half dressed—is absolutely indecent; and the motions—they are such as may not be described, with any respect for propriety, in a family newspaper. Suffice it to say that there are certain houses appropriate for such dances; but those houses have been closed by law."

Supposedly "nice" girls were smoking cigarettes—openly and defiantly, if often rather awkwardly and self-consciously. They were drinking—somewhat less openly but often all too efficaciously. There were stories of daughters of the most exemplary parents getting drunk—"blotto," as their companions cheerfully put it—on the contents of the hip flasks of the new prohibition régime, and going out joyriding with men at four in the morning. And worst of all, even at well-regulated dances they were said to retire where the eye of the sharp-sighted chaperon could not follow, and in darkened rooms or in parked cars to engage in the unspeakable practice of petting and necking.

It was not until F. Scott Fitzgerald, who had hardly graduated from Princeton and ought to know what his generation were doing, brought out *This Side of Paradise* in April, 1920, that fathers and mothers realized fully what was afoot and how long it had been going on. Apparently the "petting party" had been current as early as 1916, and was now widely established as an indoor sport. "None of the Victorian mothers—and most of the mothers were Victorian—had any idea how casually their daughters were accustomed to be kissed," wrote Mr. Fitzgerald. ". . . Amory saw girls doing things that even in his memory would have been impossible; eating three-o'clock, after-dance suppers in impossible cafés, talking of every side of life with an air half of earnestness, half of mockery, yet with a furtive excitement that Amory considered stood for a real moral let-down. But he never realized how widespread it was until he saw the cities between New York and Chicago as one vast juvenile intrigue." The book caused a shudder to run down the national spine; did not Mr. Fitzgerald represent one of his well-nurtured heroines as brazenly confessing, "I've kissed dozens of men. I suppose I'll kiss dozens more"; and another heroine as saying to a young man (*to a young man!*), "Oh, just one person in fifty has any glimmer of what sex is. I'm hipped on Freud and all that, but it's rotten that every bit of real love in the world is ninety-nine per cent passion and one little *soupçon* of jealousy"? . . .

The forces of morality rallied to the attack. Dr. Francis E. Clark, the founder and president of the Christian Endeavor Society, declared that the modern "indecent dance" was "an offense against womanly purity, the very fountainhead of our family and civil life." The new style of dancing was denounced in religious journals as "impure, polluting, corrupting, debasing, destroying spirituality, increasing carnality," and the mothers and sisters and church members of the land were called upon to admonish and instruct and raise the spiritual tone of these dreadful young people. . . . In Philadelphia a Dress Reform Committee of prominent citizens sent a questionnaire to over a thousand clergymen to ask them what would be their idea of a proper dress, and although the gentlemen of the cloth showed a distressing variety of opinion, the committee proceeded to design a "moral gown" which was endorsed by ministers of fifteen denominations. The distinguishing characteristics of this moral gown were that it was very loose-fitting, that the sleeves reached just below the elbows, and that the hem came within seven and a half inches of the floor.

Not content with example and reproof, legislators in several states introduced bills to reform feminine dress once and for all. The *New York American* reported in 1921 that a bill was pending in Utah providing fine and imprisonment for those who wore on the streets "skirts higher than three inches above the ankle." . . .

Meanwhile innumerable families were torn with dissension over cigarettes and gin and all-night automobile rides. Fathers and mothers lay awake asking themselves whether their children were not utterly lost; sons and daughters evaded questions, lied miserably and unhappily, or flared up to reply rudely that at least they were not dirty-minded hypocrites, that they saw no harm in what they were doing and proposed to go right on doing it. From those liberal clergymen and teachers who prided themselves on keeping step with all that was new, came a chorus of reassurance: these young people were at least franker and more honest than their elders had been; having experimented for themselves, would they not soon find out which standards were outworn and which represented the accumulated moral wisdom of the race? Hearing such hopeful words, many good people took heart again. Perhaps this flare-up of youthful passion was a flash in the pan, after all. Perhaps in another year or two the boys and girls would come to their senses and everything would be all right again.

They were wrong, however. For the revolt of the younger generation was only the beginning of a revolution in manners and morals that was already beginning to affect men and women of every age in every part of the country.

A number of forces were working together and interacting upon one another to make this revolution inevitable.

First of all was the state of mind brought about by the war and its conclusion. A whole generation had been infected by the eat-drink-and-be-merry-for-tomorrow-we-die spirit which accompanied the departure of the soldiers to the training camps and the fighting front. There had been an epidemic not only of abrupt war marriages, but of less conventional liaisons. In France, two million men had found themselves very close to filth and annihilation and very far from the American moral code and its defenders; prostitution had followed the flag and willing mademoiselles from Armentières had been plentiful; American girls sent over as nurses and war workers had come under the influence of continental manners and standards without being subject to the rigid protections thrown about their continental sisters of the respectable classes; and there had been a very widespread and very natural breakdown of traditional restraints and reticences and taboos. It was impossible for this generation to return unchanged when the ordeal was over. Some of them had acquired under the pressure of war-time conditions a new code which seemed to them quite defensible; millions of them had been provided with an emotional stimulant from which it was not easy to taper off. Their torn nerves craved the anodynes of speed, excitement, and passion. They found themselves expected to settle down into the humdrum routine of American life as if nothing had happened, to accept the moral dicta of elders who seemed to them still to be living in a Pollyanna land of rosy ideals which the war had killed for them. They couldn't do it, and they very disrespectfully said so.

"The older generation had certainly pretty well ruined this world before passing it on to us," wrote one of them (John F. Carter in the *Atlantic Monthly*, September, 1920), expressing accurately the sentiments of innumerable contemporaries. "They give us this thing, knocked to pieces, leaky, red-hot, threatening to blow up; and then they are surprised that we don't accept it with the same attitude of pretty, decorous enthusiasm with which they received it, way back in the 'eighties." . . .

The revolution was accelerated also by the growing independence of the American woman. She won the suffrage in 1920. She seemed, it is true, to be very little interested in it once she had it; she voted, but mostly as the unregenerate men about her did, despite the efforts of women's clubs and the League of Women Voters to awaken her to womanhood's civic opportunity; feminine candidates for office were few, and some of them—such as Governor Ma Ferguson of Texas—scarcely seemed to represent the starry-eyed spiritual influence which, it had been promised, would presently ennoble public life. Few of the younger women could rouse themselves to even a passing interest in politics: to them it was a sordid and futile business, without flavor and without hope. Nevertheless, the winning of the suffrage had its effect. It consolidated woman's position as man's equal.

Even more marked was the effect of woman's growing independence of the drudgeries of housekeeping. Smaller houses were being built, and they were easier to look after. Families were moving into apartments, and these made even less claim upon the housekeeper's time and energy. Women were learning how to make lighter work of the preparation of meals. Sales of canned foods were growing, the number of delicatessen stores had increased three times as fast as the population during the decade 1910–20, the output of bakeries increased by 60 per cent during the decade 1914–24. Much of what had once been housework was now either moving out of the home entirely or being simplified by machinery. The use of commercial laundries, for instance, increased by 57 per cent between 1914 and 1924. Electric washing-machines and electric irons were coming to the aid of those who still did their washing at home; the manager of the local electric power company at "Middletown," a typical American city, estimated in 1924 that nearly 90 per cent of the homes in the city already had electric irons. The housewife was learning to telephone her shopping orders, to get her clothes ready-made and spare herself the rigors of dressmaking, to buy a vacuum cleaner and emulate the lovely carefree girls in the magazine advertisements who banished dust with such delicate fingers. Women were slowly becoming emancipated from routine to "live their own lives."

And what were these "own lives" of theirs to be like? Well, for one thing, they could take jobs. Up to this time girls of the middle classes who had wanted to "do something" had been largely restricted to school-teaching, social-service work, nursing, stenography, and clerical work in business houses. But now they poured out of the schools and colleges into all manner of new occupations. They besieged the offices of publishers and advertisers; they went into tea-room management until there threatened to be more purveyors than consumers of chicken patties and cinnamon toast; they sold antiques, sold real estate, opened smart little shops, and finally invaded the department stores. In 1920 the department store was in the mind of the average college girl a rather bourgeois institution which employed "poor shop girls"; by the end of the decade college girls were standing in line for openings in the misses' sportswear department and even selling behind the counter in the hope that some day fortune might smile upon them and make them buyers or stylists. Small-town girls who once would have been contented to stay in Sauk Center all their days were now borrowing from father to go to New York or Chicago to seek their fortunes—in Best's or Macy's or Marshall Field's. Married women who were encumbered with children and could not seek jobs consoled themselves with the thought that home-making and child-rearing were really "professions," after all. No topic was so furiously discussed at luncheon tables from one end of the country to the other as the question whether the married woman should take a job, and whether the mother had a right to. And as for the unmarried woman, she no longer had to explain why she worked in a shop or an office; it was idleness, nowadays, that had to be defended.

With the job—or at least the sense that the job was a possibility—came a feeling of comparative economic independence. With the feeling of economic independence came a slackening of husbandly and parental authority. Maiden aunts and unmarried daughters were leaving the shelter of the family roof to install themselves in kitchenette apartments of their own. For city-dwellers the home was steadily becoming less of a shrine, more of a dormitory—a place of casual shelter where one stopped overnight on the way from the restaurant and the movie theater to the office. Yet even the job did not provide the American woman with that complete satisfaction which the management of a mechanized home no longer furnished. She still had energies and emotions to burn; she was ready for the revolution.

Like all revolutions, this one was stimulated by foreign propaganda. It came, however, not from Moscow, but from Vienna. Sigmund Freud had published his first book on psychoanalysis at the end of the nineteenth century, and he and Jung had lectured to American psychologists as early as 1909, but it was not until after the war that the Freudian gospel began to circulate to a marked extent among the American lay public. The one great intellectual force which had not suffered disrepute as a result of the war was science; the more-or-less educated public was now absorbing a quantity of popularized information about biology and anthropology which gave a general impression that men and women were merely animals of a rather intricate variety, and that moral codes had no universal validity and were often based on curious superstitions. A fertile ground was ready for the seeds of Freudianism, and presently one began to hear even from the lips of flappers that "science taught" new and disturbing things about sex. Sex, it appeared, was the central and pervasive force which moved mankind. Almost every human motive was attributable to it: if you were patriotic or liked the violin, you were in the grip of sex—in a sublimated form. The first requirement of mental health was to have an uninhibited sex life. If you would be well and happy, you must obey your libido. Such was the Freudian gospel as it imbedded itself in the American mind after being filtered through the successive minds of interpreters and popularizers and guileless readers and people who had heard guileless readers talk about it. . . .

The principal remaining forces which accelerated the revolution in manners and morals were all 100 per cent American. They were prohibition, the automobile, the confession and sex magazines, and the movies.

When the Eighteenth Amendment was ratified, prohibition seemed, . . . to have an almost united country behind it. Evasion of the law began immediately, however, and strenuous and sincere opposition to it—especially in the large cities of the North and East—quickly gathered force. The results were the bootlegger, the speakeasy, and a spirit of deliberate revolt which in many communities made drinking "the thing to do." From these facts in turn flowed further results: the increased popularity of distilled as against fermented liquors, the use of the hip-flask, the cocktail party, and the general transformation of drinking from a masculine prerogative to one shared by both sexes together. The old-time saloon had been overwhelmingly masculine; the speakeasy usually catered to both men and women. As [radio commentator] Elmer Davis put it, "The old days when father spent his evenings at Cassidy's bar with the rest of the boys are gone, and probably gone forever; Cassidy may still be in business at the old stand and father may still go down there of evenings, but since prohibition mother goes down with him." Under the new régime not only the drinks were mixed, but the company as well.

Meanwhile a new sort of freedom was being made possible by the enormous increase in the use of the automobile, and particularly of the closed car. (In 1919 hardly more than 10 per cent of the cars produced in the United States were closed; by 1924 the percentage had jumped to 43, by 1927 it had reached 82.8.) The automobile offered an almost universally available means of escaping temporarily from the supervision of parents and chaperons, or from the influence of neighborhood opinion. Boys and girls now thought nothing, as the Lynds pointed out in *Middletown,** of jumping into a car and driving off at a moment's notice—without asking anybody's permission—to a dance in another town twenty miles away, where they were strangers and enjoyed a freedom impossible among their neighbors. The closed car, moreover, was in effect a room protected from the weather which could be occupied at any time of the day or night and could be moved at will into a darkened byway or a country lane. The Lynds quoted the judge of the juvenile court in "Middletown" as declaring that the automobile had become a "house of prostitution on wheels," and cited the fact that of thirty girls brought before his court in a year on charges of sex crimes, for whom the place where the offense had occurred was recorded, nineteen were listed as having committed it in an automobile.

Finally, as the revolution began, its influence fertilized a bumper crop of sex magazines, confession magazines, and lurid motion pictures, and these in turn had their effect on a class of readers and movie-goers who had never heard and never would hear of Freud and the libido. The publishers of the sex adventure magazines, offering stories with such titles as "What I Told My Daughter the Night Before Her Marriage," "Indolent Kisses," and "Watch Your Step-Ins," learned to a nicety the gentle art of

[*Robert S. and Helen M. Lynd's pioneering sociological study of Muncie, Indiana (1929)]

arousing the reader without arousing the censor. The publishers of the confession magazines, while always instructing their authors to provide a moral ending and to utter pious sentiments, concentrated on the description of what they euphemistically called "missteps." Most of their fiction was faked to order by hack writers who could write one day "The Confessions of a Chorus Girl" and the next day recount, again in the first person, the temptations which made it easy for the taxi-driver to go wrong. Both classes of magazines became astonishingly numerous and successful. Bernarr Macfadden's *True Story*, launched as late as 1919, had over 300,000 readers by 1923; 848,000 by 1924; over a million and a half by 1925; and almost two million by 1926—a record of rapid growth probably unparalleled in magazine publishing.

Crowding the newsstands along with the sex and confession magazines were motion-picture magazines which depicted "seven movie kisses" with such captions as "Do you recognize your little friend, Mae Busch? She's had lots of kisses, but she never seems to grow *blasé*. At least you'll agree that she's giving a good imitation of a person enjoying this one." The movies themselves, drawing millions to their door every day and every night, played incessantly upon the same lucrative theme. The producers of one picture advertised "brilliant men, beautiful jazz babies, champagne baths, midnight revels, petting parties in the purple dawn, all ending in one terrific smashing climax that makes you gasp"; the venders of another promised "neckers, petters, white kisses, red kisses, pleasure-mad daughters, sensation-craving mothers, . . . the truth—bold, naked, sensational." Seldom did the films offer as much as these advertisements promised, but there was enough in some of them to cause a sixteen-year-old girl . . . to testify, "Those pictures with hot love-making in them, they make girls and boys sitting together want to get up and walk out, go off somewhere, you know. Once I walked out with a boy before the picture was even over. We took a ride. But my friend, she all the time had to get up and go out with her boy friend.". . .

Each of these diverse influences—the post-war disillusion, the new status of women, the Freudian gospel, the automobile, prohibition, the sex and confession magazines, and the movies—had its part in bringing about the revolution. Each of them, as an influence, was played upon by all the others; none of them could alone have changed to any great degree the folkways of America; together their force was irresistible.

The most conspicuous sign of what was taking place was the immense change in women's dress and appearance. . . . During the fall of 1923 and the spring of 1924, manufacturers were deluged with complaints from retailers that skirts would have to be shorter. Shorter they finally were, and still shorter. The knee-length dress proved to be exactly what women wanted. The unlucky manufacturers made valiant efforts to change the fashion. Despite all they could do, however, the knee-length skirt remained standard until the decade was approaching its end.

With the short skirt went an extraordinary change in the weight and material and amount of women's clothing. The boyishly slender figure became the aim of every woman's ambition, and the corset was so far abandoned that even in so short a period as the three years from 1924 to 1927 the combined sales of corsets and brassières in the department stores of the Cleveland Federal Reserve District fell off 11 per cent. Silk or rayon stockings and underwear supplanted cotton, to the distress of cotton manufacturers and the delight of rayon manufacturers; the production of rayon in American plants, which in 1920 had been only eight million pounds, had by 1925 reached fifty-three million pounds. The flesh-colored stockings became as standard as the short skirt. Petticoats almost vanished from the American scene; in fact, the tendency of women to drop off one layer of clothing after another became so pronounced that in 1928 the *Journal of Commerce* estimated that in 15 years the amount of material required for a woman's complete costume (exclusive of her stockings) had declined from 19¼ yards to 7 yards. . . .

Not content with the freedom of short and skimpy clothes, women sought, too, the freedom of short hair. During the early years of the decade the bobbed head—which in 1918, had been regarded . . . as a sign of radicalism—became increasingly frequent among young girls, chiefly on the ground of convenience. In May, 1922, the *American Hairdresser* predicted that the bob, which persisted in being popular, "will probably last through the summer, anyway." It not only did this, it so increased in popularity that by 1924 the same journal was forced to feature bobbed styles and give its subscribers instructions in the new art, and was reporting the progress of a lively battle between the professional hairdressers and the barbers for the cream of this booming business. The ladies' hairdressers very naturally objected to women going to barbers' shops; the barbers, on the other hand, were trying to force legislation in various states which would forbid the "hairdressing profession" to cut hair unless they were licensed as barbers. Said the *Hairdresser*, putting the matter on the loftiest basis, "The effort to bring women to barber shops for hair-cutting is against the best interests of the public, the free and easy atmosphere often prevailing in barber shops being unsuitable to the high standard of American womanhood." But all that American womanhood appeared to insist upon was the best possible shingle. In the latter years of the decade bobbed hair became almost universal among girls in their twenties, very common among women in their thirties and forties, and by no means rare among women of sixty; and for a brief period the hair was not only bobbed, but in most cases cropped close to the head like a man's. Women universally adopted the small cloche hat which fitted tightly on the bobbed head, and the manufacturer of milliner's materials joined the hair-net manufacturer, the hair-pin manu-facturer, and the cotton goods and woolen goods and corset manufacturers, among the ranks of depressed industries.

For another industry, however, the decade brought new and enormous profits. The manufacturers of cosmetics and the proprietors of beauty shops had less than nothing to complain of. The vogue of rouge and lipstick, which in 1920 had so alarmed the parents of the younger generation, spread swiftly to the remotest village. Women who in 1920 would have thought the use of paint immoral were soon applying it regularly as a matter of course and making no effort to disguise the fact; beauty shops had sprung up on every street to give "facials," to apply pomade and astringents, to make war against the wrinkles and sagging chins of age, to pluck and trim and color the eyebrows, and otherwise to enhance and restore the bloom of youth; and a strange new form of surgery, "face-lifting," took its place among the applied sciences of the day. Back in 1917, according to Frances Fisher Dubuc, only two persons in the beauty culture business had paid an income tax; by 1927 there were 18,000 firms and individuals in this field listed as income-tax payers. The "beautician" had arrived. . . .

These changes in fashion—the short skirt, the boyish form, the straight, long-waisted dresses, the frank use of paint—were signs of a real change in the American feminine ideal (as well, perhaps, as in men's idea of what was the feminine ideal.) Women were bent on freedom—freedom to work and to play without the trammels that had bound them heretofore to lives of comparative inactivity. But what they sought was not the freedom from man and his desires which had put the suffragists of an earlier day into hard straw hats and mannish suits and low-heeled shoes. The woman of the nineteen-twenties wanted to be able to allure man even on the golf links and in the office; the little flapper who shingled her hair and wore a manageable little hat and put on knickerbockers for the week-ends would not be parted from her silk stockings and her high-heeled shoes. Nor was the post-war feminine ideal one of fruitful maturity or ripened wisdom or practiced grace. On the contrary: the quest of slenderness, the flattening of the breasts, the vogue of short skirts (even when short skirts still sug-gested the appearance of a little girl), the juvenile effect of the long waist—all were signs that, consciously or unconsciously, the women of this decade worshiped not merely youth, but unripened youth: they wanted to be—or thought men wanted them to be—men's casual and light-hearted com-panions; not broad-hipped mothers of the race, but irresponsible play-mates. Youth was their pattern, but not youthful innocence: the adolescent whom they imitated was a hard-boiled adolescent, who thought not in terms of romantic love, but in terms of sex, and who made herself desirable not by that sly art which conceals art, but frankly and openly. In effect, the woman of the Postwar Decade said to man, "You are tired and disil-lusioned, you do not want the cares of a family or the companionship of mature wisdom, you want exciting play, you want the thrills of sex without their fruition, and I will give them to you." And to herself she added, "But I will be free."

One indication of the revolution in manners which her headlong pursuit of freedom brought about was her rapid acceptance of the cigarette. Within a very few years millions of American women of all ages followed the lead of the flappers of 1920 and took up smoking. Custom still generally frowned upon their doing it on the street or in the office, and in the evangelical hinterlands the old taboo died hard; but in restaurants, at dinner parties and dances, in theater lobbies, and in a hundred other places they made the air blue. Here again the trend in advertising measured the trend in public opinion. At the beginning of the decade advertisers realized that it would have been suicidal to portray a woman smoking; within a few years, however, they ventured pictures of pretty girls imploring men to blow some of the smoke their way; and by the end of the decade billboards boldly displayed a smart-looking woman cigarette in hand, and in some of the magazines, despite floods of protests from rural readers, tobacco manufacturers were announcing that "now women may enjoy a companionable smoke with their husbands and brothers." In the ten years between 1918 and 1928 the total production of cigarettes in the United States *more than doubled.* Part of this increase was doubtless due to the death of the one-time masculine prejudice against the cigarette as unmanly, for it was accompanied by somewhat of a decrease in the production of cigars and smoking tobacco as well as—mercifully—of chewing tobacco. Part of it was attributable to the fact that the convenience of the cigarette made the masculine smoker consume more tobacco than in the days when he preferred a cigar or a pipe. But the increase could never have been so large had it not been for the women who now strewed the dinner table with their ashes, snatched a puff between the acts, invaded the masculine sanctity of the club car, and forced department stores to place ornamental ash-trays between the chairs in their women's shoe departments. A formidable barrier between the sexes had broken down. The custom of separating them after formal dinners, for example, still lingered, but as an empty rite. Hosts who laid in a stock of cigars for their male guests often found them untouched; the men in the dining-room were smoking the very same brands of cigarettes that the ladies consumed in the living-room.

Of far greater social significance, however, was the fact that men and women were drinking together. Among well-to-do people the serving of cocktails before dinner became almost socially obligatory. Mixed parties swarmed up to the curtained grills of speakeasies and uttered the mystic password, and girls along with men stood at the speakeasy bar with one foot on the old brass rail. The late afternoon cocktail party became a new American institution. When dances were held in hotels, the curious and rather unsavory custom grew up of hiring hotel rooms where reliable drinks could be served in suitable privacy; guests of both sexes lounged on the beds and tossed off mixtures of high potency. As houses and apartments became smaller, the country club became the social center of the small city, the suburb, and the summer resort; and to its pretentious clubhouse, every Saturday night, drove men and women (after a round of cocktails at some-body's house) for the weekly dinner dance. Bottles of White Rock and of ginger ale decked the tables, out of capacious masculine hip pockets came flasks of gin (once the despised and rejected of bartenders, now the most popular of all liquors), and women who a few years before would have gasped at the thought that they would ever be "under the influence of alcohol" found themselves matching the men drink for drink and enjoying the uproarious release. The next day gossip would report that the reason Mrs. So-and-so disappeared from the party at eleven was because she had had too many cocktails and had been led to the dressing-room to be sick, or that somebody would have to meet the club's levy for breakage, or that Mrs. Such-and-such really oughtn't to drink so much because three cock-tails made her throw bread about the table. A passing scandal would be created by a dance at which substantial married men amused themselves by tripping up waiters, or young people bent on petting parties drove right out on the golf-links and made wheel-tracks on the eighteenth green.

Such incidents were of course exceptional and in many communities they never occurred. It was altogether probable, though the professional wets denied it, that prohibition succeeded in reducing the total amount of drinking in the country as a whole and of reducing it decidedly among the workingmen of the industrial districts. The majority of experienced college administrators agreed—rather to the annoyance of some of their under-graduates—that there was less drinking among men students than there had been before prohibition and that drinking among girl students, at least while they were in residence, hardly offered a formidable problem. Yet the fact remained that among the prosperous classes which set the standards of national social behavior, alcohol flowed more freely than ever before and lubricated an unprecedented informality—to say the least—of manners.

It lubricated, too, a new outspokenness between men and women. Thanks to the spread of scientific skepticism and especially to Sigmund Freud, the dogmas of the conservative moralists were losing force and the dogma that salvation lay in facing the facts of sex was gaining. An upheaval in values was taking place. Modesty, reticence, and chivalry were going out of style; women no longer wanted to be "ladylike" or could appeal to their daughters to be "wholesome"; it was too widely suspected that the old-fashioned lady had been a sham and that the "wholesome" girl was merely inhibiting a nasty mind and would come to no good end. "Victorian" and "Puritan" were becoming terms of opprobrium: up-to-date people thought of Victorians as old ladies with bustles and inhibitions, and of Puritans as blue-nosed, ranting spoilsports. It was better to be modern—everybody wanted to be modern—and sophisticated, and smart, to smash the conventions and to be devastatingly frank. And with a cocktail glass in one's hand it was easy at least to be frank. . . .

With the taste for strong liquors went a taste for strong language. To one's lovely dinner partner, the inevitable antithesis for "grand" and "swell" had become "lousy." An unexpected "damn" or "hell" uttered on the New York stage was no longer a signal for the sudden sharp laughter of shocked surprise; such words were becoming the commonplace of everyday talk. The barroom anecdote of the decade before now went the rounds of aristocratic bridge tables. Everyone wanted to be unshockable; . . .

With the change in manners went an inevitable change in morals. Boys and girls were becoming sophisticated about sex at an earlier age; it was symptomatic that when the authors of *Middletown* asked 241 boys and 315 girls of high-school age to mark as true or false, according to their opinion, the extreme statement, "Nine out of every ten boys and girls of high-school age have petting parties," almost precisely half of them marked it as true. How much actual intercourse there was among such young people it is of course impossible to say; but the lurid stories told by Judge [Ben] Lindsey—of girls who carried contraceptives in their vanity cases, and of "Caroline," who told the judge that fifty-eight girls of her acquaintance had had one or more sex experiences without a single pregnancy resulting—were matched by the gossip current in many a town. Whether prostitution increased or decreased during the decade is likewise uncertain; but certain it is that the prostitute was faced for the first time with an amateur competition of formidable proportions.

As for the amount of outright infidelity among married couples, one is again without reliable data, the private relations of men and women being happily beyond the reach of the statistician. The divorce rate, however, continued its steady increase; for every 100 marriages there were 8.8 divorces in 1910, 13.4 divorces in 1920, and 16.5 divorces in 1928—almost one divorce for every six marriages. There was a corresponding decline in the amount of disgrace accompanying divorce. In the urban communities men and women who had been divorced were now socially accepted without question; indeed, there was often about the divorced person just enough of an air of unconventionality, just enough of a touch of scarlet, to be considered rather dashing and desirable. Many young women probably felt as did the New York girl who said, toward the end of the decade, that she was thinking of marrying Henry, although she didn't care very much for him, because even if they didn't get along she could get a divorce and "it would be much more exciting to be a divorcée than to be an old maid."

The petting party, which in the first years of the decade had been limited to youngsters in their teens and twenties, soon made its appearance among older men and women: when the gin-flask was passed about the hotel bedroom during a dance, or the musicians stilled their saxophones during the Saturday-night party at the country club, men of affairs and women with half-grown children had their little taste of raw sex. One began to hear of young girls, intelligent and well born, who had spent week-ends with men before marriage and had told their prospective husbands everything and had been not merely forgiven, but told that there was nothing to forgive; a little "experience," these men felt, was all to the good for any girl. Millions of people were moving toward acceptance of what a *bon-vivant* of earlier days had said was his idea of the proper state of morality—"A single standard, and that a low one."

It would be easy, of course, to match every one of these cases with contrasting cases of men and women who still thought and behaved at the end of the decade exactly as the president of the Epworth League* would have wished. Two women who conducted newspaper columns of advice in affairs of the heart testified that the sort of problem which was worrying young America, to judge from their bulging correspondence, was not whether to tell the boy friend about the illegitimate child, but whether it was proper to invite the boy friend up on the porch if he hadn't yet come across with an invitation to the movies, or whether the cake at a pie social should be cut with a knife. In the hinterlands there was still plenty of old-fashioned sentimental thinking about sex, of the sort which expressed itself in the slogan of a federated women's club: "Men are God's trees, women are His flowers." There were frantic efforts to stay the tide of moral change by law, the most picturesque of these efforts being the ordinance actually passed in Norphelt, Arkansas, in 1925, which contained the following provisions:

"Section 1. Hereafter it shall be unlawful for any man and woman, male or female, to be guilty of committing the act of sexual intercourse between themselves at any place within the corporate limits of said town.

"Section 3. Section One of this ordinance shall not apply to married persons as between themselves, and their husband and wife, unless of a grossly improper and lascivious nature."

Nevertheless, there was an unmistakable and rapid trend away from the old American code toward a philosophy of sex relations and of marriage wholly new to the country: toward a feeling that the virtues of chastity and fidelity had been rated too highly, that there was something to be said

[*Methodist youth organization]

for what Mrs. Bertrand Russell defined as "the right, equally shared by men and women, to free participation in sex experience," that it was not necessary for girls to deny themselves this right before marriage or even for husbands and wives to do so after marriage. . . .

. . . The new code had been born in disillusionment, and beneath all the bravado of its exponents and the talk about entering upon a new era the disillusionment persisted. If the decade was ill-mannered, it was also unhappy. With the old order of things had gone a set of values which had given richness and meaning to life, and substitute values were not easily found. If morality was dethroned, what was to take its place? Honor, said some of the prophets of the new day: "It doesn't matter much what you do so long as you're honest about it." A brave ideal—yet it did not wholly satisfy; it was too vague, too austere, too difficult to apply. If romantic love was dethroned, what was to take its place? Sex? But as Joseph Wood Krutch explained, 'If love has come to be less often a sin, it has also come to be less often a supreme privilege." And as Walter Lippmann, in *A Preface to Morals*, added after quoting Mr. Krutch, "If you start with the belief that love is the pleasure of a moment, is it really surprising that it yields only a momentary pleasure?" The end of the pursuit of sex alone was emptiness and futility—the emptiness and futility to which Lady Brett Ashley and her friends in *The Sun Also Rises* were so tragically doomed.

There were not, to be sure, many Brett Ashleys in the United States during the Post-war Decade. Yet there were millions to whom in some degree came for a time the same disillusionment and with it the same unhappiness. They could not endure a life without values, and the only values they had been trained to understand were being undermined. Everything seemed meaningless and unimportant. Well, at least one could toss off a few drinks and get a kick out of physical passion and forget that the world was crumbling. . . . And so the saxophones wailed and the gin-flask went its rounds and the dancers made their treadmill circuit with half-closed eyes, and the outside world, so merciless and so insane, was shut away for a restless night. . . .

It takes time to build up a new code. Not until the decade was approaching its end did there appear signs that the revolutionists were once more learning to be at home in their world, to rid themselves of their obsession with sex, to adjust themselves emotionally to the change in conventions and standards, to live the freer and franker life of this new era gracefully, and to discover among the ruins of the old dispensation a new set of enduring satisfactions.

DOCUMENTS

Petting and Necking, 1924

. . . [In 1924] I was at a student conference of young women comprised of about eight hundred college girls from the middle western states. The subject of petting was very much on their minds, both as to what attitude they should take toward it with the younger girls, (being upperclassmen themselves) and also how much renunciation of this pleasurable pastime was required of them. If I recall correctly, two entire mornings were devoted to discussing the matter, two evenings, and another overflow meeting.

So far as I could judge from their discussion groups, the girls did not advise younger classmen not to pet—they merely advised them to be moderate about it, not lose their heads, not go too far—in fact the same line of conduct which is advised for moderate drinking. Learn temperance in petting, not abstinence.

Before the conference I made it my business to talk to as many college girls as possible. I consulted as many, both in groups and privately, as I had time for at the conference. And since it is all to be repeated in another state this summer, I have been doing so, when opportunity offered, ever since. Just what does petting consist in? What ages take it most seriously? Is it a factor in every party? Do "nice" girls do it, as well as those who are not so "nice"? Are they "stringing" their elders, by exaggerating the prevalence of petting, or is there more of it than they admit? These are samples of the questions I have asked, and have heard them ask each other in the discussions where I have listened in.

One fact is evident, that whether or not they pet, they hesitate to have anyone believe that they do not. It is distinctly the *mores* of the time to be considered as ardently sought after, and as not too priggish to respond. As one girl said—"I don't particularly care to be kissed by some of the fellows I know, but I'd let them do it any time rather than think I wouldn't dare. As a matter of fact, there are lots of fellows I don't kiss. It's the very young kids that never miss a chance."

That petting should lead to actual illicit relations between the petters was not advised nor countenanced among the girls with whom I discussed it. They drew the line quite sharply. That it often did so lead, they admitted, but they were not ready to allow that there were any more of such affairs than there had always been. School and college scandals, with their sudden departures and hasty marriages, have always existed to some extent, and they still do. But only accurate statistics, hard to arrive at, can prove whether or not the sex carelessness of the present day extends to an increase

SOURCE: Eleanor Wembridge, "Petting and the Campus," *Survey*, July 1, 1925, 393–95.

of sex immorality, or whether since so many more people go to college, there is an actual decrease in the amount of it, in proportion to the number of students. The girls seemed to feel that those who went too far were more fools than knaves, and that in most cases they married. They thought that hasty and secret marriages, of which most of them could report several, were foolish, but after all about as likely to turn out well as any others. Their attitude toward such contingencies was disapproval, but it was expressed with a slightly amused shrug, a shrug which one can imagine might have sat well on the shoulders of Voltaire. In fact the writer was torn, in her efforts to sum up their attitude, between classifying them as eighteenth century realists and as Greek nymphs existing before the dawn of history!

I sat with one pleasant college Amazon, a total stranger, beside a fountain in the park, while she asked if I saw any harm in her kissing a young man whom she liked, but whom she did not want to marry. "It's terribly exciting. We get such a thrill. I think it is natural to want nice men to kiss you, so why not do what is natural?" There was no embarrassment in her manner. Her eyes and her conscience were equally untroubled. I felt as if a girl from the Parthenon frieze had stepped down to ask if she might not sport in the glade with a handsome faun. Why not indeed? Only an equally direct forcing of twentieth century science on primitive simplicity could bring us even to the same level in our conversation, and at that, the stigma of impropriety seemed to fall on me, rather than on her. It was hard to tell whether her infantilism were real, or half-consciously assumed in order to have a child's license and excuse to do as she pleased. I am inclined to think that both with her and with many others, it is assumed. One girl said, "When I have had a few nights without dates I nearly go crazy. I tell my mother she must expect me to go out on a fearful necking party." In different parts of the country, *petting* and *necking* have opposite meanings. One locality calls necking (I quote their definition) "petting only from the neck up." Petting involves anything else you please. Another section reverses the distinction, and the girl in question was from the latter area. In what manner she announces to her mother her plans to neck, and in what manner her mother accepts the announcement, I cannot be sure. . . .

Moving Pictures Evoke Concern, 1922

Moving pictures, their educational influence for good or for bad, their growing importance as a factor in our civilization, the announced determination of those controlling the industry boldly to enter politics, and the desirability of regulation by law through censorship constitute a subject of acknowledged importance to the American people. . . .

The motion picture is a great invention, and it has become a powerful factor for good or bad in our civilization. It has great educational power for good or bad. It may educate young people in the ways of good citizenship or in ways of dissoluteness, extravagance, wickedness, and crime. It furnishes recreation, diversion, and amusement at a cheap price to many millions of our people—largely the young. It is the only form of amusement within the means of millions. It possesses great potential possibilities for good. It may furnish not only amusement but education of a high order.

Through motion pictures the young and the old may see depicted every good motive, laudable ambition, commendable characteristic, ennobling trait of humanity. They may be taught that honesty is the best policy; that virtue and worth are rewarded; that industry leads to success. Those who live in the country or in small interior towns, and who never visit large cities, may see pictured the skyscrapers, the crowded streets, the rush and jam of metropolitan cities. Those who live in the interior, and never see the seacoast, may see on the screen the great docks and wharves of seaports and see the loading and unloading of giant ocean steamers. Those who live in crowded cities, and never see the country or get a glimpse of country life, may have depicted to them all the beauties of rural life and scenery. All may see scenes of the luxuriant Tropics, the grandeur of Alpine Mountains, polar conditions, life in the Orient. The cities, palaces, cathedrals, ports, rural life, daily routine, scenic attractions, mode of living of every country on the globe, may be brought to our doors and eyes for a small price. The industry may be made an education to the young.

However, from all accounts, the business has been conducted, generally speaking, upon a low plane and in a decidedly sordid manner. Those who own and control the industry seem to have been of the opinion that the sensual, the sordid, the prurient, the phases of fast life, the ways of extravagance, the risqué, the paths of shady life, drew the greatest attendance and coined for them the most money, and apparently they have been out to get the coin, no matter what the effect upon the public, young or old; and when thoughtful people have suggested or advocated official censorship, in the interest of good citizenship and wholesome morals, the owners of the industry have resented it and, in effect, declared that it was

SOURCE: A speech by Senator Henry Myers, *Congressional Record,* June 29, 1922, 9655–57.

nobody's business other than theirs and concerned nobody other than them what kind of shows they produced; that if people did not like their shows they could stay away from them; that it was their business, and they would conduct it as they might please. At least they have vigorously fought all attempts at censorship and resented them. . . .

I have no doubt young criminals got their ideas of the romance of crime from moving pictures. I believe moving pictures are doing as much harm to-day as saloons did in the days of the open saloon—especially to the young. They are running day and night, Sunday and every other day, the year round, and in most jurisdictions without any regulation by censorship. I would not abolish them. They can be made a great force for good. I would close them on Sunday and regulate them week days by judicious censorship. Already some dozen or more States have censorship laws, with the right of appeal to the courts, and the movement is on in many other States.

When we look to the source of the moving pictures, the material for them, the personnel of those who pose for them, we need not wonder that many of the pictures are pernicious.

The pictures are largely furnished by such characters as Fatty Arbuckle, of unsavory fame, notorious for his scandalous debauchery and drunken orgies, one of which, attended by many "stars," resulted in the death of Virginia Rappe, a star artist; William Desmond Taylor, deceased, murdered for some mysterious cause; one Valentino, now figuring as the star character in rape and divorce sensations. Many others of like character might be mentioned.

At Hollywood, Calif., is a colony of these people, where debauchery, riotous living, drunkenness, ribaldry, dissipation, free love, seem to be conspicuous. Many of these "stars," it is reported, were formerly bartenders, butcher boys, sopers, swampers, variety actors and actresses, who may have earned $10 or $20 a week, and some of whom are now paid, it is said, salaries of something like $5,000 a month or more, and they do not know what to do with their wealth, extracted from poor people, in large part, in 25 or 50 cent admission fees, except to spend it in riotous living, dissipation, and "high rolling."

These are some of the characters from whom the young people of to-day are deriving a large part of their education, views of life, and character-forming habits. From these sources our young people gain much of their views of life, inspiration, and education. Rather a poor source is it not? Looks like there is some need for censorship, does it not? There could be some improvement, could there not? . . .

Prohibition Nonobserved, 1931

There is a mass of information before us as to a general prevalence of drinking in homes, in clubs, and in hotels; of drinking parties given and attended by persons of high standing and respectability; of drinking by tourists at winter and summer resorts; and of drinking in connection with public dinners and at conventions. In the nature of the case it is not easy to get at the exact facts in such a connection, and conditions differ somewhat in different parts of the country and even to some extent from year to year. This is true likewise with respect to drinking by women and drinking by youth, as to which also there is a great mass of evidence. In weighing this evidence much allowance must be made for the effect of new standards of independence and individual self-assertion, changed ideas as to conduct generally, and the greater emphasis on freedom and the quest for excitement since the war. As to drinking among youth, the evidence is conflicting. Votes in colleges show an attitude of hostility to or contempt for the law on the part of those who are not unlikely to be leaders in the next generation. It is safe to say that a significant change has taken place in the social attitude toward drinking. This may be seen in the views and conduct of social leaders, business and professional men in the average community. It may be seen in the tolerance of conduct at social gatherings which would not have been possible a generation ago. It is reflected in a different way of regarding drunken youth, in a change in the class of excessive drinkers, and in the increased use of distilled liquor in places and connections where formerly it was banned. It is evident that, taking the country as a whole, people of wealth, business men and professional men, and their families, and, perhaps, the higher paid workingmen and their families, are drinking in large numbers in quite frank disregard of the declared policy of the National Prohibition Act. . . .

SOURCE: U.S. Congress, House, U.S. National Commission on Law Enforcement, *Enforcement of the Prohibition Laws of the United States,* H. Doc. 722, 71st Cong., 3d sess., 1931, 21.

CHAPTER 11

The Depression Years

The crusades against changing morals and manners during the 1920s seem trivial when compared to the challenges of the Great Depression of the 1930s. Although the United States had experienced economic declines before, the Great Depression was the worst ever: nearly a quarter of the workforce was unemployed by 1933, banks failed, the stock market crashed, businesses declared bankruptcy, and families lost their homes and farms.

Caroline Bird's essay "The Discovery of Poverty" paints a vivid picture of America during Herbert Hoover's presidency in the early depression years. It describes the nature and scope of the suffering, and the attitudes and efforts of those who worked to alleviate the innumerable problems. Notice the distinctions made during the 1930s between the so-called deserving and undeserving poor and between public relief and charity. Are such distinctions made in our own time, or have the experiences of the depression modified our views about the causes of poverty and the need for public assistance? Bird points out that the Hoover administration's role in dealing with the depression amounted to little more than issuing messages of encouragement. Prior to 1933, the burden of meeting the crisis rested almost exclusively on the shoulders of local government relief agencies and voluntary charitable organizations, which lacked adequate resources to cope with the widespread need.

When relief funds ran out, families survived as best as they could. The first document consists of excerpts from the testimony of Jacob Billikoph, executive director of the Federation of Jewish Charities in Philadelphia, before a Senate sub-committee studying the issue. What light does the document shed on the reasons that millions of Americans responded so positively to Franklin Roosevelt's message of hope, and to the New Deal's programs of relief and public employment?

In addition to enduring the economic woes of the depression, America's farmers faced natural calamities. Beginning in 1934 a great drought ravaged crops and brought dust storms to a dozen states of the Midwest and Southwest. In the second document, Iowa author James Hearst recalls what happened when the dust over-spread his family's farm. Today we recognize that the great dust storms of the thirties were not entirely the fault of nature; human neglect of the environment played a role. What steps have been taken in recent decades to protect against a repetition of such disasters?

Despite their suffering, the Hearst family was able to hold on to its land; thousands of farmers fared far worse. Many landowning farmers did not possess sufficient acreage on which to support themselves. And almost half of all American farmers, sharecroppers trapped in the grip of a brutal poverty, did not own their land. Some left for the cities, while others survived on earnings that scarcely provided an adequate standard of living. Perhaps no other group caught the public eye so much as the Okies—farmers from Texas, Oklahoma, and elsewhere on the southern plains who migrated to California, driven from their homes by poverty and great clouds of dust. John Steinbeck's novel The Grapes of Wrath *brought the plight of these Dust Bowl refugees to the attention of the public, and so did the writings of political activist Carey McWilliams. The final document, a statement by McWilliams before a congressional committee, describes the conditions the Okies in California experienced. That the Okies continued to flock to and remain in California is evidence of the desperate situation from which they fled. Why did they choose California as the place to rebuild their lives?*

The New Deal programs, particularly those directed toward relief and reform, helped businesses, farmers, and workers survive the worst ravages of the 1930s, but economic woes persisted until the economic boom of World War II finally brought an end to the Great Depression.

ESSAY

The Discovery of Poverty
Caroline Bird

You could feel the Depression deepen, but you could not look out of the window and see it. Men who lost their jobs dropped out of sight. They were quiet, and you had to know just when and where to find them: at night, for instance, on the edge of town huddling for warmth around a bonfire, or even the municipal incinerator; at dawn, picking over the garbage dump for scraps of food or salvageable clothing.

In Oakland, California, they lived in sewer pipes the manufacturer could not sell. In Connellsville, Pennsylvania, unemployed steelworkers kept warm in the big ovens they had formerly coked. Outside Washington, D.C., one Bonus Marcher* slept in a barrel filled with grass, another in a piano box, a third in a coffin set on trestles. Every big city had a "Hooverville"** camp of dispossessed men living like this.

It took a knowing eye—or the eye of poverty itself—to understand or even to observe some of the action. When oranges fell off a truck, it wasn't always an accident; sometimes they were the truck driver's contribution to slum kids. A woman burning newspapers in a vacant lot might be trying to warm a baby's bottle. The ragged men standing silent as cattle, in a flatrack truck parked on a lonely public road, might be getting the bum's rush out of town. In the Southwest, freight trains were black with human bodies headed for warm weather. Railroad dicks [detectives] shooed them off at stations. Deming, New Mexico, hired a special constable to keep them out of town. When the Southern Pacific [Railroad] police ordered the men off the train, the special constable ordered them back on again.

Everyone knew of someone engaged in a desperate struggle, although most of the agony went on behind closed doors. The stories were whispered. There was something indecent about them. A well-to-do man living on the income from rental property could not collect his rents. His mortgages were foreclosed, and his houses sold for less than the debt. To make up the difference, he sold his own home. He moved himself and his

---

SOURCE: Caroline Bird, *The Invisible Scar*, Copyright © 1966 by Longman, Inc. Reprinted by permission.

*In June 1930, 20,000 World War I veterans marched on Washington demanding immediate payment of a service bonus that Congress had promised would be due them in 1945.

[**so called because people blamed the Hoover administration for failing to effectively combat the economic conditions that produced them]

wife into a nearby basement and did odd jobs for the people upstairs in exchange for a room for some of his six children. He mowed lawns, graded yards, and did whatever common labor he could find in order to pay for groceries, until his health broke down under the unaccustomed work. The doctor told him that he needed an operation and would have to rest for a year afterward.

A 72-year-old factory worker was told that he could no longer be employed because he was too old. He went home and turned on the gas. His 56-year-old widow, who had worked as a proofreader before developing heart trouble, sat alone staring at their few sticks of furniture for three days after her husband's death. Then she too turned on the gas. The neighbors smelled it in time and saved her life.

Neither the property owner nor the widow was an uncommon case. . . . These people were in trouble . . . because they were physically sick and had no money. By the charitable standards of the rich at that time, they were regarded as the "deserving poor," as distinguished from the undeserving poor, who were thought to be unwilling to work or to save.

If the "deserving poor" had been few, charitable help might have sufficed. But there were too many, and more all the time. In December 1929, three million people were out of work. The next winter, four to five million. The winter of 1931–1932, eight million. The following year, no one knew exactly how many, but all authorities agreed that additional millions were unemployed. . . . In the fall of 1932, *Fortune* thought that 34 million men, women, and children—better than a fourth of the nation—were members of families that had no regular full-time breadwinner. Estimates differed, but none included farmers unable to make both ends meet, in spite of the blessing of seven-day, sunup-to-sundown employment, or factory hands who were making out on two or three days' work a week.

There were too many in want to hide. There were too many in want to blame. And even if the poor were shiftless, a Christian country would not let them starve. "Everyone is getting along somehow," people said to each other. "After all, no one has starved." But they worried even as they spoke.

A few were ashamed to eat. The Elks in Mt. Kisco, New York, and Princeton University eating clubs were among the organizations that sent leftovers from their tables to the unemployed. A reporter on *The Brooklyn Eagle* suggested a central warehouse where families could send their leftovers for distribution to the needy. John B. Nichlos, of the Oklahoma Gas Utilities Company, worked out a leftover system in detail and urged it on Hoover's Cabinet. It provided:

> "Sanitary containers of five (5) gallons each should be secured in a large number so that four (4) will always be left in large kitchens where the restaurants are serving a volume business. The

containers should be labeled 'MEATS, BEANS, POTATOES, BREAD AND OTHER ITEMS.' Someone from the Salvation Army with a truck should pick up the loaded containers every morning and leave empty ones. The civic clubs, restaurants, the proprietors and the workers should be asked to cooperate in order to take care of all surplus food in as sanitary a way as possible. In other words, when a man finishes his meal he should not (after lighting his cigarette or cigar) leave the ashes on the food which he was unable to consume.''

Many more fortunate people turned away from the unemployed, but some tried to help in the traditional neighborly way. A Brooklyn convent put sandwiches outside its door where the needy could get them without knocking. St. Louis society women distributed unsold food from restaurants. Someone put baskets in New York City railroad stations so that commuters could donate vegetables from their gardens. In New York, Bernarr Macfadden served six-cent lunches to the unemployed and claimed he was making money. In San Francisco, the hotel and restaurant workers' union arranged for unemployed chefs and waiters to serve elegant if simple meals to the unemployed.

But there was more talk than help. A great many people spent a great deal of energy urging each other to give, to share, to hire. President Hoover led a national publicity campaign to urge people to give locally and to make jobs. At the suggestion of public-relations counsel Edward L. Bernays, the first President's Emergency Committee was named "for Employment" (PECE) to accentuate the positive. In 1931 it was reorganized more realistically as the President's Organization for Unemployment Relief (POUR). Both undertook to inspire confidence by the issuing of optimistic statements; POUR chairman Walter Gifford told a Senate committee offhandedly that he did not know how many were unemployed and did not think it was the committee's job to find out.

Local groups responded by pressing campaigns of their own to "Give-A-Job" or "Share-A-Meal" until people grew deaf to them. Carl Byoir, founder of one of the country's biggest public-relations firms, declared a "War against Depression" that proposed to wipe it out in six months by getting one million employers to make one new job each.

Results of such appeals were disappointing. Corporation executives answered the pleas of PECE and POUR by saying that they had no right to spend stockholders' money hiring men they did not need. Even in New York City, where the able and well-supported Community Service Society pioneered work relief, there were enough hungry men without money to keep 82 badly managed breadlines going, and men were selling apples on every street corner. Newspapers discovered and photographed an apple seller who was formerly a near-millionaire.

The well of private charity ran dry. A Westchester woman is said to have fired all her servants in order to have money to contribute to the unemployed. "Voluntary conscription" of wages helped steelworkers weather the first round of layoffs in little Conshohocken, Pennsylvania, but the plan broke down as there were more mouths to feed and fewer pay envelopes to conscript. Local charities everywhere were overwhelmed by 1931, and the worst was yet to come.

Kentucky coal miners suffered perhaps the most. In Harlan County there were whole towns whose people had not a cent of income. They lived on dandelions and blackberries. The women washed clothes in soap-weed suds. Dysentery bloated the stomachs of starving babies. Children were reported so famished they were chewing up their own hands. Miners tried to plant vegetables, but they were often so hungry that they ate them before they were ripe. On her first trip to the mountains, Eleanor Roosevelt saw a little boy trying to hide his pet rabbit. "He thinks we are not going to eat it," his sister told her, "but we are." In West Virginia, miners mobbed company stores demanding food. Mountain people, with no means to leave their homes, sometimes had to burn their last chairs and tables to keep warm. Local charity could not help in a place where everyone was destitute.

No national charity existed to relieve mass poverty. The American Red Cross was big and efficient, but it had been set up to mobilize outside help for "a temporary condition brought about by some uncontrollable act or acts." Chairman John Barton Payne contended that unemployment was not an "Act of God." If not controllable by the unemployed themselves, and he believed it was, it was the result of some Act of Man and so out of bounds for the Red Cross. Payne did not even want to distribute $25 million of Federal money for drought relief because drought was a natural disaster and so belonged to the Red Cross. Government help would ruin his fund drive. "Why should the Government be dealing in this sort of thing when the people have plenty of money?" But the police could not keep hungry people out of the Red Cross warehouse in Hazard, Kentucky.

A Quaker himself, Hoover went to the American Friends Service Committee. The Philadelphia Meeting developed a "concern" for the miners. Swarthmore and Haverford students ventured into the hollows, winning the confidence of suspicious miners. They systematically weighed the children, so they could feed those in greatest need first. Hoover gave them $2,500 out of his own pocket, but most of the contributions seem to have come from the Rockefellers.

"No one has starved," Hoover boasted. To prove it, he announced a decline in the death rate. It was heartening, but puzzling, too. Even the social workers could not see how the unemployed kept body and soul together, and the more they studied, the more the wonder grew. Savings, if any, went first. Then insurance was cashed. Then people borrowed from family and friends. They stopped paying rent. When evicted, they moved in with relatives. They ran up bills. It was surprising how much credit could be wangled. In 1932, about 400 families on relief in Philadelphia had managed to contract an average debt of $160, a tribute to the hearts if not the business heads of landlords and merchants. But in the end they had to eat "tight."

Every serious dieter knows how little food it takes to keep alive. One woman borrowed 50¢, bought stale bread at 3½¢ a loaf, and kept her family alive on it for 11 days. Every serious dieter knows how hunger induces total concentration on food. When eating tight, the poor thought of nothing but food, just food. They hunted food like alley cats, and in some of the same places. They haunted docks where spoiled vegetables might be thrown out and brought them home to cook up in a stew from which every member of the family would eat as little as possible, and only when very hungry. Neighbors would ask a child in for a meal or give him scraps—stale bread, bones with a bit of good meat still on them, raw potato peelings. Children would hang around grocery stores, begging a little food, running errands, or watching carts in exchange for a piece of fruit. Sometimes a member of the family would go to another part of town and beg. Anyone on the block who got hold of something big might call the neighbors in to share it. Then everyone would gorge like savages at a killing, to make up for the lean days. Enough people discovered that a five-cent candy bar can make a lunch to boom sales during the generally slow year of 1931. You get used to hunger. After the first few days it doesn't even hurt; you just get weak. When work opened up, at one point, in the Pittsburgh steel mills, men who were called back were not strong enough to do it.

Those who were still prosperous hated to think of such things and frequently succeeded in avoiding them. But professional people could not always escape. A doctor would order medicine for a charity case and then realize that there was no money to pay for it. A school doctor in Philadelphia gave a listless child a tonic to stimulate her appetite and later found that her family did not have enough to eat at home.

A reporter on *The Detroit Free Press* helped the police bring a missing boy back to a bare home on Christmas Day, 1934. He and his friends on the paper got a drugstore to open up so they could bring the boy some toys. *The Detroit Free Press* has supplied Christmas gifts for needy children every year since.

A teacher in a mountain school told a little girl who looked sick but said she was hungry to go home and eat something. "I can't," the youngster said. "It's my sister's turn to eat." In Chicago, teachers were ordered to ask what a child had had to eat before punishing him. Many of them were getting nothing but potatoes, a diet that kept their weight up, but left them listless, crotchety, and sleepy.

The police saw more than anyone else. They had to cope with the homeless men sleeping in doorways or breaking into empty buildings.

They had to find help for people who fell sick in the streets or tried to commit suicide. And it was to a cop that city people went when they were at the end of their rope and did not know what else to do. In New York City, the police kept a list of the charities to which they could direct the helpless. In 1930 they took a census of needy families, and city employees started contributing one percent of their salaries to a fund for the police to use to buy food for people they found actually starving. It was the first public confession of official responsibility for plain poverty, and it came not from the top, but from the lowest-paid civil servants, who worked down where the poor people were.

Teachers worried about the children who came to school to get warm. They organized help for youngsters who needed food and clothing before they could learn. Sometimes Boards of Education diverted school funds to feed them. Often the teachers did it on their own. In 1932, New York City schoolteachers contributed $260,000 out of their salaries in one month. Chicago teachers fed 11,000 pupils out of their own pockets in 1931, although they had not themselves been paid for months. "For God's sake, help us feed these children during the summer," Chicago's superintendent of schools begged the governor in June.

Mayors discovered the poor. Mayor Harry A. Mackey of Philadelphia used to disguise himself as a hobo to check up on the city shelters for unemployed men. Detroit's Frank Murphy invited the unemployed into his office and insisted on allowing them to demonstrate. In the fall of 1931 there were 600,000 single men with no work in Chicago. The city was bankrupt. Only state funds could keep the breadlines going. "Call out the troops before you close the relief stations," Mayor Anton Cermak told the Illinois state legislature.

Official recognition of need, and even Hoover's appeals to private local charity, raised questions of principle in the minds of those in a position to think of poverty and unemployment in the abstract. "You make a bad mistake in talking about the unemployed," a businessman told the mayor of Youngstown when he tried to raise a bond issue to finance city relief. "*Don't* emphasize hard times, and everything will be all right." Businessmen feared that the talk was bad for business. They did not like to think of hard times. Without firsthand experience, it was easy to stick to the traditional view that it was a man's own fault if he was poor, that a man ought to take care of his own family and lay aside something for a rainy day. The suspicion persisted that most of the poor were not really "deserving" of charity, that they were better off now than they had ever been.

Men of old-fashioned principles really believed that the less said about the unemployed, the faster they would get jobs. They really believed that public relief was bad for the poor because it discouraged them from looking for work or from taking it at wages that would tempt business to start up again. According to their theory, permanent mass unemployment was impossible, because there was work at some wage for every able-bodied man, if he would only find and do it. Charity was necessary, of course, for those who were really disabled through no fault of their own, but there could never be very many of these, and they should be screened carefully and given help of a kind and in a way that would keep them from asking for it as long as possible. Those who held this view were not necessarily hardhearted or self-interested. Josephine Lowell, a woman who devoted her life to the poor, issued the bluntest warning: "The presence in the community of certain persons living on public relief has the tendency to tempt others to sink to their degraded level." That was in 1884, when cities were smaller, and fewer people depended on the ups and downs of factory work. . . .

. . . Respectable folk worried about the idea of public relief, even though accepting the need for it. On opinion polls they agreed with the general proposition that public relief should be temporary, hard to get, and less than the lowest wage offered by any employer. In the North as well as in the South, relief stations were closed at harvesttime to force the unemployed to work at getting in the crops, for whatever wages farmers offered.

It was a scandal when a relief client drove an old jalopy up to the commissary to lug his groceries home. In some places, a client had to surrender his license plates in order to get relief, even if the old car meant a chance to earn small sums to pay for necessities not covered by relief. Phones went, too, even when they were a relief client's only lifeline to odd jobs. It was considered an outrage if a woman on relief had a smart-looking winter coat, or a ring, or a burial-insurance policy, or a piano. She was made to sell them for groceries before relief would help her. The search for hidden assets was thorough. One thrifty family in New York was denied relief "because it does not seem possible for this family to have managed without some other kind of assistance."

When a woman on relief had triplets, newspapers pointed out that for every 100 children born to self-supporting parents, relief parents produced 160. It was hard even for the social workers to see that big families were more apt to need relief. Almost everybody thought relief caused the poor to become irresponsible and to have children they could not support—if, in fact, they did not have babies deliberately in order to qualify. . . . During the Depression, if some way could have been found to prevent married couples on relief from indulging in sexual intercourse, there would have been those who would have demanded it.

People who took public relief were denied civil rights. Some state constitutions disqualified relief clients from voting, and as late as 1938 an opinion poll showed that one out of every three Republicans thought this was right. In some places, village taxpayers' organizations tried to keep the children of tax delinquents out of the local schools. People suspected of taking public relief were even turned away from churches.

During the first and worst years of the Depression, the only public relief was improvised by cities. Appropriations were deliberately low. If funds ran out every few months, so much the better. The poor would have to make another effort to find work. Every program was "temporary." In most cases, this was sheer necessity. Cities could not afford otherwise. Their tax bases were too narrow. Some of them had lost tax money when banks folded. Detroit could not collect property taxes because landlords could not collect the rent from their unemployed tenants. Bankrupt Chicago was living on tax anticipation warrants doled out by bankers. Some well-heeled citizens refused to pay their taxes at all. Cities cut their own employees, stopped buying library books, and shot zoo animals to divert money to relief.

State governments were not prepared to help. No state even had a Department of Welfare until Governor Franklin D. Roosevelt organized one for New York State in 1929. Cities begged for temporary loans. Bankers were generally reluctant, because cities did not have tax resources from which to pay back the money. The bankers made conditions. Everything was done on an emergency basis. In January 1932, the New York City Department of Welfare did not have postage stamps on hand to distribute a million dollars raised and lent to the city by a committee of bankers.

Cities had to ration relief. In 1932, family allowances in New York City fell to $2.39 a week, and only half of the families who could qualify were getting it. Things were worse elsewhere. In little Hamtramck, Michigan, welfare officials had to cut off all families with fewer than three children. In Detroit, allowances fell to 15¢ a day per person before running out entirely. Across the country, only about a fourth of the unemployed were able to get help, and fewer than that in many cities. Almost everywhere, aid was confined to food and fuel. Relief workers connived with clients to put off landlords. Medical care, clothing, shoes, chairs, beds, safety pins— everything else had to be scrounged or bought by doing without food. Those on relief were little better off than those who couldn't get it. Private help dwindled to six percent of the money spent on the unemployed.

Still, Hoover kept insisting, no one starved. In May 1932, Hoover's Secretary of the Interior, Dr. Ray Lyman Wilbur, reassured the National Conference of Social Workers meeting in Philadelphia. "We must set up the neglect of prosperity against the care of adversity," he philosophized. "With prosperity many parents unload the responsibilities for their children onto others. With adversity the home takes its normal place. The interest of thousands of keen and well-trained people throughout the whole country in seeing that our children are properly fed and cared for has given many of them better and more suitable food than in past good times."

Social workers were indignant. "Have you ever seen the uncontrolled trembling of parents who have starved themselves for weeks so that their children might not go hungry?" social worker Lillian Wald demanded. Others told how fathers and even older brothers and sisters hung around the street corners while the younger children were being fed, for fear they would be tempted to eat more than their share. The social workers knew the facts. They also knew newspaper reporters. In 1932, the public began to listen.

"Mrs. Green left her five small children alone one morning while she went to have her grocery order filled," one social worker reported. "While she was away the constable arrived and padlocked her house with the children inside. When she came back she heard the six-weeks-old baby crying. She did not dare touch the padlock for fear of being arrested, but she found a window open and climbed in and nursed the baby and then climbed out and appealed to the police to let her children out."

Eviction was so common that children in a Philadelphia day-care center made a game of it. They would pile all the doll furniture up first in one corner and then in another. "We ain't got no money for the rent, so we's moved into a new house," a tot explained to the teacher. "Then we got the constable on us, so we's movin' again." Philadelphia relief paid an evicted family's rent for one month in the new house. Then they were on their own. Public opinion favored the tenant. An eviction could bring on a neighborhood riot.

Landlords often let the rent go. Some of them needed relief as much as their tenants, and had a harder time qualifying for it. In Philadelphia a little girl whose father was on relief could not get milk at school, under a program for needy children, because her father "owned property." Investigators found some unemployed tenants sharing food orders with their landlords. In the country, where poor farmers had been accustomed to paying their taxes in work on the roads, tenants who could not pay their rent sometimes did the landlord's road work for him.

It was not true that "no one starved." People starved to death, and not only in Harlan County, Kentucky. The New York City Welfare Council counted 29 deaths from starvation in 1933. More than fifty other people were treated for starvation in hospitals. An additional 110, most of them children, died of malnutrition.

A father who had been turned away by a New York City welfare agency was afraid to apply for help after public relief had been set up. Social workers found one of his children dead; another, too weak to move, lay in bed with the mother; the rest huddled, shivering and hungry, around the desperate father.

A New York dentist and his wife died rather than accept charity. They left a note, and then took gas together. "The entire blame for this tragedy rests with the City of New York or whoever it is that allows free dental work in the hospital," the note read. "We want to get out of the way before we are forced to accept relief money. The City of New York is not to touch our bodies. We have a horror of charity burial. We have put the last of our money in the hands of a friend who will turn it over to my brother."

Health surveys were made to pound home the fact that poor people are sicker than the well-to-do. Doctors, nurses, teachers, and social workers warned that privation was ruining the nation's health. In 1933, the Children's Bureau reported that one in five American children was not getting enough of the right things to eat. Lower vitality, greater susceptibility to infections, slower recovery, stunting, more organic disease, a reversal of gains against tuberculosis—all were freely predicted. Medical care for the poor was sketchy. Doctors were hard hit financially, and they did not always live up to the Oath of Hippocrates. Frequently, the poor were afraid to call a doctor because they did not have money. New York City surgeons sometimes demanded cash in advance or delayed operations until the family could get money together.

Middle-class people put off the doctor and the dentist. "Illness frightens us," [novelist] John Dos Passos writes of his Depression days at Pacific Grove, California. "You have to have money to be sick—or did then. Any dentistry also was out of the question, with the result that my teeth went badly to pieces. Without dough you couldn't have a tooth filled." Hospitals could never fill the private rooms that helped to pay for their charity cases, with the result that they had fewer patients than they do now, but sicker ones. They learned to be tough in admitting people who could not pay.

The harder the middle class looked, the more critical poverty seemed. It did not seem possible that people could stand lack of regular food, unstable homes, medical neglect. The Depression would leave its mark in the future. "If we put the children in these families under a period of malnutrition such as they are going through today, what sort of people are we going to have twenty years from now?" Karl de Schweinitz of the Philadelphia Community Council asked a Senate committee in 1932. "What will we say at that time about them?"

Senator Robert M. La Follette pursued the point in the same hearing. "What do you think would happen to your standard of living and the health conditions of your dependents if you were forced to exist on $5.50 a week?" he asked Walter Gifford, president of American Telephone and Telegraph Company and chairman of POUR. Walter Gifford conceded they would be bad. Senator La Follette cited some of the evidence of overcrowding. "Do you think this is an adequate meeting of the problem of relief?" La Follette pressed.

"In prosperous times I regret to say, unfortunately, you find conditions like that," Gifford stammered. "Whether we can, as much as we might like to, under these conditions, and in these times, remedy conditions which we could not remedy in more prosperous times, I doubt."

He was right. The Depression did not depress the conditions of the poor. It merely publicized them. The poor had been poor all along. It was just that nobody had looked at them. The children of Depression grew up to be bigger and healthier than their parents, who had enjoyed the advantages of a prosperous childhood. World War II recruits were more fit in every way than doughboys drafted in World War I. The death rate did not rise in the Depression. It kept going down. The health record of the Depression parallels that of rapidly industrializing societies everywhere: infectious diseases dropped, but mental illness, suicide, and the degenerative diseases of an aging population rose. . . .

The poor survived because they knew how to be poor. The Milbank Foundation found more sickness among the poor than among the well off, but they also found that the newly poor were sicker more often than those who always had been poor. . . .

A family eating tight would stay in bed a lot. That way they would save fuel, as well as the extra food calories needed in cold weather. The experienced poor, particularly the Negroes, knew about eating the parts of the animal normally rejected. And the poor generally did not spend as much money on food as their middle-class advisers thought they should be spending.

The poor worked at keeping warm. A family with no money for the gas company would economize by cooking once a week. When it was cut off, they would cook in the furnace. They gathered scrap wood to keep the furnace going. They saved by heating only the kitchen. When fuel was low, the experienced poor would sneak into a movie house. Even if they had to spend ten cents to get in, they could sometimes keep out of the cold for two double features. When the electricity was turned off, some men found ways to steal current by tapping a neighbor's wire.

Shoes were a problem. The poor took them off when they got home, to save them. Do-it-yourself shoe-repair kits were popular with the middle class, but if you could not afford the dime-store item you could resole a pair of shoes with rubber cut from an old tire, or wear rubbers over a worn-out sole. Clothes were swapped among the family. One mother and daughter managed to get together an outfit both could wear. They took turns going to church. . . .

A year after his defeat by Roosevelt, Hoover—who had repeated so many times that no one was starving—went on a fishing trip with cartoonist "Ding" Darling in the Rocky Mountains. One morning a local man came into their camp, found Hoover awake, and led him to a shack where one child lay dead and seven others were in the last stages of starvation. Hoover took the children to a hospital, made a few phone calls, and raised a fund of $3,030 for them.

Before the Crash, it was easy for the middle classes to forget about the poor, because soon everyone was going to be rich. Some of the poor themselves were carried along on the tide of illusion. When they thought about their poverty, they thought they were exceptions, or victims of bad luck, or that it was true they did not deserve any better. Unemployment was high in the good years. Farmers, seamen, textile workers, coal miners had hard going all through the prosperous Twenties, but many believed that soon all this would change.

Before the Crash, nobody suspected how many Americans were poor. Senator Paul Douglas, then a social worker, figured that it took almost $2,500 a year to support a family of four on what he called "the American standard of living." In 1929, more than two-thirds of the people were living on that amount or less. After the Crash, manufacturers and farmers talked about overproduction, but they did not have the capacity to produce an "American standard of living" for everybody. Those who were black, or didn't speak English, were not even expected to live "like white folks."

The Depression gave the middle classes a double vision of the poor. They did not give up the notions that the poor should have saved or that they did not want to work, or that their poverty was their own fault. These were concepts hard to change. While firmly holding to these ideas, however, they saw contradictory facts before their eyes. When the Depression forced them to scrutinize the condition of the working people, they could see that wages were too low and employment too intermittent for most wageworkers to save enough money to see them through emergencies, or old age, even if banks had not failed. A favorite cartoon of the times pictured a squirrel asking an old man sitting on a park bench why he had not saved for a rainy day.

I did," said the old man.

DOCUMENTS

The Great Depression in Philadelphia, 1933

Relief stopped in Philadelphia on June 25 [1932]. For months previously 52,000 destitute families had been receiving modest grocery orders and a little milk.

The average allowance to a family at that time was about $4.35 per week, no provision being made for fuel, clothing, rent or any of the minimum accessories that go to make up the family budget.

SOURCE: Jacob Billikopf, testimony from U.S. Congress, Senate Subcommittee of the Committee on Manufacturers, Hearings, *Federal Aid for Unemployment Relief,* 72d Cong., 2d sess., 1933, 8–11.

Their rent was unpaid, their credit and their borrowing power exhausted. Most of them were absolutely dependent for existence on the food orders supplied through State funds administered by the Committee for Unemployment Relief. Then there were no more funds, and relief—except for a little milk for half-sick children, and a little Red Cross flour—was suddenly discontinued. And Philadelphia asked itself what was happening to these 52,000 families. There were no reports of people starving in the streets, and yet from what possible source were 52,000 families getting enough food to live on?

It was a fair question and the Community Council under the direction of Mr. Ewan Clague, a competent economist and in charge of its Research Bureau, set out to find the answer by a special study of 400 families who had been without relief for a period varying from 10 to 25 days. The families were not picked out as the worst cases, but as stated before were fairly typical of the 52,000.

According to Mr. Clague, and I am quoting him quite liberally, the count of the 400 families showed a total of 2,464 persons. The great majority ranged from five to eight persons per family.

In their effort to discover how these 2,464 human beings were keeping themselves alive the investigators inquired into the customary sources of family maintenance, earnings, savings, regular help from relatives, credit and, last but not least, the neighbors.

Some current income in the form of wages was reported by 128 families, though the amounts were generally small and irregular, two or three dollars a week perhaps, earned on odd jobs, by selling knickknacks on the street or by youngsters delivering papers or working nights. For the whole 128 the average wage income was $4.16 a week and 272 families of the 400 had no earnings whatsoever.

Savings were an even more slender resource. Only 54 families reported savings and most of these were nothing more than small industrial insurance policies with little or no cash surrender value, technically an asset, actually an item of expense. This does not mean that these families had not had savings—take for instance, the Baker family—father, mother, and four children. They had had $1,000 in a building and loan association which failed. They had had more than $2,000 in a savings bank, but the last cent had been withdrawn in January, 1931. They had had three insurance policies, which had been surrendered one by one. Both the father and the oldest son were tubercular, the former at the moment being an applicant for sanitarium care. This family—intelligent, clean, thrifty, and likable—one of thousands at the end of their rope—had had savings as a resource even a year ago, but not now.

The same situation, it was found, prevailed in regard to regular help from relatives. In the early stages of the depression a large proportion of relief families could count on this help in some form. But of our 400 families only 33 reported assistance from kinsfolk that could be counted on, and this assistance was slender indeed: A brother paid the rent to save eviction, a brother-in-law guaranteed the gas and electric bills, a grandmother, working as a scrubwoman, put in a small sum each week. Most of the relatives it was found were so hard pressed that it was all they could do to save themselves. As a matter of fact many relatives had moved in with the families and were recorded as members of the household.

In the absence of assets or income the next line of defense is credit. But most of the 400 families were bogged down in debt and retained only a vestige of credit. Take the item of rent or building and loan payments: Three hundred and forty-nine of the families were behind—some only a month or two, some for a year, a few for two or three years, with six months as the average for the group. . . .

Thus, then, the picture of the 400 families shaped itself. Generally no income, such as there was slight, irregular and undependable; shelter still available so long as landlords remained lenient; savings gone, credit exhausted.

But what of food, the never ending, ever pressing necessity for food? In this emergency the outstanding contribution has been made by neighbors. The poor are looking after the poor. In considerably more than a third of the 400 families the chief source of actual subsistence when grocery orders stopped was the neighbors. The supply was by no means regular or adequate but in the last analysis, when all other resources failed the neighbors rallied to tide the family over a few days. Usually it was leftovers, stale bread, meat bones for soup, a bowl of gravy. Sometimes the children are asked in for a meal. One neighbor sent two eggs a day regularly to a sick man threatened with tuberculosis. This help was the more striking since the neighbors themselves were often close to the line of destitution and could illy spare the food they shared. The primitive communism existing among these people was a constant surprise to the visitors. More than once a family lucky enough to get a good supply of food called in the entire block to share the feast. There is absolutely no doubt that entire neighborhoods were just living from day to day sharing what slight resources any one family chanced to have. Without this mutual help the situation of many of the families would have been desperate.

As a result of all these efforts, what did these families have? What meals did they get and of what did these meals consist? About 8 per cent of the total number were subsisting on one meal a day. Many more were getting only two meals a day, and still others were irregular, sometimes one meal, sometimes two, occasionally by great good fortune, three. Thirty-seven per cent of all families were not getting the normal three meals a day.

When the content of these meals is taken into consideration the facts are still more alarming. Four families had absolutely no solid food whatever—nothing but a drink, usually tea or coffee. Seventy-three others had only one food and one drink for all meals, the food in many cases being bread made from Red Cross flour. Even in the remaining cases, where there were two or three articles of food, the diets day after day and week after week consisted usually of bread, macaroni, spaghetti, potatoes, with milk for the children. Many families were getting no meat and very few vegetables. Fresh fruits were never mentioned, although it is possible that the family might pick these up in the streets occasionally.

These diets were exceedingly harmful in their immediate effects on some of the families where health problems are present. In a number of cases the children are definitely reported on a hospital diagnosis as anemic. Occasionally the adults are likewise affected. The MacIntyre family for instance: These two older people have an adopted child 8 years of age. The husband is a bricklayer by trade and the wife can do outside house-work. They have had occasional odd jobs over the past year but have been very hard pressed. For the three meals immediately preceding the visit they reported the menus as follows: Dinner, previous day, bread and coffee; breakfast, bread and coffee; lunch, corn, fish, bread, and coffee; one quart of milk for the little girl for the entire three meals.

Also their health problems were serious. The wife has had several operations, the husband is a possible tuberculosis case, and the child is underweight. All three have also been receiving medical attention from a hospital for the past three years. The little girl has been nervous, has fainted at times, and is slightly deformed from rickets. Being undernourished, she needs cod-liver oil, milk, oranges, and the food which was possible only when the family was on relief. She went to camp for two weeks and returned up to weight and in good spirits. But relief was cut off while she was away, and she came back to meals of milk, coffee, and bread. In the short time at home she had become fretful and listless, refusing to take anything but milk. This whole family promised to be in serious health difficulties if their situation were long continued.

A Memory of Drought and Depression, 1934

The worst of it began for us in 1934. I remember how the dust settled so thickly on the pastures that the cattle would not eat and cows, and calves, and steers wandered about bawling their hunger. We found it hard to believe. We all knew about dust storms in the dry plains of the Southwest,

SOURCE: James Hearst, "We All Worked Together: A Memory of Drought and Depression," *Palimpsest* 59 (May–June 1978): 67–70.

but for drought and wind and dust to sweep, like a plague, over the fertile fields of Black Hawk County, Iowa seemed a bad dream, not real. But it was real, all right.

We endured it for three years. I think it was the dust that gave Mother the shivers. She stuck paper strips along the window sills, rolled rugs against the doors, but still it sifted in, dry and fine as talcum powder but gritty to taste and touch. The dust left a film on dishes in the cupboard, on sheets folded in drawers, on woodwork and chairs, on people's faces and hair. Outside if the wind blew, visibility would be cut to a few yards. Autos ran at mid-day with their headlights turned on. Drifts of dust piled against fences like snow, sometimes two and three feet high. Years later after the ground had been plowed and planted many times, the stain could still be seen where the drifts had been.

Spring came with no rain. That was the first sign. The winter snow melted and ran off during a sudden thaw in March. The water could not soak into frozen ground and it ran off down gullies and creeks. Even then, on the bare and frozen ground, the wind chiselled furrows and filled the air with dust. In April and May the ground baked in summer temperatures. Farmers stirred the ground as little as possible, and the damp patches dried almost before they turned up. But we sowed the oats, harrowed in the clover, and planted corn when the time came. This is what farmers do.

An old farmer once said, the time to plant corn is at corn-planting time. Crops are planted in their season. This wisdom lies deep in the farmer's blood. When spring comes he rises early, looks at the sky, tests for wind and temperature and impregnates the earth with seed. He is his own almanac.

In the spring of 1934 we came in at the end of the day exhausted from the heat and flying dirt, and feeling there was no sense in what we were doing. In some places in the field where the dust devils came whirling, seeds were pulled right out of the ground. In other places the seeds lay dormant in dry earth. It takes moisture for any roots to grow, but my brother Charles did not dare set the corn planter deep enough to reach damp earth because the seeds would smother. So we hoped for rain and plowed and disced and harrowed and planted just like our neighbors without knowing what else to do.

Late in May a few showers fell and some of the kernels sprouted. But in July, when the corn needs an inch of rain every week, even the clouds burned off. The sun fired the stalks that had grown and left them waving dead white tassels with no live pollen. The ears turned out to be stubby cobs with a few kernels on them. That fall, we chopped one hundred and twenty acres of corn to fill the silo, when eight acres should have done it.

The Okies in California, 1939

The most characteristic of all housing in California in which migrants reside at the moment is the shacktown or cheap subdivision. Most of these settlements have come into existence since 1933 and the pattern which obtains is somewhat similar throughout the State. Finding it impossible to rent housing in incorporated communities on their meager incomes, migrants have created a market for a very cheap type of subdivision of which the following may be taken as being representative:

In Monterey County, according to a report of Dr. D. M. Bissell, county health officer, under date of November 28, 1939, there are approximately three well-established migrant settlements. One of these, the development around the environs of Salinas, is perhaps the oldest migrant settlement of its type in California. In connection with this development I quote a paragraph of the report of Dr. Bissell:

"This area is composed of all manners and forms of housing without a public sewer system. Roughly, 10,000 persons are renting or have established homes there. A chief element in this area is that of refugees from the Dust Bowl who inhabit a part of Alisal called Little Oklahoma. Work in lettuce harvesting and packing and sugar beet processing have attracted these people who, seeking homes in Salinas without success because they aren't available, have resorted to makeshift adobes outside the city limits. Complicating the picture is the impermeable substrata which makes septic tanks with leaching fields impractical. Sewer wells have resulted with the corresponding danger to adjacent water wells and to the water wells serving the Salinas public. Certain districts, for example, the Airport Tract and parts of Alisal, have grown into communities with quite satisfactory housing, but others as exemplified by the Graves district are characterized by shacks and lean-tos which are unfit for human habitation." . . .

Typical of the shacktown problem are two such areas near the city limits of Sacramento, one on the east side of B Street, extending from Twelfth Street to the Sacramento city dump and incinerator; and the other so-called Hoovertown, adjacent to the Sacramento River and the city filtration plant. In these two areas there were on September 17, 1939, approximately 650 inhabitants living in structures that, with scarcely a single exception, were rated by the inspectors of this division as "unfit for human occupancy." The majority of the inhabitants were white Americans, with the exception of 50 or 60 Mexican families, a few single Mexican men, and a sprinkling of Negroes. For the most part they are seasonally employed in the canneries, the fruit ranches, and the hop fields of Sacramento

SOURCE: Carey McWilliams, testimony from U.S. Congress, House Select Committee to Investigate the Interstate Migration of Destitute Citizens, *Hearings*, 76th Cong., 3d sess., 1941, 2543–44.

County. Most of the occupants are at one time or another upon relief, and there are a large number of occupants in these shacktowns from the Dust Bowl area. Describing the housing, an inspector of this division reports:

"The dwellings are built of brush, rags, sacks, boxboard, odd bits of tin and galvanized iron, pieces of canvas and whatever other material was at hand at the time of construction."

Wood floors, where they exist, are placed directly upon the ground, which because of the location of the camps with respect to the Sacramento River, is damp most of the time. To quote again from the report:

"Entire families, men, women, and children, are crowded into hovels, cooking and eating in the same room. The majority of the shacks have no sinks or cesspools for the disposal of kitchen drainage, and this, together with garbage and other refuse, is thrown on the surface of the ground."

Because of the high-water table, cesspools, where they exist, do not function properly; there is a large overflow of drainage and sewage to the surface of the ground. Many filthy shack latrines are located within a few feet of living quarters. Rents for the houses in these shacktowns range from $3 to $20 a month. In one instance a landlord rents ground space for $1.50 to $5 a month, on which tenants are permitted to erect their own dugouts. The Hooverville section is composed primarily of tents and trailers, there being approximately 125 tent structures in this area on September 17, 1939. Both areas are located in unincorporated territory. They are not subject at the present time to any State or county building regulation. In Hooverville, at the date of the inspection, many families were found that did not have even a semblance of tents or shelters. They were cooking and sleeping on the ground in the open and one water tap at an adjoining industrial plant was found to be the source of the domestic water supply for the camp. . . .

CHAPTER 12

World War II: The Home Front

The New Deal had an enormous impact on American society. For the embattled farmers and workers and their families described in the previous chapter, the federal government offered relief, mortgage aid, crop payments, and even employment—programs that helped to restore the nation's flagging morale and maintain the people's faith in their government and economic system.

Yet the New Deal programs fell short of bringing about full employment. As the essay "The Wartime Consumer" by John Morton Blum points out, real prosperity did not return until the United States entered World War II. Blum observes something else as well: the birth of a consumer society. Although the nation experienced shortages of such goods as meat, sugar, rubber, and gasoline, all of which *were rationed by the federal government, the standard of living nonetheless went up during the war. Perhaps it is more accurate to say that the consumer society developed in the 1920s, disappeared during the Great Depression, and emerged again permanently in the 1940s. What evidence of consumerism do you see in America today?*

The first document, "The Consumer's Wartime Duty" by Caroline Ware, was published early in the war and was intended to stimulate patriotism, enthusiasm, and sacrifice for the war. What efforts did she ask of American consumers? Ware and many others at the time did not see how the United States would be able to convert its economy to war purposes and still enjoy a rising standard of living; Blum's essay indicates that, in fact, Americans at home did not have to sacrifice drastically during the war. The second document, an excerpt from the U.S. Department of Labor's Women's Bureau, gives one reason for America's huge wartime production: during the war, women worked in many jobs formerly barred to them. Thus the labor shortage created by the induction of millions of men (and some women) into the armed services was relieved by women who entered the labor force. The economy could therefore produce both war goods and consumer items.

Life on the home front was touched in other ways by the war. Fatter pay envelopes were meager consolation for the families of the over one-half million servicemen who lost their lives and the thousands of others who were physically or emotionally maimed in battle. Black Americans, though experiencing improved job opportunities, continued to face intense discrimination and segregation; Japanese-Americans also suffered from such prejudice. Many children also fell victim to the disruptions of wartime society; at the height of the conflict, some localities reported increases of as much as 50 percent in the rate of juvenile delinquency. In the final document, Katherine F. Lenroot, chief of the Children's Bureau in the Department of Labor, discusses the forces that contributed to juvenile delinquency and to a relaxation of moral standards. Although many of these conditions were aggravated by the war and disappeared with the return of peace, can you identify some that persist today?

ESSAY
_____

The Wartime Consumer

John Morton Blum

By stimulating the economy, the war did wonderful things for the American people. After the drab years of depression, Americans in 1941 and thereafter found themselves enjoying conditions many of them could scarcely remember. There were plenty of jobs. Business and farm profits were rising, as were wages, salaries, and other elements of personal income. At every level of society, men and women, even children, had money to spend, for luxuries if they were rich, for amenities long denied them if they were of moderate means, for small conveniences, decent food, and some recreation if they were workers. In spite of taxes, rationing, and price and wage controls, the wartime surge of buying was exciting in part because for so long most Americans had had to stint. It was also frustrating because wartime shortages denied Americans much of what they wanted. The contemplation of the end of deprivation after the war fostered dreams that achieved a partial fulfillment in the immediate consumption of such goods as there were. While they awaited, sometimes petulantly, a postwar consumers' nirvana, while they feared a postwar depression but fussed about wartime inconvenience, Americans indulged their appetites as broadly as they could afford to.

Less than a year after the Japanese attack on Pearl Harbor, government spending had worked its miracle. The average income per family in American cities (an average based upon salaries, wages, rents, dividends, and interest) had soared above the depression levels of 1938. In Hartford, Connecticut, it had moved from $2,207 to $5,208; in Boston, from $2,455 to $3,618; in New York, from $2,760 to $4,044; in Chicago, from $3,233 to $3,776; in San Francisco, from $2,201 to $3,716; and in Los Angeles, from $2,031 to $3,469. The largest reported relative jump occurred in Washington, D.C.—from $2,227 to $5,316. . . .

Looking for better jobs, following war industries, or following servicemen to locations near their camps and training stations, Americans moved faster and in greater numbers than ever before. On the highways, buses carried peak loads of passengers—in 1942, for the first time ever, more even than the railroads. The railroads for their part filled their coaches and had demands far beyond the supply for Pullman reservations. They made money on passenger traffic in 1942 for the first time in fifteen years. River cargoes went way up; air transport went into the black in the first

SOURCE: From *V Was for Victory*, copyright © 1976 by John Morton Blum. Reprinted by permission of Harcourt Brace Jovanovich, Inc.

quarter of 1942 and stayed there. The boom cities of the South, the Southwest, and the Pacific Coast flourished. New Orleans, typical of the others, saw its population rise 20 per cent in 1942 and then keep rising. Bank deposits reached a record high. War contracts that year were huge, with Higgins Industries, builders of boats and ships, alone receiving over $700 million. And boom begot more boom, as war workers had to have $100 million worth of new housing.

Baton Rouge, Seattle, Los Angeles, Philadelphia, Detroit, and San Diego, like New Orleans and Washington, staggered under the new prosperity. Schools, short of teachers, could not absorb all the children needing schooling. Public transportation had difficulty handling all the new workers in all the new neighborhoods. There were not enough houses or apartments, too few parks and playgrounds, insufficient places at night clubs and bars. Life was hurried and strange and sometimes harassed, and for those wistful for home or old friends or a boy in uniform, Washington was only one of dozens of loneliest cities.

Shortages, rationing, the hustle and strain and anxiety of daily urban living during the war grated upon Americans. Naturally they complained, though their lot was better than that of any other people in the world, and better, too, than it had been only a few years ago. They ate bountifully. Industry and government co-operated in arranging programs that packed vitamins into workers' lunches, and provided free milk, snacks between meals, and other inducements to spur output and combat absenteeism. But appetite often overruled hunger, and well-fed workers, blue collar and white, tended to care less for the snacks they were given than for the steak they could not buy. Yet even the scarcity of steak and bacon, or, later, of cigarettes and shoes, carried its benefits. Wage earners who could not purchase what they missed instead paid off what they owed. "The pawn-broking business," the *Wall Street Journal* reported in October 1942, "has fallen upon dark days."

The race for consumer goods began right after Pearl Harbor. With incomes and prices both rising, along with rumors of impending shortages, rationing, and controls, Americans began to stock up at a record rate. A study of fourteen cities showed hoarding under way in many items: food (especially sugar, canned meats and vegetables, coffee, tea, spices, and olive oil), rubber goods (used automobile tires, gaskets for jars, garden hoses, golf balls, galoshes, girdles), household supplies (soap, linen, furniture, blankets), clothing (particularly men's suits and shoes), and a miscellany of rifles and shotgun shells, typewriters, and paper clips.

The War Production Board, anxious about wool supplies early in March 1942, issued an order forbidding men's suits to include an extra pair of trousers, a vest, patch pockets, or cuffs, and calling for the manufacture only of single-breasted and somewhat shorter jackets with narrower lapels. Those prescriptions were designed to save 40 to 50 million pounds of wool a year. To the casual observer, according to the WPB, only the absence of cuffs would be noticeable, a deliberate tactic, since "an abrupt style change," the agency feared, "would start a buying rush for 'victory suits' which would defeat the conservation aims of the order." The tactic was not wholly successful. By the beginning of April, sales of men's suits, which merchants had not hesitated to advertise, were running at three times the normal volume.

Women were also spending freely, especially women war workers, of whom some 6.5 million, most of them middle-aged and married, entered the labor force between 1941 and 1945. They had yet to question traditional attitudes toward women's roles. Except for a few feminists, they did not protest the continuing disparity between men's and women's wages or the lack of day-care centers for the children of working mothers. Instead, they accepted the conclusion of the Children's Bureau that in war, as in peace, "a mother's primary duty is to her home and children." On several accounts that conventional definition suited almost all newly employed women. They did not, for the most part, intend to remain in the working force, although after the war many of them did not leave and others soon returned. They had, in the main, a special satisfaction, a continuing sense of the importance of their wartime tasks, of the nation's need for their labor, a point that the federal government continually stressed. Perhaps most important, they were beguiled by their new income. Their earnings, supplementing the military pay or the wages of their husbands, gave their families, usually for the first time, the chance to buy, or to save in order later to buy, the conveniences, the comforts, the small luxuries that had become a part of American middle-class expectations and a mark of middle-class status. After the disheartening years of depression, the prospect of achieving that status, and the immediate excitement of available cash to spend at will, seemed to many women, as to many men, not just satisfying but almost miraculous.

By 1943, 5 million more women were employed than in 1941, and the wages of women factory operatives were up over 50 per cent for the same period. They had some $8 billion more in pocket than they had had. Retailers had doubled their sales of women's clothing and found price no barrier as women sought quality as well as quantity. As cotton, wool, and nylon supplies dropped, the government ordered a 10-per-cent reduction in the amount of cloth in a woman's bathing suit, an objective reached by banishing the billowing bathing skirts of the 1930's and concentrating on two- rather than one-piece outfits. "The difficulties and dangers of the situation are obvious," the *Wall Street Journal* observed. "But the saving has been effected—in the region of the midriff. The two-piece bathing suit now is tied in with the war as closely as the zipperless dress and the pleatless skirt." No complaints were reported about the sacrifices thus entailed.

When clothes and cars were unavailable, Americans spent their money on entertainment and recreation. The motion-picture industry by the summer of 1942 had become one of the best "war babies" on the stock market. Theater earnings climbed as war workers flocked to films. The shortages of gasoline and tire rubber added to the attraction of neighborhood theaters, where air-cooled interiors provided a substitute of a kind for a drive to the shore or mountains or a trip to a resort. Also, American producers were relieved for the while of the competition from abroad. Their only worry was a possible loss to the services of celebrated male stars. Resorts, too, did not much suffer, for trains and buses carried eager clients to them. Night clubs and cafés, in spite of rising prices, were crowded. With work weeks prolonged to accelerate war production, Sunday became a rich day for entertainment. In spite of wartime restrictions, as one report noted, "Americans are finding fun—and lots of it." Indeed, during the war New York was really "fun city." There the boom in demand for hotel rooms and seats in restaurants and theaters reflected a rising influx of servicemen, executives, and war workers seeking relaxation and amusement. . . .

There were other ways, too, of enjoying the new affluence. It was no problem to obtain scarce and rationed goods at a price in the black markets. Boneless ham in Washington, D.C. sold on the black market for $1.25 a pound, almost twice its legal ceiling price. With patience, a buyer could find nylon hose in most cities for five dollars a pair. In Philadelphia, without recourse to rationing coupons, a determined customer could buy five-dollar shoes for about seven dollars. Those "willful violations," as an official of the Office of Price Administration said, were hard to prevent, since they occurred largely within regular retail channels on the basis of quiet collusion between the merchant and his patron.

In wholly legal markets, Americans during 1942 bought $95 million worth of pharmaceuticals, $20 million more than during the previous year. That increase did not arise from an abundance of colds, indigestion, or headaches. Rather, as the druggists knew, people simply had "more money to spend." For the same reason, jewelry sales mounted, depending on local circumstances, between 20 and 100 per cent. Though the volume of business from the wealthy declined, war workers avidly purchased diminishing stocks of cigarette cases, lighters, rings, silverware, and watches, particularly jeweled models. "People are crazy with money," one Philadelphia jeweler said. "They don't care what they buy. They purchase things . . . just for the fun of spending."

Though shortages became more severe in 1944, the rush to buy continued. Over-all retail sales in the first six months were up 8 per cent compared to 1943. The average sale in department stores, two dollars before the war, became ten dollars. American men shaved more often with fresher blades in spite of the shortage of steel. Just before the new luxury tax became effective in the spring of 1944, R. H. Macy & Company enjoyed a buying wave for furs, jewelry, cosmetics, and handbags. During 1944 the food industry made significant gains in its sales of breakfast cereals, baked goods, mixes, spices, and better grades of coffee, a rationed commodity. Supermarkets—of which there had been only 4,900 in 1939—were constructed so rapidly in the face of low stocks of building materials that by 1944 there were more than 16,000. Even nature smiled: there was a record crop of cherries, quickly sold, a guarantee of "more pie all around." Well before Christmas 1944, holiday purchasing had stripped retailers' shelves. On December 7, the third anniversary of Pearl Harbor, Macy's had its biggest selling day ever. The Federal Reserve index of department-store sales for November had exceeded the high of any month in any previous year. Textiles, jewelry, and clothing moved especially fast. "People want to spend money," one store manager said, "and if they can't spend it on textiles they'll spend it on furniture; or . . . we'll find something else for them." Then as in earlier years it was "delayed consumer demand," a function of deprivation during the Depression, in the opinion of the *Wall Street Journal*, that accounted for the wartime baby boom.

There was no change in 1945. In spite of OPA curtailments of apparel production, in spite of high prices, the Easter dash for clothing again set records, up 7 to 50 per cent, depending on the city, over 1944. So, too, high prices and shortages failed to deter diners-out. One hotel menu had "ox tongues, tails, nothing between," but restaurants, like department stores, thrived.

For the well-to-do, those who were accustomed to spending, those whose possessions permitted them to spurn more jewelry or furs, the conditions that hurt the most were usually those that removed housemaids from mansions to production lines and prevented annual excursions to the Riviera or Switzerland. Both the wealthy and the comfortable who enjoyed food took solace in the tone and content of *Gourmet*, a journal born just as the war began. It was an inauspicious time for graceful eating, but *Gourmet* helped its subscribers courageously to transcend the inconveniences they faced. "Imports of European delicacies may dwindle," the first issue admitted, "but America has battalions of good foods to rush to appetite's defense." Wine connoisseurs, for one group, were advised in 1942 to turn their attention to California *vin ordinaire* and by their example to "make it clear to the great non-wine-drinking public that ordinary wines, treated with appreciation . . . constitute a gastronomic resource that is of the first order." War stopped the spice trade, but my lady could instead cultivate an herb garden and make up for lost time, as well as for a lost chef, by adapting favorite recipes to a pressure cooker. "China is helping us," *Gourmet* noted, patriotically, "we must help the Chinese"—by buying almond cookies from United China Relief. The magazine also recommended a Russian cookbook. "The money goes to help Russia," it wrote, "and give Hitler indigestion." And if an issue arrived late because of transportation difficulties, the impatient reader should "blame Japan, not us." . . .

Early in the war, in his acid and penetrating *Generation of Vipers*, Philip Wylie caught the implications of the American mood: "Our war aims remain nebulous, we are told, because nobody has yet hit upon a plan for the postwar world which satisfies the majority of the people on this all-consuming problem of goods. . . . To many, it hardly seems worthwhile fighting to live until they can be assured that their percolators will live, along with their cars, synthetic roofing, and disposable diapers."

Through the war years, advertising exploited the urge to spend, intensified it, and directed it to deferred but glowing postwar possibilities. Some advertisements might have won awards, had any been offered, for bad taste. The city of Miami, inundated with Army Air Corps and Navy personnel at its sundry training stations, nevertheless sought expense-account tourists to overcrowd its filled hotels and night clubs. "Miami's pledge to America at War" offered warmth, relaxation, and salt water as respites from hard work, respites to be won by further burdening the railroads and airlines. The presumed need for respite also inspired the United States Playing Card Company to link its product to victory. For continued strength and vitality, it was alleged, "83 per cent of the people of this nation turn to card playing for inexpensive recreation." War-related themes, like those that associated almond cookies with the Grand Alliance, led Mennen's to brag that 1,300 dermatologists serving soldiers and civilians recommended the company's shaving cream. In a similar vein, Formfit sold its brassieres "for the *support* you need these hectic days of added responsibility."

Even before the cross-channel invasion in 1944, the advertising industry had its largest budget in history and had begun to prepare the public for postwar goods. In 1942 and 1943, industry, exercising some restraints, had emphasized institutional advertising designed to keep the name of a firm in the public eye. Now the switch began to product advertising. The Ford Motor Company, Remington Rand, and W. A. Shaeffer launched campaigns for their cars, typewriters, and pens, while General Electric, continuing to urge consumers to stretch the use of their household hard goods, had copy prepared for a sales effort as soon as steel could become available. The potential market was vast. At the time of Pearl Harbor, the liquid assets of individuals came to $50 billion; by the end of 1944 that figure had reached a record $140 billion. The National Association of Savings Banks conducted a survey of depositors that showed 43 per cent eager to spend their savings for "future needs," 20.6 per cent more precisely for homes and their accoutrements, 9 per cent for automobiles. The Office of Civilian Requirements in June 1944 announced that eleven appliances led the list on Americans' postwar plans for buying, with washing machines first, followed by electric irons, refrigerators, stoves, toasters, radios, vacuum cleaners, electric fans, and hot-water heaters. Those items, advertisers had claimed throughout the war, constituted the American way of life. "Weren't you bragging just a little, Yamamoto,*" *The Saturday Evening Post* had asked. "Your people are giving their lives in useless sacrifice. Ours are fighting for a glorious future of mass employment, mass production and mass distribution and ownership." "Some day Johnny, front line observer, will climb out of his foxhole," Western Electric predicted, "into a world freed from fear of dictators. When that day comes, the telephone . . . will help to place all peoples . . . on friendly speaking terms." Johnston and Murphy promised that "when our boys come home . . . among the finer things of life they will find ready to enjoy will be Johnston and Murphy shoes. Quality unchanged." The advertisement that probably most bothered Bill Mauldin,** an advertisement neither better nor worse than dozens like it, displayed a Nash Kelvinator refrigerator as the emblem of a sentimental homecoming. The lady in the picture, chin up, spoke out for an unaltered world in which she and her heroic soldier-spouse would pick up where they had left off: "I know you'll come back to me. . . . And when you do . . . you'll find . . . everything your letters tell me you hold dear. I will be wearing the same blue dress I wore the day you went away. And on my arm the silver bracelet you gave me . . . on our anniversary. . . . Everything will be here, just as you left it" and withal a new refrigerator in the kitchen. . . .

The house and all that went into it, "the American home," best symbolized of all things material a brave new world of worldly goods. The vision was in part a fantasy woven by advertising, in part a romanticizing of desires born of depression circumstances and wartime deprivations. After the decade of the 1930's, during which new building dropped 61 per cent below construction in the preceding ten years, housing in 1940 had already become scarce and grim, especially for low-income groups. Of all available housing units, more than 14 per cent needed major repair and improvements. "Not less than 416,000 families," according to the Bureau of Labor statistics, had "established households in the backs of stores, in public buildings, warehouses, and garages, and in shacks, houseboats, barns, tents, boxcars, caves, dugouts. . . . More than four-fifths of . . . new properties . . . were beyond the reach of more than four-fifths of the families in non-farm areas."

Wartime dislocations, not least the mobilization of 13 million men, many with wives who traveled with them, further strained conditions. Over 4 million workers—with their families, some 9 million people—left their homes for employment in war plants. "Scarcely a section of the coun-

[*Japanese admiral who masterminded the attack on Pearl Harbor]
[**World War II cartoonist, creator of "Willie and Joe"]

try," one federal report noted, "or a community of any size escaped the impact of this great migration." Yet the shortage of building materials forced the War Production Board in April 1942 to ban all nondefense construction and put stringent limitations on the alteration or improvement of existing structures. By June 1945, over 98 per cent of American cities reported a shortage of single-family houses, over 90 per cent a shortage of apartments. Various estimates judged 75 per cent of all plumbing and electrical equipment and 68 per cent of all interiors to be below par. Conservation orders had also necessarily prohibited production of sinks, furniture, bedding, and electric appliances, and curtailed production of electric wiring and of plumbing and heating fixtures. . . .

Columns of letters from young couples to *Better Homes and Gardens* described the homes and furnishings and refrigerators for which the writers were saving. "I can see our house going up," one wife wrote, "stamp by stamp, bond by bond, joist by joist." Another correspondent believed "children should have the security of a home and the pride of a home that belongs to their family . . . a neighborhood where they'll be included in things because they *belong* . . . a place to which they can bring their friends." The Celotex Corporation encouraged the chorus. "As America drives under war's incentive," it advertised, "the products of our future greatness are being shaped. New wonders are coming from the men of science and industry. . . . Housing will undergo tremendous change. . . . Out of undreamed-of progress . . . will emerge your 'Miracle House' of tomorrow." It was to be "within the reach of the *average* family" but nonetheless fantastic—luminescent panels instead of incandescent bulbs, furniture and upholstery that would never wear out—the proper equivalent in a house of the new, static-free radios, new and more powerful automobiles, new tickets to a consumer's heaven. "Is This Worth Fighting For?" another advertisment asked. It then depicted an old-fashioned living room complete with fireplace and walls of western pine, the latter the product of the manufacturer who paid for the ad.

To most of the American people at home, that advertisement symbolized much of what was worth fighting for and, well before the fighting ended, what was worth spending for, whether to satisfy yearnings long unfulfilled or whether just for the fun of spending. The postwar world as most people visualized it, the Office of War Information told President Roosevelt, was "compounded largely of 1929 values and the economics of the 1920's, leavened with a hangover from . . . makeshift controls of the war." The American way of living returned, during the new prosperity of the war years, to patterns that Americans liked to believe had marked national life before the Depression, patterns they wanted to preserve and to project into the postwar period.

That way of living, they believed with sufficient cause, would also satisfy Americans in arms. After all, even Bill Mauldin did expect Willie and Joe to settle down. Where more likely, if the civilian consumer could arrange it, than in a little white house in the suburbs where a young wife wearing a pretty blue dress and an anniversary bracelet would greet her veteran husband every evening with slippers to change into from his Johnston and Murphy shoes, with a Scotch whiskey highball and a sirloin steak, all within the efficient antiseptic environment created by electric appliances that cooked the meals, did the housework, kept out the cold or heat, and left the couple free to listen to their radio. With modest alterations to suit individual tastes, with allowances for Mom's blueberry pie for dinner on alternate Sundays, that was the decent, uninspired picture, for thousands of Americans, of their postwar world.

DOCUMENTS

The Consumer's Wartime Duty, 1942

We consumers have a big job to do in this war. We can and must help our fighting men by making possible all-out production of war supplies. We can and must keep our civilian population strong and fit, our economy efficient, our nation democratic.

Everything that we do is part of this job. For every purchase we make is a claim on our nation's resources. Every article we use is part of the nation's precious supplies. Each worker and machine that is working to make things for us is one less worker and one less machine producing guns, planes, uniforms, ships, and food for our fighting men and our allies. At the same time, every home is a unit of national strength. Economic efficiency depends on our day-by-day dealings in the market place. Democracy lives or dies in our home towns.

A strong consumer front thus means that we must release all possible resources to work for our fighting men, and that we must make the best possible use of the limited supplies which our armies can spare for civilian living. It means an all-out attack on inflation, with war bonds, taxes, and effective price control. It means wise buying by consumers and careful conservation of all our possessions. It means the utmost efficiency in producing and distributing civilian goods. For the better use we can make of materials, manpower, machines and farms that are producing for us, the more we can free for military production, and the stronger we can keep ourselves and our families to meet the strains of war.

SOURCE: Abridgement of pp. 1–3, 5 from *The Consumer Goes to War: A Guide to Victory on the Home Front* by Caroline Ware (New York: Funk and Wagnalls, 1942). Reprinted by permission of Harper & Row, Publishers, Inc.

No one of us consumers can escape his wartime duty. We must be at our battle stations twenty-four hours a day—lest we leave the furnace burning too high while we sleep. . . .

We need to understand what is required of us, too, because we must reverse attitudes and habits to which we have been accustomed in the past. Our rich land of "plenty" has become a land of "scarcities." We have had too little money to buy the goods we were able to produce; now we have too much. We have been a wasteful people; overnight we must become savers. We have struggled to "keep up with the Joneses"; now both we and the Joneses must "keep down." . . .

From now on, virtually everything is going to be "scarce."

Although stores are still full of goods that were produced in 1940 and 1941 when more things were made for civilians than in any previous two years, many shelves will be bare as soon as present stocks are gone. It is not only a matter of the refrigerators, automobiles, electric toasters and other products whose production was stopped or cut to the bone in the spring of 1942. Shoes and blankets for our soldiers, food for our fighting forces and our allies demand a large part of our national ability to produce.

We can no longer deal with shortages one by one. Every new shortage creates ten or a hundred others and thus sends ripples through the whole economy. For substitutes in turn become short. The delicate balance of peacetime uses is violently upset. . . .

The Woman Worker, 1942

Half a million women were estimated early this year [1942] to be serving their country in war industries. The number of these increases day by day. In some 30 plants making small-arms and artillery ammunition, where 40,000 women were employed in the last quarter of 1941, over 70,000 are expected to be at work by late summer. In some of these the woman labor force will be doubled, in others trebled, and some will employ 10 times as many women as before. These are chiefly new jobs, not those vacated by men. Before 1941 almost no women were in aircraft.

Women in Jobs Vacated by Men

Many reports from all parts of the country show that men called to war service actually have been replaced by women in types of work formerly not done, or done only very rarely, by women, though of course there is no way to discover the full number of these. They include clerks, cashiers,

SOURCE: U.S. Department of Labor, Women's Bureau, *The Woman Worker* (Washington, D.C.: Government Printing Office, May 1942), 3–4.

and pharmacists in drug stores, theater ushers, hotel elevator operators, taxi drivers, bank tellers, electricians, acetylene welders, milling-machine operators, riveters, tool-keepers, gage checkers, gear cutters, turret and engine lathe operators. Women are operating service stations. They are replacing men as finger-print classifiers. A southern city reports a woman manager of a parking lot.

One of the country's major airfields has women on maintenance work, engaging them chiefly in cleaning spark plugs and painting luminous dials. One woman hired as a secretary now directs landings and take-offs by radio. In another city a woman has entered for the first time an airfield office as a meteorologist. Both an eastern and a southern airport have definite plans to place women in their reservations departments, and in flight watch or in the traffic operations departments, and the Civil Aeronautics Administration is considering training women as radio operators.

Women telegraph messengers now number 325 in New York City alone, and in the country as a whole 3,000 women are expected to do such work this year. In New York, they must be at least 21 years of age. Girls also are performing other messenger service, formerly done by boys, in many plants and offices. A major chemical company is now training a few women as its chemists.

Labor Shortages Open Jobs to Women

There are many types of work long done by women but in which women now are being taken on in large numbers, because of plant expansion as well as declining supply of male labor. For example, as armature winders, inspectors, power-press and drill-press operators, assemblers. Shortages of workers are reported in many places in fields usual for women; for example, in hotel and restaurant work, as retail clerks, stenographers, and as sewing-machine operators in certain great clothing centers. Shortages of school teachers are growing, because of better-paid jobs in industry as well as the drafting of men, and the National Education Association reports that the enrollment in teachers' colleges and normal schools has declined by 11 per cent. Certain of the army camps already have employed considerable numbers of women in their offices and laundries, jobs formerly done by men but of a type frequently performed by women. A woman's job at present done by men in camps is canteen work, but serious consideration is being given to employing women in this.

Unemployment of Women

Contrary to the movement of women into the manufacture of war products, and into jobs being vacated by men, runs that opposite line of women losing jobs due to curtailment of civilian goods and of critical materials. Such "priorities unemployment" became acute at certain points in the second half of 1941. Plants making many of the products curtailed employed large numbers of women—as on aluminum kitchenware, refrigerators, silk hosiery, washing machines, radios, typewriters, photographic supplies, metal toys, costume jewelry, slide and snap fasteners, and so forth. Others depend on equipment now curtailed, as for example the apparel industry threatened with shortages of steel needles and consequent danger of unemployment. In many cases it takes longer to place women than men in new jobs, since their industrial experience is less similar to the new types of work required. Moreover, some of these products are made in localities that offer women little chance of other plant jobs.

Juvenile Delinquency During the War, 1944

Delinquency is a problem that is not readily susceptible to accurate and complete statistical measurement. Certain difficulties are readily apparent. It is not possible to determine the exact extent to which the increase in delinquency cases represents actual increase or to what extent it represents greater community concern, causing greater emphasis on finding cases and on taking measures that heretofore might not have been taken. It is unquestionable that emphasis placed on the control of venereal disease has resulted in the attention of the courts being called more frequently to problems of young girls than was formerly the case. Furthermore, from the standpoint of community concern about juvenile delinquency, the many unhappy, maladjusted, and neurotic children who fail to come to the attention of agencies and courts, yet who make up a large group of individuals who are potential delinquents, easily precipitated into delinquency by unfavorable environment, are of importance equal to those already delinquent in the legal sense.

Although we may lack the means of comprehensive measurement of the problem of delinquent behavior, evidence of increases during the past few years is apparent in recent reports from varied and reliable sources. Field reports of representatives of the Children's Bureau of the United States Department of Labor and other public and private agencies, and special studies and reports of particular communities indicate that the problem is of sufficient proportions to warrant concern.

SOURCE: Testimony of Katherine Lenroot in U.S. Congress, Senate Subcommittee of the Committee on Education and Labor, Hearings, *Wartime Health and Recreation*, 78th Cong., 2nd Sess., 1944, 103–4.

Causal Factors

In wartime, as in peacetime, juvenile delinquency results from our failure to satisfy the basic needs of children and young people—the need for knowing that they are loved and cared for—the chance to take part as equals in school and recreational activities. The home and community through which these needs are met find their task more difficult by the dislocations they are undergoing in wartime.

Some of the wartime conditions which mean that homes and communities are not meeting the needs of children as well as they formerly did include the following:

Fathers are separated from their families because they are serving in the armed forces or working in distant war industries.

Mothers in large numbers are engaged in full-time employment and are therefore absent from the home most of the day.

An increasing number of children are now employed, in many instances under unwholesome conditions that impede their growth, limit their educational progress, or expose them to moral hazards.

The widespread migration of families to crowded centers of war industry has uprooted children from familiar surroundings and subjected them to life in communities where resources are overtaxed by the increased population.

Dance halls, beer parlors, and other attractions that flourish in industrial centers and near military establishments, unless kept under community control, frequently exert a harmful influence on youth.

The general spirit of excitement and adventure aroused by war, and the tension, anxiety, and apprehension felt by parents or other adults are reflected in restlessness, defiance, emotional disturbance, and other negative forms of behavior on the part of children and young people.

Conditions affecting children and young people in war-affected communities are conducive to lack of parental responsibility and resultant neglect and delinquency of children. In a report from a child-welfare worker in a southwestern State it was stated that several mothers who had followed their soldier husbands to a military camp secured work as waitresses or taxi dancers in the night cafes and left their children alone in hotel rooms without supervision. It is not surprising that such children, without protection of a secure home life, find it easy to drift into delinquency.

A typical situation reported by child-welfare workers as occurring in communities near Army camps is illustrated by the story of Julia, a 14-year-old girl found living with her girl friend aged 15, who was the wife of a soldier at the nearby camp. Both of the girls were having many soldiers visit them each night and were picked up by the police in one of the taverns near the camp. Julia told the child-welfare worker of her unhappy home situation in a dull little village in an adjoining State. She thought hitchhiking was fun and life around an Army camp exciting. . . .

CHAPTER 13

The Internment of Japanese-Americans: Executive Order 9066

During World War II, the United States government removed from their homes 110,000 West Coast immigrant and native-born Japanese and interned them in stark, isolated "relocation centers." The essay in this chapter is excerpted from "Personal Justice Denied," a 1984 report written by a group of scholars for the federal Commission on Wartime Relocation and Internment of Civilians. It examines the events and arguments leading up to President Franklin Roosevelt's signing of Executive Order 9066, under which Japanese-Americans were ordered from their homes and housed in government camps. The report also details the conditions that prevailed in the relocation centers. In reading the essay, consider why the internment occurred and the roles that wartime hysteria, greed, and racism may have played in it.

The first two documents illustrate the mood and attitudes prevalent at the time of the internment. The first is taken from the testimony presented by Earl Warren before a congressional committee meeting in San Francisco in 1942. Today Warren is best remembered as chief justice of the U.S. Supreme Court from 1953 to 1969, and as a staunch defender of civil rights. In 1942, however, he was California's attorney general and a future candidate for governor. In response to questioning regarding the civil rights of Japanese-Americans, he replied, "I believe, sir, that in time of war every citizen must give up some of his normal rights." Even if one accepts such a belief, would it excuse the treatment of Japanese-Americans during the war?

The second document is from Justice Hugo Black's majority opinion in the case of Korematsu v. United States *(1944). After reading the accounts of removal and relocation in the essay, evaluate Justice Black's statement that it is "unjustifiable to call [the relocation centers] . . . concentration camps" and his assertion that "to cast this case into outlines of racial prejudice, without reference to the real military dangers which were present, merely confuses the issue."*

Since the end of the war, racial attitudes toward Japanese-Americans, as well as other minorities, have considerably improved in the United States. In the case of Japanese-Americans, their outstanding military service during the war no doubt aided their acceptance by other Americans. The 442d Regimental Combat Team, composed almost entirely of Japanese-Americans, suffered enormous casualties in Italy and was the most decorated unit in the war.

The final document, a proclamation by President Gerald Ford in 1976, expresses the nation's regret over the wartime miscarriage of justice. Proposals to compensate financially those Japanese-Americans who were interned have yet to be approved by Congress, however. Have racial attitudes evolved enough so that Americans will abide by President Ford's resolve "that this kind of error shall never be made again"?

ESSAY

Personal Justice Denied
Commission on Wartime Relocation and Internment of Civilians

At dawn on December 7, 1941, Japan began bombing American ships and planes at Pearl Harbor. The attack took our forces by surprise. Japanese aircraft carriers and warships had left the Kurile Islands for Pearl Harbor on November 26, 1941, and Washington had sent a war warning message

SOURCE: Commission on Wartime Relocation and Internment of Civilians, *Personal Justice Denied* (Washington, D.C.: Government Printing Offices, 1984), 47–50, 83–89, 156–63, 176–78.

indicating the possibility of attack upon Pearl Harbor, the Philippines, Thailand or the Malay Peninsula. Nevertheless, the Navy and Army were unprepared and unsuspecting. After a few hours of bombing, Japan had killed or wounded over 3,500 Americans. Two battleships were destroyed, four others sunk or run aground; a number of other vessels were destroyed or badly damaged. One hundred forty-nine American airplanes had been destroyed. Japan lost only 29 planes and pilots.

That night President Roosevelt informed his Cabinet and Congressional leaders that he would seek a declaration of war. On December 8 the President addressed a joint session of Congress and expressed the nation's outraged shock at the damage which the Japanese had done on that day of infamy. The declaration of war passed with one dissenting vote. Germany and Italy followed Japan into the war on December 11.

At home in the first weeks of war the division between isolationists and America Firsters, and supporters of the western democracies, was set aside, and the country united in its determination to defeat the Axis powers. Abroad, the first weeks of war sounded a steady drumbeat of defeat, particularly as the Allies retreated before Japanese forces in the Far East. On the same day as Pearl Harbor, the Japanese struck the Malay Peninsula, Hong Kong, Wake and Midway Islands, and attacked the Philippines, destroying substantial numbers of American aircraft on the ground near Manila. The next day Thailand was invaded and within days two British battleships were sunk off Malaysia. On December 13 Guam fell, and on Christmas the Japanese captured Wake Island and occupied Hong Kong. In the previous seventeen days, Japan had made nine amphibious landings in the Philippines. General Douglas MacArthur, commanding Army forces in the islands, evacuated Manila on December 27, withdrew to the Bataan Peninsula, and set up headquarters on Corregidor. With Japan controlling all sea and air approaches to Bataan and Corregidor, after three months the troops isolated there were forced to surrender unconditionally in the worst American defeat since the Civil War. On February 27 the battle of the Java Sea resulted in another American naval defeat with the loss of thirteen Allied ships. In January and February 1942, the military position of the United States in the Pacific was bleak indeed. Reports of American battlefield deaths gave painful personal emphasis to the war news.

Pearl Harbor was a surprise. The outbreak of war was not. In December 1941 the United States was not in the state of war-readiness which those who anticipated conflict with the Axis would have wished, but it was by no means unaware of the intentions of Japan and Germany. The President had worked for some time for Lend-Lease and other measures to support the western democracies and prepare for war. In 1940, he had broadened the political base of his Cabinet, bringing in as Secretary of the Navy Frank Knox, the publisher of the Chicago *Daily News* who had been Alfred M.

Landon's vice-presidential candidate in 1936. Roosevelt drafted as Secretary of War one of the most distinguished Republican public servants of his time, Henry L. Stimson, who had served as Secretary of War under Taft and Secretary of State under Hoover. Stimson, who brought with him the standing and prestige of half a century of active service to his country, carried a particularly impressive weight of principled tradition. He brought into the War Department other, younger easterners, many of whom were fellow lawyers and Republicans. John J. McCloy came from a prominent New York law firm to become first a Special Assistant and then Assistant Secretary for War, and after the outbreak of war he was the civilian aide to Stimson responsible for Japanese American questions. Roosevelt later named Francis Biddle, a Philadelphian who was a firm defender of civil rights, as Attorney General when Robert Jackson was appointed to the Supreme Court.

Ten weeks after the outbreak of war, on February 19, 1942, President Roosevelt signed Executive Order 9066 which gave to the Secretary of War and the military commanders to whom he delegated authority, the power to exclude any persons from designated areas in order to secure national defense objectives against sabotage and espionage. The order was used, as the President, his responsible Cabinet officers and the West Coast Congressional delegation knew it would be, to exclude persons of Japanese ancestry, both American citizens and resident aliens, from the West Coast. Over the following months more than 100,000 people were ordered to leave their homes and farms and businesses. "Voluntary" resettlement of people who had been branded as potentially disloyal by the War Department and who were recognizable by their facial features was not feasible. Not surprisingly, the politicians and citizens of Wyoming or Idaho believed that their war industries, railroad lines and hydroelectric dams deserved as much protection from possible sabotage as did those on the Pacific Coast, and they opposed accepting the ethnic Japanese. Most of the evacuees were reduced to abandoning their homes and livelihoods and being transported by the government to "relocation centers" in desolate interior regions of the west.

As the Executive Order made plain, these actions were based upon "military necessity." The government has never fundamentally reviewed whether this massive eviction of an entire ethnic group was justified. In three cases the Supreme Court reviewed the Executive Order in the context of convictions for violations of military orders issued pursuant to it, but the Court chose not to review the factual basis for military decisions in wartime, accepting without close scrutiny the government's representation that exclusion and evacuation were militarily necessary. Forty years later, the nation is sufficiently concerned about the rights and liberties of its citizens and residents, that it has undertaken to examine the facts and pose to itself the question of whether, in the heat of the moment, beset by defeat and fearful of the future, it justly took the proper course for its own protection, or made an original mistake of very substantial proportion. "Peace hath her victories/No less renowned than war."

Was a policy of exclusion militarily justified as a *precautionary* measure? This is a core initial question because the government has conceded at every point that there was no evidence of actual sabotage, espionage or fifth column activity among people of Japanese descent on the West Coast in February 1942. The Commanding General of the Western Defense Command, John L. DeWitt, put the point plainly, conceding in his recommendation to the War Department "[t]he very fact that no sabotage has taken place to date." The Justice Department, defending the exclusion before the Supreme Court, made no claim that there was identifiable subversive activity. The Congress, in passing the Japanese-American Evacuation Claims Act in 1948, reiterated the point:

> [D]espite the hardships visited upon this unfortunate racial group by an act of the Government brought about by the then prevailing military necessity, there was recorded during the recent war not one act of sabotage or espionage attributable to those who were the victims of the forced relocation.

Finally, the two witnesses before the Commission [on Wartime Relocation and Internment of Civilians] who were most involved in the evacuation decision, John J. McCloy and Karl R. Bendetsen, who was first liaison between the War Department and the Western Defense Command and later General DeWitt's chief aide for the evacuation, testified that the decision was not taken on the basis of actual incidents of espionage, sabotage or fifth column activity.

One may begin, then, by examining the competent estimates of possible future danger from the ethnic Japanese, citizen and alien, on the West Coast in early 1942. This is not to suggest that a well-grounded suspicion is or should be sufficient to require an American citizen or resident alien to give up his house and farm or business to move hundreds of miles inland, bearing the stigma of being a potential danger to his fellow citizens—nor that such suspicion would justify condemnation of a racial group rather than individual review—but it does address the analysis that should be made by the War Department charged with our continental defenses. . . .

The intelligence services have the task of alerting and informing the President, the military and those charged with maintaining security about whether, where and when disruptive acts directed by an enemy may be expected. Intelligence work consists predominantly of analytical estimate, not demonstrably comprehensive knowledge—there may always be another, undiscovered ring of spies or a completely covert plan of sabotage.

Caution and prudence require that intelligence agencies throw the net of suspicion wide, and take measures to protect vital information or militarily important installations. At the same time, if intelligence is to serve the ends of a society which places central value on personal liberty, even in time of war, it must not be overwhelmed by rumors and flights of fancy which grip a fearful, jittery public. Above all, effective intelligence work demands sound judgment which is immune to the paranoia that treats everyone as a hostile suspect until his loyalty is proven. In 1942, what credible threat did Japan pose to the internal peace and security of the United States?

It was common wisdom that the Nazi invasions of Norway and Western Europe had been aided by agents and sympathizers within the country under attack—the so-called fifth column—and that the same approach should be anticipated from Japan. For this reason intelligence was developed on Axis saboteurs and potential fifth columnists as well as espionage agents. This work had been assigned to the Federal Bureau of Investigation and the Navy Department but not to the War Department. The President had developed his own informal intelligence system through John Franklin Carter, a journalist, who helped Roosevelt obtain information and estimates by exploiting sources outside the government. None of these organizations operated with the thoroughness of, say, the modern CIA, but they were the best and calmest eyes and ears the government had.

Each of these sources saw only a very limited security risk from the ethnic Japanese; none recommended a mass exclusion or detention of all people of Japanese ancestry. . . .

Under General DeWitt's guidance from the Presidio [of San Francisco, Army Headquarters on the West Coast], the War Department moved toward the momentous exclusion of American citizens from the West Coast without any thoughtful, thorough analysis of the problems, if any, of sabotage and espionage on the West Coast or of realistic solutions to those problems. In part there was an easy elision between excluding Issei* and Nisei.** The legal basis for excluding aliens was essentially unquestioned; no rigorous analysis of military necessity was needed because there were no recognized interests or rights to weigh against the interest in military security that was served by moving enemy aliens. The very word "Japanese," sometimes used to denote nationality and at other times to indicate ethnicity, allowed obvious ambiguities in discussing citizens and resident aliens. The War Department came toward the problem with a few major facts: the Japanese were winning an incredible string of victories in the Far East; the West Coast was lightly armed and defended, but now appeared

[*First-generation Japanese Americans]
[**Second-generation Japanese Americans]

far more vulnerable to Japanese raid or attack than it had been before Pearl Harbor—although General Staff estimates were that the Japanese could not make a sustained invasion on the West Coast. But after the surprise of Pearl Harbor, laymen, at least, doubted the reliability of military predictions: it was better to be safe than sorry. And laymen had a great deal to say about what the Army should do on the West Coast. . . .

It was the voices of organized interests, politicians and the press on the West Coast that DeWitt heard most clearly—and the War Department too. The first weeks after Pearl Harbor saw no extensive attacks on the ethnic Japanese, but through January and early February the storm gathered and broke. The latent anti-Japanese virus of the West Coast was brought to life by the fear and anger engendered by Pearl Harbor, stories of sabotage in Hawaii and Japan's victories in Asia. Among private groups the lead was typically taken by people with a long history of anti-Japanese agitation and by those who feared economic competition. It is difficult . . . to recreate the fear and uncertainty about the country's safety which was generally felt after Pearl Harbor; it is equally impossible to convey . . . the virulence and breadth of anti-Japanese feeling which erupted on the West Coast in January and February of 1942.

On January 2 the Joint Immigration Committee sent a manifesto to California newspapers which summed up the historical catalogue of charges against the ethnic Japanese. It put them in the new context of reported fifth column activity in Hawaii and the Philippines and a war that turned the Japanese into a problem for the nation, not California alone. Repeating the fundamental claim that the ethnic Japanese are "totally unassimilable," the manifesto declared that "those born in this country are American citizens by right of birth, but they are also Japanese citizens, liable . . . to be called to bear arms for their Emperor, either in front of, or behind, enemy lines." Japanese language schools were attacked as "a blind to cover instruction similar to that received by a young student in Japan— that his is a superior race, the divinity of the Japanese Emperor, the loyalty that every Japanese, wherever born, or residing, owes his Emperor and Japan." In these attacks the Joint Immigration Committee had the support of the Native Sons and Daughters of the Golden West and the California Department of the American Legion, which in January began to demand that "all Japanese who are known to hold dual citizenship . . . be placed in concentration camps." By early February, Earl Warren, then Attorney General of California, and U.S. Webb, a former Attorney General and coauthor of the Alien Land Law, were actively advising the Joint Immigration Committee how to persuade the federal government that all ethnic Japanese should be removed from the West Coast. . . .

These traditional voices of anti-Japanese agitation were joined by economic competitors of the Nikkei [Japanese-Americans]. The Grower-Shipper Vegetable Association was beginning to find a voice in January, although its bluntest statement can be found in a *Saturday Evening Post* article in May:

> We're charged with wanting to get rid of the Japs for selfish reasons. We might as well be honest. We do. It's a question of whether the white man lives on the Pacific Coast or the brown man. They came into this valley to work, and they stayed to take over. . . . If all the Japs were removed tomorrow, we'd never miss them in two weeks, because the white farmers can take over and produce everything the Jap grows. And we don't want them back when the war ends, either.

Through January and early February, the Western Growers Protective Association, the Grower-Shippers, and the California Farm Bureau Federation all demanded stern measures against the ethnic Japanese. All assured the newspapers and politicians to whom they wrote that the removal of the ethnic Japanese would in no way harm or diminish agricultural production.

This wave of self-assured demands for a firm solution to the "Japanese problem" encountered no vigorous, widespread defense of the Issei and Nisei. Those concerned with civil liberties and civil rights were silent. For instance, a poll of the Northern California Civil Liberties Union in the spring of 1942 showed a majority in favor of the evacuation orders.

West Coast politicians were not slow to demand action against ethnic Japanese. Fletcher Bowron, reform mayor of Los Angeles, went to Washington in mid-January to discuss with Attorney General Biddle the general protection of Los Angeles as well as the removal of all ethnic Japanese from Terminal Island in Los Angeles Harbor. By Feburary 5, in a radio address, the Mayor was unequivocally supporting mass evacuation. In the meantime, all Nisei had been removed from the city payrolls. The Los Angeles County Board of Supervisors fired all its Nisei employees and adopted a resolution urging the federal government to transport all Japanese aliens from the coast. Following Los Angeles, 16 other California counties passed formal resolutions urging evacuation; Imperial County required the fingerprinting, registration and abandoning of farming by all enemy aliens; San Francisco demanded suppression of all Japanese language newspapers. Portland, Oregon, revoked the licenses of all Japanese nationals doing business in the city. The California State Personnel Board ordered all "descendants" of enemy aliens barred from civil service positions, and Governor Olson authorized the State Department of Agriculture to revoke the produce-handling licenses of enemy aliens. Attorney General Warren found these measures unlawful, but he sympathized with their basic aim, laboring to persuade federal officials that the military should remove ethnic Japanese from what Warren thought sensitive areas on the West Coast.

In Washington, most West Coast Congressmen and Senators began to express similar views, Congressman Leland Ford of Los Angeles taking the early lead. On January 16, 1942, he wrote the Secretaries of War and Navy and the FBI Director informing them that his California mail was running heavily in favor of evacuation and internment:

> I know that there will be some complications in connection with a matter like this, particularly where there are native born Japanese, who are citizens. My suggestions in connection with this are as follows:
>
>   1. That these native born Japanese either are or are not loyal to the United States.
>   2. That all Japanese, whether citizens or not, be placed in inland concentration camps. As justification for this, I submit that if an American born Japanese, who is a citizen, is really patriotic and wishes to make his contribution to the safety and welfare of this country, right here is his opportunity to do so, namely, that by permitting himself to be placed in a concentration camp, he would be making his sacrifice and he should be willing to do it if he is patriotic and is working for us. As against his sacrifice, millions of other native born citizens are willing to lay down their lives, which is a far greater sacrifice, of course, than being placed in a concentration camp. . . .

This clamor for swift, comprehensive measures against the ethnic Japanese both reflected and was stimulated by the press. In December the West Coast press had been comparatively tolerant on the issue of the Nikkei, but by January more strident commentators were heard. John B. Hughes, who had a regular Mutual Broadcasting Company program, began a month-long series from Los Angeles which steadily attacked the ethnic Japanese, spreading rumors of espionage and fifth column activity and even suggesting that Japanese dominance of produce production was part of a master war plan.

Nurtured by fear and anger at Japanese victories in the Far East and by eagerness to strike at the enemy with whom the Nisei were now identified, calls for radical government action began to fill letters to the editor and newspaper commentary. Private employers threw many ethnic Japanese out of their jobs, while many others refused to deal with them commercially. Old stereotypes of the "yellow peril" and other forms of anti-Japanese agitation provided a ready body of lore to bolster this pseudo-patriotic cause. By the end of January the clamor for exclusion fired by race hatred and war hysteria was prominent in California newspapers. Henry McLemore, a Hearst syndicated columnist, published a vicious diatribe:

> I am for immediate removal of every Japanese on the West Coast to a point deep in the interior. I don't mean a nice part of

the interior either. Herd 'em up, pack 'em off and give 'em the inside room in the badlands. Let 'em be pinched, hurt, hungry and dead up against it . . .

Personally, I hate the Japanese. And that goes for all of them.

By the end of January the western Congressional delegation and many voices in the press and organized interest groups were pressing for evacuation or internment of aliens and citizens. The Presidio at San Francisco listened, and by January 31, General DeWitt had embraced the Representatives' view that all enemy aliens and dual citizens should be evacuated and interned; action should be taken at the earliest possible date "even if they [the aliens and dual citizens] were temporarily inconvenienced." . . .

In the face of . . . demands for evacuation and the recommendation of his Secretary of War, Roosevelt was not likely to reconsider his decision. Nevertheless, on February 17 Attorney General Biddle sent a memorandum to the President in the guise of a briefing paper for a press conference. . . . :

For several weeks there have been increasing demands for evacuation of all Japanese, aliens and citizens alike, from the West Coast states. A great many of the West Coast people distrust the Japanese, various special interests would welcome their removal from good farm land and the elimination of their competition, some of the local California radio and press have demanded evacuation, the West Coast Congressional Delegation are asking the same thing and finally, Walter Lippman [sic] and Westbrook Pegler recently have taken up the evacuation cry on the ground that attack on the West Coast and widespread sabotage is imminent. My last advice from the War Department is that there is no evidence of imminent attack and from the F.B.I. that there is no evidence of planned sabotage.

I have designated as a prohibited area every area recommended to me by the Secretary of War, through whom the Navy recommendations are also made. . . .

We are proceeding as fast as possible. To evacuate the 93,000 Japanese in California over night would materially disrupt agricultural production in which they play a large part and the farm labor now is so limited that they could not be quickly replaced. Their hurried evacuation would require thousands of troops, tie up transportation and raise very difficult questions of resettlement. Under the Constitution 60,000 of these Japanese are American citizens. If complete confusion and lowering of morale is to be avoided, so large a job must be done after careful planning. The Army has not yet advised me of its conclusion in the matter.

There is no dispute between the War, Navy, and Justice Departments. The practical and legal limits of this Department's authority which is restricted to alien enemies are clearly understood.

The Army is considering what further steps it wishes to recommend.

It is extremely dangerous for the columnists, acting as "Armchair Strategists and Junior G-Men," to suggest that an attack on the West Coast and planned sabotage is imminent when the military authorities and the F.B.I. have indicated that this is not the fact. It comes close to shouting FIRE! in the theater; and if race riots occur, these writers will bear a heavy responsibility. Either Lippman [sic] has information which the War Department and the F.B.I. apparently do not have, or is acting with dangerous irresponsibility.

No minds were changed, and by this time the Attorney General was taking coarse and threatening abuse for his unwillingness to join the stampede to mass evacuation. . . .

On February 17 [Secretary of War] Stimson recorded meeting with War Department officials to outline a proposed executive order; General Gullion undertook to have the order drafted that night: "War Department orders will fill in the application of this Presidential order. These were outlined and Gullion is also to draft them." Further, Stimson said, "It will involve the tremendous task of moving between fifty and one hundred thousand people from their homes and finding temporary support and sustenance for them in the meanwhile, and ultimately locating them in new places away from the coast." In short, whatever his views during discussion with the President a few days before, Stimson now contemplated a mass move.

On February 18, 1942, Stimson met about the executive order with Biddle, Ennis, Rowe, and Tom Clark of the Department of Justice; and Robert Patterson, Under Secretary of War; McCloy; Gullion; and Bendetsen from the War Department. Stimson wrote:

> Biddle, McCloy and Gullion had done a good piece of work in breaking down the issues between the Departments the night before, and a draft of a presidential executive order had been drawn by Biddle based upon that conference and the preceding conference I had had yesterday. We went over them. I made a few suggestions and then approved it. This marks a long step forward towards a solution of a very dangerous and vexing problem. But I have no illusions as to the magnitude of the task that lies before us and the wails which will go up in relation to some of the actions which will be taken under it.

The Attorney General remembered the tenor of the meeting somewhat differently, but, writing in his autobiography, agreed about the result:

> Rowe and Ennis argued strongly against [the Executive Order]. But the decision had been made by the President. It was, he said,

a matter of military judgment. I did not think I should oppose it any further. The Department of Justice, as I had made it clear to him from the beginning, was opposed to and would have nothing to do with the evacuation.

In Los Angeles on the night of February 19, the United Citizens Federation, representing a wide range of pro-Nisei interests, held its first meeting of more than a thousand people. Plans were laid to persuade the press, the politicians and the government that their attacks upon the ethnic Japanese were unfounded. It was too late.

Earlier in the day, President Roosevelt had signed Executive Order 9066. The Order directed the Secretary of War and military commanders designated by him, whenever it was deemed necessary or desirable, to prescribe military areas "with respect to which, the right of any person to enter, remain in, or leave shall be subject to whatever restrictions the Secretary of War or the appropriate Military Commander may impose in his discretion." There was no direct mention of American citizens of Japanese descent, but unquestionably the Order was directed squarely at those Americans. A few months later, when there was talk of the War Department using the Executive Order to move Germans and Italians on the East Coast, the President wrote Stimson that he considered enemy alien control to be "primarily a civilian matter except of course in the case of the Japanese mass evacuation on the Pacific Coast."

The next day, to underscore the government's new-found unity on this decision, Attorney General Biddle sent to the President's personal attention a memorandum justifying the Executive Order and its broad grant of powers to the military. . . . :

This authority gives very broad powers to the Secretary of War and the Military Commanders. These powers are broad enough to permit them to exclude any particular individual from military areas. They could also evacuate groups of persons based on a reasonable classification. The order is not limited to aliens but includes citizens so that it can be exercised with respect to Japanese, irrespective of their citizenship.

The decision of safety of the nation in time of war is necessarily for the Military authorities. Authority over the movement of persons, whether citizens or noncitizens, may be exercised in time of war. . . . This authority is no more than declaratory of the power of the President, in time of war, with reference to all areas, sea or land.

The President is authorized in acting under his general war powers without further legislation. The exercise of the power can meet the specific situation and, of course, cannot be considered as any punitive measure against any particular nationalities. It is rather a precautionary measure to protect the national safety. It is not based on any legal theory but on the facts that the unrestricted movement of certain racial classes, whether American citizens or aliens, in specified defense areas may lead to serious disturbances. These disturbances cannot be controlled by police protection and have the threat of injury to our war effort. A condition and not a theory confronts the nation.

After the decision, there was no further dissent at the highest levels of the federal government. The War Department stood behind the facts and the Justice Department stood behind the law which were the foundation of the Executive Order. . . .

WRA [the War Relocation Authority] had to move quickly in finding centers to house 120,000 people and in developing policies and procedures for handling the evacuees soon to come under its jurisdiction. The President had stressed the need for immediate action; both the War Department and the WRA were anxious to remove the evacuees from the primitive, make-shift assembly centers.

Selecting the sites for the relocation centers proved complicated. Two sites had been chosen by military authorities before the WRA was born. Eight more locations were needed—designed to be "areas where the evacuees might settle down to a more stable kind of life until plans could be developed for their permanent relocation in communities outside the evacuated areas." Site selection required the War Department and the WRA to agree, although each had different interests. The WRA retained the portion of its early plan that called for large-scale agricultural programs in which evacuees would clear, develop and cultivate the land. Thus, the centers had to be on federal land so that improvements would become a public benefit. The Army, now face-to-face with the actual movement of people, no longer advocated freedom of movement outside the Western Defense Command. It became concerned about security and insisted that sites be located at a safe distance from "strategic installations," a term that included power lines and reservoirs. The Army also wanted each camp to have a population of at least 5,000 so that the number of guards could be minimized. To be habitable, the centers had to have suitable transportation, power and water facilities. By June 5, after considering 300 proposed sites and negotiating with many potentially affected state and local government officials, the WRA chose the final eight sites.

More than any other single factor, the requirement for large tracts of land virtually guaranteed that the sites would be inhospitable. As [historian] Roger Daniels explained it: "That these areas were still vacant land in 1942, land that the ever-voracious pioneers and developers had either passed by or abandoned, speaks volumes about their attractiveness."

The sites were indeed unattractive. Manzanar [California] and Poston [Arizona], selected by the Army, were in the desert. Although both could eventually produce crops, extensive irrigation would be needed, and Poston's climate was particularly harsh. Six other sites were also arid desert. Gila River, near Phoenix, suffered almost as severely from the heat. Minidoka [Idaho] and Heart Mountain [Wyoming], the two northernmost centers, were known for hard winters and severe dust storms. Tule Lake [California] was the most developed site; located in a dry lake bed, much of it was ready for planting. Topaz [Utah] was covered in greasewood brush. Granada [Colorado] was little better, although there was some provision for irrigation. The last two centers—Rohwer and Jerome in Arkansas—were entirely different. Located in swampland, the sites were heavily wooded, with severe drainage problems. . . .

Having selected the sites, the WRA's second job was to develop the policies and procedures that would control the lives of evacuees. This was begun almost immediately, with help from the JACL*. In his April 6 letter to Eisenhower,** Masaoka set forth a long list of recommendations for regulating life in the camps and stressed, among other things, the importance of respecting the citizenship of the Nisei, protecting the health of elderly Issei, providing educational opportunities, and recognizing that the evacuees were "American" in their outlook and wanted to make a contribution to the war effort. The first set of policies issued May 29 were labelled by the Director "tentative, still fairly crude, and subject to immediate change." Further, they did not reach the centers until three weeks after the first groups had arrived. They were not clarified until August, when over half the evacuee population had been transferred to the centers. Given the limited time available and the novelty of WRA's task as both jailer and advocate for the evacuees, it is not surprising that the agency was not fully prepared. Still, the fact that WRA was not able to provide dependable answers to basic questions about how the centers would be managed probably fed the disaffection that increasingly characterized reactions to the relocation centers.

The confluence of diverse political interests had again conspired against the evacuees. The new centers at which they were arriving were barely an improvement over the assembly centers they had left. The increased freedom and possible resettlement they had anticipated had been reversed in favor of confinement. And the rules that would govern their lives were uncertain or non-existent. . . .

Except at Manzanar, which was built as an assembly center and transferred to the WRA for use as a relocation center, all the relocation camps were built from scratch. Thus, the design and facilities were relatively standard. By agreement with the WRA, the camps were built by the War

[*Japanese-American Citizens League, headed by Bill Masaoka]
[**Milton Eisenhower was in charge of the camps during their early operation.]

Department according to its own specifications. Barbed-wire fences, watch-towers, and armed guards surrounded the residential and administrative areas of most camps.

The military police and administrative personnel had separate quarters, more spacious and better furnished. At most centers, evacuees built the administrative housing, which had not been included in the original construction contracts. At Topaz, Gladys Bell and her family, who were with the administrative staff, had an entire four-room barrack complete with piano. At Manzanar, staff houses were painted and had residential cooling systems, refrigerators, indoor toilets and baths.

Arrangements for the evacuees were not comparable. The basic organizational unit was once again the "block," consisting of about 12 to 14 barracks, a mess hall, baths, showers, toilets, a laundry and a recreation hall. Each barrack was about 20 by 100 to 120 feet, divided into four or six rooms, each from 20 by 16 to 20 by 25 feet. Each room housed at least one family, even if the family was very large. Even at the end of 1942, in 928 cases, two families shared a 20 by 25-foot room.

Construction was of the kind used to house soldiers overseas—the so-called "theatre of operations" type, modified somewhat to accommodate women and children. The barracks were built of planks nailed to studs and covered with tarpaper. In some places the green wood warped quickly, cracking walls and floors. Congressman Leland Ford said of the Manzanar barracks that "on dusty days, one might just as well be outside as inside." "So much of our work was done sloppily," Dean Meeker testified of Heart Mountain:

> I can remember the foreman's comment when he found cracks in the building. He said, "Well, I guess those Japs will be stuffing their underwear in there to keep the wind out."
>
> In my defense, I will say I applied a bit more diligence and care to my work when I realized people would actually have to survive a Wyoming winter in this housing. We all knew that there was no way anyone accustomed to California weather could possibly survive a Wyoming winter in those barracks. If they were from California, they probably didn't even own the proper clothing for a winter in Cody.

No inside walls or ceilings were included in the original plans. As part of a winterization program, however, evacuee construction crews eventually added firboard ceilings and inside walls in many of the centers.

A visiting reporter from *The San Francisco Chronicle* described quarters at Tule Lake:

> Room size—about 15 by 25, considered too big for two reporters.
>   Condition—dirty.

Contents—two Army cots, each with two Army blankets, one pillow, some sheets and pillow cases (these came as a courtesy from the management), and a coal-burning stove (no coal). There were no dishes, rugs, curtains, or housekeeping equipment of any kind. (We had in addition one sawhorse and three pieces of wood, which the management did not explain.)

The furnishings at other camps were similar. At Minidoka, arriving evacuees found two stacked canvas cots, a pot-bellied stove and a light bulb hanging from the ceiling; at Topaz, cots, two blankets, a pot-bellied stove and some cotton mattresses. Rooms had no running water, which had to be carried from community facilities. Running back and forth from the laundry room to rinse and launder soiled diapers was a particular inconvenience. . . .

Others, however, found not even the minimal comforts that had been planned for them. An unrealistic schedule combined with wartime shortages of labor and materials meant that the WRA had difficulty meeting its construction schedule. In most cases, the barracks were completed, but at some centers evacuees lived without electric light, adequate toilets or laundry facilities. . . .

Mess halls planned for about 300 people had to handle 600 or 900 for short periods. Three months after the project opened, Manzanar still lacked equipment for 16 of 36 messhalls. At Gila:

There were 7,700 people crowded into space designed for 5,000. They were housed in messhalls, recreation halls, and even latrines. As many as 25 persons lived in a space intended for four.

As at the assembly centers, one result was that evacuees were often denied privacy in even the most intimate aspects of their lives. . . . Even when families had separate quarters, the partitions between rooms failed to give much privacy. Gladys Bell described the situation at Topaz:

[T]he evacuees . . . had only one room, unless there were around ten in the family. Their rooms had a pot-bellied stove, a single electric light hanging from the ceiling, an Army cot for each person and a blanket for the bed. Each barrack had six rooms with only three flues. This meant that a hole had to be cut through the wall of one room for the stovepipe to join the chimney of the next room. The hole was large so that the wall would not burn. As a result, everything said and some things whispered were easily heard by people living in the next room. Sometimes the family would be a couple with four children living next to an older couple, perhaps of a different religion, older ideas and with a difference in all ways of life—such as music.

253

Despite these wretched conditions the evacuees again began to rebuild their lives. Several evacuees recall "foraging for bits of wallboard and wood" and dodging guards to get materials from the scrap lumber piles to build shelves and furniture. . . . Eventually, rooms were partitioned and shelves, tables, chairs and other furniture appeared. Paint and cloth for curtains and spreads came from mail order houses at evacuee expense. Flowers bloomed and rock gardens emerged; tree and shrubs were planted. Many evacuees grew victory gardens. One described the change:

> [W]hen we entered camp, it was a barren desert. When we left camp, it was a garden that had been built up without tools, it was green around the camp with vegetation, flowers, and also with artificial lakes, and that's how we left it.

The success of evacuees' efforts to improve their surroundings, however, was always tempered by the harsh climate. In the western camps, particularly Heart Mountain, Poston, Topaz and Minidoka, dust was a principal problem. Monica Sone described her first day at Minidoka:

> [W]e were given a rousing welcome by a dust storm. . . . We felt as if we were standing in a gigantic sand-mixing machine as the sixty-mile gale lifted the loose earth up into the sky, obliterating everything. Sand filled our mouths and nostrils and stung our faces and hands like a thousand darting needles. Henry and Father pushed on ahead while Mother, Sumi and I followed, hanging onto their jackets, banging suitcases into each other. At last we staggered into our room, gasping and blinded. We sat on our suitcases to rest, peeling off our jackets and scarves. The window panels rattled madly, and the dust poured through the cracks like smoke. Now and then when the wind subsided, I saw other evacuees, hanging on to their suitcases, heads bent against the stinging dust. The wind whipped their scarves and towels from their heads and zipped them out of sight.

In desert camps, the evacuees met severe extremes of temperature as well. In winter it reached 35 degrees below zero and summers brought temperature as high as 115°. Because the desert did not cool off at night, evacuees would splash water on their cots to be cool enough to sleep. Rattlesnakes and desert wildlife added danger to discomfort.

The Arkansas camps had equally unpleasant weather. Winters were cold and snowy while summers were unbearably hot and humid, heavy with chiggers and clouds of mosquitos. . . .

The WRA walked a fine line in providing for evacuees' basic needs. On the one hand was their genuine sympathy for the excluded people. On the other was a well-founded apprehension that the press and the politicians would seek out and denounce any evidence that evacuees were being treated generously. WRA's compromise was to strive for a system that would provide a healthy but Spartan environment. They did not always succeed, and it was usually the evacuees who suffered when they failed.

The meal system was institutional—food served in messhalls at designated times. Lines were long and tables crowded. Special arrangements were made for infants, the sick or elderly, but, as in most institutions, they were developed from necessity, not convenience. There were formula kitchens for the babies, to which their mothers brought them at designated times; some mothers walked many "blocks" as often as six times a day to get their infants fed when the camps first opened. Others bought hot plates to make formula, but without running water this system was almost as unsatisfactory. The arrangements for those on restricted diets were difficult. The diet kitchens were often located in the administration complex, far from the residential area; the sick and the elderly had to walk as much as a mile three times a day to get their special food.

Food quality and quantity varied among centers, generally improving in the later months as evacuees began to produce it themselves. The WRA's expressed policy was that evacuees were entitled to the same treatment as other American citizens: WRA was to provide an adequate diet; foods rationed to the public would be available to evacuees in the same quantities. The reality, however, was very different. Weiners, dry fish, rice, macaroni and pickled vegetables are among the foods evacuees recall eating most frequently. Meatless days were regular at some centers—two or three times a week, and many items were unavailable. Continuing dairy shortages meant that, at most centers, fluid milk was served only to those with special needs, while at others, there was watery skim milk. In fact, no really appetizing meals could be produced regularly under a requirement that feeding the evacuees could not cost more than rations for the Army, which were set at 50 cents per person per day. Actual costs per evacuee were approximately 45 cents per person per day; sometimes they fell as low as 31 cents.

In January 1943, after accusations that evacuees were being coddled, the WRA adopted new policies which showed that their fear of adverse publicity had overcome any humanitarian impulse. "At no time would evacuees' food have higher specifications than or exceed in quantity what the civil population may obtain in the open market." Centers were ordered to submit their planned menus for each 30-day period to Washington for advance approval to make sure that the public was adequately informed of WRA feeding policies and procedures. Perhaps the best that can be said of the meal system is that no one starved.

No one froze either. As winter approached, many evacuees were unprepared, either because they had brought no warm clothing due to baggage limitations or because they did not own such clothing, never having needed it at home. In response, the WRA provided monthly clothing allowances and distributed surplus clothing. Each employed evacuee and his or her dependents were supposed to receive from $2 to $3.75 each month, depending on the evacuee's age and the climate of the center. The system, however, did not work well because the shorthanded WRA assigned it to an inexperienced, overworked staff, which was unable to handle the additional workload, and delays continually frustrated evacuees at the mercy of the WRA for their survival. The surplus distribution became the principal source of warm clothing during the first winter, when need was greatest. The clothes were old GI peajackets and uniforms, sizes 38 to 44. However unattractive, they were warm and a source of great amusement. . . .

Discontent over camp living conditions was inevitable. Housing and food were poor. Suspicion that staff was stealing and selling food was widespread. Wages and clothing allowances were delayed. For many older residents, there were no jobs. WRA had promised that household goods would be brought to evacuees as soon as they arrived; months later, none had come. They were continual shortages of equipment and material for education and recreation. WRA had promised that one of its first jobs would be to build schools and furnish school equipment, but priority often went instead to improving quarters for WRA personnel.

Fear, uncertainty and the monotony of enforced idleness aggravated tension. At the older centers, WRA policies had not been set when evacuees arrived, and there were no answers to many of their questions. They feared the future—not only what would happen after the war, but also whether there would be enough food or quality medical care at the centers. Many had lost income and property, which left them few resources to fall back on. They feared the "outside." Relations with outside communities were poor, and evacuees knew that some towns had passed resolutions against the free movement of evacuees. Local communities and politicians had investigated the camps for evidence of "coddling."

Evacuees feared and resented the changes forced by life in the centers, particularly the breakdown of family authority, created in part by a situation in which children no longer depended so heavily on their parents. Family separation was common, and mass living discouraged normal communication and family activity. Perhaps most difficult, the position of the head of the family had been weakened. No longer the breadwinner providing food and shelter, he had been supplanted by the government; his authority over the family and his ability to lead and discipline were diminished. Children unsettlingly found their parents as helpless as they.

At the root of it all, evacuees resented being prisoners against whom no crime was charged and for whom there was no recourse. Armed guards patrolled their community and searched their packages. No evacuee could have a camera. Even beer was prohibited. For a long time, no evacuee could leave the center, except for emergency reasons, and then only in the company of someone who was not of Japanese ancestry. Evacuee positions were subordinate to WRA personnel, regardless of ability, and wages were low. At some centers, project officials actively tried to maintain class and role distinctions, forbidding WRA personnel and evacuees to eat in the same messhall, for example. . . .

DOCUMENTS

In Support of Evacuation, 1942

ATTORNEY GENERAL WARREN. For some time I have been of the opinion that the solution of our alien enemy problem with all its ramifications, which include the descendants of aliens, is not only a Federal problem but is a military problem. We believe that all of the decisions in that regard must be made by the military command that is charged with the security of this area. I am convinced that the fifth-column activities of our enemy call for the participation of people who are in fact American citizens, and that if we are to deal realistically with the problem we must realize that we will be obliged in time of stress to deal with subversive elements of our own citizenry. . . .

A wave of organized sabotage in California accompanied by an actual air raid or even by a prolonged black-out could not only be more destructive to life and property but could result in retarding the entire war effort of this Nation far more than the treacherous bombing of Pearl Harbor.

I hesitate to think what the result would be of the destruction of any of our big airplane factories in this State. It will interest you to know that some of our airplane factories in this State are entirely surrounded by Japanese land ownership or occupancy. It is a situation that is fraught with the greatest danger and under no circumstances should it ever be permitted to exist. . . .

Unfortunately, however, many of our people and some of our authorities and, I am afraid, many of our people in other parts of the country are of the opinion that because we have had no sabotage and no fifth column activities in this State since the beginning of the war, that means that none have been planned for us. But I take the view that that is the most ominous sign in our whole situation. It convinces me more than perhaps any other factor that the sabotage that we are to get, the fifth column activities that we are to get, are timed just like Pearl Harbor was

SOURCE: Testimony of Earl Warren, U.S. Congress, House Select Committee Investigating National Defense, *San Francisco Hearing*, 77th Cong., 2d sess., 11009–19.

timed and just like the invasion of France, and of Denmark, and of Norway, and all of those other countries. . . .

I want to say that the consensus of opinion among the law-enforcement officers of this State is that there is more potential danger among the group of Japanese who are born in this country than from the alien Japanese who were born in Japan. That might seem an anomaly to some people, but the fact is that, in the first place, there are twice as many of them. There are 33,000 aliens and there are 66,000 born in this country.

In the second place, most of the Japanese who were born in Japan are over 55 years of age. There has been practically no migration to this country since 1924. But in some instances the children of those people have been sent to Japan for their education, either in whole or in part, and while they are over there they are indoctrinated with the idea of Japanese imperialism. They receive their religious instruction which ties up their religion with their Emperor, and they come back here imbued with the ideas and the policies of Imperial Japan. . . .

We believe that when we are dealing with the Caucasian race we have methods that will test the loyalty of them, and we believe that we can, in dealing with the Germans and the Italians, arrive at some fairly sound conclusions because of our knowledge of the way they live in the community and have lived for many years. But when we deal with the Japanese we are in an entirely different field and we cannot form any opinion that we believe to be sound. . . .

MR. [JOHN] SPARKMAN. I have noticed suggestions in newspaper stories. I noticed a telegram this morning with reference to the civil rights of these people. What do you have to say about that?

ATTORNEY GENERAL WARREN. I believe, sir, that in time of war every citizen must give up some of his normal rights.

Exclusion and Internment Upheld, 1944

The petitioner, an American citizen of Japanese descent, was convicted in a federal district court for remaining in San Leandro, California, a "Military Area," contrary to Civilian Exclusion Order No. 34 of the Commanding General of the Western Command, U.S. Army, which directed that after May 9, 1942, all persons of Japanese ancestry should be excluded from that area. No question was raised as to petitioner's loyalty to the United States. . . .

Like curfew, exclusion of those of Japanese origin was deemed necessary because of the presence of an unascertained number of disloyal

SOURCE: Justice Hugo Black's majority opinion in *Korematsu v. United States,* 323 U.S. 214 (1944).

members of the group, most of whom we have no doubt were loyal to this country. It was because we could not reject the finding of the military authorities that it was impossible to bring about an immediate segregation of the disloyal from the loyal that we sustained the validity of the curfew order as applying to the whole group. In the instant case, temporary exclusion of the entire group was rested by the military on the ground. The judgment that exclusion of the whole group was for the same reason a military imperative answers the contention that the exclusion was in the nature of group punishment based on antagonism to those of Japanese origin. That there were members of the group who retained loyalties to Japan has been confirmed by investigations made subsequent to the exclusion. Approximately five thousand American citizens of Japanese ancestry refused to swear unqualified allegiance to the United States and to renounce allegiance to the Japanese Emperor, and several thousand evacuees requested repatriation to Japan. . . .

It is said that we are dealing here with the case of imprisonment of a citizen in a concentration camp solely because of his ancestry, without evidence or inquiry concerning his loyalty and good disposition towards the United States. Our task would be simple, our duty clear, were this a case involving the imprisonment of a loyal citizen in a concentration camp because of racial prejudice. Regardless of the true nature of the assembly and relocation centers—and we deem it unjustifiable to call them concentration camps with all the ugly connotations that term implies—we are dealing specifically with nothing but an exclusion order. To cast this case into outlines of racial prejudice, without reference to the real military dangers which were presented, merely confuses the issue. Korematsu was not excluded from the Military Area because of hostility to him or his race. He was excluded because we are at war with the Japanese Empire, because the properly constituted military authorities feared an invasion of our West Coast and felt constrained to take proper security measures, because they decided that the military urgency of the situation demanded that all citizens of Japanese ancestry be segregated from the West Coast temporarily, and finally, because Congress, reposing its confidence in this time of war in our military leaders—as inevitably it must—determined that they should have the power to do just this. There was some evidence of disloyalty on the part of some, the military authorities considered that the need for action was great, and time was short. We cannot—by availing ourselves of the calm perspective of hindsight—now say that at that time these actions were unjustified.

An American Promise, 1976

By the President of the United States of America: A Proclamation

February 19 is the anniversary of a very, very sad day in American history. It was on that date in 1942 that Executive Order 9066 was issued resulting in the uprooting of many, many loyal Americans. Over 100,000 persons of Japanese ancestry were removed from their homes, detained in special camps, and eventually relocated.

We now know what we should have known then—not only was that evacuation wrong but Japanese-Americans were and are loyal Americans. On the battlefield and at home the names of Japanese-Americans have been and continue to be written in America's history for the sacrifices and the contributions they have made to the well-being and to the security of this, our common Nation.

Executive Order 9066 ceased to be effective at the end of World War II. Because there was no formal statement of its termination, there remains some concern among Japanese-Americans that there yet may be some life in that obsolete document. The proclamation [4417] that I am signing here today should remove all doubt on that matter.

I call upon the American people to affirm with me the unhyphenated American promise that we have learned from the tragedy of that long ago experience—forever to treasure liberty and justice for each individual American and resolve that this kind of error shall never be made again.

SOURCE: From *Public Papers of the Presidents*, Gerald R. Ford, 1976–1977 (Washington, D.C.: Government Printing Office, February 19, 1976), 110.

CHAPTER 14

Moving to Suburbia: Dreams and Discontents

World War II set off an economic boom marked by the steady growth of family and individual incomes that lasted, with few interruptions, until 1973. Never before had the nation experienced such prosperity. Never before had material products that Americans associated with "the good life"—automobiles, dishwashers, stereos, televisions and more—become so readily available to large segments of the population.

The keystone of the middle-class dream was home ownership. During the 1930s and 1940s the lyrics of popular ballads like "My Blue Heaven" had expressed the desire for a bungalow in the suburbs, in which husband, wife, and children would live an idyllic life. But wartime demands for the construction of military bases and for defense industries had brought private home building, already slowed by the Depression, to a virtual halt. Within a few years of the war's end, however, the building boom was under way. Kenneth Jackson's essay "The Baby Boom and the Age of Subdivision" describes how the postwar demand for suburban housing, fueled by veterans and their growing families, was served by government assistance

261

and enterprising builders. Among the latter, William Levitt was possibly the most ingenious; and the housing tracts he built, called Levittowns, came to symbolize post-World War II construction. Which innovations in home construction and community planning were most likely responsible for establishing Levitt's reputation?

Jackson describes not only the creation of postwar suburbs but also the life-styles that characterized those communities. Although large numbers of people voted their approval of suburban life by their decisions to relocate their families, the movement was not without critics. The homogeneity and conformity of housing developments were frequent targets, as illustrated by the first document, Malvina Reynolds's popular song of the early 1960s, "Little Boxes." Does it give a fair picture of the suburbs?

The second document, from the best-selling book The Feminine Mystique *by feminist Betty Friedan, singles out for attack another aspect of suburban life, which the author calls "The Problem That Has No Name." What did Friedan see as the impact of suburbanization on the American housewife? Did the problem she discusses arise because of suburban development, or because of larger cultural changes that took place in cities as well as in suburbs?*

The final document is from a New York Times *article written on the occasion of the first Levittown's thirtieth anniversary. In the piece, both William Levitt and a local real estate broker enthusiastically proclaim Levittown a success. What is your assessment of suburban living in terms of fulfilling physical, social, and emotional needs?*

ESSAY

The Baby Boom and the Age of the Subdivision

Kenneth Jackson

What the Blandings wanted . . . was simple enough:
a two-story house in quiet, modern good taste, . . . a good-
sized living room with a fire place, a dining room, pantry,
and kitchen, a small lavatory, four bedrooms and
accompanying baths, . . . a roomy cellar . . . plenty of
closets.

—Eric Hodgins,
Mr. Blandings Builds His Dream House (1939)

No man who owns his own house and lot can be a
Communist. He has too much to do.

—William J. Levitt, 1948

At 7 P.M. (Eastern time) on August 14, 1945, radio stations across the nation
interrupted normal programming for President Harry S. Truman's announcement of the surrender of Japan. It was a moment in time that those
who experienced it will never forget. World War II was over. Across the
nation, Americans gathered to celebrate their victory. In New York City
two million people converged on Times Square as though it were New
Year's Eve. In smaller cities and towns, the response was no less tumultuous, as spontaneous cheers, horns, sirens, and church bells telegraphed
the news to every household and hamlet, convincing even small children
that it was a very special day. To the average person, the most important
consequence of victory was not the end of shortages, not the restructuring
of international boundaries or reparations payments or big power politics,
but the survival of husbands and sons. Some women regretted that their
first decent-paying, responsible jobs would be taken away by returning
veterans. Most, however, felt a collective sigh of relief. Normal family life
could resume. The long vigil was over. Their men would be coming home.

In truth, the United States was no better prepared for peace than it
had been for war when the German *Wehrmacht* crossed the Polish frontier
in the predawn hours of September 1, 1939. For more than five years
military necessity had taken priority over consumer goods, and by 1945
almost everyone had a long list of unfilled material wants.

SOURCE: Kenneth Jackson, *Crabgrass Frontier: The Suburbanization of America,* Copyright ©
1985 by Kenneth Jackson. Reprinted by permission of Oxford University Press, Inc.

Housing was the area of most pressing need. Through sixteen years of depression and war, the residential construction industry had been dormant, with new home starts averaging less than 100,000 per year. Almost one million people had migrated to defense areas in the early 1940s, but new housing for them was designated as "temporary," in part as an economy move and in part because the real-estate lobby did not want emergency housing converted to permanent use after the war. Meanwhile, the marriage rate, after a decade of decline, had begun a steep rise in 1940, as war became increasingly likely and the possibility of separation added a spur to decision-making. In addition, married servicemen received an additional fifty dollars per month allotment, which went directly to the wives. Soon thereafter, the birth rate began to climb, reaching 22 per 1,000 in 1943, the highest in two decades. Many of the newcomers were "good-bye babies," conceived just before the husbands shipped out, partly because of an absence of birth control, partly because the wife's allotment check would be increased with each child, and partly as a tangible reminder of a father who could not know when, or if, he would return. During the war, government and industry both played up the suburban house to the families of absent servicemen, and between 1941 and 1946 some of the nation's most promising architects published their "dream houses" in a series in the *Ladies' Home Journal*.

After the war, both the marriage and the birth rates continued at a high level. In individual terms, this rise in family formation coupled with the decline in housing starts meant that there were virtually no homes for sale or apartments for rent at war's end. Continuing a trend begun during the Great Depression, six million families were doubling up with relatives or friends by 1947, and another 500,000 were occupying quonset huts or temporary quarters. Neither figure included families living in substandard dwellings or those in desperate need of more room. In Chicago, 250 former trolley cars were sold as homes. In New York City a newly wed couple set up housekeeping for two days in a department store window in hopes that the publicity would help them find an apartment. In Omaha a newspaper advertisement proposed: "Big Ice Box, 7 × 17 feet, could be fixed up to live in." In Atlanta the city bought 100 trailers for veterans. In North Dakota surplus grain bins were turned into apartments. In brief, the demand for housing was unprecedented.

The federal government responded to an immediate need for five million new homes by underwriting a vast new construction program. In the decade after the war Congress regularly approved billions of dollars worth of additional mortgage insurance for the Federal Housing Administration. Even more important was the Servicemen's Readjustment Act of 1944, which created a Veterans Administration mortgage program similar to that of FHA. This law gave official endorsement and support to the view that the 16 million GI's of World War II should return to civilian life with a home of their own. Also, it accepted the builders' contention that they needed an end to government controls but not to government insurance on their investments in residential construction. According to novelist John Keats, "The real estate boys read the Bill, looked at one another in happy amazement, and the dry, rasping noise they made rubbing their hands together could have been heard as far away as Tawi Tawi."

It is not recorded how far the noise carried, but anyone in the residential construction business had ample reason to rub their hands. The assurance of federal mortgage guarantees—at whatever price the builder set—stimulated an unprecedented building boom. Single-family housing starts spurted from only 114,000 in 1944, to 937,000 in 1946, to 1,183,000 in 1948, and to 1,692,000 in 1950, an all-time high. However, . . . what distinguished the period was an increase in the number, importance, and size of large builders. Residential construction in the United States had always been highly fragmented in comparison with other industries, and dominated by small and poorly organized house builders who had to subcontract much of the work because their low volume did not justify the hiring of all the craftsmen needed to put up a dwelling. In housing, as in other areas of the economy, World War II was beneficial to large businesses. Whereas before 1945, the typical contractor had put up fewer than five houses per year, by 1959, the median single-family builder put up twenty-two structures. As early as 1949, fully 70 percent of new homes were constructed by only 10 percent of the firms (a percentage that would remain roughly stable for the next three decades), and by 1955 subdivisions accounted for more than three-quarters of all new housing in metropolitan areas.

Viewed from an international perspective, however, the building of homes in the United States remained a small-scale enterprise. In 1969, for example, the percentage of all new units built by builders of more than 500 units per year was only 8.1 percent in the United States, compared with 24 percent in Great Britain and 33 percent in France. World War II, therefore, did not transform the American housing industry as radically as it did that of Europe.

The family that had the greatest impact on postwar housing in the United States was Abraham Levitt and his sons, William and Alfred, who ultimately built more than 140,000 houses and turned a cottage industry into a major manufacturing process. They began on a small scale on Long Island in 1929 and concentrated for years on substantial houses in Rockville Center. Increasing their pace in 1934 with a 200-unit subdivision called "Strathmore" in Manhasset, the Levitts continued to focus on the upper-middle class and marketed their tudor-style houses at between $9,100 and $18,500. Private commissions and smaller subdivisions carried the firm through the remainder of the prewar period.

In 1941 Levitt and Sons received a government contract for 1,600 (later increased to 2,350) war workers' homes in Norfolk, Virginia. The effort was a nightmare, but the brothers learned how to lay dozens of concrete foundations in a single day and to preassemble uniform walls and roofs. Additional contracts for more federal housing in Portsmouth, Virginia, and for barracks for shipyard workers at Pearl Harbor provided supplemental experience, as did William's service with the Navy Seabees from 1943 to 1945. Thus, the Levitts were among the nation's largest home builders even before construction of the first Levittown.

Returning to Long Island after the war, the Levitts built 2,250 houses in Roslyn in 1946 in the $17,500 to $23,500 price range, well beyond the means of the average veteran. In that same year, however, they began the acquisition of 4,000 acres of potato farms in the Town of Hempstead, where they planned the biggest private housing project in American history.

The formula for Island Trees, soon renamed Levittown, was simple. After bulldozing the land and removing the trees, trucks carefully dropped off building materials at precise 60-foot intervals. Each house was built on a concrete slab (no cellar); the floors were of asphalt and the walls of composition rock-board. Plywood replaced ¾-inch strip lap, ¾-inch double lap was changed to ⅜-inch for roofing, and the horse and scoop were replaced by the bulldozer. New power hand tools like saws, routers, and nailers helped increase worker productivity. Freight cars loaded with lumber went directly into a cutting yard where one man cut parts for ten houses in one day.

The construction process itself was divided into twenty-seven distinct steps—beginning with laying the foundation and ending with a clean sweep of the new home. Crews were trained to do one job—one day the white-paint men, then the red-paint men, then the tile layers. Every possible part, and especially the most difficult ones, were preassembled in central shops, whereas most builders did it on site. Thus, the Levitts reduced the skilled component to 20–40 percent. The five-day work week was standard, but they were the five days during which building was possible; Saturday and Sunday were considered to be the days when it rained. In the process, the Levitts defied unions and union work rules (against spray painting, for example) and insisted that subcontractors work only for them. Vertical integration also meant that the firm made its own concrete, grew its own timber, and cut its own lumber. It also bought all appliances from wholly owned subsidiaries. More than thirty houses went up each day at the peak of production.

Initially limited to veterans, this first "Levittown" was twenty-five miles east of Manhattan and particularly attractive to new families that had been formed during and just after the war. Squashed in with their in-laws or in tiny apartments where landlords frowned on children, the GI's looked upon Levittown as the answer to their most pressing need. Months before the first three hundred Levitt houses were occupied in October 1947, customers stood in line for the four-room Cape Cod box renting at sixty dollars per month. The first eighteen hundred houses were initially available only for rental, with an option to buy after a year's residence. Because the total for mortgage, interest, principal, and taxes was *less* than the rent, almost everyone bought; after 1949 all units were for sale only. So many of the purchasers were young families that the first issue of *Island Trees*, the community newspaper, opined that "our lives are held closely together because most of us are within the same age bracket, in similar income groups, live in almost identical houses and have common problems." And so many babies were born to them that the suburb came to be known as "Fertility Valley" and "The Rabbit Hutch."

Ultimately encompassing more than 17,400 separate houses and 82,000 residents, Levittown was the largest housing development ever put up by a single builder, and it served the American dream-house market at close to the lowest prices the industry could attain. The typical Cape Cod was down-to-earth and unpretentious; the intention was not to stir the imagination, but to provide the best shelter at the least price. Each dwelling included a twelve-by-sixteen-foot living-room with a fireplace, one bath, and two bedrooms (about 750 square feet), with easy expansion possibilities upstairs in the unfinished attic or outward into the yard. Most importantly, the floor plan was practical and well-designed, with the kitchen moved to the front of the house near the entrance so that mothers could watch their children from kitchen windows and do their washing and cooking with a minimum of movement. Similarly, the living room was placed in the rear and given a picture window overlooking the back yard. This early Levitt house was as basic to post–World War II suburban development as the Model T had been to the automobile. In each case, the actual design features were less important than the fact that they were mass-produced and thus priced within the reach of the middle class.

William Jaird Levitt, who assumed primary operating responsibility for the firm soon after the war, disposed of houses as quickly as other men disposed of cars. Pricing his Cape Cods at $7,990 (the earliest models went for $6,990) and his ranches at $9,500, he promised no down payment, no closing costs, and "no hidden extras." With FHA and VA "production advances," Levitt boasted the largest line of credit ever offered a private home builder. He simplified the paperwork required for purchase and reduced the entire financing and titling transaction to two half-hour steps. His full-page advertisements offered a sweetener to eliminate lingering resistance—a Bendix washer was included in the purchase price. Other inducements included an eight-inch television set (for which the family would pay for the next thirty years). So efficient was the operation that *Harper's Magazine* reported in 1948 that Levitt undersold his nearest competition by $1,500 and still made a $1,000 profit on each house. As *New York Times'* architecture critic Paul Goldberger has noted, "Levittown houses were social creations more than architectural ones—they turned the detached, single-family house from a distant dream to a real possibility for thousands of middle-class American families."

Buyers received more than shelter for their money. When the initial families arrived with their baby strollers and play pens, there were no trees, schools, churches, or private telephones. Grocery shopping was a planned adventure, and picking up the mail required sloshing through the mud to Hicksville. The Levitts planted apple, cherry, and evergreen trees on each plot, however, and the development ultimately assumed a more parklike appearance. To facilitate development as a garden community, streets were curvilinear (and invariably called "roads" or "lanes"), and through traffic was shunted to peripheral thoroughfares. Nine swimming pools, sixty playgrounds, ten baseball diamonds, and seven "village greens" provided open space and recreational opportunities. The Levitts forbade fences (a practice later ignored) and permitted outdoor clothes drying only on specially designed, collapsible racks. They even supervised lawn-cutting for the first few years—doing the jobs themselves if necessary and sending the laggard families the bill.

Architectural critics, many of whom were unaccustomed to the tastes or resources of moderate-income people, were generally unimpressed by the repetitious houses on 60-by-100-foot "cookie cutter lots" and referred to Levittown as "degraded in conception and impoverished in form." From the Wantagh Parkway, the town stretched away to the east as far as the eye could see, house after identical house, a horizon broken only by telephone poles. Paul Goldberger, who admired the individual designs, thought that the whole was "an urban planning disaster," while [social critic] Lewis Mumford complained that Levittown's narrow range of house type and income range resulted in a one-class community and a backward design. He noted that the Levitts used "new-fashioned methods to compound old-fashioned mistakes."

But Levittown was a huge popular success where it counted—in the marketplace. On a single day in March 1949, fourteen hundred contracts were drawn, some with families that had been in line for four days. "I truly loved it," recalled one early resident. "When they built the Village Green, our big event was walking down there for ice cream."

In the 1950s the Levitts shifted their attention from Long Island to an equally large project near Philadelphia. Located on former broccoli and spinach farms in lower Bucks County, Pennsylvania, this new Levittown was built within a few miles of the new Fairless Works of the United States Steel Corporation, where the largest percentage of the community's residents were employed. It was composed on eight master blocks, each of about one square mile and focusing on its own recreational facilities. Totaling about 16,000 homes when completed late in the decade, the town included light industry and a big, 55-acre shopping center. According to Levitt, "We planned every foot of it—every store, filling station, school, house, apartment, church, color, tree, and shrub."

268

In the 1960s, the Levitt forces shifted once again, this time to Willing-boro, New Jersey, where a third Levittown was constructed within distant commuting range of Philadelphia. This last town was the focus of Herbert Gans's well-known account of *The Levittowners*. The Cape Cod remained the basic style, but Levitt improved the older models to resemble more closely the pseudo-colonial design that was so popular in the Northeast.

If imitation is the sincerest form of flattery, then William Levitt has been much honored in the past forty years. His replacement of basement foundations with the radiantly heated concrete slab was being widely cop-ied as early as 1950. Levitt did not actually pioneer many of the mass-production techniques—the use of plywood, particle board, and gypsum board, as well as power hand tools like saws, routers, and nailers, for example—but his developments were so widely publicized that in every large metropolitan area, large builders appeared who adopted similar methods. . . .

FHA and VA programs made possible the financing of their immense developments. Title VI of the National Housing Act of 1934 allowed a builder to insure 90 percent of the mortgage of a house costing up to nine thousand dollars. Most importantly, an ambitious entrepreneur could get an FHA "commitment" to insure the mortgage, and then use that "com-mitment" to sign himself up as a temporary mortgagor. The mortgage lender (a bank or savings and loan institution) would then make "pro-duction advances" to the contractor as the work progressed, so that the builder needed to invest very little of his own hard cash. Previously, even the largest builders could not bring together the capital to undertake thou-sand-house developments. FHA alone insured three thousand houses in Henry J. Kaiser's Panorama City, California; five thousand in Frank Sharp's Oak Forest; and eight thousand in Klutznick's Park Forest project.

However financed and by whomever built, the new subdivisions that were typical of American urban development between 1945 and 1973 tended to share five common characteristics. The first was peripheral lo-cation. A Bureau of Labor Statistics survey of home building in 1946–1947 in six metropolitan regions determined that the suburbs accounted for at least 62 percent of construction. By 1950 the national suburban growth rate was ten times that of central cities, and in 1954 the editors of *Fortune* estimated that 9 million people had moved to the suburbs in the previous decade. The inner cities did have some empty lots—serviced by sewers, electrical connections, gas lines, and streets—available for development. But the filling-in process was not amenable to mass production techniques, and it satisfied neither the economic nor the psychological temper of the times.

The few new neighborhoods that were located within the boundaries of major cities tended also to be on the open land at the edges of the built-up sections. In New York City, the only area in the 1946–1947 study where city construction was greater than that of the suburbs, the big growth was on the outer edges of Queens, a borough that had been largely undeveloped in 1945. In Memphis new development moved east out Summer, Poplar, Walnut Grove, and Park Avenues, where FHA and VA subdivisions advertised "No Down Payment" or "One Dollar Down" on giant billboards. In Los Angeles, the fastest-growing American city in the immediate postwar period, the area of rapid building focused on the San Fernando Valley, a vast space that had remained largely vacant since its annexation to the city in 1915. In Philadelphia thousands of new houses were put up in farming areas that had legally been part of the city since 1854, but which in fact had functioned as agricultural settlements for generations.

The second major characteristic of the postwar suburbs was their relatively low density. In all except the most isolated instances, the row house completely lost favor; between 1946 and 1956, about 97 percent of all new single-family dwellings were completely detached, surrounded on every side by their own plots. Typical lot sizes were relatively uniform around the country, averaging between ⅕ (80 by 100 feet) and ⅒ (40 by 100 feet) of an acre and varying more with distance from the center than by region. Moreover, the new subdivisions alloted a higher proportion of their land area to streets and open spaces. Levittown, Long Island, for example, was settled at a density of 10,500 per square mile, which was about average for postwar suburbs but less than half as dense as the streetcar suburbs of a half-century earlier. This design of new neighborhoods on the assumption that residents would have automobiles meant that those without cars faced severe handicaps in access to jobs and shopping facilities.

This low-density pattern was in marked contrast with Europe. In war-ravaged countries east of the Rhine River, the concentration upon apartment buildings can be explained by the overriding necessity to provide shelter quickly for masses of displaced and homeless people. But in comparatively unscathed France, Denmark, and Spain, the single-family house was also a rarity. In Sweden, Stockholm committed itself to a suburban pattern along subway lines, a decision that implied a high-density residential pattern. Nowhere in Europe was there the land, the money, or the tradition for single-family home construction.

The third major characteristic of the postwar suburbs was their architectural similarity. A few custom homes were built for the rich, and mobile homes gained popularity with the poor and the transient, but for most American families in search of a new place to live some form of tract house was the most likely option. In order to simplify their production methods and reduce design fees, most of the larger developers offered no more than a half-dozen basic house plans, and some offered half that number. The result was a monotony and repetition that was especially stark in the early years of the subdivision, before the individual owners had transformed their homes and yards according to personal taste.

But the architectural similarity extended beyond the particular tract to the nation as a whole. Historically, each region of the country had developed an indigenous residential style—the colonial-style homes of New England, the row houses of Atlantic coastal cities, the famous Charleston town houses with their ends to the street, the raised plantation homes of the damp bayou country of Louisiana, and the encircled patios and massive walls of the Southwest. This regionalism of design extended to relatively small areas; early in the twentieth century a house on the South Carolina coast looked quite different from a house in the Piedmont a few hundred miles away.

This tradition began eroding after World War I, when the American dream house became . . . the Cape Cod cottage, a quaint one-and-a-half-story dwelling. This design remained popular into the post–World War II years, when Levittown featured it as a bargain for veterans. In subsequent years, one fad after another became the rage. First, it was the split-level, then the ranch, then the modified colonial. In each case, the style tended to find support throughout the continent, so that by the 1960s the casual suburban visitor would have a difficult time deciphering whether she was in the environs of Boston or Dallas.

The ranch style, in particular, was evocative of the expansive mood of the post–World War II suburbs and of the disappearing regionality of style. It was almost as popular in Westchester County as in Los Angeles County. Remotely derived from the adobe dwellings of the Spanish colonial tradition and more directly derived from the famed prairie houses of [architect] Frank Lloyd Wright, with their low-pitched roofs, deep eaves, and pronounced horizontal lines, the typical ranch style houses of the 1950s were no larger than the average home a generation earlier. But the one-level ranch house suggested spacious living and an easy relationship with the outdoors. Mothers with small children did not have to contend with stairs. Most importantly, the postwar ranch home represented newness. In 1945 the publisher of the *Saturday Evening Post* reported that only 14 percent of the population wanted to live in an apartment or a "used" house. Whatever the style, the post–World War II house, in contrast to its turn-of-the-century predecessor, had no hall, no parlor, no stairs, and no porch. And the portion of the structure that projected farthest toward the street was the garage.

The fourth characteristic of post–World War II housing was its easy availability and thus its reduced suggestion of wealth. To be sure, upper-income suburbs and developments sprouted across the land, and some set high standards of style and design. Typically, they offered expansive lots, spacious and individualized designs, and affluent neighbors. But the most important income development of the period was the lowering of the threshold of purchase. At every previous time in American history, and indeed for the 1980s as well, the successful acquisition of a family home required savings and effort of a major order. After World War II, however, because of mass-production techniques, government financing, high wages, and low interest rates, it was quite simply cheaper to buy new housing in the suburbs than it was to reinvest in central city properties or to rent at the market price.

The fifth and perhaps most important characteristic of the postwar suburb was economic and racial homogeneity. The sorting out of families by income and color began even before the Civil War and was stimulated by the growth of the factory system. This pattern was noticeable in both the exclusive Main Line suburbs of Philadelphia and New York and in the more bourgeois streetcar developments which were part of every city. The automobile accentuated this discriminatory "Jim Crow" pattern. In Atlanta where large numbers of whites flocked to the fast-growing and wealthy suburbs north of the city in the 1920s, [it was] reported that: "By 1930, if racism could be measured in miles and minutes, blacks and whites were more segregated in the city of Atlanta than ever before." But many pre-1930 suburbs—places like Greenwich, Connecticut; Englewood, New Jersey; Evanston, Illinois; and Chestnut Hill, Massachusetts—maintained an exclusive image despite the presence of low-income or minority groups living in slums near or within the community.

The post-1945 developments took place against a background of the decline of factory-dominated cities. What was unusual in the new circumstances was not the presence of discrimination—Jews and Catholics as well as blacks had been excluded from certain neighborhoods for generations—but the thoroughness of the physical separation which it entailed. The Levitt organization, which was no more culpable in this regard than any other urban or suburban firm, publicly and officially refused to sell to blacks for two decades after the war. Nor did resellers deal with minorities. As William Levitt explained, "We can solve a housing problem, or we can try to solve a racial problem. But we cannot combine the two." Not surprisingly, in 1960 not a single one of the Long Island Levittown's 82,000 residents was black.

The economic and age homogeneity of large subdivisions and sometimes entire suburbs was almost as complete as the racial distinction. Although this tendency had been present even in the nineteenth century, the introduction of zoning—beginning with a New York City ordinance in 1916—served the general purpose of preserving residential class segregation and property values. In theory zoning was designed to protect the interests of all citizens by limiting land speculation and congestion. And it was popular. Although it represented an extraordinary growth of municipal power, nearly everyone supported zoning. By 1926 seventy-six cities had adopted ordinances similar to that of New York. By 1936, 1,322 cities (85 percent of the total) had them, and zoning laws were affecting more property than all national laws relating to business.

In actuality zoning was a device to keep poor people and obnoxious industries out of affluent areas. And in time, it also became a cudgel used by suburban areas to whack the central city. Advocates of land-use restrictions in overwhelming proportion were residents of the fringe. They sought through minimum lot and set-back requirements to insure that only members of acceptable social classes could settle in their privileged sanctuaries. Southern cities even used zoning to enforce racial segregation. And in suburbs everywhere, North and South, zoning was used by the people who already lived within the arbitrary boundaries of a community as a method of keeping everyone else out. Apartments, factories, and "blight," euphemisms for blacks and people of limited means, were rigidly excluded.

While zoning provided a way for suburban areas to become secure enclaves for the well-to-do, it forced the city to provide economic facilities for the whole area and homes for people the suburbs refused to admit. Simply put, land-use restrictions tended to protect residential interests in the suburbs and commercial interests in the cities because the residents of the core usually lived on land owned by absentee landlords who were more interested in financial returns than neighborhood preferences. For the man who owned land but did not live on it, the ideal situation was to have his parcel of earth zoned for commercial or industrial use. With more options, the property often gained in value. In Chicago, for example, three times as much land was zoned for commercial use as could ever have been profitably employed for such purposes. This overzoning prevented inner-city residents from receiving the same protection from commercial incursions as was afforded suburbanites. Instead of becoming a useful tool for the rational ordering of land in metropolitan areas, zoning became a way for suburbs to pirate from the city only its desirable functions and residents. Suburban governments became like so many residential hotels, fighting for the upper-income trade while trying to force the deadbeats to go elsewhere.

Because zoning restrictions typically excluded all apartments and houses and lots of less than a certain number of square feet, new home purchasers were often from a similar income and social group. In this regard, the postwar suburbs were no different from many nineteenth-century neighborhoods when they were first built. Moreover, Levittown was originally a mix of young professionals and lower-middle-class blue-collar workers.

As the aspiring professionals moved out, however, Levittown became a community of the most class-stratifying sort possible. This phenomenon was the subject of one of the most important books of the 1950s. Focusing on a 2,400-acre project put up by the former Public Housing Administrator Phillip Klutznick, William H. Whyte's *The Organization Man* sent shudders through armchair sociologists. Although Whyte found that Park Forest, Illinois, offered its residents "leadership training" and an "ability to chew

273

on real problems," the basic portrait was unflattering. Reporting excessive conformity and a mindless conservatism, he showed Park Foresters to be almost interchangeable as they fought their way up the corporate ladder, and his "organization man" stereotype unfortunately became the norm for judging similar communities throughout the nation.

By 1961, when President John F. Kennedy proclaimed his New Frontier and challenged Americans to send a man to the moon within the decade, his countrymen had already remade the nation's metropolitan areas in the short space of sixteen years. From Boston to Los Angeles, vast new subdivisions and virtually new towns sprawled where a generation earlier nature had held sway. In an era of low inflation, plentiful energy, federal subsidies, and expansive optimism, Americans showed the way to a more abundant and more perfect lifestyle. Almost every contractor-built, post–World War II home had central heating, indoor plumbing, telephones, automatic stoves, refrigerators, and washing machines.

There was a darker side to the outward movement. By making it possible for young couples to have separate households of their own, abundance further weakened the extended family in America and ordained that most children would grow up in intimate contact only with their parents and siblings. The housing arrangements of the new prosperity were evident as early as 1950. In that year there were 45,983,000 dwelling units to accommodate the 38,310,000, families in the United States and 84 percent of American households reported less than one person per room.

Critics regarded the peripheral environment as devastating particularly to women and children. The suburban world was a female world, especially during the day. Betty Friedan's 1968 classic *The Feminine Mystique* challenged the notion that the American dream home was emotionally fulfilling for women. As Gwendolyn Wright has observed, their isolation from work opportunities and from contact with employed adults led to stifled frustration and deep psychological problems. Similarly, Sidonie M. Gruenberg warned in the *New York Times Magazine* that "Mass produced, standardized housing breeds standardized individuals, too—especially among youngsters." Offering neither the urbanity and sophistication of the city nor the tranquility and repose of the farm, the suburb came to be regarded less as an intelligent compromise than a cultural, economic, and emotional wasteland. No observer was more critical than Lewis Mumford, however. In his 1961 analysis of *The City in History*, which covered the entire sweep of civilization, the famed author reiterated sentiments he had first expressed more than four decades earlier and scorned the new developments which were surrounding every American city:

In the mass movement into suburban areas a new kind of community was produced, which caricatured both the historic city and

the archetypal suburban refuge: a multitude of uniform, uniden-
tifiable houses, lined up inflexibly, at uniform distances, on uniform roads, in a treeless communal waste, inhabited by people of
the same class, the same income, the same age group, witnessing
the same television performances, eating the same tasteless pre-
fabricated foods, from the same freezers, conforming in every outward and inward respect to a common mold, manufactured in the
central metropolis. Thus, the ultimate effect of the suburban escape
in our own time is, ironically, a low-grade uniform environment
from which escape is impossible.

Secondly, because the federally supported home-building boom was
of such enormous proportions, the new houses of the suburbs were a major
cause of the decline of central cities. Because FHA and VA terms for new
construction were so favorable as to make the suburbs accessible to almost
all white, middle-income families, the inner-city housing market was deprived of the purchasers who could perhaps have supplied an appropriate
demand for the evacuated neighborhoods.

The young families who joyously moved into the new homes of the
suburbs were not terribly concerned about the problems of the inner-city
housing market or the snobbish views of Lewis Mumford and other social
critics. They were concerned about their hopes and their dreams. They
were looking for good schools, private space, and personal safety, and
places like Levittown could provide those amenities on a scale and at a
price that crowded city neighborhoods, both in the Old World and in the
New, could not match. The single-family tract house—post–World War II
style—whatever its aesthetic failings, offered growing families a private
haven in a heartless world. If the dream did not include minorities or the
elderly, if it was accompanied by the isolation of nuclear families, by the
decline of public transportation, and by the deterioration of urban neighborhoods, the creation of good, inexpensive suburban housing on an unprecedented scale was a unique achievement in the world.

DOCUMENTS

Little Boxes, 1962

Little boxes on the hillside, little boxes made of ticky tacky,
Little boxes on the hillside, little boxes all the same.
There's a green one and a pink one and a blue one and a yellow
  one,
And they're all made out of ticky tacky and they all look just the
  same.

SOURCE: Words and music by Malvina Reynolds, © 1962 by Schroder Music Co. (ASCAP).
Used by permission; all rights reserved.

And the people in the houses all went to the university
Where they were put in boxes and they came out all the same;
And there's doctors, and there's lawyers and there's business
    executives
And they're all made out of ticky tacky and they all look just the
    same.

And they all play on the golf course and drink their martini dry
And they all have pretty children and the children go to school
And the children go to summer camp and then to the university
Where they are all put in boxes and they come out all the same.

Coda (retard like a music box running down)

The Problem That Has No Name, 1963

The suburban housewife—she was the dream image of the young American women and the envy, it was said, of women all over the world. The American housewife—freed by science and labor-saving appliances from the drudgery, the dangers of childbirth and the illnesses of her grandmother. She was healthy, beautiful, educated, concerned only about her husband, her children, her home. She had found true feminine fulfillment. As a housewife and mother, she was respected as a full and equal partner to man in his world. She was free to choose automobiles, clothes, appliances, supermarkets; she had everything that women ever dreamed of.

In the fifteen years after World War II, this mystique of feminine fulfillment became the cherished and self-perpetuating core of contemporary American culture. Millions of women lived their lives in the image of those pretty pictures of the American suburban housewife, kissing their husbands goodbye in front of the picture window, depositing their station-wagonsful of children at school, and smiling as they ran the new electric waxer over the spotless kitchen floor. They baked their own bread, sewed their own and their children's clothes, kept their new washing machines and dryers running all day. They changed the sheets on the beds twice a week instead of once, took the rug-hooking class in adult education, and pitied their poor frustrated mothers, who had dreamed of having a career. Their only dream was to be perfect wives and mothers; their highest ambition to have five children and a beautiful house, their only fight to get and keep their husbands. They had no thought for the unfeminine prob-

SOURCE: Reprinted from *The Feminine Mystique* by Betty Friedan, by permission of W. W. Norton & Co., Inc. Copyright © 1983, 1974, 1973, 1963 by Betty Friedan.

lems of the world outside the home; they wanted the men to make the major decisions. They gloried in their role as women, and wrote proudly on the census blank: "Occupation: housewife."

For over fifteen years, the words written for women, and the words women used when they talked to each other, while their husbands sat on the other side of the room and talked shop or politics or septic tanks, were about problems with their children, or how to keep their husbands happy, or improve their children's school, or cook chicken or make slipcovers. Nobody argued whether women were inferior or superior to men; they were simply different. Words like "emancipation" and "career" sounded strange and embarrassing; no one had used them for years. When a French-woman named Simone de Beauvoir wrote a book called *The Second Sex*, an American critic commented that she obviously "didn't know what life was all about," and besides, she was talking about French women. The "woman problem" in America no longer existed.

If a woman had a problem in the 1950's and 1960's, she knew that something must be wrong with her marriage, or with herself. Other women were satisfied with their lives, she thought. What kind of a woman was she if she did not feel this mysterious fulfillment waxing the kitchen floor? She was so ashamed to admit her dissatisfaction that she never knew how many other women shared it. If she tried to tell her husband, he didn't understand what she was talking about. She did not really understand it herself. For over fifteen years women in America found it harder to talk about this problem than about sex. Even the psychoanalysts had no name for it. When a woman went to a psychiatrist for help, as many women did, she would say, "I'm so ashamed," or "I must be hopelessly neurotic." "I don't know what's wrong with women today," a suburban psychiatrist said uneasily. "I only know something is wrong because most of my patients happen to be women. And their problem isn't sexual." Most women with this problem did not go to see a psychoanalyst, however. "There's nothing wrong really," they kept telling themselves. "There isn't any problem."

But on an April morning in 1959, I heard a mother of four, having coffee with four other mothers in a suburban development fifteen miles from New York, say in a tone of quiet desperation, "the problem." And the others knew, without words, that she was not talking about a problem with her husband, or her children, or her home. Suddenly they realized they all shared the same problem, the problem that has no name. They began, hesitantly, to talk about it. Later, after they had picked up their children at nursery school and taken them home to nap, two of the women cried, in sheer relief, just to know they were not alone.

Gradually I came to realize that the problem that has no name was shared by countless women in America. As a magazine writer I often interviewed women about problems with their children, or their marriages, or their houses, or their communities. But after a while I began to recognize the telltale signs of this other problem. I saw the same signs in suburban ranch houses and split-levels on Long Island and in New Jersey and Westchester County; in colonial houses in a small Massachusetts town; on patios in Memphis; in suburban and city apartments; in living rooms in the Midwest. Sometimes I sensed the problem, not as a reporter, but as a suburban housewife, for during this time I was also bringing up my own three children in Rockland County, New York. I heard echoes of the problem in college dormitories and semiprivate maternity wards, at PTA meetings and luncheons of the League of Women Voters, at suburban cocktail parties, in station wagons waiting for trains, and in snatches of conversation overheard at Schrafft's. The groping words I heard from other women, on quiet afternoons when children were at school or on quiet evenings when husbands worked late, I think I understood first as a woman long before I understood their larger social and psychological implications. . . .

If I am right, the problem that has no name stirring in the minds of so many American women today is not a matter of loss of femininity or too much education, or the demands of domesticity. It is far more important than anyone recognizes. It is the key to these other new and old problems which have been torturing women and their husbands and children, and puzzling their doctors and educators for years. It may well be the key to our future as a nation and a culture. We can no longer ignore that voice within women that says: "I want something more than my husband and my children and my home."

Mr. Levitt Remembers, 1977

. . . "Before I went into the service," Mr. Levitt said, "a broker came to me and told me about 1,200 acres that were available farther out on the Island." Mr. Levitt grinned at the idea of considering Levittown "farther out on the Island" today, but at the time his vantage point was as a moderately successful builder in such established communities as Roslyn, Manhasset and Rockville Centre.

"It was potato fields," Mr. Levitt said, "and the broker said that he could work out a deal whereby I'd pay $225 an acre for the first parcel of 200 acres, with the price increasing in steps each time I exercised an option for another 200-acre parcel."

SOURCE: "Levittown 30 Years Later," by Irvin Molotsky, October 2, 1977. Copyright © 1977 by The New York Times Company. Reprinted by permission.

Eventually, Mr. Levitt assembled a total of 7,000 acres by buying adjacent land. "My God," Mr. Levitt recalls having thought, "how could anyone live out here and work in New York?"

But it was a rhetorical thought, because Mr. Levitt had already made his decision to build homes for the families of returned veterans who were living with their parents or in crowded apartments.

But before he could build Levittown, Mr. Levitt had to get the approval of the Town of Hempstead, because, although Levittown houses have had the New Yorker cartoon reputation for sameness, they were different in a very significant way, at least different from most housing built in the United States up until then. They had no basements.

Why? "It was for cost and speed," Mr. Levitt said. "We were in a hurry. It takes time to dig cellars, and we wanted to build at least 150 houses a week."

Levitt & Sons needed to build swiftly so it could use the rents or down payments from every new occupant to finance the construction of the next houses. By the time the construction got into high gear, 36 houses were being built every day.

"In 1929, Levitt & Sons built 18 houses in Rockville Centre," Mr. Levitt noted. "By 1947, we were building 18 every day before noon and then 18 more in the afternoon." . . .

"Today the cellar is a rarity—all over the world," Mr. Levitt said, but in 1947 a house was expected to have a basement. "We filed plans and the Hempstead Town building inspector turned them down," he added. "He objected to our plans on what he called general principles, so we applied for an amendment to the building code."

"We put out the word to veterans that they should attend the hearing and *Newsday* ran a couple of strong editorials early on saying that our ideas were right. Thanks to the newspaper articles, it seemed that all the veterans in Nassau County came to the hearing at Town Hall."

"They crowded the hearing room and they crowded the hallways. There were so many people in Town Hall that they overflowed and blocked Front Street. A. Holly Patterson, the Town Supervisor, wanted to table the matter, but the veterans refused to go home and the town board was forced to vote, and they passed it."

The first occupant moved into a Levitt house on Oct. 1, 1947, which was 30 years ago yesterday and the focal point of Levittown's anniversary celebration.

"The early people can recall the furor," William C. Bryson, editor of *The Levittown Tribune,* recalled the other day. "Levitt was creating a slum, they said. Now, after 20 years, we know that Levittown is a success. What used to be mud and dirt are now green lawns with large trees. Levittown helped G.I.'s fulfill their dream to buy a house they could afford."

Everyone seems to agree that there are no slums in Levittown. "The critics are being dumbfounded," Mr. Levitt said. "Critics like Lewis Mumford said that we were creating slums, but we weren't."

Joseph A. Bell, a real-estate broker with the Vigilant Realty office in Levittown, said, "Most of the peole in real estate, including me, thought 30 years ago—when I started in this business—that Levittown was going to become a shanty town. We were wrong."

Mr. Bell added that although Levittown houses were no longer considered in the cheap range—a recent Sunday newspaper carried 25 ads for Levittown houses with the average price around $36,000—"this area is still the best investment for the money."

Asked to cite the community's advantages, Mr. Bell listed good schools, closeness to the city—the commuting range seems to have moved 30 miles to the east in the last 30 years—shopping and swimming pools. He added, "The houses are built very well."

"The best endorsement I can offer is my daughter," Mr. Bell said. "Ten years ago, after looking for a house for a year, she and her husband came to me and said they would settle for a Levittown house. It was a compromise, but they've never regretted it."

Speaking with the terseness of a long-time Levittown realty man, Mr. Bell summed up his daughter's house this way: "It's a 1951 Levitt ranch in the D section."

The 'D Section'

The D section?

"Of course," said Francine Truglio, Mr. Bell's daughter. "All the streets in the neighborhood start with a D."

Mrs. Truglio lives on Daffodil Lane with her husband and two children. The other streets in the neighborhood—the D section—are Duckpond Drive North, Duckpond Drive East and Duckpond Drive South (if there ever was a duck pond there, no one remembers it), plus Downhill Lane, Duck Lane, Dell Lane, Deep Lane, Dahlia Lane, Disc Lane, Dome Lane and Deer Lane.

There are 82 streets and lanes beginning with the letter S, from Saddle Lane to Sycamore Lane—and it was possible to build the 17,447 Levitt houses (as well as 3,500 erected nearby by other builders) without having to scrape up a single street name beginning with an X or a Y. There is a token Z—Zenith Lane.

Is this what led to all of those New Yorker cartoons of people (usually men) staggering (usually inebriated) into a look-alike house (never their own)?

Mr. Levitt, 30 years later, was still eager to defend the Levittown policy of enforcing a certain sameness.

"The restrictions against building without permission from us ran out years ago, but they were necessary," Mr. Levitt said. "The covenants protected the homeowners against what other people might build next door. We barred people from stringing out clotheslines in their backyards, because they were unsightly."

Those restrictions have long since ended. Mrs. Truglio has lived in Levittown for more than 10 years and she never heard of the old restrictions against clotheslines. . . .

CHAPTER 15

The Black Struggle for Equality

Not all groups shared equally in the nation's economic growth after World War II. Blacks who had migrated to the North in search of a better life were often sorely disappointed at what they found. Many of those who remained in the South as sharecroppers and tenants were forced off the land by federal government programs that encouraged farmers to leave their fields fallow, and by new machinery that increasingly replaced human labor. In addition, blacks in both the North and South encountered discrimination in employment, housing, schools, and public facilities. Segregation and disenfranchisement were most severe in the South, where they were imposed and enforced as policies of local and state governments.

In the mid-1950s, a struggle for racial equality and civil rights emerged. Jane Stevenson's essay, "Rosa Parks Wouldn't Budge," brings to life the story of the 1955 bus boycott in Montgomery, Alabama, the event generally credited with launching the renewed crusade and the career of its great leader, Martin Luther King, Jr. What factors made Montgomery's bus system an "appropriate target for *the integration movement"?* In what ways were the tactics employed by the boy-cotters illustrative of King's philosophy of militant nonviolence?

Stevenson points out that plans for concerted black action against racial dis-crimination followed the U.S. Supreme Court's anti-segregation ruling of May 1954 in Brown v. Board of Education. The first document presents excerpts from Chief Justice Earl Warren's statement of the unanimous opinion. What were the key points in the Court's sweeping condemnation of school segregation?

Although the Supreme Court's decision in Brown, and later the Montgomery bus boycott cases, won widespread support among whites as well as blacks, many white Americans, particularly in the South, were determined to maintain segre-gation and to deny blacks political and social equality. As the civil rights movement grew, segregationist opposition became more intense and violent. Ironically, as this violence and the contrasting nonviolent resistance of the civil rights activists were brought by television into homes throughout the nation, popular support for black demands increased. Congress finally responded, passing the Civil Rights Act of 1964 and the Voting Rights Act of 1965. The speech by Congressman Jamie Whitten of Mississippi in the second document expresses sentiments typical of those who opposed the 1964 Civil Rights Act. Compare Whitten's arguments with those of Justice Warren in the Brown decision.

Following Supreme Court decisions, presidential action, and the enactment of civil rights laws, the southern states finally began to desegregate public facilities. Blacks also registered to vote in growing numbers in the South, and many won election to local, state, and federal offices. The final document, from a 1983 U.S. Civil Rights Commission report, indicates how much the racial climate in the South had changed. At the same time, however, it notes ways in which segregation and discrimination still existed in the rural Alabama counties the Commission had investigated. What does that report identify as the most significant remaining barriers to the achievement of racial equality?

ESSAY

Rosa Parks Wouldn't Budge

Jane Stevenson

A neatly dressed, middle-aged black woman was riding home on a Montgomery, Alabama, bus on the evening of Thursday, December 1, 1955. Her lap was full of groceries, which she was going to have to carry home from the bus stop, and her feet were tired from a long day's work.

Mrs. Rosa Parks was sitting in the first row of seats behind the section marked "Whites Only." When she chose this seat, there had been plenty of empty ones both in front of and behind the "Great Divide." Now they were all occupied, and black passengers were standing in the aisle at the rear.

Then two white men got aboard. They dropped their dimes into the fare box. The driver called over his shoulder, "Niggers move back." Three of the passengers obediently rose from their seats in the black section and stood in the aisle. Rosa Parks did not.

Even when the driver repeated his order and heads turned to see who was "making trouble," she sat as if she hadn't heard. The driver swore under his breath, pulled over to the curb, put on the brakes, and came to stand above her.

"I said to move back. You hear?"

All conversation stopped. No one dared move. Mrs. Parks continued to stare out the window at the darkness. The driver waited. Sounds of other traffic dramatized the silence in the bus.

It was a historic moment: the birth of a movement that was to challenge and ultimately change the social patterns that had established themselves in most Americans' minds as a way of life which was traditional and deeply rooted in the South.

Actually, that tradition of racial segregation—loosely nicknamed Jim Crow—was not as venerable as most of its adherents believed. Many segregation laws—especially those concerned with public transportation—only dated from the turn of the twentieth century, and at the start had been resisted, through boycotts, by southern blacks, sometimes successfully. But by 1906 resistance had worn itself out. And in the intervening fifty years the memory had also worn itself out. E. D. Nixon, the man who proposed the Montgomery bus boycott of 1955–56, had never heard of the successful Montgomery bus boycott of 1900–1902. In fact he

SOURCE: Jane Stevenson, "Rosa Parks Wouldn't Budge," *American Heritage* 23 (February 1972): 56–64, 85. Copyright © *American Heritage,* a division of Forbes Inc. Reprinted with permission from *American Heritage.*

did not even know that boycotts were again being tried—without much success—in a few southern cities; for example, Baton Rouge.

Nixon was a leader of the Brotherhood of Sleeping Car Porters and one of the founders of both the Alabama state and the Montgomery city branches of the National Association for the Advancement of Colored People [NAACP]. For almost a year before the night of Mrs. Parks's refusal to give up her seat, he had been trying to persuade Montgomery's black community that "the only way to make the power structure do away with segregation on the buses was to take some money out of their pockets."

Few aspects of Jim Crow life were as galling to Montgomery blacks as travel on the city's bus line, which most of them had to use to get to and from work, school, and the central shopping district. There were runs on which a white passenger was a curiosity. Yet the first four rows of seats (ten places) were permanently reserved for whites. And blacks sitting behind those rows could be told to vacate their seats if whites got on after the reserved section was filled.

Blacks also had to endure discourtesy and sometimes hostility from many drivers, all of whom were white. Some used insulting language; others picked quarrels and put blacks off the bus for real or imagined offenses. Some played a peculiarly tormenting practical joke. Since all fares had to be deposited in the box beside the driver, every passenger had to get on by the front door. Blacks then had to get off the bus and board from the rear. The game was to wait until a black passenger got outside, slam the two doors, and drive off, leaving him standing on the curb without his dime.

Resentment was wide and deep in the black community. Some whites, too, were known to disapprove of the bus drivers' harassments. And even among the die-hard segregationists, the mixing of races on a public bus was hardly the emotionally charged issue that integrated schools, or parks, or swimming pools, were. For all these reasons, in the months following the United States Surpeme Court ruling of May, 1954, against segregated schools in *Brown v. Board of Education*, black leaders all over the South had been arguing that city bus lines were the next appropriate target for the integration movement.

In Montgomery three individual blacks, all women, had refused to give up their seats when ordered. In each case Nixon and the Montgomery NAACP had vainly tried to rally the black community to some sort of effective protest.

The most nearly successful attempt had been organized in March, 1955, after one of these three, a fifteen-year-old high school girl named Claudette Colvin, had been arrested and removed in handcuffs. An *ad hoc* committee of prominent Negro leaders had called on the manager of the bus company and on the City Commission, which governed Montgomery, to protest the way she had been treated and the whole system that led to such acts of spontaneous defiance. Three demands had been formulated: a guarantee of courtesy by drivers; a first-come first-served seating policy; and the hiring of Negro drivers on runs predominantly in Negro areas.

The proposed seating plan would not have ended segregation on the buses. It only required that when all seats were filled (blacks having seated themselves from the back forward and whites from the front backward), the next passengers to board would have to stand, no matter what the color of their skins. Such plans were in use in other southern cities, and the manager of the Montgomery City Lines was willing to go along with the idea until he consulted the company's attorney, Jack Crenshaw, who declared that the company was obligated to abide by the law, which was "clear on the principle of segregated seating."

In fact, it was not at all clear. Alabama state law did require clearly segregated white and black sections, but the Montgomery city code had a provision that no passenger could be required to give up his seat if another was not available. And there was sound legal opinion to the effect that within the city's limits the Montgomery statute took precedence over state law.

Nevertheless, Crenshaw's ruling stiffened the company's resistance. Hope of a legal challenge died when Claudette Colvin's parents refused to let her appear in court. Then community interest cooled to such a degree that the next woman who refused to move back received no organized support at all.

No one knew this background better than Mrs. Parks, who had worked with Nixon on many projects in the NAACP. She could hardly have hoped that her gesture was going to work any profound change in the status quo. She didn't move—as she explained later—because she was "bone weary" and suddenly fed up with being imposed upon. Yet circumstances would render her arrest the spark that lit the fires of resistance.

When E.D. Nixon got home that evening, his wife told him that Mrs. Parks had called from the city jail. Nixon telephoned the desk sergeant to ask about the charges and bail, and was refused the information, as an "unauthorized person." Ordinarily his next step would have been to call a young black Montgomery lawyer named Fred Gray, with whom he had worked on some NAACP cases. But Gray happened to be out of town. So Nixon turned instead to Clifford Durr, a distinguished white Alabamian who had recently returned to private law practice after twenty years in Washington, D.C. Durr had been on the legal staff of the Reconstruction Finance Corporation in the early New Deal years; later he had served as general counsel for the Defense Plant Corporation; and finally he had been a member of the Federal Communications Commission. He and his wife Virginia were part of a small group of southern white liberals who met, with black counterparts, under the aegis of the Alabama Council on Human

Relations, to find ways of improving the South's racial picture. Nixon had come to know and trust them both.

"I called Mr. Durr," Nixon remembered later, "and he called down to the jail and they told him what the charge was. Bail was about $50, so I could make that all right." Then Nixon drove the attorney and his wife (who was a friend of Rosa Parks's) down to the jail. "I made the bond," Nixon told an interviewer, "and we got Mrs. Parks out. We carried her on home, and had coffee and talked."

Over coffee, Durr explained the legal alternatives as he saw them: Mrs. Parks could be defended "on the facts." She had not violated the Montgomery city code because there was no other seat available. He thought such a case could be won, but no challenge to segregation was involved. On the other hand, her attorney could challenge the constitutionality of the Alabama state law. That would mean a protracted and expensive battle, with no possible hope of victory short of a successsful appeal to the United States Supreme Court. But a victory there would strike a major blow against Jim Crow.

Such a fight would need the backing of some national organization like the NAACP. Above all, it would take all the community support that Montgomery's blacks could mobilize.

Fired by the prospect Durr outlined, Nixon went home and told his wife, "I think we got us our test case at last." As he saw it, Fred Gray would take Rosa Parks's case and "do like Mr. Durr said. Go up all the way!" Meantime, he added, "What we got to do now is see about getting folks to stay off those buses Monday when Mrs. Parks comes up in Recorder's Court."

Mrs. Nixon told her husband he was "just plain crazy." "If headaches was selling for a dollar a dozen," she said, "you'd be the guy who'd go into a drug store and ask the man to put some in a bag." She didn't believe sympathy for Mrs. Parks was going to keep people off the buses "when it's as cold as this, and Christmas coming on."

There was some cause for pessimism. Montgomery's black community of fifty thousand persons was, in one observer's phrase, "as caste-ridden as any country in the world except India." No issue and no leader had yet managed to bring anything resembling unity out of its political, religious, economic, and cultural diversity. There might be strong support for Mrs. Parks in the professional group (made up in the main of faculty members from Alabama State College), but those people did not use public transportation. The working people, who did, depended on the buses to get to their jobs and on their jobs to feed and shelter their families. The risk of losing even a single day's pay was too much to ask of the head of a household already living on the edge of poverty.

But Nixon was determined to ask just that and more. Before he went to bed that night he planned a meeting of some forty people for the next day at the Dexter Avenue Baptist Church, a leaflet calling for a one-day bus boycott, and a Monday evening mass meeting to organize further action. He hoped to find a leader to carry on while he was out of town on his job.

Among the local blacks whom Nixon summoned was the Reverend Ralph Abernathy, a militant young Baptist preacher wholeheartedly in agreement with the plan and eager to get to work. There was also the Reverend H. H. Hubbard, head of the Baptist Ministerial Alliance. The Baptists were the largest denomination in the black community, so Hubbard's promise to cooperate in notifying his associates was crucial, and Nixon was elated to get it. Thus encouraged, he called young Dr. Martin Luther King, Jr., the new pastor of the Dexter Avenue church.

It was a fateful contact. Neither man could foresee that it would put young Dr. King on the road to national and historic importance, a Nobel Prize, and, ultimately, death at an assassin's hand. The future leader was then merely a recently arrived young minister of a fashionable Negro church in a southern town, well educated in the North, with a doctorate from Boston University, but with no other distinctions or activist record. Busy with his new duties, in fact, and the responsibilities of a young baby at home, he had only recently turned down the presidency of the local NAACP, and he told Nixon that while the protest organizers were welcome to meet in his church, he was not sure of his own participation. But he soon changed his mind and, with it, his destiny.

The meeting of more than forty people that afternoon quickly agreed to a one-day boycott of the city buses on the day of Mrs. Parks's trial. When it came to agreeing on demands, however, the initial unity was threatening to dissolve until someone pointed out that demands were unimportant compared to the practical problem of spreading the word quickly. There was no black "ghetto" in Montgomery. Negroes lived everywhere in and around the city. A volunteer phone committee could start work at once, but many black families were without phones—and radios or TV sets—and did not take newspapers. Leaflets, which Abernathy had wanted mimeographed immediately on hearing from Nixon, could be passed out at stores where Saturday shoppers congregated. Announcements could be made from church pulpits on Sunday, provided that every minister in town could be persuaded that the notice was important enough not to be ignored.

Transportation was a more serious problem. The first draft of the leaflet said: ". . . *take a car, or share a ride, or walk.*" But thousands lived too far from their jobs to walk, had no car, and knew no one with whom to share. For them some alternative way of getting to work on Monday had to be found, or the protest would not achieve the 50 per cent cut in company revenues that was the agreed target.

Someone suggested appealing to the Negro cab companies, asking them to pick up pedestrians and carry them to their destination for the ten-cent bus fare. (Segregation was so complete in Montgomery that only cabs driven by blacks and marked "Colored" were permitted to carry black passengers. The eighteen such companies and their 210 black drivers would prove a strong help in the first days of the boycott.)

By the time the meeting adjourned, assignments for phoning, distributing leaflets, and reaching ministers and the cab companies had been handed out, and morale was high. Some optimist even suggested that the passenger load of the bus lines might be cut as much as 60 or 65 per cent! Then, two events took place on Sunday that increased the chances of such success. The first was the result of a Friday encounter between E. D. Nixon and a reporter from the Montgomery *Advertiser* named Joe Azbell. The *Advertiser*, Montgomery's major journal, was seen by everyone, white and black, who read the papers in the city. It was by chance that Nixon ran into the white reporter, whom he knew to be friendly. Nixon told him he would give him a hot tip, but warned: "I don't expect to cooperate with anybody who's going to write some sort of degrading story about Negroes."

Azbell promised to write a useful story, if any. Then Nixon told him about Mrs. Parks's action and the planned boycott. Both men agreed that the story should not be attributed to Nixon, but that Azbell should "find" one of the leaflets on some city sidewalk. Sure enough, Sunday morning's *Advertiser* carried a two-column, front-page story, presumably given to the paper by an indignant white woman who had got it from her illiterate maid. The tone was properly disapproving ("Just listen to what the Negroes are up to now!"). But Azbell had kept the bargain, and as Nixon had anticipated, "every preacher in town saw it before he went into his pulpit that morning," and found it important enough to announce.

The other helpful event was a radio announcement by Montgomery's police commissioner that two motorcycle policemen would be assigned to follow every bus on Monday, "to protect anyone who wished to ride from harassment by goon squads." This, it was believed, had the effect of frightening some waverers away from the bus stops.

It was dark when the first buses began to roll on Monday, December 5. Dr. King and his wife, Coretta, who lived a few yards from a stop on one of the predominantly Negro runs, were up at dawn to see how the prospects for a 60 per cent reduction looked.

The early buses were usually crowded with black domestic workers on their way to make breakfast in white kitchens. Today, the first bus was empty. The Kings stayed at the window until the next bus passed. It, too, was empty. The third had two passengers, both white.

As the sky brightened, those of the planning committee with cars cruised the streets in different parts of town. What they saw was amazing. Sidewalks were crowded with black pedestrians. College and high school students were thumbing rides. Cars driven by blacks were overloaded with ride-sharers. There were a few old-fashioned horse-drawn buggies on the street, and one man was seen riding a mule. Youngsters waved in derisive humor at motorcycle policemen behind most of the buses. Some walkers—with up to six miles to go—sang as they trudged along. As King later wrote in his book, *Stride Toward Freedom*: "A miracle had taken place. The once dormant and quiescent Negro community was now fully awake."

At 9:30 A.M. the drama shifted to the courtroom, as Mrs. Parks's case was called. Fred Gray adhered to the line Durr had suggested. He ignored the conflict of state and local laws, and argued instead that segregation on public transportation was a violation of the spirit and letter of the United States Constitution. Without comment on Gray's argument, the judge found Mrs. Parks guilty and fined her ten dollars and court costs, which brought the total to something like fourteen dollars. Gray announced that his client would appeal the verdict, and she was released on bail. Now it was time for a third act: the mass meeting scheduled for 7 P.M. at the Holt Street Baptist Church.

But first, Nixon and Abernathy talked over the needs of the future. These included long-term plans and a permanent organization to carry on the fight. Nixon proposed to call it the Montgomery Citizens' Council, but Abernathy thought that sounded like the White Citizens' Councils that were springing up in opposition to school desegregation. His own suggestion was the Montgomery Improvement Association, and Nixon agreed to go along. They also agreed to ask the meeting to approve of repeating the demands made in Claudette Colvin's case—which fell short of total integration. And then, Abernathy raised the potentially touchy issue of leadership. "Brother Nixon, you're going to serve as president, aren't you?"

"Not unless you all turn down the man I have in mind. That's this young reverend, Martin Luther King, Jr."

Abernathy was surprised. King was not only young—not quite twenty-seven years old—but very new to the area. To nominate him would be to pass over a number of other, older ministers, many of whom had good qualifications.

"I'll tell you my reasons," Nixon said. "First, there's the way he talks. Day I first heard him preach, I turned to the fellow sitting next to me and I said, 'I don't know just how I'm going to do it, but one day I'm going to hook him to the stars!' "

King's education equipped him to talk to Montgomery's white leaders in their own terms. King had a reputation for courage, too. As Nixon said, "You knew he wasn't any white man's nigger." And he had not been in Montgomery long enough to become entangled in any of the factional struggles that divided the black community.

Abernathy agreed that King was a good choice, but thought he would decline. So it was decided to nominate him without warning at a session of the "planning committee"—which would frame resolutions to present to the mass meeting. King was so astonished by the very fact of his election—it was unanimous—that he put up no resistance, confessing later that if he had had time to think, he would have almost certainly refused. Immediately afterward he received a tough assignment: presenting to the crowd not merely the routine matters of choosing a name and officers but the hard choice of whether to continue the boycott or merely threaten to renew it if demands were not met. That decision, clearly, had to be made by those who would carry it out: the thousands of humble people who had walked on this cold, gray morning. Many of them would be present at the Holt Street Baptist Church, and they would there be asked to vote on whether they could sustain their incredible initial momentum by approving a recommendation to continue.

By the seven o'clock meeting time there was not a seat empty in the Holt Street church. Loudspeakers had been installed on the roof to accommodate latecomers who might not find room inside. It took Dr. King fifteen minutes to work his way through the crowd from his car, and ten more to get to the platform after he was inside. The audience was singing "Onward, Christian Soldiers" when he joined Nixon, Abernathy, a number of other ministers, Mrs. Parks, and Fred Gray. After the ritual of prayer and scripture reading—with which all such meetings open in the South—and an ovation for Mrs. Parks, E. D. Nixon rose, glancing at Montgomery's police commissioner, whom he saw seated in one of the pews.

"Before you brothers and sisters get comfortable in your seats," Nixon began, "I want to say if anybody here is afraid, he better take his hat and go home. This is going to be a long, drawn-out affair, and before it's over, somebody's going to die."

There were loud amens, but no one reached for his hat. Nixon then delivered a rouser in favor of continuing the boycott, ending with the challenge: "We've worn aprons long enough. It's time for us to take them off!"

The next speaker was Martin Luther King, Jr. He came to the rostrum almost completely unprepared for what he knew by now would be one of the most important addresses of his life. There had hardly been time in the two hours since he had been given this task to think through the basic purpose of his speech. His analysis had gone as far as dividing it into two possibly contradictory aims: the first, to drain off the anger of those who were "tired of being kicked about by the brutal feet of oppression"—anger that might lead to violence of which he disapproved; and a second, to "keep them courageous and prepared for action." Or, as he put it in another place, the problem was to be militant and moderate at the same time. To make things more difficult, he would have to face the microphones and lights of television crews, for news of the morning's action had focussed national attention on Montgomery.

King rose to the moment. Pulpit oratory, once a typical American art, is obsolete in most parts of the country today. But it lingers on in the black

South, and King's sermon was a classic production. Stating the Christian case for nonviolent protest, he said: "We have been amazingly patient . . . but we come here tonight to be saved from that patience that makes us patient with anything less than freedom and justice." Though he roused his audience at first by shouting, "We are tired. Tired of being segregated and humiliated," he brought them down to calmness again by declaring, "Once again we must hear the words of Jesus. 'Love your enemies. Bless them that curse you. Pray for them that despitefully use you.' If we fail to do this, our protest will end up as a meaningless drama on the stage of history. . . . We must not become bitter and end up by hating our white brothers." And in a final chord, he wooed them to their better selves.

"If you will protest courageously, and yet with dignity and Christian love, future historians will say, 'There lived a great people—a black people—who injected new meaning and dignity into the veins of civilization.' This is our challenge and our overwhelming responsibility."

The audience rose, cheering, and one elderly woman remembered afterward the feeling that she "saw angels standing all around him when he finished, and they were lifting him up on their wings!"

Even before Ralph Abernathy read the recommendation, the verdict was in. It was, in Clifford Durr's recollection, "a grass roots verdict if there ever was one. Some of the [black] middle-class professionals were saying, 'Well, we showed them this morning.' But the maids and the cooks, the ones who had done the walking, were saying, 'We haven't showed them a thing yet! But we're going to stay off those buses until they make up their minds to treat us decently.' "

For the first few days this unanimous determination created a euphoric optimism. In view of the unprecedented effectiveness of the boycott and the willingness of the Montgomery Improvement Association [M.I.A.] to settle for a partial victory such as first-come first-served seating through separate doors, it was generally believed that there would be a negotiated settlement. But on Thursday, December 8, when Abernathy's committee met with the City Commission, the bus company attorney, Jack Crenshaw, once more insisted that the Alabama law required continued total segregation. City officials were taking a hard line, too. It was clear that they did not want a Negro victory to stimulate further challenges. And a hint was dropped of strong action to come. The city code set a minimum cab fare of forty-five cents per passenger. Negro taxi companies might soon be forbidden to take passengers at ten cents per trip. The next day that threat did materialize. But fortunately, on Thursday evening there had been one of the twice-weekly meetings planned for the boycott's duration as a way of exchanging information, squelching rumors, boosting morale, and ratifying decisions. Anticipating the city's action, the chairman had appealed for volunteer drivers. One hundred and fifty names were handed in. Next,

Rufus Lewis's Transportation Committee sat up all night, working out the details of a system which utilized the whole intricate network of black institutions that had grown up under the hothouse conditions of total segregation.

On Tuesday, just a week after the first day of the boycott, thousands of leaflets were ready for distribution, showing on a map of the city the location of forty-eight dispatch and forty-two pick-up stations, with the hours at which each would be operative. There were plenty of problems still. Dispatch stations for sending people off to work were easy to locate in Negro neighborhoods, and churches could shelter riders who had to wait in bad weather. But after-hours pick-up stations had to be in less friendly territory. Without the intimate knowledge of Montgomery's white neighborhoods supplied by black mail carriers, this part of the plan would have been impossible to design. There were never quite enough volunteer dispatchers at rush hours. Cars sometimes broke down, and so, occasionally, did the tempers of passengers and drivers. But overall, the car pools worked as well as, if not better than, the old bus system. And their impact as a unifying force in the black community was incalculable.

It was expensive, but help came from two unexpected sources. As the "Montgomery Story" was spread throughout the country by the news media, contributions began coming in to the M.I.A. from cities in the North and West. Black churches took up collections to buy station wagons, which were presented to Montgomery churches of the same denominations for car-pool use.

The load was also lightened by some white Montgomery housewives, who entered into a sort of conspiracy with their black domestics. Accepting the police commissioner's fiction about "goon squads," these women began to drive their maids and cooks to and from work, "to protect them from harassment." When the mayor protested that this gave aid and comfort to the boycott, ladies wrote letters to the newspaper suggesting that he provide them with other help before telling them how to run their households.

As weeks went by without the blacks yielding, threats of violence began to be directed against the leadership of the M.I.A. King, Abernathy, Nixon, and other officers started to receive hate mail and phone calls warning them to "get out of town or else. . . ." Then, on January 30, the ugliness erupted.

On that night, while Dr. King was attending one of the regular mass meetings, a bomb tossed onto the porch of his house exploded seconds later with a shattering roar. Having heard the thud as the missile landed, Mrs. King and a visiting friend had moved quickly toward the rear of the house. They and the Kings's infant daughter escaped injury. But it looked for a time as if the chief casualty of the night would be the concept of nonviolence to which the Negroes had so far been held by their leaders.

Rushing home, King found an angry crowd milling on his lawn. As he stepped from his car, he heard one black man offer to shoot it out with a white policeman who was trying to push him back. Mayor W. A. "Jackie" Gayle and Police Commissioner Clyde Sellers were on hand, along with white reporters and the police. The mood of the crowd was so hostile that all of them later reported having felt that a race riot was a distinct and immediate possibility.

Dr. King went into his house, assured himself that his family was all right, and then came back to speak to the crowd. His voice was unusually quiet, and everyone else stopped speaking or moving, to listen.

"My wife and baby are all right," he told them. "I want you to go home and put down your weapons. We cannot solve this problem through retaliatory violence. . . . We must love our white brothers no matter what they do to us. We must make them know that we love them. Jesus still cries out across the centuries, 'Love your enemies.' This is what we must live by." Then, his voice swelling with emotion, he added: "Remember, if I am stopped, this movement will not stop, because God is with this movement."

It was another miracle of oratory, in a different style from his Holt Street speech. This time there was no applause. Simply, at his request, the crowd began to melt away, and with it, the tension. King even got them to listen quietly as the mayor promised a reward for information leading to the arrest of the bombers. But it had been a close thing. A small incident could have brought bloodshed. Calm returned, although two nights later a bomb landed—harmlessly—in the Nixons' yard.

After that climactic moment, there was a year-long struggle marked by court actions, by feats of improvisation that kept the M.I.A.'s transportation system rolling, and finally by fresh bombings.

Perhaps the most significant and least publicized action on the legal front was the petition on behalf of the M.I.A. for a hearing on the constitutionality of the Alabama segregation law before a three-judge federal court. This tactic was first suggested by Clifford Durr. About mid-April he realized that something more would be needed than Mrs. Parks's appeal, which was before the Alabama court of appeals, to carry the case to the top. The Supreme Court could not render a decision "on the merits" until the Alabama court had spoken—almost certainly against Rosa Parks. . . .

Durr therefore suggested to Fred Gray that he petition for a special three-judge federal court and ask it for an injunction against discrimination in seating, on the grounds that it was a violation of rights guaranteed in the Constitution. Such a panel was allowable in a federal action challenging a state law. And its rulings could be appealed directly to the Supreme Court.

Gray went to work at once, made contact with the New York and Washington branches of the NAACP, got some high-powered co-counsel, and filed his petition. The hearing was set for early in May. The court was composed of Richard T. Rives, at the time judge of the United States Circuit Court for the district including Alabama, who was the presiding justice;

Judge Frank Johnson, an indigenous "Andrew Jackson Republican" (in Durr's words) from the northern part of Alabama; and Judge Seybourne Lynn of Birmingham.

Within three weeks, two of the three white southern judges—Johnson and Rives—outvoted their colleague and ruled in favor of Gray's petition. Rives, who wrote the majority opinion, was threatened, obliged to listen to sermons attacking the federal judiciary in the Montgomery church he attended, and had garbage dumped on his son's grave in a local cemetery. Johnson took similar abuse. But the strategem was successful.

The federal question was raised at last. For the city of Montgomery appealed the ruling "on the merits," and the state of Alabama joined in the appeal; the matter now went onto the Supreme Court's docket. . . .

Montgomery authorities were meanwhile harassing the car pools. A car full of riders would be flagged down; the inspecting officer would find one or more violations of the state safety standards—weak brakes, poorly aligned headlights, or something else. The driver would be forced to abandon his vehicle, and a city wrecker would be called to tow it away (at the owner's expense) for repairs (also at his expense) in a city-approved shop. A similar tactic was the arbitrary cancellation of black auto-owners' insurance.

But all this was only prelude to the main attack. On October 30 Mayor Gayle directed the city's legal department to request an injunction "to stop the operation of the car pools or transportation systems growing out of the bus boycott," and to collect damages of fifteen thousand dollars for loss of tax revenues. Fred Gray's counterpetition to prevent the city's interference on behalf of the bus company was denied. A hearing was set for November 13.

There was no question in the minds of the M.I.A. leaders that this was, as King confessed to a mass meeting on the second of November, a bad moment. The city was certain to get its injunction, and to end the car pools would hopelessly undercut the boycott. He tried to rally confidence by saying, "This may well be the darkest hour before dawn. We have moved all these months with . . . daring faith. . . . We must go on with that same faith. . . ."

November 13 found the main contestants on both sides in court for the injunction hearing. The same judge who had tried Mrs. Parks a year earlier was listening to the arguments when, some time around noon, there was an interruption.

The two attorneys for the city, the mayor, and the police commissioner were all called out of the court, and there was an excited buzzing at the press table. One of the reporters brought over to the defense table a copy of a message just received over the wire service teletype machine:

The United States Supreme Court today affirmed a decision of a special three-judge U.S. District Court declaring Alabama's state and local laws requiring segregation on buses unconstitutional. The Supreme Court acted without listening to any argument; it simply said, "the motion to affirm is granted and the Judgment is affirmed."

Legally, the struggle was over. The black-led and black-supported boycott, rising out of Mrs. Parks's spontaneous act, had resulted in the highest court's driving another nail in the coffin of legalized segregation. But life follows law slowly. It took a month more for the judicial mandate actually to reach Montgomery. In that time the injunction against the car pools was granted. So blacks, still staying off the buses, walked many extra miles when no alternative arrangements were possible.

The interval was used to prepare the black community for the first day of the new dispensation. Sheets of suggestions on how to behave "in a loving manner" were distributed. Role-playing sessions were held in black churches. Among whites reactions varied. The City Commission received front-page coverage to proclaim its "determination [to] do all in its power to oppose the integration of the Negro race with the white race in Montgomery . . . [and] stand like a rock against social equality, intermarriage and mixing of the races under God's creation and plan." But the fateful December 21, the day of official desegregation, came and went with what the Montgomery *Advertiser* called " a calm but cautious acceptance of this significant change in Montgomery's way of life." Black and white ministers sat together undisturbed in what had been the "Whites Only" section. Drivers were uniformly courteous. Most white passengers chose to ignore the innovation; those who made nasty remarks were in turn ignored by the blacks. . . .

Ahead lay many events [in the struggle for civil rights]: sit-ins, freedom rides, gunfire on the campus of the University of Mississippi, the March on Washington, the Civil Rights and Voting Rights acts of 1964 and 1965, the summers of rioting in northern cities—and then, the murder of Martin Luther King, Jr., in a Memphis motel. Perhaps it would take the decade of the seventies to discover the full meaning of the record that began with the Montgomery boycott. But in that January of 1957, as integrated buses rolled down the streets of the Confederacy's first capital, over which the Stars and Bars still flew, almost everyone must have sensed that a new page in the history of black (and white) Americans had been turned.

DOCUMENTS

School Segregation
Ruled Unconstitutional, 1954

Today, education is perhaps the most important function of state and local governments. Compulsory school attendance laws and the great expenditures for education both demonstrate our recognition of the importance of education to our democratic society. It is required in the performance of our most basic public responsibilities, even service in the armed forces. It is the very foundation of good citizenship. Today it is a principal instrument in awakening the child to cultural values, in preparing him for later professional training, and in helping him to adjust normally to his environment. In these days, it is doubtful that any child may reasonably be expected to succeed in life if he is denied the opportunity of an education. Such an opportunity, where the state has undertaken to provide it, is a right which must be made available to all on equal terms.

We come then to the question presented: Does segregation of children in public schools solely on the basis of race, even though the physical facilities and other "tangible" factors may be equal, deprive the children of the minority group of equal education opportunities? We believe that it does.

In *Sweatt* v. *Painter*, . . . in finding that segregated law school for Negroes could not provide them equal educational opportunities, this Court relied in large part on "those qualities which are incapable of objective measurement but which make for greatness in a law school." In *McLaurin* v. *Oklahoma State Regents*, . . . the Court, in requiring that a Negro admitted to a white graduate school be treated like all other students, again resorted to intangible considerations: ". . . his ability to study, to engage in discussions and exchange views with other students, and, in general, to learn his profession." Such considerations apply with added force to children in grade and high schools. To separate them from others of similar age and qualifications solely because of their race generates a feeling of inferiority as to their status in the community that may affect their hearts and minds in a way unlikely ever to be undone. The effect of this separation on their educational opportunities was well stated by a finding in the Kansas case by a court which nevertheless felt compelled to rule against the Negro plaintiffs:

> Segregation of white and colored children in public schools has a detrimental effect upon the colored children. The impact is greater

SOURCE: Chief Justice Earl Warren's majority opinion in *Brown* v. *Board of Education of Topeka*, 347 U.S. 483 (1954).

when it has the sanction of the law; for the policy of separating the races is usually interpreted as denoting the inferiority of the negro group. A sense of inferiority affects the motivation of the child to learn. Segregation with the sanction of law, therefore, has a tendency to [retard] the educational and mental development of negro children and to deprive them of some of the benefits they would receive in a racial[ly] integrated school system.

. . . We conclude that in the field of public education the doctrine of "separate but equal" has no place. Separate educational facilities are inherently unequal. Therefore, we hold that the plaintiffs and others similarly situated for whom the actions have been brought are, by reason of the segregation complained of, deprived of the equal protection of the laws guaranteed by the Fourteenth Amendment. . . .

Opposition to the Civil Rights Bill, 1964

Truly . . . this is a sad day. As a student of law, and a practicing lawyer, I never dreamed that the day would ever come when more than two-thirds of the Congress—Senate and House—would virtually destroy the Constitution, violating every intent of the founders of our Republic.

For 10 years the executive and judiciary departments have had a virtual partnership to set up a dictatorship. Here, today the Congress gets in on the act, says, "Me, too," and ratifies the unconstitutional acts which have gone before.

Present conditions are so similar to the days just preceding the Civil War, we should pause to remember that heart-breaking conflict, which pitted brother against brother, and father against son—today, it is section against section, and those who need to straighten out their own sections, cover up by going to mine.

As we look back upon those troubled times we can see that sound leaders of both sides deplored any effort to settle the issue by armed conflict. Unfortunately, the radicals of that day prevented a peaceful solution. Then, as now, they were not satisfied to run their own local affairs, but insisted that all other sections conform to their pattern. A terrible war resulted. . . .

Instead of forcing integration upon the Southern States, truly it would be well for the rest of the country to learn from the States of the South

SOURCE: Speech of Congressman James Whitten in *Congressional Record*, July 2, 1964, 15886–87.

that the way for peace and harmony is to provide for separate but equal facilities and protect each race in the enjoyment of its own way of life. . . .

You may well ask why the Supreme Court rendered the unanimous decision in the Brown integration case. It was probably argued that if we do not bring about integration in the United States, we will lose the contest with Russia throughout the world; and if we do not do this, Russia will eventually conquer the world. It was said by the press, "If Russia takes over here, the first thing they will do is set up a dictatorship. If Russia takes over," they charged, "they will do away with the right to trial by jury." "Yes," they said, "if we do not integrate, Russia will force on us a system similar to Hitler's in Germany or Stalin's in Russia."

What did they do in Germany and Russia? What was the source of their absolute control of those nations? Why, they had the courts issue decrees, then they used troops and government officers to enforce the decrees.

Have we not done that here? We have seen the Supreme Court, unwilling to wait for constitutional amendment in the regular process, change the Constitution. We have seen the President send troops and Federal officials to enforce such decrees. Our Government does itself what we feared Russia might do.

We were told we have to integrate all the races of the United States or we cannot hold the friendship of the people of India, China, Japan, Africa, and all the rest. If that be true, why have China and Japan been at dagger's point throughout history? Talk about India—in spite of what you read, we know in many areas people of the same color cannot even touch each other.

The agitation is right here at home. People are using the threat of Russia here in the United States to accomplish their personal desires and actually to impose the Russian system of required conformity upon us.

My friends, history clearly shows an individual must have pride or he makes no real progress. A family must have pride or it goes down the scale. So it is with countries. So it is with race. Any race, whatever it may be, which feels it must be intermixed with another acknowledges its own lack. Such a race will not serve itself well, nor that with which it wishes to intermix.

Integration, where it has taken place, has only led to great turmoil. We all know that if you go into some sections of New York City at night you take your life in your hands; and you may be in danger there in the daytime. You can not go to certain areas of Chicago without danger to life and limb. The same is true of most of our major cities. Rape, murder, and robbery are commonplace in some areas of Washington. . . .

In recent weeks we have seen agitators deliberately go into areas of the South for the admitted purpose of violating laws of the States which have never been held to be beyond the power of such States, but rather have been held to be within the power; and then we have seen the Federal Government move its force in to protect such individuals in their avowed purpose of testing existing laws.

What if it were the law against murder they wished to test, or rape, or treason? Is there one rule in the Federal Government for laws the executive or the judiciary likes and another for the laws they do not like? . . .

I am proud that the people of my section are showing real self-restraint under trying circumstances. I hope time will show you who support this bill, that you are wrong; that those on the Supreme Court who have led this Nation down the road to state socialism are wrong; and that the present judicial dictatorship of the Supreme Court, supported by the executive branch, and here affirmed by this Congress, is all wrong and that this act will be repealed; that the rights of individuals to accumulate and control one's own property, the right to choose one's own customers, one's own companions and one's friends, regardless of color will be reestablished. Only then . . . will our Nation endure.

Rural Alabama Revisited, 1983

In 1958 and 1968, the [U.S. Civil Rights] Commission found that blacks suffered from discrimination and segregation in every facet of life. This cycle of unequal opportunities in employment, education, health, and other areas lasted from cradle to grave and from generation to generation.

In 1982 the Commission decided to reexamine the 16-county area [in Alabama studied previously] to determine the extent of changes in education, employment, and health conditions for blacks since 1968. The purpose of the study is to determine whether disparities between blacks as compared to whites continue and whether discriminatory barriers to equal opportunity remain. The 1982 report on rural Alabama did not use hearings, but field investigations to assess education, employment, and health conditions for blacks relative to whites since 1968 in 6 of the 16 counties. The Commission believed that certain events had occurred since 1968 that should have improved conditions for blacks in the counties. For example:

- School desegregation cases, which ordered Alabama school districts to desegregate their student bodies and faculties and take other affirmative steps to ensure equal educational opportunity, had been implemented.
- Federal funds for education, health care, and other areas had been made available to the region.

SOURCE: U.S. Civil Rights Commission, *Fifteen Years Ago . . . Rural Alabama Revisited* (Washington, D.C.: Government Printing Office, 1983), iii–iv, 82, 84.

- Alabama had undertaken an intensive campaign to attract industry that was moving to the "Sunbelt."
- Health statistics showed that infant mortality rates had decreased significantly for blacks in the region.

With these changes, it was hoped that discriminatory barriers had been dismantled and that there had been improvements in the quality of life for blacks relative to whites in the 16 counties since the last Commission hearing. . . .

In the 15 years since the Commission's hearing in Montgomery, the 16-county region has remained an economically depressed area, especially for blacks.

- The black unemployment rate remains two to three times higher than that of whites.
- Blacks are employed generally in the lowest paying jobs and are largely undereducated and unskilled.
- Median family income for blacks is only half that of whites.
- Poverty rates for blacks remain as much as 5 times those of whites.
- The percentage of blacks over 25 years of age who have graduated from high school is approximately half that of whites.
- New industries that have located in Alabama since 1968 have bypassed the 16-county area to a large extent, particularly in those counties where the population is majority-black and blacks have political control.
- Although the infant mortality rate for blacks has decreased, the black infant mortality rates continue to be much higher than those of whites.

In the six counties visited by Commission staff, educational, employment, and health conditions and services have improved for blacks, but there has been little change in conditions for blacks relative to whites.

As a result of the Voting Rights Act, blacks have been elected to a wide variety of political offices in five of the six counties, particularly where they represent a majority of the population. Currently, a majority of the county commissioners and school board members in the four majority-black counties—Greene, Macon, Lowndes, and Sumter—are black. However, these political gains have produced little real power. The authority of these officials is basically limited to the distribution of minimal county revenues as well as Federal funds; black officials make decisions regarding the policies of public institutions such as the schools, health clinics, and other county services.

Whites maintain control over the major financial resources and institutions in these counties, affording whites considerable power. Whites in majority-black counties also have withdrawn from the public schools and other institutions controlled by blacks, and have established and promoted segregated institutions in the counties.

Segregation, institutional and social, existed in the South until the passage of civil rights legislation. Although *de jure* segregation ended, segregation as a practice evolved into its present form—"neosegregation." Under neosegregation, blacks and whites accept the separation of the races as a way of life. For example, it has become generally accepted that blacks attend public schools and whites attend private academies. Therefore, a dual system in education still prevails; however, today it is not viewed by blacks or whites to be harmful or discriminatory in effect. Neosegregation appears to be more pervasive in the predominantly black counties where blacks have political control. Within these counties, whites have segregated themselves from blacks in many aspects of life. . . .

It is clear from the evidence gathered that much remains to be done if equal opportunity in education, employment, and health care is to be achieved in this area of the Nation.

CHAPTER 16

The Revival of Feminism

When women gained the vote in 1920, the women's movement that had long sought this goal—dating back to the mid-nineteenth century—became dormant for several decades. Yet this victory by no means marked the end of the struggle for equality of opportunity and treatment for women. The franchise gained women entry to the voting booth, but few won elective office. Women still found most of their employment opportunities in the traditional, low-paying, "feminine" occupations, and their wages were typically lower than those of men with similar experience, education, skill, and responsibility. Moreover, during the Great Depression, married women discovered that many employers were reluctant to hire them, insisting that during the crisis men must be given preference for whatever jobs were available.

In 1923 a group of women led by Alice Paul proposed an amendment to the Constitution designed to ensure sexual equality. This equal rights amendment (ERA) is reproduced in the first document. The idea lay dormant for nearly half a century until the resurgence of the women's movement in the 1960s, detailed in William Chafe's essay "The Revival of Feminism." How does Chafe account for

304

the renewed strength of the movement at that time? What, in addition to adoption of the amendment, does the essay identify as key objectives of the "new feminism"?

By 1970 the ERA had again become a live issue. The second document is a statement in support of the amendment before a Senate committee by the well-known feminist writer and editor Gloria Steinem. To what extent and in what ways might the ERA affect the conditions Steinem describes?

In 1972 Congress approved the ERA by the necessary two-thirds margin, and opinion polls indicated support for the amendment by a vast majority of the American public. Nevertheless, the amendment failed to receive ratification by the required three-quarters of the states. Opposition centered in the South, several western states, Missouri, and Illinois. The third document, a speech by Senator Sam Ervin of North Carolina during the senatorial debates on the amendment, provides an example of the kinds of arguments offered in opposition. Would his position find support today?

The defeat of the ERA, although a major setback, was not fatal to the women's movement. A growing number of women ran for and were elected to office after 1970. And in 1984, for the first time, a woman, Geraldine Ferraro, was selected as a vice-presidential candidate. Encouraged by the spirit of feminism, and aided by civil rights legislation, favorable court decisions, and government-directed affirmative action programs, increasing numbers of women have entered what had been traditional male occupations. In 1960 only 3.5 percent of lawyers were women, compared to 14 percent in 1982. Among physicians, 6.8 percent were women in 1960; by 1982 the figure had risen to 14.3 percent.

In the area of equal pay for equal work, however, by the mid-1980s a substantial gap still existed between the wages of men and women. The last document reveals another disturbing development in American society: the increasing number of female-headed, impoverished households. What does this report by the Commission on Civil Rights identify as the chief causes and consequences of this trend?

E S S A Y

The Revival of Feminism

William H. Chafe

HELMER: Before all else, you are a wife and mother.
NORA: That I no longer believe. I believe that before all
else, I am a human being, just as much as you are—or at
least that I should try to become one.

Henrik Ibsen, *A Doll's House* (1879)

In the fall of 1962, the editors of *Harpers* observed a curious phenomenon. An extraordinary number of women seemed "ardently determined to extend their vocation beyond the bedroom, kitchen and nursery," but very few showed any interest in feminism. Both observations were essentially correct. In the years during and after World War II, millions of women had left the home to take jobs, but the expansion of their "sphere" occurred without fanfare and was not accompanied by any organized effort to challenge traditional definitions of woman's place. If many women were dissatisfied with what one housewife called the endless routine of "dishwashing, picking up, ironing, and folding diapers," they kept their frustration to themselves. Women examined their futures privately and with an unmilitant air. They had not yet developed a sense of collective grievance.

Eight years later, feminism competed with the Vietnam war, student revolts, and inflation for headlines in the daily press. Female activists picketed the Miss America contest, stormed meetings of professional associations to demand equal employment opportunities, and forced their way into male bars and restaurants in New York. They called a national strike, wrote about the oppression of a "sexual politics," and sat in at editorial offices of *Newsweek* and *Ladies Home Journal*. At times, it seemed that the media had been taken over by women's liberation, so often did female activists appear on network television and in national magazines. In an era punctuated by protest, feminism had once again come into its own. If not all women subscribed to the new fight for equality, an energetic minority nevertheless believed that the time had come to finish the task of gaining for women the same rights that men had.

The evolution of any protest movement is a complicated phenomenon. In general, however, at least three preconditions are required: first, a point

SOURCE: William H. Chafe, *The American Woman: Her Changing Social, Economic and Political Role, 1920–1970*, copyright © 1972 by William H. Chafe. Reprinted by permission of Oxford University Press, Inc.

of view around which to organize; second, a positive response by a portion of the aggrieved group; and third, a social atmosphere which is conducive to reform. To an extent unmatched since the last days of the suffrage fight, all three elements came together in the American woman's movement during the 1960's. Articulate feminists presented a cogent indictment of society's treatment of women. A substantial number of females who had already experienced profound change in their lives were responsive to the call to end discrimination. And the society at large was peculiarly attuned to the need for guaranteeing equality to all its citizens. No one development by itself could have explained the rebirth of the woman's movement, but all three together created a context in which, for the first time in half a century, feminism became a force to be reckoned with in American society.

The ideological keynote of the feminist revival was sounded in 1963 by Betty Friedan. In the years after World War II, she charged, American women had been victimized by a set of ideas—a "feminine mystique"—which permeated society and defined female happiness as total involvement in the roles of wife and mother. Advertisers manipulated women into believing that they could achieve fulfillment by using the latest model vacuum cleaner or bleaching their clothes a purer white. Women's magazines romanticized domesticity and presented an image of woman as "gaily content in a world of bedroom, kitchen, sex, babies and home." And psychiatrists like Marynia Farnham and Helene Deutsch popularized the notion that any woman dissatisfied with a full-time occupation as housewife was somehow emotionally maladjusted. As a result, Friedan declared, a woman's horizons were circumscribed from childhood on by the assumption that her highest function in life was to care for her husband and rear their children. In effect, the home had become a "comfortable concentration camp" which infantilized its female inhabitants and forced them to "give up their adult frame of reference." Just as Victorian culture had repressed the need of women to express themselves sexually, modern culture denied them the opportunity to use their minds.

Despite some exaggerations, Friedan articulated a point of view which struck a responsive chord, and within a year others presented a similar position. Adopting a more academic perspective, Ellen and Kenneth Keniston placed particular emphasis on the fact that young girls had no positive models of career women to emulate. "The most effective forms of oppression are those with which the victim covertly cooperates," they declared, and women provided a case in point. Denied any culturally approved alternative to homemaking, most females internalized society's view of their place and accepted a "voluntary servitude" in the home rather than risk losing their femininity. Alice Rossi made the same point. "There are few Noras in contemporary society," she observed, "because women have deluded themselves that a doll's house is large enough to find complete fulfillment within it."

All the feminists agreed that the limitations placed on women's activities had a profoundly destructive effect. When a woman's sole focus of interest was the home, they claimed, she was forced to overcompensate for her lack of power in other areas by establishing an emotional tyranny over her husband and children. Females who made a full-time occupation of motherhood, Alice Rossi declared, treated their children "like hothouse plants" and tried to live vicariously "in and through them." Consequently, youngsters were stifled and prevented from growing into autonomous personalities. At the same time, the conditions of suburban living made it difficult for a wife to achieve the marital fulfillment which the "mystique" led her to expect. Husbands were away 80 per cent of the time, and it was almost impossible for a wife to derive the same measure of satisfaction from the few hours a couple spent together that a man found in the full variety of his occupational and social experiences. The family thus became a breeding ground of discontent and unhappiness. Female neurosis skyrocketed, divorces multiplied, and a generation of children grew up spoiled and dependent.

Ultimately, however, the feminists traced the "woman problem" to the fact that females were denied the same opportunity as men to develop an identity of their own. The success of any interpersonal relationship depended on the autonomy and strength of each participant. Yet in many cases, cultural conditioning had prevented women from achieving a sense of themselves as persons. While men were encouraged to fashion their own destinies, females were confined to those roles which were rooted in their biological functions. Assigned to a place solely on the basis of sex, women were kept from seeing themselves as unique human beings, distinct from others. All females participated equally in the undifferentiated roles of housewife and mother, but many lacked a more precise image of themselves as individuals. As one young mother wrote:

> I've tried everything women are supposed to do—hobbies, gardening, pickling, canning, and being very social with my neighbors. . . . I can do it all, and I like it, but it doesn't leave you anything to think about—any feeling of who you are. . . . I love the kids and Bob and my home. . . . But I'm desperate. I begin to feel that I have no personality. I'm a server of food and putter-on of pants and a bedmaker, somebody who can be called on when you want something. But who am I?

To the feminists, the question struck at the core of the alienation of modern women and could be answered only if wives and mother rejected cultural stereotypes and developed a life of their own outside the home. A career, the feminists claimed, had two advantages. First, it would allow women to realize their potential as individuals in the wider society. And second, it was the only way by which they could achieve the personal recognition and identity essential to a healthy family life. A study of Vassar students had shown that women with professional aspirations experienced fewer problems of personal adjustment and enjoyed a greater degree of self-fulfillment than those who rejected a career and opted for a life in the home. Another survey by Abraham H. Maslow disclosed that "high dominance" women—those who were aggressive and assertive—had a better sex life and less neurosis than "low dominance" women who more closely conformed to cultural stereotypes. Wives and mothers with careers, Alice Rossi declared, would demand less of their husbands, provide a "living model" of independence and responsibility to their children, and regain a sense of their own worth as persons. With an independent existence outside the home, they would cease to be parasites living off the activities of those around them and instead become full and equal partners in the family community.

To a remarkable extent, the new feminists presented a uniform analysis of women's position in contemporary society. They all believed that the women's rights movement had suffered a grievous setback in the years after 1945, that the "feminine mystique" had forced females to accept a "voluntary servitude" in the home, and that women could break out of their "prison" only if they developed outside interests and rectified the imbalance of social and family relationships. To that end, they urged a radical modification of cultural stereotypes, the creation of new community institutions like child-care centers, and a concerted campaign by women to develop a "lifelong commitment" to the professions or business.

Unfortunately, the feminists also shared in common several misconceptions. To begin with, they assumed that all homemakers secretly resented their position and if given a chance would automatically decide to pursue a career. While such an assumption might describe some women, it certainly did not apply to all. The challenges of a full social life, volunteer work, good cooking, and enlightened child care provided many women with a diverse and rewarding existence—one which they would not choose to sacrifice even if the opportunity presented itself. Such women may have "voluntarily" accepted a life in the home, but their condition was not that of servitude nor could they honestly be described as oppressed. A 1962 Gallup Poll, for example, showed that three out of five women were "fairly satisfied" with their achievements, and believed that they were happier than their mothers.

Second, the feminist analysis betrayed the same middle-class bias which had characterized the women's rights movement from its inception. Even if many housewives were discontented, very few had either the training or motivation to follow a career in business or the professions. Such an option existed only for the best educated and most dedicated segment of the female population; it did not represent a realistic alternative for most women. Furthermore, Friedan and the other feminists concentrated their attention on suburban, college graduates who by definition had been exposed at least briefly to the possibility of a different way of life. Millions of lower-class women, on the other hand, lacked both the sophistication and experience to envision the possibility of an alternative life style. Such women agreed without hesitation that their husbands' sphere of responsibility should remain separate from their own. The wife of the blue-collar worker rarely asked the question "Who am I?", first, because it never occurred to her, and, second, because she already knew the answer. Brought up to be a wife and mother, she accepted her ascribed status as both natural and right.

Finally, contemporary feminists often showed an appalling ignorance of history in their contention that the "feminine mystique" represented a post–World War II phenomenon. The "cult of true womanhood" pervaded nineteenth-century culture, and the ideology of the "mystique" dominated the editorial policy of women's magazines in the twentieth century long before 1945. Indeed, the consistency of anti-feminist arguments constitutes one of the most striking facts of the entire debate in America over woman's place. When Adlai Stevenson told the graduates of Smith in 1955 that their political task was to "influence man and boy" through the "humble role of housewife," he was essentially repeating a point of view which had been expressed for centuries. Similarly, women had been told for over a hundred years that equality would lead to the destruction of the home and the family. There was nothing necessarily new about the feminine mystique, nor could it be said that women in the 1950's were more "victimized" than they had been at other times in history. The feminists had simply given fresh expression to an old problem.

Nevertheless, the fact that the problem was discovered anew represented a development of critical importance. As a result of the feminists' contribution, a cogent if controversial viewpoint emerged around which to build a movement of popular protest. Talk about female discontent had been rife for years, but for the first time in a generation dissatisfied women had a focus for their anger. Friedan, in particular, exerted a significant influence. With eloquence and passion, she dramatized through case studies the boredom and alienation of those afflicted by "the problem that has no name." In addition, she was able to take her readers behind the scenes to editorial offices and advertising firms where they could see first hand the way in which the image of the feminine mystique was formed. It was hard not to be outraged after reading how advertising men—who themselves viewed housework as menial—tried to sell cleaning products as an answer to drudgery and as a means of expressing creativity. If, as Friedan claimed, the women frustrated by such manipulation were legion, her book helped to crystallize a sense of grievance and to provide an ideological position with which the discontented could identify. *The Feminine Mystique* sold more than a million copies, and, if not all its readers agreed with the conclusions, they could not help but re-examine their own lives in light of the questions it raised.

No protest movement occurs in a vacuum, however, and it is unlikely that feminism could have gained the energy it did during the 1960's had not Americans been preoccupied with the demand to eliminate prejudice and discrimination. Historically, women's rights advocates had succeeded in focusing attention on their grievances only at a time of generalized social reform. The feminist movement began when abolitionism provided female activists with an opportunity to organize and exposed them directly to the physical and psychological reality of discrimination based on sex. For nearly forty years after the Civil War, the movement was stagnant and isolated. The advent of Progressivism offered another vehicle for advance, and in a generation dedicated to ending social injustice women's rights leaders succeeded in placing suffrage on the agenda of reform and in building a national coalition sufficient to win enactment of the Nineteenth Amendment. On both occasions, women themselves played an important part in creating the atmosphere of reform, but their own cause benefited most from the climate of opinion which resulted.

It was not surprising, therefore, that the revival of the woman's movement in the 1960's coincided with another national crusade to redress the grievances of oppressed minority groups. The civil rights revolution dramatized the immorality of discriminating against any group of people on the basis of physical characteristics. It provided a model of moral indignation and tactical action which women (as well as Indians and Mexican-Americans) quickly adopted as their own. And it spawned a generation of young female leaders who determined to remove the stumbling block of discrimination from their own path at the same time that they fought for the liberation of their black brothers and sisters. Like their abolitionist ancestors, many latent feminists fully realized the extent of their own oppression only through the "sexism" of their male civil rights colleagues. Forced to do menial women's work, and denied an equal voice in policy-making councils ("the position of women in our movement should be prone," black leader Stokely Carmichael said), they rapidly concluded that their own freedom was also on the line, and set out to win it. Whenever America became sensitive to the issue of human rights, it seemed, the woman's movement acquired new support in one way or another, and the 1960's proved no exception to the rule. The civil rights movement did not cause the revival of feminism, but it did help to create a set of favorable circumstances.

The most important precondition for the resurgence of the woman's movement, however, was the amount of change which had already occurred among American females. If women had been as oppressed as the feminists claimed, no amount of rhetoric could have aroused them from their captivity. Social scientists have pointed out that rebellions almost never occur among people enslaved in a "closed system," especially in a concentration camp. Rather, revolutions begin in response to "rising expectations," after a group has started on the road to improvement and become aware of its relative deprivation. It is reasonable to assume, therefore, that, unless substantial shifts had already taken place in women's lives, the ideology of the feminists would have fallen on barren ground. There was little in the writings of Friedan or Rossi which had not been anticipated in one form or another by Charlotte Perkins Gilman.* Yet Gilman never received the enthusiastic reception accorded her latter-day successors. One explanation, it would seem, is that Gilman spoke to an audience which, by virtue of the social structure of the time, was incapable of hearing her message, while Friedan and her colleagues addressed a society which was more prepared to listen. It would be an exaggeration to say that the ideology of the feminists was simply catching up with reality. But if reality had not already altered considerably—if women had not already departed in such great numbers from their traditional sphere—it is doubtful that the feminists' call for further change would have met with the response it did.

In fact, a strong case could be made that the changes which had occurred directly set the stage for the possibility of feminist success. To begin with, over 40 per cent of all women—including wives—held jobs by the end of the 1960's. Included in that number were a substantial number of middle-class women (41 per cent of those whose husbands earned from $8,000–10,000) and approximately 50 per cent of all mothers with children six to eighteen years old. For the first time in the nation's history, almost half the adolescent girls in the country were growing up with examples in their own homes of women who combined outside employment with marriage. To be sure, very few of these women occupied positions which could be described as executive, but they did have interests outside the home and clearly contradicted the image of the captive housewife.

In addition, the evidence suggested that many working mothers already provided a positive model to their children. Repeated surveys of elementary and high school students showed that children of mothers who held jobs approved of maternal employment and that the girls intended to work after they married and had children. Significantly, adolescent females were more likely to name their mother as the person they most admired if she worked than if she did not work. "The [employed] mother," Lois Hoffman has written, "may represent to her daughter a person who has achieved success in areas that are, in some respects, more salient to a growing girl than household skills." Alice Rossi noted that, if a woman

---

[*militant feminist of the early twentieth century]

had a career, she "might finally provide her children with . . . a healthy dose of inattention, and a chance for adolescence to be a period of fruitful immaturity and growth." But surveys by social scientists indicated that many working mothers were already imparting lessons of self-reliance to their teenage children and that part-time and voluntary employment in particular seemed to foster a heathier child-mother relationship. The family, in the eyes of many experts, was becoming less child-centered and more person-centered, largely as a result of the growing interest of mothers in activities outside the home.

Not surprisingly, maternal employment also exerted considerable influence on the female child's self-image. Most sociologists agree that children learn their future sex roles by observing their parents. Since mothers who worked presented a different role model than most housewives, their children grew up with a substantially revised image of what it meant to be a woman. On a battery of tests administered to female students, daughters of working mothers scored lower on scales of traditional femininity, viewed the female role as less restricted to the home, and believed that both men *and* women participated in and enjoyed a variety of work, household, and recreational experiences. To some extent, the results of maternal employment differed according to the age and sex of the child and the social class of the mother. Women with pre-school children, for example, often felt guilty about not fulfilling their maternal responsibilities and tended to compensate by over-protecting their children. Similarly, in lower-class households where mothers were forced to work because of economic need, maternal employment sometimes reflected negatively on the father's ability as a provider, causing male children to become more dependent, withdrawn, and passive. The evidence indicated, however, that, in most families where both spouses worked, the presence of a working mother had no deleterious effect on the emotional or mental development of children, but instead encouraged young girls in particular to perceive sexual spheres as overlapping. It was likely that, as more and more mothers took jobs, a new generation of daughters would appear, with a commitment to function just as fully in the world outside the home as their brothers.

Finally, female employment seemed to have a salutary effect on the attitudes of both men and women toward equality. Not only did female workers themselves increasingly value their jobs as an opportunity for self-expression and personal recognition, but, in addition, their husbands gave signs of shifting their philosophy on issues involving women's rights. A survey of households in a Western city showed that husbands of working wives were more likely than husbands of non-working wives to favor equal pay (62 per cent versus 49 per cent), to believe that sexual intercourse should occur only when both partners desired it (68 per cent versus 50 per cent), to think that men should help around the house "all the time" (29 per cent versus 13 per cent), and to indicate a willingness to make sacrifices for a wife's career (20 per cent versus 8 per cent). The figures were not overwhelming, and it was possible that a husband's attitudes either preceded or were independent of a wife's working pattern. But together with other data which showed a close relationship between women's work and the companionate family the survey results gave support to the suggestion that female employment, in its own way, was causing a profound modification in relationships between the sexes.

On balance, then, it appeared that the ground was well prepared for a revival of the woman's movement. If the feminists had been correct in their analysis, almost all women might have been expected to cling to their traditional roles, afraid to leave the hearth because of the oppobrium attached to any vocation other than homemaking. The evidence indicated, however, that, despite the popularity of the feminine mystique, a dramatic change in the content of women's sphere had already taken place. Women's rights advocates were correct in claiming that little progress had occurred in areas such as professional opportunities, community services, and fair pay. But they vastly exaggerated the degree of women's servitude. As [sociologist] David Reisman noted in 1964, "there is much less resignation and inhibition among women [today than in my mother's generation]. . . . Instead, there is an effort to lead a multi-dimensional life." If the barriers to equality had not been eliminated, women nevertheless enjoyed more freedom than ever before, and the extent to which ideas and expectations were shifting—especially among the young—created the context in which a renewed drive for equality was possible.

In response to such developments, the woman's movement came to life in the mid-1960's. At first slowly, then with growing confidence and strength, feminist leaders established new organizations to carry on the battle for equal rights. Like most social movements, the new feminism was comprised of different constituencies. On the "right" wing was the National Organization for Women (NOW) formed in 1966 by Betty Friedan. Supported primarily by well-educated professional women, NOW represented a reformist approach to equality and acted on the assumption that the social structure could be changed from within through legislation and persuasion. Women's liberation groups, in contrast, were made up mostly of younger, more radical women, many of whom had been involved in the peace, civil rights, and student movements, and who were convinced that revolutionary change offered the only answer to sexual inequality. Through such mechanisms as "consciousness-raising"—a process in which small groups of women share their common experiences—members of women's liberation sought to understand the depth of what it means to be female and to explore ways of overcoming the sources of oppression in their lives.

Although the diffuse structure of the movement encouraged division and controversy, most feminists subscribed to a core set of demands which constituted the essence of their program. All insisted on an end to job discrimination, all supported the repeal of abortion laws, and all urged the creation of twenty-four-hour-a-day child-care centers. Most important, all wanted an end to class treatment, to the idea that women, because of their sex, should automatically be expected to do the housework, act as secretaries at meetings, or rear children. Women were individuals, they claimed, not sex objects or servants, and wherever a female was assigned a place on the basis of sex alone, whether at a news magazine where women were "researchers" rather than "reporters," or in the home where husbands expected wives to get up with the baby at night, discrimination existed and had to be rooted out. Critics of the movement frequently dismissed women's liberation as a middle-class fad which was irrelevant to the real problems of society, but, in fact, feminist proposals spoke to all women and, if implemented, were more likely to benefit the ghetto-dweller than the affluent resident of the suburb.

Perhaps the most notable characteristic of the movement was its ability to make news. In an era dominated by the mass media, the feminists displayed consummate skill in drawing public attention to themselves and "raising" America's consciousness to the inequalities from which women suffered. Television might spotlight the more spectacular tactics of the movement such as sit-ins or boycotts, but it also dealt seriously with more substantive concerns. Every network (and most magazines) devoted special programs to the reasons for the feminist protest, and enterprising reporters ferreted out impressive documentation to support charges of sex discrimination. Unequal pay, the tragedy of unwanted pregnancies which could not legally be terminated, and the frustration of many women with domesticity—all were given nationwide exposure. The success of the feminists in attracting publicity alerted millions of uninvolved women to the possibility that they too might be victims of discrimination. Many females might have rejected the idea that they were an "oppressed class," but, as they talked about the effort by feminists to "liberate" them, the likelihood increased that they would discern examples of inequality and prejudice in their own lives and develop a heightened sense of sex solidarity.

Significantly, the resurgence of feminism coincided with other signs of independence among American women. The *New York Times* reported that a "new breed of middle class women" was emerging and that suburban housewives who had previously stayed at home all day were seeking jobs, going back to school, and engaging in volunteer work. Both the Protestant and Catholic churches were confronted by an increasing militancy among women who demanded equal recognition. A leader of American Baptist women threatened a floor fight if a female was not included in the top hierarchy of the Baptist convention, and angry nuns insisted on an end to supervision by priests. The feminist message also met with an enthusiastic response among the young women of "middle America." Representatives of the Future Homemakers of America declared that women's liberation had exerted a "definite influence" on their 600,000 members. Teenage girls still wanted to marry and have children, FHA leaders noted, but they now believed that fulfillment as women could come only if they also worked in a gainful occupation. Although such reports were obviously impressionistic, two studies of teenage girls in Georgia and Washington state showed that a sizable majority planned to hold jobs after they married and that less than 25 per cent definitely anticipated *not* being employed.

A 1970 Gallup Poll confirmed that many women—especially the well educated—were developing greater sensitivity to their rights. Although 65 per cent of the respondents believed that women were generally given an even break with men, a majority also declared that females were discriminated against in business and in the professions. Eight years earlier, in a similar poll, less than 30 per cent felt that females suffered from job discrimination, and only 39 per cent said that women were underpaid. More important, the level of discontent in 1970 rose appreciably among women with a college education. Almost half the college respondents (47 per cent) asserted that women did not receive an even break with men, and 75 per cent declared that women were discriminated against in gaining executive positions (significantly, 70 per cent of women with college degrees were in the labor force by the end of the decade). In a parallel finding, [social scientist] Mirra Komarovsky discovered that women who were married to blue-collar workers and who had a high school diploma were far more likely to demand that their husbands share in domestic and child-rearing responsibilities than those with only elementary schooling. Education thus appeared to be another critical variable in fostering self-awareness among females and correlated directly with perceptions of inequality.

Perhaps the greatest evidence that the woman's movement had made an impact was the increased attention it received from politicians. For more than four decades after passage of the suffrage, feminist demands had largely been ignored by government leaders. By the late 1960's, however, a change in attitude began to appear. After having been bottled up in committee for forty-seven years, the Equal Rights Amendment to the Constitution was brought before the House of Representatives where it received enthusiastic support. James Hodgson, Richard Nixon's Secretary of Labor, announced in 1970 that federal contracts would henceforth contain a clause mandating the employment of a certain quota of women. Attorney General John Mitchell initiated federal suits under Title VII of the 1964 Civil Rights Act to end job discrimination against women in such large corporations as Libby-Corning Glass and American Telephone and Telegraph. And under feminist pressure, the Nixon Administration required 2,000 colleges and universities to turn over their personnel files to the federal government so that it could determine whether females were victims of prejudice in hiring and wages.

The same effort to respond to the demands of the woman's movement occurred at other levels of government. Despite the vigorous opposition of the Catholic Church, abortion reform laws were passed in seventeen states. By 1970, over 200,000 women were receiving legal abortions annually—a 1,000 per cent increase over two years earlier. Candidates for public office made support of women's rights a major plank of their platforms. Municipal leaders instructed department chiefs to seek out qualified women for executive posts. And school boards began to change their rules on such things as who could take home economics and shop courses, and who could play on athletic squads. If women's liberationists scorned some of the actions as corrupt tokenism, the fact remained that their movement had become big enough in the eyes of political leaders to merit co-opting.

Nevertheless, there was little reason to be over-optimistic. Although some progress had been made on laws involving job discrimination, resistance to change mounted as the stakes became higher and more deeply entrenched social values were challenged. Once again, the child-care issue symbolized the difficulties faced by women's rights advocates. When Congress enacted a massive day-care program designed to make child-care facilities available to every working mother in the country, President Nixon vetoed the measure, declaring that it would commit "the vast moral authority of the national Government to the side of communal approaches to child-rearing. . . ." The family, Nixon insisted, was "the keystone of our civilization," and enlightened public policy required that it be strengthened rather than weakened. On a second controversial issue, Nixon issued an emotional statement opposing abortion reform and defending the rights of unborn fetuses, thereby lending his support to those in the various states who were striving to overturn liberalized abortion statutes. Thus, while feminists and their sympathizers could draw some encouragement from the progress which had taken place, opposition to change remained both strong and effective.

In most ways, then, the fight had just begun. Radical feminists would not be satisfied with halfway measures or limited legislative reforms. They desired drastic change, the end of a system which assumed that men were powerful and women weak, males aggressive and females passive. American culture, [feminist] Kate Millett wrote, was permeated by an oppressive ideology in which all that could "be described as distinctly human . . . [was] reserved for the male." If politics meant power, then women were still disenfranchised. Even in "liberal" households, they were expected to do the dirtiest chores, take primary responsibility for rearing the children, and put their aspirations behind those of their husbands. For Millett and her allies, the answer had to be revolution—the abolition of patriarchy, an end to the family as presently constituted, and replacement of the traditional socialization process. Emancipation could be achieved only when every vestige of sexual stereotyping had been eliminated, when "masculine" and "feminine" spheres disappeared, and members of each sex were free to develop as individuals.

In a very real sense, the woman's movement had gone full cycle. The women who started feminism in the nineteenth century had ideas which were similar in substance, if not in tone, to those of their successors. They too wanted an end to the notion that women should occupy a separate sphere, and they too insisted on every person's right to be a human being first and a man or a woman second. "Whatsoever it is morally right for a man to do it is morally right for a woman to do," [abolitionist] Sarah Grimké wrote in 1838. And Margaret Fuller* added: "What Woman needs . . . is as a nature to grow, as an intellect to discern, as a soul to live freely. . . . We would have every arbitrary barrier thrown down. We would have every path laid open to Woman as well as to Man." More than a century later, the same plea echoed across the country. Sometimes raucous, often bitter, it nevertheless had the strength of appealing to the basic principle that every human being is unique and sacred and has an inalienable right to determine his or her own destiny.

Whether the new feminism could succeed where its predecessors had failed was an open question. It seemed unlikely that the vast majority of Americans were yet ready to accept the ramifications of complete sexual equality. The nuclear family, the concept of maternal responsibility for child-rearing, the importance of privatism—all were cherished values and all to some extent stood in the way of the revolution envisioned by women's rights advocates. On the other hand, the signs of change were manifold. The number of three and four year olds in nursery schools or kindergartens doubled between 1965 and 1970. Nearly 70 per cent of all women approved in principle the idea of day-care centers. And most young people gave at least verbal allegiance to the values associated with sexual equality. The proportion of women living alone or with roommates rose 50 per cent during the 1960's, and the increase was 109 per cent for those in the crucial marrying range of twenty to thirty-four years old. A Barnard senior, the *New York Times* reported, was introduced to friends "as the only girl at Barnard who's getting married," and applications by women students to professional schools mounted. If such facts were any index, it seemed that fewer women saw marriage and motherhood as their only vocation, and that young mothers were increasingly prepared to utilize day-care facilities so that they could resume careers in the world outside the home.

Whatever the case, there could be little question at the end of the 1960's that feminism had once again become a vital force in American society. Women's liberation groups spread from the city to the suburbs. Groups of welfare mothers, airline stewardesses, and female soldiers all asserted their right to equal treatment with men. And officials in government and

[*1810–1850, feminist, critic, and journalist]

business went out of their way to give at least the appearance of meeting feminist demands. America might not be ready for the revolutionary ideas of the more extreme feminists, but more and more women were demonstrating an acute consciousness of the need to end discrimination based on sex. The future was uncertain, but as the nation entered a new decade, feminism exhibited a strength, vitality, and appeal which had not been seen in the United States for half a century.

DOCUMENTS

The Equal Rights Amendment, 1923

Sec. 1. Equality of rights under the law shall not be denied or abridged by the United States or by any State on account of sex.

Sec. 2. The Congress shall have the power to enforce, by appropriate legislation, the provisions of this article.

Sec. 3. This amendment shall take effect two years after the date of ratification.

In Support of ERA, 1970

My name is Gloria Steinem. I am a writer and editor. I have worked in several political campaigns, and am currently a member of the Policy Council of the Democratic National Committee.

During twelve years of working for a living, I've experienced much of the legal and social discrimination reserved for women in this country. I have been refused service in public restaurants, ordered out of public gathering places, and turned away from apartment rentals; all for the clearly-stated sole reason that I am a woman. And all without the legal remedies available to blacks and other minorities. I have been excluded from professional groups, writing assignments on so-called "unfeminine" subjects such as politics, full participation in the Democratic Party, jury

SOURCE: U.S. Congress, House of Representatives Joint Resolution 208, 92d Cong., 1st sess. (1971), 1, 23.

SOURCE: testimony of Gloria Steinem, U.S. Congress, Senate Committee on the Judiciary, Subcommittee on Constitutional Amendments, Hearings, *The "Equal Rights" Amendment*, 91st Cong., 2d sess., 1970, 335–37.

duty, and even from such small male privileges as discounts on airline fares. Most important to me, I have been denied a society in which women are encouraged, or even allowed, to think of themselves as first-class citizens and responsible human beings.

However, after two years of researching the status of American women, I have discovered that I am very, very lucky. Most women, both wage-earners and housewives, routinely suffer more humiliation and injustice than I do.

As a freelance writer, I don't work in the male-dominated hierarchy of an office. (Women, like blacks and other visibly-different minorities, do better in individual professions such as the arts, sports, or domestic work; anything in which they don't have authority over white males.) I am not one of the millions of women who must support a family. Therefore, I haven't had to go on welfare because there are no day care centers for my children while I work, and I haven't had to submit to the humiliating welfare inquiries about my private and sexual life, inquiries from which men are exempt. I haven't had to brave the sex bias of labor unions and employers, only to see my family subsist on a median salary 40% less than the male median salary.

I hope this committee will hear the personal, daily injustices suffered by many women—professionals and day laborers, women housebound by welfare as well as suburbia. We have all been silent for too long. We won't be silent anymore.

The truth is that all our problems stem from the same sex-based myths. We may appear before you as white radicals or the middle-aged middleclass or black soul sisters, but we are *all* sisters in fighting against these outdated myths. Like racial myths, they have been reflected in our laws. Let me list a few:

That Women Are Biologically Inferior to Men

In fact, an equally good case can be made for the reverse. Women live longer than men, even when the men are not subject to business pressures. Women survived Nazi concentration camps better, keep cooler heads in emergencies currently studied by disaster-researchers, are protected against heart attacks by their female sex hormones, and are so much more durable at every stage of life that nature must conceive 20 to 50 percent more males in order to keep some balance going.

Man's hunting activities are forever being pointed to as tribal proof of superiority. But while he was hunting, women built houses, tilled the fields, developed animal husbandry, and perfected language. Men, being all alone in the bush, often developed into a creature [*sic*] as strong as women, fleeter of foot, but not very bright.

However, I don't want to prove the superiority of one sex to another. That would only be repeating a male mistake. English scientists once definitively proved, after all, that the English were descended from the angels, while the Irish were descended from the apes: it was the rationale for England's domination of Ireland for more than a century. The point is that science is used to support current myth and economics almost as much as the church was.

What we do know is that the difference *between* two races or two sexes is much smaller than the differences to be found *within* each group. Therefore, in spite of the slide show on female inferiorities that I understand was shown to you yesterday, the law makes much more sense when it treats individuals, not groups bundled together by some condition of birth.

A word should be said about Dr. Freud, the great 19th Century perpetuator of female inferiority. Many of the differences he assumed to be biological, and therefore changeless, have turned out to be societal, and have already changed. . . .

That Women Are Already Treated Equally In This Society

I'm sure there has been ample testimony to prove that equal pay for equal work, equal chance for advancement, and equal training or encouragement is obscenely scarce in every field, even those—like food and fashion industries—that are supposedly "feminine."

A deeper result of social and legal injustice, however, is what sociologists refer to as "Internalized Aggression." Victims of aggression absorb the myth of their own inferiority, and come to believe that their group is in fact second class.

Women suffer this secondclass treatment from the moment they are born. They are expected to *be* rather than achieve, to function biologically rather than learn. A brother, whatever his intellect, is more likely to get the family's encouragement and education money, while girls are often pressured to conceal ambition and intelligence, to "Uncle Tom."

I interviewed a New York public school teacher who told me about a black teenager's desire to be a doctor. With all the barriers in mind, she suggested he be a veterinarian instead.

The same day, a high school teacher mentioned a girl who wanted to be a doctor. The teacher said, "How about a nurse—"

Teachers, parents, and the Supreme Court may exude a protective, well-meaning rationale, but limiting the individual's ambition is doing no one a favor. Certainly not this country. It needs all the talent it can get.

That American Women Hold Great Economic Power

51% of all shareholders in this country are women. That's a favorite male-chauvinist statistic. However, the number of shares they hold is so small that the total is only 18% of all shares. Even those holdings are often controlled by men.

Similarly, only 5% of all the people in the country who receive $10,000 a year or more, earned or otherwise, are women. And that includes all the famous rich widows.

The constantly-repeated myth of our economic power seems less testimony to our real power than to the resentment of what little power we do have.

That Children Must Have Full-Time Mothers

American mothers spend more time with their homes and children than those of any other society we know about. In the past, joint families, servants, a prevalent system in which grandparents raised the children, or family field work in the agrarian systems—all these factors contributed more to child care than the labor-saving devices of which we are so proud.

The truth is that most American children seem to be suffering from too much Mother, and too little Father. Part of the program of Women's Liberation is a return of fathers to their children. If laws permit women equal work and pay opportunities, men will then be relieved of their role as sole breadwinner. Fewer ulcers, fewer hours of meaningless work, equal responsibility for his own children: these are a few of the reasons that Women's Liberation is Men's Liberation, too.

As for the psychic health of the children, studies show that the quality of time spent by parents is more important than the quantity. The most damaged children were not those whose mothers worked, but those whose mothers preferred to work but stayed home out of role-playing desire to be a "good mother."

That the Women's Movement Is Not Political, Won't Last, or Is Somehow Not "Serious"

When black people leave their 19th Century roles, they are feared. When women dare to leave theirs, they are ridiculed. We understand this, and accept the burden of ridicule. It won't keep us quiet anymore.

Similarly, it shouldn't deceive male observers into thinking this is somehow a joke. We are 51% of the population, we are essentially united on these issues across boundaries of class or race or age, and we may well end by changing this society more than the civil rights movement. That is an apt parallel. We, too, have our right wing and left wing, our separatists, gradualists, and Uncle Toms. But we are changing our own consciousness, and that of the country. [Friedrich] Engels noted the relationship of the authoritarian, nuclear family to capitalism: the father as capitalist, the mother as means of production, and the children as labor. He said the family would change as the economic system did, and that seems to have happened, whether we want to admit it or not. Women's bodies will no longer be owned by the state for the production of workers and soldiers:

birth control and abortion are facts of everyday life. The new family is an egalitarian family.

Gunnar Myrdal noted thirty years ago the parallel between women and Negroes in this country. Both suffered from such restricting social myths as: smaller brains, passive natures, inability to govern themselves (and certainly not white men), sex objects only, childlike natures, special skills and the like. When evaluating a general statement about women, it might be valuable to substitute "black people" for "women"—just to test the prejudice at work.

And it might be valuable to do this Constitutionally as well. Neither group is going to be content as a cheap labor pool anymore. And neither is going to be content without full Constitutional rights.

Finally, I would like to say one thing about this time in which I am testifying.

I had deep misgivings about discussing this topic when National Guardsmen are occupying our campuses, the country is being turned against itself in a terrible polarization, and America is enlarging an already inhuman and unjustifiable war.* But it seems to me that much of the trouble this country is in has to do with the Masculine Mystique; with the myth that masculinity somehow depends on the subjugation of other people. It is a bi-partisan problem: both our past and current Presidents seem to be victims of this myth, and to behave accordingly.

Women are not more moral than men. We are only uncorrupted by power. But we do not want to imitate men, to join this country as it is, and I think our very participation will change it. Perhaps women elected leaders—and there will be many more of them—will not be so likely to dominate black people or yellow people or men; anybody who looks different from us.

After all, we won't have our masculinity to prove.

Opposition to ERA, 1972

If the equal rights amendment becomes law, it will put Congress in a straitjacket and will say to Congress, "You cannot draft anybody or send anybody into combat against an enemy unless you draft men and women alike and send them into combat under exactly the same conditions."

[*In 1970, many colleges were centers of the struggle for civil rights for women and minorities and of the anti-Vietnam War movement.]

SOURCE: Speech by Senator Sam Ervin in the *Congressional Record*, March 21, 1972, 9333–35.

Frankly, I do not think that any man who has been subjected to combat in the armed services is in favor of drafting the daughters of America and subjecting them to the experience which combat gives to men.

I had the privilege of serving in a division which suffered 5,000 casualties in battle and suffered 20,000 casualties in wounds. I had the privilege of serving in a company which suffered 96 battle deaths and had only two men who served with it any length of time who were not killed or wounded.

I have seen the bodies of mortal casualties lying upon the field of battle many hours after they had suffered death in battle, and have witnessed the beginning of the putrefying process which the bodies of the dead go through in returning to dust. I have seen bodies of my comrades mangled and their limbs torn asunder.

I agree with the Senator from Indiana that if absolute necessity should require that women fight a foreign foe in order that our country not be destroyed, I could be reconciled to it. But as long as my country has a total population of more than 200 million and as long as it has the millions of young men who are able to fight for my country, I shall adamantly oppose any proposal that the Congress of the United States be deprived of the power to provide for the drafting of men unless it drafts women under exactly the same conditions.

I am going to talk about the privacy question later, when I offer an amendment on that subject. At that time, I expect to show that the supporters of this amendment do not know what its effect will be on the privacy of men and women and boys and girls. . . .

Mr. President, there are 32,975,000 women of the age of 16 years and up in the United States who are either employed or seeking employment outside their homes. A very small percentage of these women are business and professional women.

I am told that this amendment is backed by business and professional women. From my association with women in North Carolina, I confess that I am of the opinion that only a relatively small percentage of business and professional women favor this amendment.

The Senator from North Carolina realizes that society imposes discrimination in employment upon many women, both in respect to the compensation they receive and their promotional opportunities. These discriminations which are imposed upon women in this respect by the traditional customs and usages of society are not discriminations created by law and, for this reason, the equal rights amendment will not abolish discriminations of that character.

All of us who are familiar with the legislative action of the Congress and of the States in recent years know that Congress and the States have enacted much enlightened legislation which puts an end, if such legislation is properly invoked and enforced, to many of the discriminations against women in employment.

Moreover, the President of the United States and every department and agency of the Federal Government, and many of the executive agencies and departments of many States, have issued regulations prohibiting discrimination against women in employment in Federal and State services.

There is one group of women, however, who need no laws and need no regulations to abolish legally imposed discriminations against them.

That group is composed of business and professional women. Insofar as the law itself is concerned, business and professional women have the absolute legal right at the present moment, and without the equal rights amendment, to compete with men in all of the business or commercial activities of life. I wish to say, as I said in my opening remarks, that the submission of the equal rights amendment by Congress to the States and the ratification of the equal rights amendment by 38 States will not add one job or title to the position of business and professional women insofar as their legal rights to engage in business or commercial enterprises is concerned.

You know, Mr. President, the American people have a simplistic faith in law. Our great national delusion is based on the fact that we have a childlike faith that anything wrong in our civilization can be abolished by law and that all of life's problems lend themselves to legal solutions. It is doubtful whether many of the people who are in custody in institutions for the mentally ill in our land suffer under a greater delusion than that.

If this amendment is submitted by Congress to the States and is ratified by 38 States and made a part of the Constitution, all of the problems which life presents to women will remain. New problems will undoubtedly be presented to women from time to time by life. The chief effect of the equal rights amendment will be to handicap Congress and the legislatures of the 50 States in their efforts to solve the problems because the equal rights amendment says to the Congress and to the States that they must ignore the existence of sex when they attempt to solve the problems of women as well as when they undertake to solve the problems of men.

The most important fact in life is sex. No greater folly could be perpetrated than to place in the Constitution of the United States an amendment which says that Congress and the 50 States must absolutely ignore the existence of sex when they fashion the laws to solve the problems of men and women, all of whom belong to a sex.

Women and Poverty, 1982

For millions of black and Hispanic women and their children, poverty is still very much a part of American life. The magnitude of the problem is appalling. In 1981, 27 percent of all black and Hispanic children were poor. The poverty rate for persons in female-headed families with children was 68 percent for blacks and 67 percent for Hispanics. For the mothers of these children, poverty is not an illusion; it is a painful reality fraught with deprivations not only for themselves but also for those whose future is in their hands.

The specter of poverty is no less real for white female heads of household and their children. Minority women and their children, however, are disproportionately subjected to the ravages of poverty, which severely hamper achievement of their fullest potential. . . .

During the last several decades, many woman and their dependent children have experienced economic hardship. The phenomenal growth of female householder families, stemming in part from increasing marital disruption and out-of-wedlock births, has forced many women to be both chief parent and chief provider. The continuing trend in teenage childbearing out of wedlock is cause for concern. Teenage mothers often must interrupt or discontinue their education, thereby making the acquisition of marketable employment skills more difficult. If unable to find adequate and affordable child care, the teenage mother and those who experience marital disruption may be forced to rely upon public assistance for basic needs.

Female-headed families are disproportionately impoverished. Families headed by women with no husband present constituted 47 percent of all families below the poverty line in 1981. Minority female heads of household experience even higher levels of deprivation. More than half (53 percent) of all female-headed black and Spanish-origin families were below the poverty line. The vulnerability of female-headed families, particularly minorities, to economic adversity and the surprising number of households having some recent contact with welfare programs underline the importance of these programs.

Disproportionate numbers of America's poor in the early 1980s are women. The demographic data that reflect these trends suggest that more of the same may lie ahead.

SOURCE: U.S. Commission on Civil Rights, *Statement on the Equal Rights Amendment* (Washington, D.C.: Government Printing Office, 1982), 14, 62.

PART II

Suggestions for Further Reading

Some of the changes in American society during the 1920s are covered in Lois Banner, *The American Beauty: A Social History through Two Centuries of the American Idea, Ideal, and Image of the Beautiful Woman* (1983) and William Leuchtenburg, *Perils of Prosperity, 1914–1932* (1958). A good study on prohibition is Andrew Sinclair, *Era of Excess: A Social History of the Prohibition Movement* (1964). On the Ku Klux Klan, see Kenneth Jackson, *The Ku Klux Klan in the Cities, 1915–1930* (1967) and David Chalmers, *Hooded Americanism: The First Century of the Ku Klux Klan* (1965). Paula Fass, *The Damned and the Beautiful: American Youth in the 1920s* (1977) is valuable, as is J. Stanley Lemons, *The Woman Citizen: Social Feminism in the 1920s* (1973). A classic study of that era is Helen Merrill Lynd and Robert S. Lynd, *Middletown: A Study of Contemporary American Culture* (1929).

On the Great Depression, a good introduction is Robert S. McElvaine, *The Great Depression: America, 1929–1941* (1984). Also of use are Caroline Bird, *The Invisible Scar: The Great Depression and What It Did to American Life, From Then Until Now* (1966); Donald Worster, *Dust Bowl: The South Plains in the 1930s* (1979); and William Leuchtenburg, *Franklin Roosevelt and the New Deal* (1963). For women during the 1930s, see Susan Ware, *Holding Their Own: American Women in the 1930s* (1982). On blacks, see Nancy Weiss, *Farewell to the Party of Lincoln: Black Politics in the Age of FDR* (1983). A good picture of life in one American community can be found in Robert Lynd and Helen Lynd, *Middletown in Transition: A Study in Cultural Conflict* (1937).

America during World War II has been receiving increasing attention. A good introduction is Peter Lingeman, *Don't You Know There Is a War On?* (1970). Another general work is Richard Polenberg, *War and Society* (1972). On the Japanese-Americans, see Peter Irons, *Justice at War* (1983) and Roger Daniels, *Concentration Camps, U.S.A.* (1970). On women during the war, see D'Ann Campbell, *Woman at War with America: Private Lives in a Patriotic Cause* (1984) and Maureen Honey, *Creating Rosie the Riveter: Class, Gender and Propaganda during World War II* (1984).

For changes during the war and after, see Kenneth Jackson, *Crabgrass Frontier: The Suburbanization of the United States* (1985) and Gavin Wright, *Old South, New South: Revolutions in the Southern Economy Since the Civil War* (1986). On suburbs, see Herbert J. Gans, *The Levittowners: Ways of Life and Politics in a New Suburban Community* (1982); Gwendolyn Wright, *Building the Dream: A Social History of Housing in America* (1981); and William Dobriner, *Class in Suburbia* (1963).

For the civil rights movement and the status of blacks after 1945, an overall view is Harvard Sitkoff, *The Struggle for Black Equality, 1954–1980* (1981). On the background of the *Brown v. Board of Education* decision, see

Richard Kruger, *Simple Justice: The History of Brown vs. Board of Education: Black America's Struggle for Equality* (1976). A moving biography of Martin Luther King, Jr., is Stephen Oates, *Let the Trumpet Sound: The Life of Martin Luther King* (1982). The process of ghettoization is discussed in Arnold Hirsch, *Making the Second Ghetto: Race and Housing in Chicago, 1940–1960* (1983). A controversial book about black progress is William Wilson, *The Declining Significance of Race: Blacks and Changing American Institutions* (1978). A more balanced account is Reynolds Farley, *Blacks and Whites* (1984).

For American women in recent years, the best introduction is William Chafe, *The American Woman: Her Changing Social, Economic, and Political Role, 1920–1970* (1972). Jacqueline Jones, *Labor of Love, Labor of Sorrow* (1985) is also useful, as is Alice Kessler-Harris, *Out to Work* (1982). Also helpful are Sara Evans, *Personal Politics: The Roots of Women's Liberation in the Civil Rights Movement and the New Left* (1979); Carol Stack, *All Our Kin: Strategies for Survival in a Black Community* (1974); and Susan Estabrook Kennedy, *If All We Did Was to Weep at Home: A History of White Working-Class Women in America* (1979).

1 2 3 4 5 6 7 8 9 0